# RELIGION
## AND THE
# RADICAL
# REPUBLICAN
# MOVEMENT
## 1860-1870

# RELIGION
## AND THE
# RADICAL
# REPUBLICAN
# MOVEMENT
# 1860-1870

## Victor B. Howard

THE UNIVERSITY PRESS OF KENTUCKY

Copyright © 1990 by The University Press of Kentucky
Scholarly publisher for the Commonwealth,
serving Bellarmine College, Berea College, Centre
College of Kentucky, Eastern Kentucky University,
The Filson Club, Georgetown College, Kentucky
Historical Society, Kentucky State University,
Morehead State University, Murray State University,
Northern Kentucky University, Transylvania University,
University of Kentucky, University of Louisville,
and Western Kentucky University.

*Editorial and Sales Offices:* Lexington, Kentucky 40506-0336

**Library of Congress Cataloging-in-Publication Data**
Howard, Victor B.
  Religion and the radical Republican movement, 1860-1870 / Victor
B. Howard.
     p. cm.
  Includes bibliographical references.
  ISBN 0-8131-1702-X (alk. paper)
    1. United States—Politics and government—Civil War, 1861-1865.
2. United States—History—Civil War, 1861-1865—Religious aspects.
3. Reconstruction.   4. United States—Politics and
government—1865-1877.   5. Slavery and the church—United States.
6. Slavery—United States—Emancipation.   7. Church and state—
United States—History—19th century.   I. Title.
973.7—dc20                                                89-49233
                                                              CIP

To my wife, Wilma,
and my children,
Linda and Lawrence

# Contents

# Preface

This book is a study of the interplay of religion and politics during the Civil War era. More specifically it examines the extent to which religion set the moral tone of the North during the period 1860-1870. The study focuses on the growing influence of the evangelical and liberal churches during the period. This influence was largely exerted through the agency of the radical Republicans, a faction that took an extreme position on war measures and on reconstruction after the war. I have examined the degree to which radicalism was inspired by moral motivation and the action that followed the moral commitment.

The quest for source material to undertake this task took me to many religious as well as political depositories. This work would have been impossible without the cooperation of the staff of the Camden-Carroll Library, Morehead State University, particularly of the inter-library loan librarians, Betty Lane, and Carol Nutter. I wish to express my gratitude to the Manuscript Division and the Interlibrary Loan Division of the Library of Congress. I owe a debt of gratitude to the libraries of the following institutions: the American Antiquarian Society, the Amistad Research Center, Berea College, Boston Public Library, Calasis Free Public Library, Chicago Historical Society, Indiana Historical Society, Cincinnati Historical Society, Columbia University, Connecticut Historical Society, Cornell University, DePauw University, Drew University, Emory University, Essex Institute, Pennsylvania Historical Society, Knox College, Massachusetts Historical Society, Minnesota Historical Society, New York Historical Society, Oberlin College, Radcliffe College, Syracuse University, University of Kentucky, Earlham College, University of Michigan, University of Rochester, University of Tennessee, University of West Virginia, Yale University, Western Reserve Historical Society, and Worcester Historical Society. Special thanks are due to the Connecticut State Library, Detroit Public Library, Houghton Library of Harvard University, Huntington Library, Illinois State Historical Library, Indiana State Historical Library, Iowa State Historical Library, New York Public Library,

New York State Historical Library, Ohio State Historical Library, Rutherford B. Hayes Library, and the Wisconsin State Historical Library.

This volume would not have been possible without the assistance of the libraries and archives of many divinity schools and religious institutions, including: American Baptist Historical Society, United Methodist Archives Center, Wesleyan Methodist Church Archives, Free Methodist Church Archives, Ohio Wesleyan University Library, Presbyterian Historical Society, the Congregational Library of the American Congregational Association, Asbury Theological Seminary, Lutheran Theological Seminary, Harvard Divinity School, Yale University Divinity School, Southern Baptist Theological Seminary, Historical Commission of the Southern Baptist Sunday School Board, Chicago Theological Seminary, Friends Historical Library of Swarthmore, McCormick Theological Seminary, Union Theological Seminary, General Theological Seminary, and Garrett-Evangelical-Seabury-Western Theological Seminaries United Library.

I am indebted to more than a hundred county historical societies and county libraries that furnished me with xeroxed records of county histories, obituaries and local church records that helped me to identify the religious affiliations of individuals who registered their convictions on the moral questions that were debated during the Civil War era.

I wish to express my thanks to Allan Bogue, who graciously shared his material on the religious affiliations of the United States senators during the Civil War era. I am indebted to the American Philosophical Society for granting me the Penrose Award for research in the early stages of this project. The Morehead State University Faculty Research Committee made generous research grants to help finance the travel necessary for my research and financed the typing of the monograph. I am indebted to Carolyn H. Hamilton who typed the manuscript with accuracy and patience. Wilma B. Howard read all that was written, offered frank and critical suggestions on revision, and proofread all drafts of the manuscript.

# Introduction

This book seeks to examine the influence of the churches in shaping the course of the Civil War and the extent to which the religious community conditioned the character and course of Reconstruction. The clergy and the Protestant churches played a significant role in molding and supporting Radical Reconstruction. The Northern Protestant church was the conscience of the Republican party and was recognized as the mainstay of the radical program. Henry Wilson, a Congregational layman, declared, during the war, that the Republican party "contained more . . . moral . . . worth than was ever embodied in any political organization in any land . . . , created by no man . . . , brought into being by Almighty God himself."[1] The radicals of the Civil War era were either Christian reformers of the prewar years who had tried to remove slavery by moral suasion or men who were influenced to take a radical stand during the late antebellum period because of the maturity of their own moral imperative or of that of the churches. The reason was that the radical Christians saw the war as God's judgment on slaveholders and as His means of purging the nation of its greatest sin.[2] Kenneth Stampp called attention to the fact that churches furnished the chief institutional vicinage in which the antislavery impulse throve during the Civil War and Reconstruction.

In the antebellum era, secessions from the evangelical religious denominations created three radical antislavery churches—the Wesleyan Methodist Connection, the Free Methodist Church, and the Free Presbyterian Church. Sectional schisms separated several of the evangelical churches as a result of the slavery controversy. The Old and New School Presbyterians divided because of doctrinal differences and the slavery question in 1837. The Methodist Episcopal Church, South, separated from the Methodist Episcopal Church in 1844, and the Southern Baptists separated from the Northern church and established the Southern Baptist Convention in 1845. In 1857 the Southern synods of the New School Presbyterian Church withdrew from the General Assembly because of the slavery controversy in the General Assembly.

In 1861 the Southern synods left the Old School Presbyterian General Assembly when the majority passed a loyalty resolution.[3]

Military conflict between the North and the South in 1861 caused the Congregational Church, the Methodist Episcopal Church (North), the Baptists, and the New School Presbyterians to move rapidly to a radical position urging emancipation. Only the Roman Catholic Church was able to remain neutral. The General Synod of the Lutheran Church delayed condemning secession until 1862 and never fully adopted an advanced radical position. The Dutch Reform Church followed a similar course.[4] The Episcopal Church refrained from condemning secession and failed to adopt radical measures throughout the war. The Old School Presbyterian Church refused to pass measures in the General Assembly against slavery or the Southern people until 1864, when the General Assembly resolved that slavery should be removed.[5] The Disciples of Christ refused to adopt resolutions in sympathy with the Union in their missionary meeting in 1861 but in 1863 declared their opposition to the rebellion. Eventually the Northern associations were able to take an advanced position without splitting the church because the Disciples had no national governing body.[6] The liberal Christians—the Universalists and the Unitarians—took a radical position somewhat later than the evangelical radicals, and the Universalists preceded the Unitarians. By the end of the war, only the Catholics and Episcopalians had failed to condemn slavery and to call for its destruction.[7]

The radical Christians were the clergymen and lay leaders who believed that their first duty was to free society from all vestiges of the slavery system. Many of them gave priority to emancipation over saving the Union, but most of them considered emancipation the first essential step in saving the Union. Although they were never fully unified, they revised their program as the war progressed. It became their ultimate goal to make blacks equal partners in the democratic life of the nation. The evangelical community was convinced that republicanism was viable only when the nation was internally disciplined by the moral sanction of religion. Radical Christians considered pure Christianity and republicanism impossible as long as slavery existed.[8]

The radical Christians were Christian reformers who had come under the influence of the radical spirit that marked religious life and characterized the antebellum reform movement in the decade after 1825. Some radical Christians identified with the abolition movement and came out of the church; others remained in the church but worked to cleanse it. Most radical Christians were satisfied to advocate containment of slavery within existing boundaries, during the antebellum years, for fear of breaking up the Union. Still, they saw the Civil War as a new stage of the old struggle and were convinced that the time had come to abolish slavery. Many had supported the Liberty and Free Soil movements, but moderates on the slavery question were recruited in 1854 and after the outbreak of the Civil War. All of the radicals manifested a Christian abhorrence for slavery and believed that they would suffer retribution if slavery was not removed. The radical Christians were imbued with the concept that the total life of man must be converted and sin in its every manifestation eliminated. They believed not only that Christians were responsible for cleansing themselves but that the church had been commissioned to purify the nation. The radical Christians who had come out of the traditional churches as well as those within these churches regarded the duty and task of reforming the world as having been vested in the church by God. The war had come, in their view, because the nation had tolerated slavery. The people were being punished for that sin. Failure to terminate slavery and to grant Christian equality would bring down greater retribution on the nation. The greatest percentage of radical Christians was found in the evangelical churches. They were less numerous in the liberal churches. Almost all of the members of the Wesleyan Methodists, Free Will Baptists, United Presbyterians, Free Methodists, and Free Presbyterians were radical Christians. As the war continued, the radical Christians came to control the Methodist Episcopal, Baptist, Congregational, and New School Presbyterian churches. Radical Christians were found in very small numbers in the Episcopal, Old School Presbyterian, and Christian churches.

The political abolitionists, the Garrisonian abolitionists, and the more recent Radical Republicans formed the core of the crusade against slavery by the eve of the Civil War. For all practical purposes the factions were identical during the war.[9] The Radical Republicans were the spokesmen and representatives of the evangelical and liberal churches. Some Radical Republicans were the driving forces in shaping the political opinion of their constituents. George Julian, Charles Sumner, Samuel Pomeroy, and William Kelley were men who aroused the emotions of the moral community. Other Radical Republicans acted more as the barometer of radical constituents. Lyman Trumbull and John Sherman tended to mirror the radical voters and reacted to their sentiments.[10] Most Radical Republicans were church members, but since human motivation is essentially subjective, the precise nature of the impetus for all radical action is difficult to determine. Human motivation often has many causes. Most radicals were principled, self-righteous men with a Christian concern for their duties to the freedmen and a commitment to equal rights. Some radicals were motivated by shades of antisouthernism, hatred of the Southern aristocracy, and nationalism. That the Republicans were devoted to principles is clear from their commitment to equal rights and to blacks despite the political expediency of overlooking these issues. Religion was undoubtedly a significant component in the value system of most Radical Republicans.[11] The Radical Republicans were most nearly united by their devotion to religion and their moral commitment.

From the rocky coast of New England to the woodlands of Minnesota, on the political platform as well as from the pulpit, clergymen thundered the message: this is a holy war! The Civil War was a moral war, not because all the evil was on one side, but because the conflict sprang from a moral dilemma which Americans could no longer escape, evade, or compromise.[12] The clergy read political tracts from the pulpit, told congregations how to vote, and warned that God would be vengeful if the radical program was not carried out. The crusading zeal and energies of the clergy were not limited to the pulpit; they also entered the political arena. The first objective was the emancipation of the slaves. Following the adoption of the Emancipation Proclamation, the majority of churches supported the Radical Republicans. After the assassination of Lincoln the evangelical and liberal churches gave overwhelming support to the Radical Republicans in Congress.[13]

The radical Christians believed they should make Reconstruction an extension of the wartime issues so that the fruits of military victory would not be lost. Their goals of freedom were as sacred as the Holy Writ. Black suffrage became a religious duty. In most Northern states the evangelical and liberal churches were in the vanguard of the radical movement for black suffrage.[14] The clergy supported harsh, vindictive measures for the punishment of the South. Ministers claimed that God and Christian justice to the rebels, Christian charity, and mercy to the black man demanded it. They believed that the Southern leaders should be brought to penitence and reformed and that reconciliation should begin only after this change of heart had taken place. So devoted were the clergy and Protestant churches to the radical congressional program that a majority of them supported the most questionable measure of Radical Reconstruction, the impeachment of the president.

The religious journals and the denominational press kept the duty to reform the South before the clergy and congregations. On every issue that came before the nation during the Civil War era, The religious press went on record espousing freedom and justice. The *New York Independent* proved to be the single most influential journal, but the Methodist press influenced the Protestant mind more powerfully than any other denominational press.[15]

The evangelical and liberal church conferences and associations devoted a large proportion of their time to measures in support of the Republican party. These convocations were so unanimous that there was no extensive debate on measures. After 1861, debate concerning the South and slavery was heated and prolonged only in the national convention of the Episcopal Church. The radical Christians and the Radical Republicans did not secure all they wanted, but they played a significant part in keeping the Republican party goals focused on black rights when it was politically expedient to forget about the party's commitment.

Edward Gibbon found the Christians to be the most radical element in society during the early history of Christianity in the first century. The Christian doctrine was a radical concept in the materialistic society of that period. The Golden Rule, fellowship of all mankind, with Christian justice and charity to all, was a radical idea when it was applied in the mid-nineteenth-century Protestant church, with its middle-class morals and values.[16] James Ford Rhodes recognized the moral forces at work in the Civil War and gave weight to them,[17] but in the decades preceding World War II, the revisionist historians concentrated on the economic and political factors involved in the Civil War and Reconstruction and ignored the moral factors. These historians portrayed the radicals as agents of greedy, exploitive capitalism. The silence on the moral and humanitarian aspects of the Civil War was broken in the 1960s. James McPherson did pioneer work when he published his impressive *The Struggle for Equality* (1964), demonstrating that the abolitionist crusades for racial justice reached maturity and the high point of effectiveness during the Civil War era. In his *American Crisis* (1963), W.R. Brock declared that the radical faction of the Republican party had consisted of principled men. In the same year John and LaWanda Cox challenged the thesis that the Republican party had been the selfish pawn of exploitive economic interests and that its actions had represented political expediency. Their thesis in *Politics, Principles, and Prejudice* was that the Republican party had been a party of principles. Glenn Linden verified this fact in a quantitative study entitled *Politics or Principle* (1976). Hans Trefousse praised the essential morality and humanity of the vanguard for racial justice in *The Radical Republicans* (1969).

Michael Benedict demonstrated in his *Compromise of Principles* (1974) that the radicals did not get all they wanted and had to settle for a program that was less radical than many had hoped it would be. Allan Bogue, in a masterly quantitative study, *The Earnest Men* (1981), found the radicals in the Senate to have been very earnest indeed about the problem of slavery and black justice. None of these historians, however, made an in-depth study of the relations of religion and politics during the Civil War.

It has been my purpose to show how the church and state interacted in their response to the slavery problem. I have specifically investigated the relation of the radical Christians to the Radical Republicans. It is my conclusion that the radical Christians significantly affected the course of the Civil War and Reconstruction and greatly influenced the men of principle.

# CHAPTER ONE

# Moral Inevitability and Military Necessity

The election of 1860 came at a time when the nation had endured long months of almost unbearable tension. The American people had scarcely recovered from the economic panic of 1857 when they were deeply moved by a religious revival that roused emotions to a fever pitch and left many people with the feeling that the country was burdened with a grave national sin. The horrors of John Brown's raid lingered in the thoughts, if not in the words, of the people. This was a dangerous time for a presidential election.[1]

The election campaign of 1860 took place in a milieu dominated by a transcending moral issue. In 1949 Arthur Schlesinger, Jr., observed that slavery forced upon every one, both those living at the time and those writing about it later, "the necessity for moral judgment." The antislavery Christians had already made the same judgment before 1860 and would soon gradually convert moderates to their view. Evangelical Christians in the Civil War era were strong believers in postmillennialism, which taught that Christ would come again only after a millennium of prolonged progress and reform. Many expected the millennium to grow out of nineteenth-century revivals. Revivals were expected to bring radical social reforms, including the end of slavery. To many observers, the nation seemed to stand on the brink of an apocalyptic and providential era. Antislavery Christians saw the growth of reform and the progress of antislavery opinion as part of the program to prepare the nation for the advent of the great millennial age. In May 1860, Charles C. Sholes, a Unitarian layman, believed the country was on the eve of a moral uprising. "I see distinctly now a Providence in the election of James Buchanan" in order that "the cup of iniquity . . . might be filled to overflowing" and the people aroused to a full sense of the wrongs, "wickedness and nefarious designs of the slave oligarchy" so that the people would be driven to take radical measures against slavery.[2]

After Lincoln's nomination by the Republican National Convention in May, the Protestant clergy, sectarian journals, and benevolent societies used their influence to help secure his election. In some districts of the North, the election campaign assumed the character of a religious crusade. In Michigan and Massachusetts, prominent laymen were campaigning for office in state elections. Republican gubernatorial Unitarian candidates John Andrew of Massachusetts and Austin Blair of Michigan were campaigning for election. They were Radical Republicans who were abolitionists in all but name. Andrew was a leading layman in the church of the radical James Freeman Clark, and Blair frequently delivered addresses from the pulpit. In Wisconsin and Illinois, antislavery Christians were actively campaigning in the field. Congressman John Wentworth declared that John Brown and Charles Sumner were apostles of freedom who were, like John the Baptist, crying in the wilderness. They paved the way for Lincoln, who "will break every yoke and let the oppressed go free," Wentworth said. He was a long-time member of the Second Presbyterian Church of Chicago.[3]

In June, Henry Dexter, editor of the *Boston Congregationalist*, urged his readers "to carry religion into politics" as a duty of their faith, and in July the Congregational *New York Independent* implored the faithful to arouse the "conscience of the nation against the iniquity of slavery," because there would be "a moral power in political action" which would never rest until the federal government had ceased to be connected with the institution. Eight weeks before the election, Theodore Tilton instructed the readers of the *Independent* regarding "the imperative duty" to rid the nation of slavery as much as "to pray and labor for the conversion of souls." Christians should guard the ballot box "with holy jealousy" because it would decide the great issue.[4] The clergy, Christian laymen, sectarian press, and religious conventions and conferences supported the Republican candidates as they had during the election of 1856. Dale Baum found that roughly three of every four Congregationalists who voted in 1860 cast ballots for Lincoln. The evangelical clergy supported Lincoln in even greater numbers.[5]

With the election of Lincoln over, sectional tension increased, hastening the final division of the Union. The American Anti-Slavery Society planned a convention in Boston in December to strengthen the forces against the growing spirit of compromise and asked antislavery clergy and laymen how slavery could be abolished. Joshua Giddings, an elder in the Congregational Church and president of a local Bible society, believed that slavery could be abolished only "by the advancement of Christian civilization" and the operation of "truth and justice upon the public conscience." Henry H. Garnett, a black Calvinist clergyman, was convinced that God would end slavery in his own righteous way. Christian men need only wait for the signs and cooperate with the Providence of God. Conservatives denounced the antislavery Christians as the cause of the secession movement and urged that the antislavery convention be suppressed. The Conservatives hoped for concessions to the South, which they felt would be prevented by the radical meetings. When the antislavery meeting convened, the mayor of Boston promptly suppressed it, and a mob broke up a religious meeting in Boston that was commemorating the martyrdom of John Brown. Many liberals denounced these offenses against freedom of speech, but Elizabeth C. Stanton was sure the rioters were doing work necessary for abolition. Despite the growing concern with concessions to the South, Henry Crapo, the next radical governor of Michigan, wrote to his son: "I say no concessions." Crapo was a vestryman in the Congregational Church and a long-time member of a local missionary society in Michigan.[6]

Union meetings were held by commercial people in eastern cities. The conservative clergymen gathered in several churches for prayer meetings to promote conciliation. Early in January 1861, Buchanan spoke to Congress. He insisted that the North had no more right to interfere with slavery in the South than with similar institutions in Russia or Brazil. He laid the blame for secession on the violent agitation in the North. Many Democratic journals insisted that the Northern clergy had brought on the war by their violent agitation. Most clergy refuted the charge, but Granville Moody, a Methodist minister, proudly maintained that it was true. Buchanan proclaimed a national fast day for January 4, 1861, so that the people could repent their individual sins and pray for peace. Nothing was said of slavery. "Let us implore Him [God] to remove from our hearts the false pride of opinion," Buchanan pleaded. The radical press denounced the proclamation, which made no mention of slavery, and radical governors of eastern states issued their own proclamations asking the people to pray that their national leaders would have sufficient courage to maintain the government inviolate and to uphold the Constitution.[7]

A large number of clergy in the North had, for a decade, already taken to the public platform as political spokesmen against slavery, and many radical ministers refused to comply with the president's proclamation. Charles Beecher, of the First Congregational Church in Georgetown, Massachusetts, held an earlier fast day and preached against Buchanan's proclamation. "Let us take such a position as becomes believing men . . . who expect to meet in eternity," he advised his congregation. At the end of the service the congregation passed resolutions accusing Buchanan of a treacherous conspiracy with rebels to overthrow the government. A Baptist minister in Holden, Massachusetts, refused to observe Buchanan's proclamation. He also held an earlier fast day and accused the South of being unwilling to continue the Union "unless it carried slavery on its shoulder. I could as soon pray that Satan might be prospered and his kingdom come. Let there be not another inch of concession given." God willed that slavery cease, he insisted, and the violent commotions might be an answer to the many prayers for deliverance from slavery.[8]

The initial step in urging conciliation of the South had been taken by Buchanan's own denomination, the Old School Presbyterian Church. A circular letter had been addressed to the clergymen of the South, signed by more than thirty distinguished divines, of whom more than half were Old School Presbyterians from the East. The *New York Observer*, an Old School journal, then suggested that the moderator of the Old School Church call for a day of prayer for the country. When Buchanan's proclamation was issued, the moderator concurred. Episcopal, Dutch Reformed, Old School Presbyterian, and some conservative Unitarian clergy preached conciliatory sermons that avoided mentioning the slavery question and urged prayer for peace and national harmony. Henry Bellows, a conservative Unitarian clergyman, blamed much of the nation's trouble on insulting and inflammatory sermons from the pulpit. Reverend Stephen H. Tyng, of New York, one of the most outspoken antislavery Episcopal clergymen in the East, read Bishop Simon Potter's circular letter counseling Christians to work for conciliation and compromise with the South. Tyng had nothing to say personally.[9]

As information was received about Lincoln's cabinet selections, antislavery Christians expressed reservations about some of Lincoln's conservative choices. Charles D. Cleveland, a Presbyterian layman from Philadelphia and vice president of the American Missionary Association (AMA), urged Lincoln to choose cabinet advisers with the "purest moral integrity" and expressed the hope that Simon Cameron would not be an official adviser because he would "give no moral power" to the cabinet. Other laymen, clergy, and antislavery Christians protested against the appointment of Cameron and expressed concern that the government be placed on the highest moral plane.[10]

In his inaugural address, March 4, 1861, Lincoln repeated his campaign pledge that there would be "no purpose, directly or indirectly, to interfere with the institution of slavery in the States where it exists." After the attack on Fort Sumter on April 12, radical Christians took a different view. Charles L. Brace, a Congregational clergyman and secretary of the Children's Aid Society, began bombarding the New York and Boston newspapers with correspondence saying that the war against the South should be made a holy war and that the soldiers should be taught that, like the English Puritans, they were serving God. The New England Conference of the Methodist Episcopal Church and the New York Welsh Congregational Church came out against further compromises with slavery. After the Unitarian *Christian Inquirer* insisted that the Civil War should deliver the death blow to slavery, James Freeman Clarke published his letter to Senator Charles Sumner, explaining why no compromise could be made with slavery. Clarke and others were simply expressing the idea John Quincy Adams had popularized earlier in the century, that the constitutional protection of slavery would cease to exist in the advent of war.[11]

In May, Henry Ward Beecher informed a correspondent that slavery should be destroyed. Several other Congregational clergymen took the same stand publicly. During the same month, under the lead of S.S. Jocelyn, secretary to the AMA, a petition for the abolition of slavery was circulated and was sent to Lincoln from the First Congregational Church of Brooklyn. A similar petition, which noted that slavery could be abolished by the war powers of the president, was circulated in the region of Jewett City, Connecticut, by the Congregationalists of the county, and the Congregational Association of Connecticut informed Lincoln that it reverently waited on the providence of God to remove slavery. From the Northwest came a memorial drawn up by the Fox River Congregational Association, Illinois, affirming that its members did not want the war to end until slavery had been completely eradicated. The General Association of Congregational Churches of Illinois passed resolutions to the same effect, which were sent to Lincoln.[12]

In his July 4 message to Congress, Lincoln reiterated his inaugural pledge that he would not indirectly or directly interfere with slavery. By this time antislavery Christians increasingly feared a compromise with slavery. George B. Cheever, pastor of the Congregational Church of the Puritans and president of the Church Anti-Slavery Society, took every occasion to persuade the nation that the war would cease if slavery were completely abolished by the federal government. If the government did not deal with the cause of the war, the nation should expect the retribution of God, he warned. Benjamin Aydelotte, a Presbyterian minister in Cincinnati, expressed the same opinion to his associates, and Moncure Conway spent the summer months of 1861 trying to persuade the Christian population of the same idea. Quick and decisive action was necessary, argued Conway, if the nation was to be redeemed. Horace Greeley, editor of the *New York Tribune* and an antislavery Universalist who was often a delegate to the Universalist National Convention, optimistically assured Conway that the "Father of all Good" would work out his holy ends and added that, although the end of slavery might be postponed and obscured, "this *Rebellion seals the doom of slavery.*"[13]

During the summer of 1861, the slowness of the Union forces to act, the apparent lethargy of the administration, and the failure to adopt a progressive policy concerning slavery suggested to many that a compromise with the South might be in the making. Defeat in the battle of Bull Run, July 21, 1861, heightened this fear, and the battle's effect was instantly reflected in the almost unanimous passage on July 22 of the Crittenden Resolution, which confirmed Lincoln's pledge not to interfere with the domestic institution. The reaction of antislavery religious sentiment was immediate. The annual conferences of the Methodist Episcopal Church resolved that they were unalterably opposed to all compromises with the South and slavery. A Methodist minister from Indiana expressed uneasiness about the lack of a government policy concerning slavery. He wrote to the *Western Christian Advocate* that only one of ten clergymen believed the war was being waged against slavery.[14]

On August 30, 1861, General John Frémont issued a proclamation freeing all slaves owned by persons in the state of Missouri who were resisting the United States. Gerrit Smith began writing to Lincoln that rebellion would have been dealt a death blow in the beginning if slavery had been abolished by the federal government. When Smith received the news, he wrote: "This step . . . is the first unqualifiedly and purely right one" which had taken place during the war. In DeKalb, Illinois, evangelical ministers of several denominations met and signed a memorial to Frémont, declaring their "unspeakable satisfaction and gratitude to God" for his immortal act. The Fox River Presbytery (Illinois) took similar action. Radical antislavery Christians were jubilant, but their mood quickly changed when, on September 2, Lincoln suggested Frémont modify his proclamation to conform with the Confiscation Act of August 6 and on September 11 ordered the change. Reaction to Lincoln's order was not long in coming. A radical Congregationalist and president of the County Sunday School Society of Kalamazoo, Michigan, wrote to Lincoln that the president's "order had sent much pain through Christian hearts." He beseeched Lincoln "in the fear of God and love of your country" to retract the order. A group of Christians of several denominations, of which the majority were Methodists, met in Coldwater, Michigan, and approved a memorial to Lincoln stating that they "fully approved" Frémont's proclamation and opposed the president's order modifying the general's edict. The memorial read: "Leave the consequence to God, after you have performed your duty." A leading member of the Plymouth Congregational Church of Janesville, Wisconsin, and a son-in-law of Reverend Henry Cowles, editor of the *Oberlin Evangelist*, informed Lincoln that his order would anger a multitude of like-minded people.[15]

Kentucky responded violently to Fremont's proclamation and demanded that Lincoln order its withdrawal. When Frémont's decree was canceled, Ohio reacted bitterly against what many called Kentucky's blackmail. A citizen of Chillicothe, Ohio, protested against the modification of Frémont's proclamation and insisted that its purpose had been to appease Kentucky so that the state would not leave the Union. "Go forward, and quell insurrection," he advised, "Leave the consequence to God, after you have performed your duty." Another citizen of Chillicothe wrote to Lincoln in the same vein. "Pursue the right, looking to God to reward the right," he counseled. Lincoln was informed by still another Ohioan that ninety-nine out of every hundred people had been pained by his order. "I firmly believe you are an instrument in the hands of Providence to preserve this Glorious Government," and the peculiar institution must not be permitted to stand in the way, he wrote to Lincoln.[16]

A Congregational missionary in Illinois reported to the missionary society's secretaries that the proclamation by Frémont had elicited much enthusiasm in his Illinois missionary field. By interfering with the proclamation, Kentucky "had risked the retribution of Egypt of old." He was convinced that the country "must return to God and humanity." A Methodist clergyman of Illinois wrote to Lincoln, expressing opposition to the president's order and added: "I pray that God will enable you to do your whole duty without fear of consequences." A clergyman from southern Illinois wrote to Lincoln, "For God's sake, for humanity's sake, for our nation's sake" support Fremont. "The only people supporting the president's order in southern Illinois," he added, were the "foulmouthed men who cried negro preachers to us poor Republicans in the campaign" of 1860.[17]

The Sunday after Frémont issued his proclamation, Reverend Conway praised the noble act: "God grant that it may flash through the land and light the train of liberty. . . . when the war is up to the standard of John C. Frémont, the country will be saved." After Lincoln revoked the proclamation, Conway informed Charles Summer: "I cannot convey to you the burning sense of wrong which is filling the hearts of our people here, as they gradually come to see that there is no President of the United States—only a President of Kentucky." Early in October, in a letter to the *Christian Inquirer*, Conway informed the East of the protest in the West because of Lincoln's order. "A hard burning feeling existed," in the West because Frémont's proclamation had been revoked, he asserted. A vast, indignant meeting of benevolent and religious people took place in Cincinnati. The meeting passed resolutions declaring that the cowardly and unworthy way in which the government dealt with Frémont "justifies the people in the worst fears of the designs of the administration." Conway argued that the conflict should be made into "a noble war of humanity." He prophesied that "the policy of the administration would be swept away, or else the Government." In Cincinnati, George Hoadly, a Unitarian layman, wrote Chase: "I pray God to forgive my vote" for Lincoln. William M. Dickson, a liberal Cincinnati Episcopalian, concluded that there was a growing sentiment in the North "to make war upon slavery." He was convinced it would come to that.[18]

Erastus Wright, a Springfield layman of the Christian Church and friend of Lincoln, informed the president that Frémont's proclamation was the chief topic of discussion at the Illinois state fair where "99 of every 100 said Amen!" He warned Lincoln: "It is a fearful thing to contend against God." Three days later John L. Scripps of Chicago advised Lincoln that it was not politically wise to appease Kentucky slaveholders with an act that was "repugnant to the twenty millions of loyal people." He regarded the war as a God-given opportunity for the nation "to wipe out forever that execrable institution." If the opportunity was lost, he believed, "swift and terrible retribution" would overtake the country. Scripp's father was a prominent member of the Methodist Church, and the son was a Christian gentleman, although he did not become a member of the Methodist Church until later. The Republican *Rock River Democrat* complained that nothing Lincoln had done since his inauguration had caused "such heartfelt regret to people of the West" as the President's repudiation of Frémont's order. A Christian citizen from Greene County, Illinois, called Lincoln's order a decree that gave "aid and comfort to the enemy."[19]

In the fall of 1861 when the western annual conferences of the Methodist Episcopal Church began their meetings, the reaction was severe. Before Lincoln issued his binding order, the Conferences of Cincinnati, Illinois, and Central Ohio had expressed cordial approval of Frémont's proclamation. The Upper Iowa Conference hoped that the next Congress would pass a law recognizing and embracing the principles set forth in Frémont's recent proclamation. When the Rock River, Illinois, Conference met, a minister called for three cheers for Frémont's proclamation. They were given with a hearty good will by all present. The Michigan Conference approved Frémont's policy regarding slavery because it was pleasing to God, and the Detroit Conference passed similar resolutions the same week. No other church officially supported Frémont as much as the western conferences of the Methodist Episcopal Church. Lincoln's conservative friend Orville Browning was influenced by this reaction in the West to the president's order when he insisted that Frémont's removal would damage both "the administration and the cause."[20] The Baptist associations made no reference to Frémont, but many called for an end to slavery. The evangelical ministers of the Congregational, Baptist, and Methodist churches met in Hamilton, Illinois, and petitioned Lincoln "in God's name and in the name of justice and humanity" to sustain Frémont. Early in October, Reverend John Fee, a refugee from Kentucky, met in Preble County, Ohio, with clergy, lay officers, and members of the Lutheran, United Brethren, Presbyterian, and Christian churches and petitioned Lincoln to remove his restriction against Frémont's proclamation.[21]

The reaction to Lincoln's order was less severe in the East than in the West. Although the majority of protests against the nullification of Frémont's order came from the Northwest, Christians from the rest of the North were by no means silent. Deacon James Allen, one of the founders of the Central Congregational Church of Bangor, Maine, told Lincoln that everyone in Bangor, apart from a few secessionists, favored Frémont's proclamation. James Russell Lowell asked Salmon Chase, "How many times are we to save Kentucky and lose our self-respect?"[22] The Methodist *Christian Advocate and Journal* of New York praised Frémont for his energy. The Congregational *Maine Evangelist* insisted that slavery must be put down one way or another; as long as the proclamation was in effect, criticism of Frémont was splitting hairs.

Charles Sumner, a hesitant and uncertain Unitarian, was probably the best-informed lawmaker concerning the moral reaction to the revocation of Frémont's proclamation. He was distressed by Lincoln's order. "How vain to have the power of a god and not use it godlike," Sumner complained to a friend.[23]

Clergymen in New York and Boston preached a series of sermons criticizing Lincoln and praised Frémont's proclamation. Charles Brace wrote to the *Independent* that finally, in the providence of God, the time had come to strike a death blow at slavery. He urged Greeley to carry more articles in the *Tribune* urging abolition. Greeley responded that the *Tribune* would print articles as was good for the cause. "I still think the Lord means to rid us of slavery in some manner which will render His hand in the work more visible," he added. Greeley was a member of E.H. Chapin's Universalist Church and firmly believed in the providential work of God. In Boston, George L. Stearns, a prominent antislavery Unitarian and Sunday school superintendent, had convinced his Quaker friend John G. Whittier that it was the proper time to strike at slavery. For the second time, the First Congregational Church of Brooklyn petitioned the president to carry out immediate and total abolition so that the country could "escape the righteous retribution" of God.[24]

Several religious bodies asked Lincoln to call a fast day for prayer to God for guidance. Lincoln called for a day of observance on September 26. Since Frémont's proclamation and Lincoln's subsequent order were on the minds of many people, antislavery radical Christians used the occasion to urge emancipation. In Pontiac, Michigan, regular union church meetings were planned, but discord broke out because the Presbyterian minister objected to the Congregational minister's preaching emancipation when the meeting was held in the Presbyterian church. The sentiment in favor of emancipation had grown so much that, according to a Baptist minister in New Bedford, Massachusetts, the next Congress would have to abolish slavery. William N. Patton, an antislavery Congregational clergyman and vice president of the antislavery AMA, called for the end of slavery in a fast day sermon. The congregation sent Lincoln resolutions calling for an antislavery policy. Two weeks later, the Congregational Triennial Convention met in Chicago and urged all conferences to petition the next Congress to suppress slavery.[25]

Frémont's proclamation was one of the critical turning points in the war on slavery. Its importance was heightened by the publication of Conway's *Rejected Stone* in October, shortly after Lincoln had can-

celed Fremont's proclamation. Lydia Child, an abolitionist and liberal
Christian, called the publication "the most powerful utterance the
crisis had called forth." It simultaneously evoked providential justi-
fication and millennial hope. The publication became a wartime antislavery bible. The theme of the pamphlet was familiar to Conway's
lecture audiences: slavery was the single issue of a holy war. The
proclamation and the book had the effect of welding the evangelical
denominations together into an antislavery force.[26]

Lincoln's order caused many religious people to fear that the administration would compromise with the South on slavery. The order
thus prompted sermons, memorials, and resolutions from religious
bodies. The Baptists were the most active and persistent in alerting
their members to the danger of compromise. Strong opposition was
also found among other evangelical denominations and antislavery
Christians. For example, an Iowa missionary for the American Home
Missionary Society (AHMS) was short and to the point in his correspondence to the secretary of the society: "We must have no more
compromises."[27] As late as December, Benjamin Wade, who professed
no religious connection but traveled in religious circles, warned an
Oberlin antislavery Congregationalist that the executive department
would prolong the war until the people would become weary and "yield
to a disgraceful compromise."[28]

The idea that emancipation was a necessary step before military
success could be achieved became popular in religious circles long
before it was discussed as a political or military concept. The First
Congregational Church proposed it in a petition of May 14. As a result
of Lincoln's order, many church groups became committed to military
necessity as the course of providential deliverance from slavery. In
September, the *Congregational Journal* of Concord, New Hampshire,
agreed that the government could not abolish slavery by a civil measure
because it did not have the constitutional power, but the editor added:
"What Gen. Fremont has done in Missouri, may become a matter not
only of military necessity in other states, but one of the most effectual
measures of suppressing rebellion." On October 1, the Reformed Presbytery of Pittsburgh explained military necessity as a war power which
presented no constitutional problems. "Military authority takes the
place of all municipal institutions—*Slavery among the rest*," and the
president has "the power to order universal emancipation" as an emergency of War. They deprecated "any executive interference to nullify
any such proclamations which have been made or yet may be made."
Three days later, the First United Presbyterian Synod of the West ap-

proved manumission by military proclamation and the confiscation of all property of those resisting the government. The Synod of the United Presbyterian Church passed similar resolutions and selected a committee to present them to Lincoln.[29] In November, Reverend George B. Cheever, in a sermon before his Church of the Puritans, insisted that a proclamation against slavery as a military necessity under the war powers would deliver the country from all treason. Reverend Asa D. Smith, a member of the executive committee of the AHMS, echoed his sentiments. Charles Sumner changed his tactics to accord with the radical religious movement. "You will observe that I propose no crusade for abolition," he wrote in November. Emancipation "is to be presented strictly as a measure of military necessity rather than on grounds of philanthropy."[30]

The Confiscation Act of August 6, 1861, had provided that the labor for their owner of slaves engaged in hostile military service would be forfeited, but the law was indefinite as to the manner of forfeiture. The president and the army left the law vague and made no aggressive effort to enforce it. Fremont's proclamation had forced Lincoln to take a stand, since he had clearly confirmed in his annual message to Congress in December 1861 that slaves used in hostile military service would no longer be slaves and steps would be taken for colonization. The struggle thus took on a hesitant but nevertheless real character that anticipated emancipation. The reaction of the moral community pushed both Congress and the administration toward a deeper commitment to make war on slavery and toward the passage of the second Confiscation Act in July 1862.[31]

On September 5, 1861, Senator Orville Browning had a conversation with Frémont. The general assured Browning that he would adhere to his proclamation and carry out the policy he had commenced. Browning forwarded this information to Lincoln. A humiliating defeat and surrender came at Lexington, Missouri, on September 20. The situation became more complicated when Frémont arrested Frank Blair on October 27, 1861. Frémont had once more offended the conservative Republicans. John A. Gurley, a Universalist clergyman, formerly editor of the moderately antislavery *Star of the West* and currently congressman from Ohio, wrote to Lincoln from St. Louis. He warned Lincoln that his administration was "sleeping on a volcano" in Missouri. "A despotism and reign of terror have been established in this city almost equal to that in revolutionary France," he commented. Gurley said he had strong reasons for believing that Frémont did not intend to yield his command if Lincoln requested it, and Gurley wrote that Lincoln's order had been disregarded. On November 2, Frémont was removed from his command in the Department of the West, and the whole issue was revived. George Templeton Strong, a moderate antislavery Episcopalian, wrote in his diary: "The criticisms on his memorable proclamation are absurd. . . . Why should it [the Government] treat rebel slave property with more delicate consideration than other property of rebels?"[32]

On November 13, Col. John Cochrane, a nephew of Gerrit Smith, made a speech in which he took a stand in favor of the military necessity of unconditional emancipation. Secretary Simon Cameron was present and spoke approvingly of Cochrane's doctrine, which included arming slaves for military service. When Cameron issued the annual report of the War Department on December 1, the document advocated emancipation and the arming of slaves. Lincoln immediately forced the secretary to withdraw the report. After the newspapers reported this development, many antislavery clergymen interpreted Cameron's act as evidence of a developing providence. Robert Collyer, a radical Unitarian clergyman from Chicago, praised the act as the most significant development for abolition since the beginning of the war.[33]

The Young Men's Republican Association met on November 27 in Cooper's Institute. The meeting was dominated by the pulpit and antislavery Christians, and measures were adopted that held to the doctrine enunciated by Frémont and more recently by Colonel Cochrane and Cameron respecting slavery. The resolutions foreshadowed the eventual rooting out of slavery as a result of moral and military necessity.[34] The Thanksgiving Day 1861 sermons continued in the same spirit. Many of the sermons throughout the country appealed for emancipation as a military necessity. Kingston Goddard, a Presbyterian clergyman, advised his Cincinnati congregation that, from all points of view, slavery must be put down. Dr. Tyng in his Thanksgiving sermon informed his St. George congregation that the war could be ended by abolishing slavery.[35]

One of the most significant developments in the emancipation struggle came when Dr. John Evans, a prominent antislavery Methodist layman, in reply to a proslavery letter, expressed the belief that the federal government should in all cases favor freedom over slavery. As a result, Evans became engaged in a controversy with Democratic Judge Walter B. Scates of the Illinois Supreme Court. The debate continued for several weeks in the *Chicago Journal*. Evans maintained that a vigorous prosecution of the war required that all means be used, including the confiscation of slave property.[36]

Lincoln's December message to Congress was disappointing to antislavery Christians. The president's only reference to emancipation was a recommendation that territory be acquired for the colonization of slaves freed by the Confiscation Act. "We are unfortunate," Lydia Maria Child commented to a Quaker friend, "in the men we have placed in power. Lincoln is narrow-minded, shortsighted and obstinate." The *Christian Times and Illinois Baptist* was less pessimistic. The editor saw the people progressing toward inevitable emancipation. Providence was more powerful than presidents or cabinets, wrote the editor, and "every day brings emancipation closer." By the end of 1861, antislavery Christians had shaped religious opinion so much that their influence was greater. This change was due not least to the fact that antislavery Christians had established a weekly meeting in the Smithsonian Institute over which the Unitarian Reverend John Pierpont presided. A Sunday service was held in the Hall of Representatives, and outstanding antislavery clergymen spoke at these meetings, which many congressmen, the president, and the cabinet attended. The speakers in these forums influenced the civil government considerably. The group that was receptive to the message of the radical Christians was becoming more visible. Senator Timothy Howe, a radical Unitarian, saw it taking shape. "Everything about us portends the coming of a rupture in the ranks of the war party," he wrote to his daughter, "Emancipation . . . will be the watchword and the efforts of one faction." The same month Strong recorded in his diary: "Signs multiply of an opposition party, founded on anti-slavery feeling stronger than that of the Administration."[37]

The radical antislavery Christians were far ahead of the platform of 1860, which declared that the party was for "the maintenance inviolate of the rights of the State, and especially the right of each State to . . . control its own domestic institutions . . . exclusively." Lincoln, on the other hand, was still in harmony with the platform. In his December message he had warned Congress about "radical and extreme measures."[38]

Antislavery Christians were beginning to realize in late 1861 that the war was a complicated affair in which moral considerations were modified by the political and military realities. The road to emancipation would not be short and easy, but they were optimistic that the millennium was close at hand. Evangelical millenialism—with the imminent arrival of the Kingdom of God upon the earth, as prophesied in the Book of Revelation—was never more vividly invoked than during the days of the Civil War. The cause of the Union was one with the advance of Christ's approaching millennial kingdom.[39] George Bancroft expressed sentiments that were widespread in the North when he told Lincoln that the war was "the instrument of Divine Providence to root out social slavery."[40]

The radical Christians were the most forthright and unrestrained citizens of the religious community. By the end of 1861 they dominated religious opinion and were united in their ultimate goals. The administration realized that the radical Christians represented a force that must be contended with and appeased. Lincoln, however, had not yet formulated a policy that would meet the demands of radical Christians and still keep the North united so that restoration would be feasible.

# CHAPTER TWO

# Radical Christians and the Emancipation Proclamation

On December 3, 1861, Lincoln sent his first annual message to Congress. He proposed that money be appropriated to establish a colony where forfeited slaves would be sent along with free blacks who chose to be colonized. "In considering the policy to be adopted for suppressing the insurrection, I have been anxious and careful that the inevitable conflict for this purpose shall not degenerate into a violent and remorseless revolutionary struggle," he explained, "I have . . . thought it proper to keep the integrity of the union prominent as the primary object of the contest on our part, leaving all questions which are not of vital military importance to the more deliberate action of the legislature."[1]

The antislavery Christians became more disillusioned with Lincoln during December 1861. James C. Conkling, a lawyer and ruling elder in a Springfield, Illinois, Presbyterian church, was disappointed with Lincoln's December message. The president's noncommittal policy did not satisfy him; Lincoln's address was "entirely destitute of that high toned sentiment which ought to have pervaded a message at such a critical period as this," he complained. A Radical Republican characterized the message as not having "one single manly, bold, dignified position," and an Aurora, Illinois, physician and Episcopal layman reported that Lincoln's message "disgusts the whole of us." Reverend J.M. Sturtevant, the Congregational president of Illinois College, who knew Lincoln well, was also disappointed with the message. "Why should we pour out our blood" for the purpose of holding our fellowmen "in unrighteous bondage to the enemies of our country?" he complained to Trumbull. Wait Talcott, a Congregational layman, warned Trumbull that there was danger of "being sold out to the Slave Power."[2]

By the end of 1861 and early in 1862, antislavery religious sentiment began to influence both Congress and the president. When Congress reassembled in December 1861, fifty-three House Republicans who had voted for the Crittenden resolution in July changed their votes, and the House refused to reaffirm the resolution. Congress was responding to the message of petitions and memorials of religious bodies. By mid-January no fewer than seven different bills dealing with emancipation and confiscation had been reported out of committee. The influence of the church became so prominent that the issue of the clergy's role in politics came to the front as it had in 1860. A Methodist clergyman writing in the *Christian Advocate* defended the right of the sectarian press and the pulpit to discuss politics when moral questions were involved. He predicted that the church would become more conspicuous in political campaigns in the future. George B. Cheever was by far the most active clergyman in delivering political sermons from the pulpit. On January 16, 1862, one of his sermons, "The Slaves are Free by Virtue of the Rebellion and the Government is bound to Protect Them" appeared in the *New York Independent*. By freeing the slaves, the government could strike a just blow and put "our cause unquestionably on the side of righteousness and God," he wrote; "the slaves of the rebellious slaveholding states are, by virtue of the rebellion, free. . . . The President . . . and every member of his Cabinet is a man-stealer," he added, if they did not by proclamation forbid interference with slaves seeking freedom. The Presbytery of Monmouth, Illinois, of the United Presbyterian Church, sympathized with this view. It instructed its members to give their vote only to candidates who met scriptural standards and asked the General Assembly to issue a circular letter on the matter. When Lincoln called a fast day on April 30, political sermons were preached from many pulpits encouraging the radical antislavery position. The pastor of the Congregational Church of Tallmadge, Ohio, counseled his congregation that "rigid morality," which included regard for the rights of humanity, should be firmly insisted upon as a qualification for office, just as "intellectual competency" was required for an officeholder. Democratic newspapers raged against pulpit politics. The editor of the *Boston Courier* complained that sermons in New England were degenerating into stump speeches. A Republican convention could hardly be found, he asserted, that did not have one or more of the "most active and noisy members" who were clergymen.[3]

Early in 1862 antislavery Christians increased propaganda for the cause in Washington. In January, Cheever received an invitation from George Julian, Owen Lovejoy, and others to speak in Washington. He spoke at the Smithsonian Institution on January 10 and assured his audience that the rebellion would not be crushed until slavery was struck down. "Marching orders" must come from God, he said. So impressive was Cheever's denunciation of the war policy that thirty senators and congressmen immediately extended an invitation to Cheever to lecture on several Sabbaths during the winter. Cheever, Theodore Tilton, William Goodell, and twenty-four other antislavery Christians drafted a petition to Congress saying that slavery should be abolished and that the government had no obligation to protect it. Cheever was followed at the Smithsonian Institution one week later by Conway, who convincingly assured the audience that emancipation alone could secure peace. In February, Cheever returned to Washington and gave lectures at the Smithsonian Institution, in the hall of the House of Representatives, and in the Unitarian church. Of the speech in the House, Julian later said it was "the most terrific arraignment of slavery I ever listened to." The significance and influence of the Washington Lecture Association can be judged by the efforts of the conservatives to close government facilities to antislavery sermons and lectures. Failing that, unsuccessful efforts were made to purge the lecture list. Radical Christians were aware that they were winning the battle of opinion. In one of his anonymous letters to the *New York Tribune*, Conway wrote confidently that Washington was beginning to "recognize the trumpet of Judgment Day." The Washington Lecture Association took steps to publish the Smithsonian lectures in a book for wider circulation.[4]

At this time Cheever and Conway were in the vanguard of antislavery Christians in shaping religious opinion on slavery and emancipation. Cheever spoke extensively in the East during the early months of 1862. Conway spent much time lecturing in the West late in 1861 and spoke widely in the East early in 1862 with a new lecture, "The Golden Hour," that described the present as the ideal time for emancipation. His new lecture was soon published. In Boston Conway told the Emancipation League of an interview with the president. "Mr. Lincoln would like to have God on his side, but he *must* have Kentucky," he declared. Conway's eastern tour culminated in lectures in the Church of the Puritans in New York and in the Boston Music Hall. Conway urged the people to do their utmost to compel the president and cabinet to adopt emancipation. While he was in the East, Conway corresponded with the *Cincinnati Gazette* and sent anonymous antislavery dispatches to the *New York Tribune*. George Cheever sponsored a massive petition drive throughout the eastern region, urging Congress and the president to abolish slavery, and he planned a national convention to meet in Washington to promote emancipation. Cheever promoted emancipation through testimonials before legislatures, by letters to the editors of several newspapers, and by using *Principia* in New York as his official organ from 1862 to the end of the war. The antislavery Christians in the West were beginning to express new concern about what they considered the proslavery stance of the administration. Richard Smith, a Presbyterian layman and editor and part owner of the *Cincinnati Gazette*, believed that the country had irreparably "lost confidence" in Lincoln. He added: "His policy, no policy, or want of pluck has brought the country to the verge of ruin, until the Northern people, and especially those who elected him president, are seriously talking about a revolution." After the president's message of March 7, urging voluntary and compensated emancipation, "Deacon" Smith observed that the president was "now getting very popular" as a result of his proposed emancipation measures.[5]

Early in 1862 strong support for emancipation came from the *Congregational Journal*, the *Zion's Herald and Wesleyan Journal*, the *Presbyterian Quarterly Review*, the *Religious Telegraph* of the United Brethren, and the *Christian Advocate and Journal*, which now took the position that God's providence required abolition or the Union would be dissolved.[6] The antislavery radical Christians and the moderates had made a great impact on the government by the time Lincoln delivered his message to Congress on March 6, 1862. The president proposed the adoption by Congress of a joint resolution providing for gradual emancipation initiated by the states, with compensation from the federal government. Recognizing the growing influence of the moral community, Lincoln asked Charles Sumner to review the message before it was sent to Congress.[7]

A large group, composed of antislavery lay leaders and clergy of various denominations, met at Cooper Institute on the evening of March 6. Conway and others spoke, and resolutions unanimously adopted declared it a supreme duty to make peace only after slavery had been exterminated throughout the land. The resolutions sent to Lincoln were signed by a committee of nine clergymen from six denominations and by two prominent laymen. There was no evidence that the meeting rejected Lincoln's moderate start on a solution to a difficult problem.[8]

Beecher and Tilton praised Lincoln's proposal. "It is a noble moral act. . . . Slavery is doomed," editorialized the *Independent*. Greeley advised his editor S.H. Gay: "Write a joyful and moderate leader for tomorrow backing up . . . Old Abe." "God be praised," declared the *Christian Advocate and Journal,* and the New England Conference of the Methodist Episcopal Church hailed Lincoln's proposal as the beginning of an auspicious era. The Methodist clergyman John McClintock wrote from Paris that Lincoln's proposal was "a master-piece" exalting the cause of the church, and he hoped that Congress would quickly agree.[9]

On the day after Lincoln's message, Conway wrote to his wife from New York that the president's message was a wedge that attested to the president's "knowledge of rail-splitting." Four days later the Massachusetts *Fall River News* reported that in a lecture in the Fall River City Hall, Conway had insisted that immediate emancipation was the only true panacea, but he characterized the president's message as "the entering wedge of this perplexing question." A missionary in Wisconsin for the AMA was similarly optimistic about the message as a progressive measure. He believed that the president's decision backed by Congress would soon lead to the end of slavery, but universal emancipation would have suited him better. A Methodist minister from Pennsylvania found nothing about Lincoln's proposal to criticize. He praised Waitman Willey, a Methodist Congressman from West Virginia, for endorsing Lincoln's proposition. Others welcomed Lincoln's suggestion but saw it as only a first halting step. A Quaker couple from Boston wrote Lincoln that the proposal was a move in the right direction.[10] It was generally assumed that Lincoln's message was the first step toward the eventual abolition of slavery.

The Methodist Episcopal Conferences of New York, New England, and North Indiana; the General Synod of the Reformed Presbyterian Church; the General Synod of the Evangelical Lutheran Church; and the Franckean Evangelic Lutheran Synod heartily endorsed the proposition.[11] Many Baptist associations met in the week after Lincoln's message and strongly supported the president. The Berkshire (Massachusetts), Ashford (Connecticut), and Central Union Baptist associations expressed gratitude for the president's timely and righteous proposal. The Pittsburgh, the Broome and Tioga, and the St. Joseph River Baptist associations resolved that if Congress did not respond to the proposal, the people should demand action. Benjamin Wade had his ear tuned to the messages of the religious societies. On the floor of Congress he told his fellow senators, "God and nature have determined the question, and we shall not affect it much either way. . . . The hand of God was never more obvious than in this rebellion. . . . You cannot escape from this war without . . . emancipation. . . . It will not be because I am going to preach it . . . , but it is because I see the hand of God, taking hold of your own delinquency to overrule for good what . . . rulers meant for evil. . . . Pro-slavery men . . . suppose that the Ruler of the universe is a pro-slavery Being; but . . . He is at least a gradual emancipationist." Wade expressed the views of many moderate and radical Christians inside and outside the government. Joshua Giddings, who had always sought "the approbation of God" and his "own conscience before consulting his constituents," informed Milton Sutliff, a radical Congregational laymen, that radical Christians should "make *principle* the object not party, but until we strike at the vital element of the rebellion, it will not be put down." According to Giddings, Christians throughout the Union believed that duty called on the nation to "plunge the dagger of justice through the very heart of slavery" to strike down the "institution which had waged war upon Christianity."[12]

The presence of slavery in Washington had always irritated antislavery Christians. In January an editorial in the *Independent* asserted that slavery should "at once and peremptorily" be removed from the capital. Reverend John McClintock concluded that such a move would go a long way in removing the spell which slavery had cast over public men. A Baptist minister in Boston spent his whole sermon on a Sunday in April advocating an end to slavery in Washington. When a bill to abolish slavery in the District of Columbia was introduced in Congress in March, the *Independent* observed that the moral effects of removal would be incalculable. The reaction of the Free Will Baptist *Morning Star* was "Let the blow be struck!" but the publication warned that the work could not be confined to the capital. After the bill had passed, the editor reminded his readers that the work could hardly stop with abolition in Washington. When the Senate approved the bill, the New England Methodist Episcopal Church "hailed with joy" the Senate's action. After the bill had been sent to the president, the *Independent* carried a prayful editorial: "Washington is Free." The *Western Christian Advocate*'s response was: "Thank God the reproach is wiped out. Washington is Free." A wide representation of evangelical conferences and associations praised Congress and Lincoln for abolishing slavery in the District of Columbia. When the American Anti-Slavery Society met in May, Cheever told the assembly that the emancipation of slaves in the capital was "the greatest triumph thus far against slavery." Another Congregational clergyman asserted that the victory was worth all the misery the war had caused thus far. Most of the radical Christians were not willing to relax, and a New England Quaker wrote a friend that the end of slavery in Washington should spur Christians to strive for universal emancipation.[13]

On May 9, 1862, General David Hunter, of the Department of the South, ordered the emancipation and arming of all slaves in his department. Hunter was a Presbyterian layman and the son of a Presbyterian clergyman who had served as a chaplain in the army during David's youth. Governor Andrew informed Secretary of War Edwin Stanton: "If the President will sustain General Hunter, and recognize *all* men, even black men . . . , and let them fight with God and human nature on their side, the roads will swarm . . . with multitudes whom New England would pour out to obey your call." On Sunday, May 18, Cheever told his congregation that Lincoln's revocation of the proclamation would be "an insult to the country, a disgrace to himself and the government," and Conway assured his friends on the same day: "The President cannot annul the order of Gen. Hunter without being pilloried in history as the man who reenslaved nearly a million human beings." That night Conway held a meeting in his church in Cincinnati to defend Hunter's proclamation. Chase fired off a letter to Lincoln, insisting that it was "of the highest importance" the the order not be revoked. Lincoln nevertheless revoked it three days later. Governor Andrew was quick to protest the president's order because he felt slaves ought to be allowed to fight with God and humanity. Andrew's letter was published in New England newspapers, and a Unitarian clergyman informed Andrew that it had been widely praised in Massachusetts. At a Methodist camp meeting the governor said he had notices that, from the day when Lincoln had repudiated Hunter's order, "the blessing of God" had been "withdrawn from our arms." Many clergymen and laymen openly agreed with Andrew's righteous and patriotic sentiments. In an editorial in the *New York Tribune*, Greeley warned the administration that "man may hesitate or vacillate, but the judgment of God is sure, and under that judgment Slavery reels to its certain downfall."[14]

Antislavery Christians with the army in the West protested the revocation of Hunter's order. A Presbyterian from Illinois wrote his congressman that loyal men of all parties now accepted the idea of unconditional surrender and no compromise. Every means that would promote the cause should be used. Reverend Mansfield French, a Methodist clergyman, worked among the slaves at Hilton Head, South Carolina, in Hunter's department and knew the general well. He informed Chase that the order was necessary to crush the rebellion and to give the country "a pure and righteous peace." He added that Hunter was one of a few men who had "the moral courage to do right and meet the consequence," one who "feared God and loved man." Hunter informed Reverend Stephen Tyng that "nothing can give us permanent peace but a successful prosecution of the war, with every weapon . . . at our command." A benevolent man from western Pennsylvania asserted in a letter to Chase that if Frémont's proclamation had been applied in the occupied parts of the South, the rebellion would have been "virtually ended" by now. Edward D. Mansfield, a ruling elder in the Presbyterian church, urged Chase to use his influence to arm slaves by local military orders. Henry H. Crapo felt that the time had come for a more radical stance. The Christian antislavery position hardened after the revoking of Hunter's order. The moderate Presbyterian minister George Duffield informed his son, Colonel W.W. Duffield, that there should be no more conciliation.[15]

The Progressive Friends of Pennsylvania took a radical antislavery position. They pleaded for immediate emancipation and criticized the revocation of Frémont's and Hunter's proclamation. The Genesee Convention of the Free Methodist Church advised its members that the Free Methodist Church had "no sympathy with the pro-slavery policy" of some of the national leaders, and they condemned the failure to support the policies of Generals Frémont, John Phelps, and Hunter. When the General Conference of Congregational Churches of Illinois met, it passed measures urging the the rebel states be reduced to territories. The ultraradical posture of the conference was due to the revocation of Hunter's proclamation. The Walworth (Wisconsin) Baptist Association regretted the president's partiality to the institution of slavery. At least six other Baptist associations meeting in June went on record as believing that it was necessary to crush slavery.[16]

In an editorial on the revocation of Hunter's order, the *Northern Independent Methodist* concluded that if Lincoln did not order the immediate enlistment of every able-bodied black man, "We shall regard him as the deadliest enemy of his country." The editor of the *Independent* tried to calm the growing hostility to the government; while Lincoln had revoked Hunter's order, it noted, he had been "very careful not to reject the principle" of military emancipation. Lincoln had combined the rejection of Hunter's order with an appeal for gradual emancipation. Some thought the appeal for gradual emancipation incorporated in the revocation of Hunter's order foreshadowed the intention of Lincoln to exercise that right.[17]

The agitation for a new confiscation act began after Frémont's order had been revoked. In March 1862, T.M. Eddy, editor of the *Northwest Christian Advocate*, asserted that the hesitancy of Congress to adopt a law of confiscation was amazing because the people believed that the Rebels had forfeited all rights, and "slavery should be struck quickly and fearlessly." The *Independent* was irritated by the strange delay in Congress concerning consideration of a confiscation act. William B. Dodge, an antislavery Congregational clergyman, urged his congressman to support such a bill. "God requires, and the great majority of the people demand" a new confiscation act, he pleaded. A trustee of a Baptist Church in Illinois wrote to the same congressman of his growing impatience with the persistence of the proslavery policy. He believed God would punish the nation until all the rebel property had been confiscated. From Kentucky a Congregational missionary for the AMA who was familiar with opinion in Ohio informed the secretaries of the association that confiscation was the real question before the people.[18]

Antislavery Christians in the East were just as impatient for congressional action. A Methodist lay leader from Pennsylvania informed Wade that the people were tiring of congressional delays and of the army's slowness in confiscating slaves. After Wade spoke in favor of a confiscation bill that was before the Senate early in May, a Congregational clergyman thanked him and expressed the belief that the new bill would lead to emancipation and save the country. Tilton, speaking before the American Anti-Slavery Society, did not believe that the confiscation bill would tend to wipe out slavery. Nothing short of an emancipation edict would end slavery, he argued. Presbyterian Senator Lyman Trumbull wrote to his wife after passage of the confiscation bill in the Senate and expressed confidence that the law would be effective if Lincoln replaced George McClellan with William Halleck.[19]

On July 15 a giant Loyal meeting of benevolent and religious leaders was held in Union Square, New York City. Slavery received much attention. L.C. Crittenden, a protégé of Chase and an officer in the Treasury Department, charged that the North had been fighting the Rebels as well as Providence for sixteen months. It was the "design of Providence that Slavery should die," he insisted. Rufus Clark, a Congregational clergyman, asserted that the ideas of Frémont had been incorporated in the proposed Confiscation Act. It was "one of the eternal decrees of Providence that . . . slavery should end" by the close of the war, Clark maintained. Roswell Hitchcock of the Union Theological Seminary asserted that the North should use all the tools with which "Providence has clothed us . . . ; black, white and gray shall fight," he said.[20]

The Second Confiscation Act, providing that slaves of Rebels would be freed, passed on July 17, 1862. Christopher R. Robert, a ruling elder in the Presbyterian church and treasurer of the AHMS, insisted that Lincoln should issue a proclamation in accordance with the provisions of the Confiscation Act. He was very disappointed with the progress of the antislavery developments. Robert told Chase that blacks should be used as soldiers. In the wake of developments after December 1862, Samuel Plumb, a Calvinist antislavery Christian of Oberlin, considered Lincoln weak and ineffective. Plumb was mortified by Lincoln's July 12 appeal to the border states to initiate gradual emancipation. "Nothing but the abolition of slavery will save us," he prophesied. From Illinois a professing Christian advised Governor Richard Yates that the Confiscation Act, emancipation, and all other effective methods should be used to combat treason.[21]

The annual conferences of the Wesleyan Methodist Church sent memorials to Lincoln urging him to faithfully execute the Confiscation Act. The Cincinnati Conferences of the Methodist Episcopal Church entreated Lincoln to carry out the Confiscation Act "fully and promptly," and the West Wisconsin Conference of the Methodist Episcopal Church rejoiced at the passage of the act and urged Lincoln to move on to full emancipation which would "fill Heaven with joy and hell with terror."[22]

Lincoln had decided on military emancipation immediately after the border states had rejected compensated gradual emancipation on July 12, 1862. He had progressed far along the road to emancipation in the last six months. McClellan, however, still advocated noninterference with slavery, as he had at the beginning of the war. The antislavery religious people had no confidence in confiscation of slaves by an army under the control of McClellan. On July 11, Lincoln called Henry Halleck from the West to become general in chief of all the armies. The Keokuk (Iowa) Baptist Association, which was convinced that there could be no peace without abolition, rejoiced in the changes that were made in the army, and the Davenport (Iowa) Baptist Association believed that the time had come to solve the "whole negro question." The association hoped the president would take action against slavery according to God's purpose within sixty days after passage of the Confiscation Act. Speaking before a Sabbath school celebration, an Ohio Methodist minister suggested that Lincoln should issue a proclamation immediately and give the Rebels sixty or ninety days before the Confiscation Act was applied.[23] The antislavery Christians were swept along with the current of the new sentiment. "We shall take square ground up on confiscation and the use of all the elements which God and nature have placed in our hands to crush the Rebellion," radical Zachariah Chandler, a Presbyterian senator, wrote Trumbull.[24]

Many antislavery Christians were despondent and dissatisfied with the slow progress of the administration's antislavery measures after the passage of the Second Confiscation Act. R.C. Parsons, a ruling elder of a Presbyterian church in Ohio, anxiously inquired of Chase about the failure of the administration to move toward emancipation. "The slavery question perplexes the President almost as much as ever and yet I think he is about to emerge from the obscurities where he has been groping into somewhat clearer light," Chase confided to his Ohio friend. Chase revealed that Lincoln planned to free the slaves of all Rebels unless they resumed allegiance within sixty days. Reuben Hitchcock, a radical Presbyterian layman, believed that "all the means of the government must be employed, and that right speedily," and thereafter God would help the nation. A Christian layman wrote to Albert Riddle, a Radical Republican, that the people were discouraged because Congress and the president had not acted more forcefully against slavery. Nothing short of a stringent Confiscation Act and freeing the slaves of rebels will satisfy our people," he insisted. Parker Pillsbury wrote to Tilton that God had done his last kind and compassionate work. "He has combined our interest with our duty. . . . We can now abolish slavery on the same principle that we burn bridges in War. . . . It is for our safety—it is a 'military necessity.' " The proclamation issued July 25 to carry out the Confiscation Act was considered an uncertain and timorous policy, a halfway measure. It never specifically mentioned slavery. The people were also depressed by the ignominious defeat at the Second Battle of Bull Run on August 30. An Ohio legislator informed Chase that he had traveled over Ohio for the past two weeks and had found people everywhere complaining about the administration and its failure to use implements that God had provided. At the end of July, Sidney Gay, Greeley's antislavery editor, sent Lincoln an anonymous letter addressed to the *New York Tribune* from a former New York congressman. According to the writer, New Yorkers feared that the administration's policy would sap the nation's strength until the country was exhausted and the administration was obliged to compromise with the Rebels. Gay did not publish the letter, but he suggested that the growing volume of such correspondence indicated that the administration should act against slavery.[25]

Despondency was increasing in the executive department of the government. W.A. Crofutt, secretary of the Washington Lecture Association and a worker in the Treasury Department, in a letter to Ignatius Donnelly, an antislavery congressman, declared it common knowledge that the war was "a peace measure; end it without ending slavery, and that peace will be a war measure! . . . God help us, if he [Lincoln] do not soon open his eyes!" Early in August, at an anniversary meeting of the Abolition of Slavery in the West Indies, Conway accused the president of being "the stumbling block" to freedom.[26]

Lincoln's August 14 address on colonization of blacks, made before a delegation of Negroes, caused fear and uncertainty. The *Congregationalist* suggested that Lincoln follow the direction of Providence and forget about colonization. On August 12, Chase declared that Lincoln was taking the right path, but when he heard that Lincoln endorsed colonization, Chase wrote in his diary: "How much better would be a manly protest against prejudice. . . . A military order, emancipating at least the slaves of South Carolina, Georgia and the Gulf States, would do more to terminate the war and ensure . . . peace than anything else that can be devised." McClintock wrote an associate that "altogether, morally and militarily, it seems that everything is going wrong." He wrote that the president told the blacks in substance that "they had no choice but slavery or exile."[27]

Greeley's letter to Lincoln entitled "The Prayer of Twenty Millions," printed in the *Tribune* for August 20, echoed much of the despair. Greeley accused Lincoln of being "strangely and disastrously remiss" in executing the Confiscation Act, because of "a perilous deference to rebel slavery" arising from the influence of the border states. The people require, said Greeley, "a frank, . . . unqualified, ungrudging execution of the laws of the land, more especially of the Confiscation Act." Lincoln replied: "My paramount object in this struggle *is* to save the Union, and is *not* either to save or destroy slavery. If I could save the union without freeing any slave, I would do it, and if I could save it by freeing *all* the slaves, I would do it; and if I could save it be freeing some and leaving others alone I would also do that." Greeley's letter had confined itself to suggesting that Lincoln honestly enforce the Confiscation Act and other laws, but by answering it as if Greeley had demanded abolition, Lincoln had adroitly used Greeley to gauge the public temper. The president was holding to his position of gradual emancipation despite the fact that he had written the first draft of the Emancipation Proclamation at least six weeks before he replied to Greeley.[28]

The editor of the *Evangelist*, a New School Presbyterian journal, would have liked Lincoln to speak in "bolder tones against slavery" when he answered Greeley, but since many Christians believed there could be no peace without the abolition of slavery, the editor felt Lincoln would be compelled by the logic of events to take higher ground.[29] In another letter to Lincoln, S.I. Prime, editor of the conservative Old School Presbyterian *New York Observer*, the Republican party was described as composed of two factions, the Constitutional party, which would remove slavery by constitutional means, and the Revolutionary party, which would achieve abolition by unconstitutional means. The leaders of the Revolutionary party filled thousands of pulpits, Prime asserted, and the party "has already marked you [Lincoln] for destruction." Some Old School Presbyterians did not share Prime's sentiment. On the day Prime wrote his letter to Lincoln, the Old School Synod of Buffalo insisted that it was "the duty of every Christian patriot . . . to use every means He [God] has put in our power for the suppression of the rebellion." A Middlebury College Alumni Meeting unanimously adopted and sent to Lincoln resolutions expressing the view that "every attribute of the Deity must be armed against our enemies." The resolution committee consisted entirely of clergy and Christian laymen, primarily of Congregational and Episcopal membership.[30]

Most evangelical Christians now supported the radical movement and were demanding that broader and more radical measures be taken against slavery. For example, the Baptist associations that met during the first half of September demanded speedy immediate or universal emancipation, as no peace could be secured without abolition.[31] On August 27, the prestigious Congregational Park Street Church in Boston sent Lincoln a petition with twenty-one signatures calling for emancipation in accordance with divine injunction because permanent peace was impossible while slavery existed. The Christian Citizens of Washington County, Pennsylvania, the General Association of Congregational and Presbyterian Ministers of New Hampshire, and the Presbyterian Synods of Genesee, New York, and Wisconsin urged Lincoln to use the war power to abolish slavery. In an editorial, Beecher advised Lincoln that it would require no more force to destroy slavery and the rebellion together.[32]

On September 7, Christian Citizens of Chicago in a memorial urged Lincoln to abolish slavery on moral and political grounds and as a matter of military necessity because God demanded it. Twelve clergymen and thirty-two laymen signed the memorial, and a committee was selected to deliver it. The meeting, the memorial, and the deputation of Chicago Christians received wide publicity. Similar meetings took place in three cities in Illinois and one each in New York, Iowa, and Wisconsin. The Protestant Methodist Church of Northern Illinois held a similar meeting of Protestant Methodists. All sent memorials to Lincoln. A liberal Christian suggested to Governor Andrew that a committee representing a thousand churches should be sent to Washington.[33]

The *Christian Instructor and United Presbyterian* urged universal emancipation but concluded that it should be based on military necessity, and the *Northwestern Christian Advocate* came out for universal emancipation throughout the land in response to the will of God and the people. The Methodist Episcopal Conference of Iowa held that the president should use all the means God had placed in his hands, and it demanded universal emancipation by the president using his war powers. The Synod of the Reformed Church earnestly urged upon the president "the importance of enforcing the proclamation of the Confiscation Act" with all the power vested in him.[34]

On July 13, Lincoln privately told Seward and Gideon Welles that he had decided to issue an emancipation proclamation. On July 22 he convened the cabinet to inform the members of his decision. Taking the advice of Seward, Lincoln laid aside his proclamation to wait for a military victory. The Battle of Antietam was fought September 17, and Lincoln called his cabinet together to read the proclamation on September 22. The president claimed to have made a vow to regard a victory in the battle as an indication of divine will, and he now called it his duty to move forward in the cause of emancipation. "God had decided this question in favor of the slave," he said.[35]

The proclamation was a war measure, but humanitarian considerations entered into the president's decision. Earlier, when Lincoln was much depressed, he had told his friend Joshua Speed that he had done nothing to make any human being remember that he had ever lived. A few days before Lincoln issued the preliminary Emancipation Proclamation he reminded Speed of the conversation and said he believed that the edict would secure his place in history. Yet twice in December, Sumner had pleaded with Lincoln to acknowledge that the proclamation, in addition to being an "act of military necessity, . . . was an act of justice and humanity, which must have the blessings of a benevolent God." Chase suggested the addition to the proclamation of a final paragraph stating that the proclamation was "sincerely believed to be an act of justice, warranted by the Constitution." Lincoln wrote, "I invoke the considerate judgment of mankind, and the gracious favor of almighty God."[36]

Religious conferences and associations were almost unanimous in rejoicing when the proclamation was issued. The General Association of Illinois Baptists called the proclamation "not only a military necessity but a moral and religious obligation." The Woodstock, Vermont, Baptist Association approved the proclamation and concluded that the President was "God's appointed agent." Senator James Doolittle, a delegate to the Wisconsin State Baptist Association, told the Wisconsin Baptists that the finger of God had withheld victory from the Union army until the Proclamation had been issued.[37]

Evangelical and liberal sectarian journals were united in praising the Emancipation Proclamation. A few religious journals wished that the proclamation had included slaves in all slave states, that the proclamation's provisions had been immediate instead of preliminary, and that moral as well as military necessity had been cited as a reason for issuing the edict. The *Pittsburgh Christian Advocate* asserted that the proclamation placed the government on the side of right and humanity: "God . . . will now fight for the nation as He has not yet fought for it." The editor of the *Christian Times and Illinois Baptist* regarded the proclamation "as the turning point of the war." Only the Old School *Philadelphia Presbyterian*, the *New York Observer*, and the Dutch Reformed *Christian Intelligencer* published the edict without comment, perhaps from hesitation or reticence regarding their own views. Eventually all sectarian journals fully accepted the edict.[38]

A few ultraradical clergymen did not see the proclamation as reflecting the design of providence. In the week after the proclamation was issued, George Cheever, one of the few evangelical clerical critics, delivered a message that he characterized as coming from God for the "undecided and unfaithful rulers" who had betrayed truth. He called the proclamation nothing but a bribe to win back the slaveholding states. On November 22, Cheever in a long letter urged Lincoln to make the proclamation immediate and universal. For his part, Conway went on the lecture circuit in December 1862 with a new sermon, "The Unrecognized Gift of God to America." He was the chief spokesman for a delegation that protested the failure of the military to carry out emancipation under the Confiscation Act. William Goodell, another ultraradical, was critical of the proclamation. He called Lincoln's edict "a two-sided" proclamation that offered a bribe with one hand and a threat with the other.[39]

James F. Clarke took a similar ultraradical stance. He told his Boston congregation that the proclamation should have been made immediate and "put on principles of justice and right, not on mere war necessity."[40] Joseph Medill, editor of the *Chicago Tribune*, felt that the Proclamation should have brought immediate action. He attended a Unitarian church whose pastor was the radical Robert Collyer. Medill wrote to a friend: Lincoln "issued his Proclamation and then sat down on his d—— content, but proclamations, like faith with out works, are dead." John Wilson, a liberal Episcopal lawyer of Illinois, lamented the delay in putting the proclamation into effect. Wilson informed the governor of Illinois that he thought "it should have gone in force at once." Henry Bellows told the Unitarian convention in Brooklyn in October: "God means not to let us off with any half-way work." Bellows asserted that he would take the most radical ground possible and conduct a war of "subjugation or the extermination of all persons who wish to maintain the slave power . . . to get rid of slave-holders, whether it be constitutional or not."[41] Since the beginning of the war Bellows had shifted from a confirmed conservative position to a radical one.

The ranks of the radical Christians had grown since the beginning of the Civil War. The failure of the government to take decisive action against slavery caused the moral community to adopt a more radical stance. Failure to win decisive military victories caused many to believe that God was exacting retribution from the North because slavery had not been abolished. The clergy decided that God had a controversy with his people and that persistent defeats were divine warning that the Union would not be saved without abolition in the North. The Civil War was viewed as God's foreordained plan of preparation for the millennium. A Brooklyn Methodist minister called the Civil War the "first great conflict to precede the millennium." With the promulgation of the Emancipation Proclamation, the barrier to the new age was broken down. Churchmen praised the moral efficacy and justice of emancipation as they had never before praised an act of the government. Moral opposition to slavery had helped to bring on the war, and in 1862 it helped to commit Congress and the president to an anti-slavery policy.[42]

With the outbreak of the Civil War, the clergy became less powerful as businessmen, politicians, generals, and editors assumed greater social and economic importance. After twenty months of war without decisive Union army successes, the nation was ready to examine the moral question of slavery in relation to the conflict. As a result the clergy and the church found themselves in a new position of prestige and power.[43]

The Northern clergymen were an important factor in the pressure upon the president to emancipate and free the slaves. The moral revolt against fighting the war and protecting slavery prevented the government from continuing the policy of 1861. Moral pressure was as significant as military necessity, and the radical Christians were an important force in suggesting military necessity.[44]

# CHAPTER THREE

# The Election of 1862

After the Confiscation Act of July 1862 had passed, the sentiments of the radicals changed considerably. An antislavery citizen wrote to Wade the following week that the Radical party had an opportunity, first, to do "justice to a poor oppressed and down trodden" people and, second, to win "the gratitude and support of voters."[1] Medill also saw that confiscation and emancipation measures would become a political issue when they were adopted. "We can make ten times as strong a fight to uphold a measure once passed as to advocate it before it is a law." He urged Trumbull to pass confiscation measures and emancipation and "let the Democrats go before the people on the issue of reenslavement."[2]

The radicals had been urging the administration to put God in the government as a necessary step in preserving the nation, but after having secured the enactment of the Confiscation Act and the adoption of the preliminary Emancipation Proclamation, they continued to pressure the administration and to prepare for the midterm election.[3] As early as July 4, a pastor of a Presbyterian church in Perry County, Pennsylvania, advised his congregation that if they voted for none but good men, the "wire-working politicians" would be forced to offer morally sound candidates. "In a crisis like ours, men must take sides, and if they are not for the Union they are against it."[4]

In August the religious journals began to prepare their readers for the election. The smaller Calvinist churches were in the forefront of the effort to persuade their members to vote only for antislavery candidates. The western corresponding editor of the *Christian Instructor and United Presbyterian* alerted Christian citizens to their great responsibility. "Let every Christian all over our land see to it," he wrote, "that henceforth they will aid in putting into office only such as are possessed of at least stern morality and integrity, if not of Christian principles." Even the editor of the Old School *Presbyterian Standard* agreed, as the election approached, that a higher moral tone was needed. In September, the editor of the *Christian Intelligencer* warned his readers that it was wrong to stay away from the polls. "We contend," he said, "that Christian men are bound by their obligation to religion, to their country, and hopes of men, to exert to the utmost of their power all their influence in our civil affairs." The *Independent* informed its readers that the altar and ballot box would "stand or fall together."[5] In response, the Democratic press accused the Protestant clergy and journals of preaching politics. A writer in *Harper's Weekly* pointed out that the people who condemned "political preaching" belonged to a party whose discipline required the support of slavery, and who therefore insisted that because politics touched slavery it ceased to be a moral question.[6]

When annual conferences and associations met in the autumn of 1862, concern was expressed about the election. The Methodist Episcopal Conference of Wisconsin, which met early in September, averred that the election to public office, and the appointment to military authority, of men of immoral habits of life was fraught with danger and shame to the land and should be discouraged in all legitimate ways by all honest and upright people.[7] The Methodists were not alone in taking a more radical position in Wisconsin. Early in September, Charles L. Scholes, a Unitarian layman, informed his senator, James Doolittle, that Republicans had advanced in Wisconsin from opposition to the extension of slavery to "*death to slavery*, and nothing shorter." An Illinois radical expressed the need for additional action by Lincoln as evidence of his "devotion to the true principle in this great war."[8]

As the midterm election approached, many religious associations began to express their moral objective in civil or political terms. According to the Dodge (Wisconsin) Baptist Association, "to save the Union is a noble work; but the salvation and enthronement of a great moral principle which is really more warred against than is the Union, seems to us the paramount duty of the hour." The Columbus (Ohio) Baptist Association considered its weapons of warfare to be spiritual, not carnal, moral, not political, and remarked that in the crisis of the country it was the duty of the people of God to remember their government.[9] In Worcester, Massachusetts, a Baptist minister was more specific about politics. Reverend Merrill Richardson of Worcester was one of the main speakers before the Massachusetts Republican Convention. "God gives us certain means, let us use them," Richardson told his audience. He felt certain that nine out of ten among the people demanded that slaves be used as a means of suppressing the rebellion.

A Baptist writer in the October issue of the Baptist *Christian Review* assured his readers that "the majesty and power of God's onward-marching providence" would carry the nation forward to a righteous success and triumph.[10]

The preliminary proclamation added a new dimension to the election campaign. With a stroke of his pen Lincoln had shifted the chief issue of the political contest from national sovereignty to human liberty. The proclamation had abundant unpredictable political consequences. After it had been issued, ministers began to counsel their congregations to lay aside their party differences and unite to secure the safety of the nation. The composition of the next Congress became a vital concern. The Pittsburgh Presbyterian Presbytery unanimously called for radical measures and pledged itself to sustain the president and the government.[11] The New School Presbyterian Synod of Illinois believed it "the duty of all good men to frown upon all attempts to weaken confidence in the Government."[12] The Illinois Methodist Episcopal Conference expressed the warmest sympathies and heartiest cooperation with the government in using all means sanctioned by the word of God in striking down slavery.[13]

The Democrats focused their political attacks on the Republican racial policies. They claimed that the Republican measures would inevitably lead to social equality. While Republican politicians tried to dodge the emancipation issue, the antislavery religious leaders made emancipation the primary reason for supporting the Republicans. The editor of the *Western Christian Advocate* met the Democrats on their own grounds and argued that slavery, not emancipation, promoted social equality and amalgamation. The Michigan Methodist Episcopal Conference heartily approved the proclamation and tried to make public opinion favorable to it. Other religious bodies adopted similar measures.[14]

Some religious synods and conferences directed their energies toward the electorate and political parties. The Illinois Conference of the Methodist Episcopal Church informed the public that they held in "the deepest abhorrence the course of any public servant who by his votes or speeches, or influences, had endeavored to embarrass the Government in crushing the rebellion at any cost." The Western Indiana Conference of the Methodist Episcopal Church disclaimed "all sympathy with any organization which does not heartily cooperate with the Government for the preservation of the liberties of the people and the maintenance of the Federal Constitution."[15]

The Presbyterian Synod of Pennsylvania urged all "loyal people to mark with their complete abhorrence" all who resist the efforts of the government "to suppress the rebellion." The Synod of Pittsburgh took a more determined stand. The synod warned that "political infidelity and spurious and hypocritical Christianity had joined hands," causing God to have a controversy with the nation. The proclamation and the election of 1862 offered a chance to remove the scourge. Many western synods urged the people to support the government. A few Presbyterian members protested such measures on the grounds that the synods had meddled in a political question, and a larger number of Methodists complained about the political measures adopted by their church.[16]

The Democrats played up racial prejudice for all it was worth. The *New York Tribune* called Democratic propaganda "an appeal to that cruel and ungenerous prejudice against color which still remains to disgrace our civilization and to impeach our Christianity." Democrats capitalized on the fact that Negro refugees migrated to the Northwest. The secretary of war played into the hands of the Democrats by sending hundreds of fugitive slaves into Illinois.[17] Religious journals attempted to counteract the Democratic propaganda. The editor of the *Western Christian Advocate* argued that emancipation would stop the tide of black immigration to the North.[18] Lyman Abbott assured his Indiana congregation that emancipation would end the flow of the blacks to the free states.[19]

Episcopal and Old School Presbyterian journals in the East were silent on the political issue. The conservative Protestant Episcopal Church met in general convention during October 1862, and the question of politics came up for discussion when the committee on the state of the country made its report. Bishop Thomas Clark of Rhode Island argued that members must avoid political discussion as they always had, but he insisted that declaring support for the government did not involve a clergyman in politics. The convention adopted measures stating that it was the whole duty of members of the church, as citizens, to sustain and defend the nation but that as deputies to the church council, which had renounced all political association and action, they should pray for their country's guidance by the wisdom of God.[20] The Methodist Episcopal Church contrasted with the Protestant Episcopal Church. On the eve of the election, "An Appeal to Christian and Patriotic Women Upon Their Duties in Relation to the War," in the *Ladies' Repository,* urged Christian women to form local investigative squads to ferret out those who opposed the war and expose them to public pressure by branding them as traitors. *"Detect and expose the covert traitors in your neighborhood. . . . Hunt them out.*

Make the place, the society, the neighborhood too hot for them. Let them know that you have taken the precise gauge of their patriotism and honesty, and that it is about time for them to go and join the rebels," urged the author.[21]

As the election approached, the sectarian press instructed the faithful in more precise language. The *Christian Instructor* thundered: "Men of God! . . . Stand up for Jesus and help to exalt no man to power and influence who will not stand up for Jesus with you."[22] A few days before the election, the *Independent* declared that no one who wanted to see the government victorious in the conflict with the rebellion should vote for the Democratic party. Three days later, in a sermon entitled "The Duties of the Crisis," Beecher counseled his congregation, "Every idea of God's providence . . . exhorts us not to yield, not to compromise. . . . Vote for freedom." A practicing Christian from Upper Alton, Illinois, considered the stakes higher. He informed Richard Yates, governor of Illinois, that he could not perceive a greater, more odious reason for the "chastising hand" of God than the triumph of the Democratic party.[23]

Although most active Christians were in sympathy with emancipation, many Old School Presbyterians and conservative Episcopalians probably voted with the Democrats. The active religious people were in a minority in the country, but since most Christians had contacts with like-minded citizens and read newspapers that were in harmony with their sentiments, they were badly informed about the reality of the canvass. The Methodist minister John McClintock, viewing the election campaign from France, did not believe that "the proslavery platform" would carry a single Northern state. The Unitarian divine Henry W. Bellows, in New York, was more informed. He feared that the Democrats might be victorious, but he hoped for a union of Republican and antislavery Democrats of the type who had voted for the abolition of slavery in the District of Columbia. Oliver Johnson, a Quaker abolitionist, was more optimistic than Bellows: "I am confident that they [the Democrats] will be overwhelmed, that the vast majority of the Northern people will sustain the President."[24] Some clergymen vacillated between optimism and pessimism, according to the news of the day.

In Massachusetts the conservative Republicans organized a People's party to try to overthrow the radicals and replace Sumner because of his radical position on emancipation. Sumner's term expired in March 1863. The possibility that Sumner's election was in doubt because of the Democrats and that the conservative Republicans might control the legislature aroused the moral forces in Massachusetts to enthusiastic action. Ministers, editors of the religious press, and Sunday school teachers mounted the political stump to support him. They were aware that Sumner would vigorously resist all attacks on the supremacy of the moral sense, and they were convinced of his strong religious faith. All doubt quickly evaporated. A Massachusetts Congregational clergyman felt that Charles Sumner should be encouraged to take a more radical stand so that the administration in Washington would "be *fully* and *heartily* sustained" after issuance of the Emancipation Proclamation; the rebellion could then be put down without fear of "any compromise whatever."[25]

Antislavery Christians urged clergymen and prominent laymen to stand for election with some results. Unitarians Reverend Thomas S. King of California and Reverend John A. Gurley of Ohio ran for Congress without success. Clergymen and former ministers also ran for state legislatures. Reverend Sereno Howe, an antislavery Baptist minister, was elected to the Massachusetts legislature, where he was a leader of the antislavery forces.[26]

There were some defections from the ranks of the Republican party among the evangelical denominations, especially the Methodist churches in the West. An antislavery Methodist clergyman from Indiana wrote in his diary that the Democrats were successful in his part of the county. He had concluded that many Republicans voted the Democratic ticket as a result of "the first reaction" to the Emancipation Proclamation. Another Indiana antislavery Methodist clergyman recorded in his diary that a church trustee was so opposed to his antislavery sermons that he would not permit repairs to the church. The trustee said the people did not want a preacher. "The country . . . had been ruined by abolition preachers, and he was going to withdraw from the whole concern." An Indianapolis Baptist minister recalled later that his printed sermon declaring that slavery was the cause of the Civil War had been forbidden on the streets of the city. His church was eventually burned because emancipation was taught from the pulpit. The General Convention of the Methodist Protestant Church was so concerned about discord in the church following the election that after approving the proclamation, those in attendance "earnestly deprecated the dissension and division in the Church." There was "strong evidence of sympathy with the enemy in our midst," the convention reported. Even some administration supporters in Congress expressed reservations about the proclamation. Representative C.D. Hubbard, a Methodist layman from West Virginia, wrote his son:

"I regard the President's proclamation as the worst error he has made."[27]

The bitterness of the Democratic opposition to the proclamation and the determination to make slavery the chief issue of the election forced the Republicans to take measures to meet the threat. The radical antislavery Republicans confronted the crucial issue directly. Theodore Weld, the most powerful lecturer of the Anti-Slavery Society in the 1830s, lectured with great effect from Pennsylvania to Massachusetts.[28] The Republicans found an earnest and convincing speaker in Anna E. Dickinson, a Quaker girl who perfected her style while speaking among the Quakers.[29] Weld and Dickinson started lecturing too late to have much effect on the election of 1862.

The country did not have a unified polling date in 1862. New Hampshire, Connecticut, and Rhode Island voted in the spring; Pennsylvania, Ohio, and Indiana held their elections in October; and elsewhere votes were cast in November. Massachusetts, New York, and New Jersey elected governors, and all of these states chose Congressmen. In Pennsylvania, Ohio, and Indiana, the Democrats polled a majority of the House seats, while Michigan, Iowa, and California went for the Republicans. The Republicans retained control of Congress in 1862 by only a slight margin. The Democrats made a net gain of thirty-two seats in the House of Representatives. The Democrats also won governorships in New York and New Jersey and gained control of the legislatures of Indiana and New York. If the election was a referendum on emancipation and the conduct of Lincoln as president, a majority of the Northern votes endorsed these policies. If the proclamation gained votes for the administration in New England, northern Ohio, and Michigan, it lost votes in southern Ohio, Indiana, and Illinois. The Emancipation Proclamation was the chief cause of the Republican party's reverses after 1860. Other causes were opposition to arbitrary arrests, suspension of habeas corpus privileges, military failures, and factional discord within the party. In Ohio, the arrest of several citizens during the summer and fall laid the administration open to the charge of violating constitutional rights.[30]

The political reverses and losses from the congressional majority of 1860 led to a fear that the administration might compromise with the South. Even before the election, Henry Bellows feared that loss of the election would weaken the policy of the administration and lead to fatal compromises with the Rebels. After the election setback in New York, a Boston clergyman admitted to Bellows that he, like many others, felt "very despondent," fearing that a dishonorable peace was possible. Trumbull was uneasy about the future after the election. He wrote Chandler: "I fear a humiliating compromise." George Bancroft was afraid that the antislavery Republicans would cease to have access to Lincoln after the election and the government would revert to a conservative position. "How can we reach the President with advice?" he queried Francis Lieber. "He is ignorant, self-willed, and is surrounded by men, some of whom are as ignorant as himself." The Philadelphia Baptist Association was uneasy about the possibility that the administration would make a negotiated peace and went on record as opposing a compromise peace.[31]

Some pessimistic antislavery Christians worried that the proclamation would never be enforced. For some this anxiety increased as time passed. Harriet Beecher Stowe doubted that the proclamation was real and wanted to find out by going to Washington and seeing Lincoln and others. She came away optimistic that the president would stand firm on the proclamation and that the border states would accede to his proposition.[32] Ralph Plumb, a Calvinist layman from Oberlin, was also optimistic because the North now had an idea and a cause. This hero of the Wellington Rescue explained that, before the proclamation, the South had been fighting for nationality and the North for subjugation. Many antislavery Christians expressed disappointment with the progress concerning emancipation. Garrison hoped the final edict would grant immediate and complete emancipation, but he pessimistically concluded that the president could "do nothing in a direct manner, but only by circumlocution and delay. How prompt was his action against Fremont and Hunter." Oliver Johnson could assure Garrison that, from all he could learn, "the President is not contemplating any change of policy so far as emancipation is concerned, in consequence of the recent election," for the removal of McClellan indicated that he had abandoned "all attempts to conciliate the proslavery Democracy." From Rochester, Sallie Holley, the daughter of one of the leading Calvinist abolitionists of the 1830s, wrote to her Quaker friend Abby Foster: "How cold the President's Proclamation is."[33]

A radical Christian from Wisconsin became so disillusioned with Lincoln's slavery policy that he wrote to the editor of *The Principia* that unless Congress took "a different position" and adopted "a different policy from our President and his cabinet, I fear the judgments of God will follow us, until our republic is subverted." Others felt the same way. A group of antislavery men in the East decided not "to waste much more ammunition upon the President." George Ward Nichols, a liberal Episcopal layman, informed Governor Andrew that they were preparing "an Emancipation Act which may be passed by the next Congress."[34] When Congress convened in December 1862 for its lame-duck session, the Republicans affirmed the Emancipation Proclamation by a straight party vote when they adopted a resolution endorsing it.[35] Cheever suggested the format of an Emancipation Act that Congressman James Ashley and others supported, but Congress adjourned without passing the act.[36]

Nevertheless, rumors were widespread that Lincoln would withdraw the Emancipation Proclamation. These rumors gained force from Lincoln's message to Congress on December 1. The president recommended to Congress a constitutional amendment for compensated, gradual emancipation in every state where slavery existed. The gradual emancipation extended slavery to 1900, when servitude would cease. The uneasy radicals reasoned that if Lincoln had intended to issue the edict, he would not have proposed the constitutional amendment for gradual emancipation.[37]

The president's message struck a sharp blow to the antislavery Christians' hopes and expectations. Moncure Conway, the editor of the *Boston Commonwealth*, an unofficial Unitarian journal, wrote, "The President says that Slavery is the cause of the War; the cause of its continuance; that we can have no peace so long as it exists. Then his proposition can only amount to a proposition to continue the war until the year 1900." Parker Pillsbury told Tilton that in his opinion "God has no better opinion of our President than he had of Pharaoh and . . . until we talk of something besides compensation and colonisation [sic] then . . . the true believer . . . has little over which to be 'cheery' or hopeful or happy."[38] The antislavery Unitarian Congressman James Ashley was "greatly disappointed" when he first read the message, but after he had talked with the president, he wrote, "I felt confident that *in heart he was far in advance of the message.*" If Lincoln remained unconvinced that he should go through with the final proclamation on January 1, 1863, the ignominious defeat of the Union forces at the Battle of Fredericksburg on December 13 finally settled the question in his mind.[39]

The Old School Presbyterian journals were not disturbed by Lincoln's December message. The *Presbyter* considered the proposal of Lincoln's message likely to have good effect on the rebel states because they undoubtedly saw that slavery was doomed, and if they acted, they would receive aid.[40] The *New York Observer* approved of Lincoln's plan and was disappointed that it had not met with more favor. By seeking an amendment to the Constitution to carry out gradual compensated emancipation, Lincoln was emphatically protesting "the plans of the modern immediate emancipation school."[41]

An antislavery Christian considered Lincoln committed to a glorious work. "We know the revolution now inaugurated cannot and will not go backward. Retributive Justice is now at work, and thank God the Union will yet be preserved," he assured Representative Ignatius Donnelly. According to Henry Ward Beecher, the people had found out that "there is no wisdom in conservatism and that radicalism was what they wanted. Radicalism which shall strike at the root of evil." He had confidence that the president would carry out emancipation as scheduled. Reverend George Putnam, a moderate Unitarian clergyman of Massachusetts, took strong ground in support of the proclamation in a sermon. He told his congregation that he had never been an abolitionist in the usual sense. "But if now the Almighty Providence itself has become manifestly and actively [an] Abolitionist, we shall have to follow its leading and fall in with its purpose. . . . God will not be crossed nor defeated." In a Thanksgiving sermon, Reverend Edwin F. Hatfield, a New School Presbyterian clergyman, saw the proclamation as the work of God. "The hand of God is clearly discernable," he asserted. "When this great act of justice had been wrung from us, how clearly is the hand of God to be seen in arresting the triumph of the conspirators." He concluded that the administration could not retreat.[42]

As January 1, 1863, began to draw near, many radical Christians became more fearful of the influence of the conservative Republicans. Governor Israel Washburn of Maine expressed uneasiness to Vice President Hannibal Hamlin: "Does the President mean to give in—if so, . . . Heaven won't save him." Hamlin, a liberal Unitarian, sympathized with Washburn's concern. He felt that the federal government should use "every means of war" that God had put in its hands.[43] An antislavery Episcopalian pleaded with Zachariah Chandler, "For *God's sake* don't let the President back down on his proclamation,"[44] and a Methodist layman informed Wade that the president's proposal for gradual emancipation did not meet with the approval of his circle. The thought of keeping slavery for years "would be painful and almost unendurable. . . . The President has a right from military necessity to emancipate all of the slaves at once and I believe there never was a greater necessity than the present."[45]

In speaking to Trumbull late in December, an antislavery Republican expressed uneasiness about the fate of the proclamation. He was concerned that the proslavery sympathizers in the cabinet might persuade Lincoln not to issue the edict on January 1. Other antislavery men were troubled by the same uncertainty. Congressman Charles Sedgwick wrote Forbes: "Some doubt that Lincoln's intention is to issue the proclamation of 1st. January; I do not. Many assert, more fear, that it will be essentially modified from what is promised. I do not fear this; but what I do fear is, that he will stop with the proclamation and take no active and vigorous measures to insure its efficacy." Sedgwick pressed Forbes to come to Washington and use his influence with Lincoln to get him to issue the proclamation and see that it was enforced. Forbes belonged to a group of radical Christians and humanitarians in the East that had been organized in 1861 by George Stearns to persuade the public that an emancipation policy was "a necessity to bring the war to a close, and that without it there can be no reasonable hope of a speedy restoration of peace" without abolishing slavery. They had been publishing articles, circulars, and pamphlets to influence public opinion. John M. Forbes and John Andrew considered sending a delegation of clergy and laity to urge the president to follow through with his intention to issue the proclamation. They contacted William Fessenden and several others who doubted the president's intention and believed that a strong delegation was needed. The clergymen met and drew up a memorial, which Forbes sent to Sumner, who presented it to Lincoln. Representative Samuel Hooper informed Andrew from Washington that, according to the best intelligence, the proclamation would be issued.[46]

Antislavery and Christian people of New Bedford drew up a memorial approving the prospective proclamation and encouraged Lincoln. Senator Samuel P. Fessenden, an antislavery Episcopalian, presented a similar paper from concerned citizens and Christians of Rockland, Maine. Senator James Harlan, an antislavery Methodist, offered one from the Quakers of Prairie Grove, Iowa.[47] Edward M. Mansfield, a Presbyterian journalist, writing anonymously under the pen name "EDM," in an article entitled "The Proclamation," suggested, "Providence brings upon a nation either great calamities or awful phenomena." He was convinced that the proclamation would be issued.[48]

On December 22, 1862, antislavery ministers of various denominations met in Cheever's Church of the Puritans to consider the duty of the churches and ministers in the present state of the country. A committee produced a memorial to the president and Congress, begging "in the name of God that a decree" be enacted and executed "immediately establishing universal freedom." Cheever, Goodell, and Nathan Brown, a Baptist, were chosen as a delegation to deliver the memorial to Lincoln. The delegation arrived in Washington the last day of the year and were courteously received by the president, who listened patiently to their memorial. The deputation took the position that the president, in war and in peace, had full power to abolish slavery. The memorial called for universal and immediate emancipation. The petition of the committee was without effect; the president had already decided upon the terms of the proclamation.[49]

Approximately forty conservative and moderate clergymen met at Cooper Institute in New York on the same day that the radicals met in the Church of the Puritans. The purpose of the Cooper Institute meeting was to find ways to sustain the president. A committee, chaired by Reverend Asa Smith, was appointed to draw up resolutions. The measure that was adopted declared slavery to be the main cause of the rebellion and war and asserted that no permanent peace could be established until slavery had been abolished from the land. A second committee was appointed to draw up a resolution urging the president to carry out the proclamation to its fullest extent. Unauthorized publicity was given to the first meeting, and two or three hundred people appeared at a second meeting, but the chairman limited participation and voting members to those who had been present at the first. The committee selected to draw up a memorial reported that none had been prepared because word had come from Washington that no action was needed. After the chairman of the committee moved adjournment, some antislavery clergyman proposed to hold a rump session but were told that they were not authorized to use the hall.[50]

The Emancipation Proclamation partly reflected the nature of the war. In addition, however, it answered military imperatives and the moral demand of antislavery Christians. Lincoln told Sumner that he "could not stop the Proclamation if he would, and would not if he could."[51] The radical Christian sentiment in Washington in late December was overwhelming in its intensity.

The final draft of the proclamation did not mention Lincoln's earlier proposals of compensation and colonization. The president had abandoned them altogether. The preliminary proclamation had promised that the slaves would be "forever free," but in the final draft Lincoln was content to say the slaves "are, and henceforward shall be, free," and the omission of "forever" seemed to make the proclamation less permanent. The preliminary proclamation said nothing about using slaves as soldiers, but in the final edict slaves were to be received into the military service. The president was simply using authority that had been granted by Congress in 1862 to strike a blow against the Confederacy. The antislavery Christians had mixed feelings about the proclamation, but they were aware the president had placed himself firmly on the side of freedom. They enjoyed unprecedented influence and prestige in church and state relations.[52]

# CHAPTER FOUR

# Rise Up O Man of God!

The Emancipation Proclamation ushered in an economic and political revolution. The most radical Christians wanted to inaugurate a social revolution as well. The antislavery Presbyterian divine John Rankin rejoiced that the Proclamation had ended the system of slavery as Heaven had ordained; he lamented that it was not broad enough to cover the whole field of oppression. Theodore Tilton informed the readers of the *Independent* that the war against rebellion was "a struggle for social equality, for rights, for justice, for freedom." A Congregational clergyman declared in a sermon to his parishioners in Westboro, Massachusetts, that slaves freed by the proclamation should receive "perfect equality with all other people!"[1]

Although Lincoln had stressed that the Emancipation Proclamation responded to military necessity, moral and humanitarian factors were significant. Lincoln accepted Chase's suggested closing for the document, which was moral in tone. The president wrote that the emancipation of the slave was "sincerely believed to be an act of justice." In the same sentence he invoked "the considerate judgment of mankind and the gracious favor of Almighty God."[2] This wording elevated the proclamation above any other war measure in tone. With Chase's final paragraph, the war became more than a conflict in which the integrity and unity of the nation were at stake. The war became a battle for the freedom of mankind.

The proclamation was generally well received by the churchgoing people. On January 1 Henry W. Beecher offered a Thanksgiving sermon on the proclamation. "Now," he told his congregation, "we are to see what radicals can do to heal the nation." Cheever delivered a sermon the Sunday after the proclamation had been issued. He believed the Almighty had forced the edict on the people, whom He was determined to save. G.R. Crooks, a Methodist divine, predicted that all Christians would "become Radical Republicans sooner or later." Tilton declared in the *Independent* that "the safety of the nation" demanded the destruction of slavery. He regretted that the proclamation was not universal, but he had faith that God would correct the omission. Tilton had been on the lecture trail in late December, urging the people to stand firm and to permit no compromise with slavery. On January 1, an emancipation jubilee was held in New York. Simon S. Jocelyn pleaded with his radical audience to stand firm. "If there had been an emancipation proclamation at the time Fort Sumter fell the war would have been over in three months," Jocelyn complained. R.C. Waterston, an antislavery Congregational minister and a director of the Church Anti-Slavery Society, praised Lincoln's edict. "This is a great Era! A sublime period in History! The Proclamation is grand. The President has done nobly," he wrote enthusiastically to Sumner. Rudolf Schleiden, the minister of the Republic of Bremen, concluded that the president's decision to issue the edict seemed "to have been caused chiefly by the apprehension that the extreme Republican Party would attempt to overthrow him if he reneged." The German minister was aware that the radicals were irked because Seward and Blair seemed to be controlling the president.[3]

The Emancipation Proclamation included a provision that all ablebodied men could be received in the military service. Calvin Fletcher, of Indianapolis, a Presbyterian layman, was no doubt thinking of black soldiers when he penned in his diary: "Who knows but God may yet raise up a Moses whom we shall fear and respect and that he will give his countrymen character and standing even among the whites." The possibility that the army might use black soldiers stirred the imagination of antislavery Christians. Dr. Tyng was one of the first people to advocate the use of black troops. Blacks had "a right to this privilege of defending themselves," Tyng argued. When Stevens's bill to raise Negro regiments passed in the House, Congressman William P. Cutler, an active Presbyterian layman and a trustee of Marietta College, recorded in his diary, "This vote is a recognition of the Negros *manhood*—such as has never before been made by this nation. We say in the hour of peril—come save us. '*Our God is marching on.*'" Sumner had made a speech in Faneuil Hall in Boston in October 1862 justifying the use of black troops. On February 6, 1863, he introduced a bill providing for black enlistment, but there was no action on the bill in the committee.[4] Mention of the use of black troops produced a racial emotional reaction among the conservative Democrats.

On the Sunday after issuance of the Emancipation Proclamation, clergymen throughout the country preached antislavery sermons.

Henry Ward Beecher saw a similarity between the United States and the Egypt of old. "We refused to hear the voice of God saying, 'Let my people go,' until now." Beecher answered the complaint that the Proclamation did not free a single slave by arguing that the decree gave "liberty a moral recognition." William Channing delivered a sermon in the Senate chamber and told the audience that the proclamation had changed the conflict into a struggle over principles. The conflict should be seen as a "war of light and darkness" as God saw it from the start. The proclamation had transformed the war into a moral crusade, and a Methodist minister in Wisconsin testified to the fact that the supposed sin of supporting Copperheadism received no sympathy. The Wisconsin Methodist Conference, "recognizing human freedom as the issue in the conflict, . . . deemed it alike the duty of the citizen and the Christian to prosecute the war."[5]

The Democratic press and politicians met the sermons of the clergy with vengeance. Counterattacks by the Democrats were led by Samuel S. Cox, a congressman from Ohio. In the lame-duck session of Congress, Cox promised all-out opposition to the Emancipation Proclamation unless it was confirmed by the states. He warned that the country must return to the time-honored system of compromise. On January 14, 1863, Cox delivered a speech before the Democratic Union Association of New York entitled "Puritanism in Politics." He denounced Puritanism as a reptile that must be crushed. "The tendency of New England Puritanical policy," he reasoned, "was to make Government a moral reform society. . . . Every Sabbath you have a sermon from Dr. Cheever, demonstrating that our failures in battle are owing to the displeasure of God, because of the sin of Slavery." The clergymen and the religious press responded to Cox's attack on the church. Months later, after the debate had ebbed, the *Zion's Herald* carried an editorial entitled "Puritanism in Politics." In it the editor explained, "Puritanism in politics means conscience or the fear of God in Civil Affairs, and is . . . the only salt that can preserve the State from despotism, anarchy and ruin."[6] The editor of the *Pittsburgh Christian Advocate* responded to the attack by counseling the clergy to "let morals rise superior to politics, and wield a controlling influence in all the affairs of Government. This is the only solution."[7]

After the final decree had been issued in January 1863, the radical Christians launched a vigorous counterattack. During the second week of January, many sectarian newspapers carried an editorial on the proclamation. The *Christian Advocate and Journal* criticized the proclamation because it had not been adopted earlier and because it liberated only three-fourths of the slaves. The Congregational *Boston Recorder* considered the proclamation of greatest value as a link in the chain of God's providential causes which were working to eradicate the system of oppression. The editor of the *Evangelist* concluded his editorial by writing, "We believe devoutly that the measure is wise and just, and that its effect will be to hasten the close of the war." The *Independent* viewed the proclamation as "law of the highest moral achievement." The editor of the *Christian Inquirer* praised Lincoln for lifting "the weight of the country . . . from the neck of the slave." William Goodell wished the proclamation had gone farther. Goodell, the editor of *Principia*, complained that an authority who could freely grant freedom to three-fourths of the slaves was "competent to proclaim freedom to the remaining one fourth." But Goodell conceded that the proclamation put the "nation indisputably on the side of justice and right." The *Morning Star* hailed the edict as the precursor of a great day "dawning upon the country and the world."[8]

Faith in the power of God's Providence became stronger as the events of the war developed. The *Christian Advocate and Journal* explained that it "required little wisdom to see the moving of His hand" in the war and "less to see the design to be ultimately accomplished." The *Boston Recorder* was sure "Providence was revealing a sign that . . . God" was about "to give great success, and another probationary trial of the nation" because the end of slavery was on the way to solution. Edmund Fairchild, a Free Will Baptist and president of Hillsdale College, was also sure that God had intervened. Fairchild delivered a sermon in the representative hall of the Michigan state legislature and assured his listeners that "the day of our redemption draweth nigh. . . . Justice . . . and Right and Heaven are with us!"[9]

Reverend Roswell Hitchcock delivered a Washington's Birthday address in which he revealed that he was shifting toward radicalism. He told his audience that "the best way to conquer aristocracy would be to knock out its under-pinning—Slavery." John McClintock was also critical of Lincoln. "If he [Lincoln] had nerve enough to issue the proclamation at the very beginning of the War," he wrote his daughter, "the rebellion would never had assumed the proportion it has." Governor Andrew had mixed feelings. He called the decree "a poor *document*, but a mighty *act*"; and Samuel May, Jr., conceded that the proclamation had a number of defects but informed a correspondent: "I cannot stop to dwell on these. Joy, gratitude, thanksgiving, renewed hope and courage fill my soul."[10]

After the Battle of Fredericksburg on December 13, 1862, there was much anguish and despair in the North. Five days later, Lincoln expressed the depth of his despair in speaking to a friend. "We are now on the brink of destruction. It appears to me the Almighty is against us, and I can hardly see a ray of hope." For much of the North the gloom extended through the winter of 1862-63. Fessenden thought that much of the fault rested with the cabinet. "The simple truth is," he wrote his family, "there never was such a shambling, half and half set of incapables collected in one government before since the world began." Congressman William P. Cutler, an Ohio Congregationalist, was of the same mind. He wrote in his diary for January 26, 1863: "To human vision all is dark and it would almost seem that God works for the rebels and keeps alive their cause. . . . How striking is the want of a leader. The nation is without a head."[11] A New York Methodist layman lamented to John McClintock in Paris, "Our poor country is in a deplorable condition. The conduct of the war does not inspire confidence in the authorities. The public mind is divided." Congressman James Pike, an antislavery Baptist layman, also viewed the administration with a critical eye. He wrote to Fessenden: "The President's emancipation policy wobbles insecurely, for the 'paltering policy' is no policy."[12] The next day, January 14, Representative James Wilson of Iowa, chairman of the Judiciary Committee, reported an amendment to the Constitution declaring slavery forever prohibited in the United States. It was the first attempt to abolish slavery by amending the Constitution.[13]

Lincoln was still promoting gradual emancipation for the border states. On January 29, 1863, Senator Trumbull proposed a bill to supply Missouri with $20 million to be used to free its slaves in thirteen years. The Presbyterian Trumbull explained the reason for backing the bill: "I am not prepared to say that because we cannot have immediate emancipation, therefore we will do nothing for gradual emancipation."[14] In February, Sumner, Fessenden, and Henry Wilson organized to resist Lincoln's plan for gradual compensated emancipation in Missouri. To Sumner, gradual emancipation in Missouri would serve as a precedent for gradual emancipation in the secession states. Sumner explained that men "forgot that God is bound by no compromise and that sooner or later, He will insist that justice shall be done." The bill passed the House, but in the Senate met opposition from Sumner and other radicals. Sumner expressed the belief that emancipation could not be effective unless it was immediate. He "did not understand a war measure which was to go into effect ten years from now . . . , a gradual war measure." The radicals amended the bill so that it was unacceptable to Missouri. The Methodist *Northern Independent* hoped no state would ever be "so mean as to accept the President's plan, and saddle their costly iniquity upon the nation at large."[15] The organized resistance to an "unfaithful" and "disgraceful peace" extended beyond Congress. Senator Samuel Pomeroy, a Congregational layman who was ready to aid all evangelical religious groups working for the cause of freedom, was chairman of a secret vigilance committee that had "sworn to each other and to Almighty God" that it would resist all efforts by Lincoln and the conservatives to make a dishonorable peace. The committee corresponded with other committees in the Northern states.[16]

The antislavery and radical Christians were sure they were in the minority early in 1863. Efforts were made to place gifted and sincere lecturers in the field to overtake the proslavery forces before the elections of that year. Moncure Conway, who was editing the *Boston Commonwealth* and was preaching every Sunday and lecturing two nights every week, was persuaded to enlarge his field of activity. Eastern antislavery Unitarians were bitter about Lincoln's selection of a military governor in North Carolina. Conway had no trouble in mobilizing them against a mild Reconstruction, and a delegation was sent to Washington to protest the developments. He spoke in the Senate chamber and two days later delivered a new lecture entitled "The Unrecognized Gift of God in America: The Negro as the Savior of the Nation." The delegation, under the leadership of Senator Wilson, consulted with Lincoln the same evening. Back in Boston, Conway delivered a new lecture in Boston's Music Hall on February 22. In the lecture, "The Vacant Throne of Washington," he complained that "we find *no man,* in the station of power and influence, adequate to the work," and no political leaders had come forward to save the nation. In March, Conway was off to address political meetings in New Hampshire.[17]

In March 1863 New Hampshire became the first state to hold a major election. All eyes focused on the state to see whether the trend of 1862 would continue. Anna E. Dickinson reached Massachusetts in December 1862 and continued lecturing, sometimes twice a day, for several weeks. She defended Lincoln's administration for twenty nights, pleading with the people to support it at the ballot box.[18] Dickinson arrived in Connecticut two weeks before the Connecticut campaign closed and opened her canvass in Touro Hall, Hartford. After lecturing in Connecticut for two weeks, she turned to Massachusetts, New York, and Pennsylvania to close out her election campaign.[19] Theodore Weld, an antislavery lecturer in the 1830s, toured New England for seven months in 1863, speaking once and sometimes twice a day. On February 2, Weld wrote to James M. McKim, a Pennsylvania abolitionist, that he had been asked to go to New Hampshire to lecture on the crisis and to promote the election of a member of Congress and the Republican candidate for governor. After a lecturing in Massachusetts and Rhode Island, Weld turned north to lecture in New Hampshire. He returned home for a short rest, then moved west to lecture in New York, Pennsylvania, and Ohio. Theodore Tilton also lectured effectively during the campaign in New York City, New Jersey, and Pennsylvania.[20]

The Garrisonians had been instrumental in recruiting both Weld and Dickinson, who tipped the balance in New Hampshire. They swung the necessary votes in this crucial contest and possibly turned the electoral tide by beating down an antiwar governor in New Hampshire. Other factors in the Republican victory were federal patronage and the furloughing of soldiers so that they could go home to vote. The presence of a third-party war Democratic candidate in the election possibly denied the Peace Democrats a majority and threw the contest into the legislature, where the Republican candidate was elected. In Connecticut, Dickinson's two-week engagement at the end of the canvass contributed to the Republicans' 51.6 percent majority. The National Union League and the Loyal League rallied support against the Peace party. New Hampshire and Connecticut were a crucial challenge to the Republicans. If the Peace Democrats had won in New Hampshire and Connecticut, they would certainly have been able to go into the other elections with an advantage.[21]

Aware of the depth of the opposition to emancipation, the antislavery Christians and sectarian press started early in 1863 to exert their influence on politics. On January 14, the Baptist *Christian Times* instructed the clergy that it was "a sacred religious obligation to stand for freedom" and support the government in the present crisis.[22] In February the Baptist *New York Recorder and Examiner* also advised clergy to apply biblical truths to public questions. The ministers should make preaching effective by letting "the light of truth fall upon public iniquity." The *Pittsburgh Christian Advocate* insisted that morals should wield a controlling influence in all affairs of the government. The faithful should see that "high and low places of the government are occupied by men of integrity and unblemished moral character."[23]

T.M. Eddy, editor of the Methodist *Northwest Christian Advocate*, observed that if religious men had carried their religion to political meetings and to the polls, national troubles could have been prevented. Those who had neglected the duty of suffrage should repent "in sackcloth and ashes." The editor of the radical *American Baptist* insisted that the Copperheads who sought to subvert the Emancipation Act and change the constitution into a proslavery instrument were aiding and abetting the enemy. The editor of the *Boston Recorder* counseled his readers: "We must carry religion into every department of life—into business, education and politics."[24]

The pulpit matched the press in calling on the people to carry their religion into politics. The Protestant clergy, in most cases voicing the feelings of their congregations, were so strongly Unionist that many of them prayed for a Republican victory. The *Western Christian Advocate* became practically a Union party organ in response to the Methodist clergy's radical response. In a Democratic convention in Butler County, Ohio, on March 4, 1863, the Democrats registered their grievances by charging that the clergy was "the devil's select and inspired representative, preaching hate, envy, malice, vengeance, blood and murder, instead of love, charity and the doctrine of Christ." A Methodist pastor told his congregation, "We *must reform or die! ...* We must infuse more of the spirit of Christianity into American politics. ... We have as a nation fallen into a mournful apostasy on the *subject of human* rights." But he observed that the church was everywhere taking higher ground than formerly.[25]

The military failure of the North was the chief reason for the attitude of urgency in the church. The loss of the Battle of Chancellorsville, May 2-6, 1863, strengthened the conviction in the antislavery religious mind that society should be reformed. After the loss of the Battle of Chancellorsville by Joseph Hooker, the Quaker James S. Gibbons wrote in his journal: "A gloomy morning and the end of our hopes for Hooker's campaign. ... It is doubtless right that we shall be humiliated, until we do justice to the negro."[26] Bryon Sunderland informed his Washington Presbyterian congregation that choosing a government was no longer just a question of religious duty. "Those who at heart have no allegiance to the Government should be put beyond the lines. ... If we mean to put away ... the abominable thing ... , we must recur to the law of the Bible." The New School Presbyterian General Assembly took virtually the same position later in May when it resolved that "all attempts to resist, or set aside the action, to oppose, or embarrass the measures which it may adopt to assert its lawful authority ... are to be regarded as treason against the nation, as giving aid and comfort to its enemies, and as rebellion against God." The charge of treason was leveled against every citizen who did not enthusiastically support the war and the president.[27]

The criticism of the clergy became more extensive as the election drew near. George Hepworth, a Unitarian preacher from Boston, dwelled on political subjects in his sermons and public lectures as well as at Republican rallies. An editor of the *Democratic Boston Post* and an editor of the Republican *Boston Journal* were members of his congregation, which made for controversial and spicy reading in the daily press.[28] John Cross of Iowa gave his congregation liberal doses of antislavery and antirebellion rhetoric; his sermons frequently departed from the position of his church.[29] The Old School Presbyterian *New York Observer* criticized a senator who would not vote for peace while a single slave remained in the land and, even more, disapproved of a Presbyterian minister who said that no person sharing the views of the Democrats Horatio Seymour, Clement Vallandigham, and Fernando Wood could call himself a patriot.[30]

The religious conferences and associations took a stronger position in defense of the Republican party after the adoption of the Emancipation Proclamation. The Methodist Episcopal conferences were among the most vocal. For example, the Pittsburgh conference repelled "with Christian manliness" and heroic firmness the virulent assaults of corrupt and scheming politicians on the Christian pulpit, press, and church. The New York Methodist Conference charged with "covert treason" those who, "influenced by political affinities or southern sympathies," used the "pretext of discriminating between the administration and government" to oppose almost every warlike measure. The conference report created, according to critics, a scene of wild enthusiasm. The clergy rose en masse and marked its approval of the measures with cheers, clapping, and foot stamping.[31] Reverend T.A. Lovejoy, a Methodist minister of the New York East conference, was assigned to a church that refused to receive him unless he promised not to preach political sermons. Lovejoy refused to pledge and was transferred. When the conference met, his peers heartily approved of his position, and a collection of $238.50 was taken up for him. Lovejoy's charge was not the typical Methodist church. When the Wyoming conference (Pennsylvania) met, the bishop found it difficult to place two or three Democratic preachers who were charged with political heresy. Popular sentiment in favor of the Union was so great in many churches that the slightest suspicion of Southern sympathies was sufficient to close every door against a preacher, however unexceptionable he might otherwise be. Even silence on the subject was scarcely tolerated.[32] The Northern Ohio Methodist Episcopal Conference pronounced it the duty of all men "irrespective of party affiliation" to sustain the administration. A reporter for the *Mt. Vernon Republican* (Ohio) was impressed by the unanimity of the conference. He declared that at least forty-nine of fifty ministers in attendance were committed Republicans.[33]

Other church bodies expressed stronger sentiments. All extant Baptist records reveal that the Baptist associations pledged their support to the administration or the government. Many went beyond a general statement of support or prayer for the rulers. The Baptist Church of White Creek, Wisconsin, denounced the "obnoxious" and "despicable" Copperheads, and the New London (Connecticut) Baptist Association deprecated the party spirit, which would weaken the president's hand and circumvent his efforts to put down the rebellion.[34] The Congregational and Presbyterian Convention of Wisconsin and the Michigan and Ohio Congregational associations pledged to sustain the administration with all their influence. The Presbytery of Columbus considered it a duty of every minister to sustain the administration by preaching and prayers.[35] The General Conference of Evangelical Associations took a forthright stand. The association considered political partisanship where religion and country were sacrificed to party interests as entirely unworthy of Christian citizenship. The Rhode Island and Massachusetts Christian Conference was even more straightforward. The conference declared that all who sympathized with the Rebels should be excluded from fellowship in the church.[36]

Trumbull became uneasy about the forthcoming elections early in August. He asked Chandler whether he thought the administration would "patch up a compromise with traitors?" Chandler was full of optimism. "We have in my judgment reached the critical point in the war. . . . The Slavery question is settling itself with great rapidity. Every negro regiment of a thousand men presents just one thousand unanswerable arguments against the revocation of the President's Proclamation." Chandler brushed aside the idea that Lincoln might try to appease the opposition. "I have little fear that the President will recede. He is as stubborn as a mule when he gets his back up and it is up now on the Proclamation." In March, Giddings feared that Lincoln might try to negotiate a compromise peace and that the Republican party would "fall to pieces," bringing the Democrats to power and allowing slavery to remain intact. In July, however, Giddings believed that Providence and the "unchanging law that has borne us on thus far" would continue in its course. Chase saw need to strengthen the proclamation by a new document or a change in the organic law. He wrote to a correspondent in the summer of 1863 that he wanted the proclamation to have "some words . . . recognizing . . . the liberation of the slave in the rebel states and the *permanence* of that liberation." But the antislavery congressmen did not rest on their laurels. Julian, Wade, and Chandler stumped the Northwest, bringing the moral issue before the people, but they concentrated on Ohio, where the most significant contest was taking place. Radical General Benjamin Franklin Butler was secured to speak in Ohio, and Reverend H.W. Chapin also spoke there. In September, Wade spoke at a political rally in Marietta, Ohio. He reminded the crowd that he had been called a radical and conceded that some would be frightened by radicalism. "But I believe that all who have benefited the world, from Jesus Christ to Martin Luther and George Washington, have been branded as Radicals." He announced to his audience with pride, "I am a Radical and glory in it." Realizing that the Ohio contest would be critical, Professor John Morgan of Oberlin College tried to persuade Theodore Weld to return in the autumn to stump the state. George Cheever was called to lecture in Ohio, and many less well known divines spoke in the western states.[37]

Ohio was critical in the election because the Democrats of Ohio had nominated Clement Vallandigham, a Peace Democrat, for governor at their convention in June, 1863. Vallandigham had been imprisoned for speaking against the war and was later exiled to Canada. He was an Old School Presbyterian. John Brough, his Republican opponent, lacked a religious affiliation. Reverend James L. Vallandigham, a brother of Clement and an Old School Presbyterian, was arrested at his home in Newark, New Jersey, during the canvass of the election of 1863 for criticizing Lincoln and praying for peace.[38] The Republicans used the churches to influence public opinion against Clement Vallandigham. Many clergymen regarded him as a traitor and believed it their duty to support the Republicans in conferences, synods, and associations. The Western Reserve (Ohio) Convention of the United Brethren advised its members that it would be "incompatible with the principles and spirit of the United Brethren Church . . . to vote for C.L. Vallandigham." The *Religious Telescope* of Dayton, Ohio, the organ of the United Brethren, endorsed the Republican position.[39]

The Ohio Congregational Conference supported the Lincoln administration in "the righteousness of the war" and condemned the "fractious spirit of the Democrats."[40] The United Presbyterian Presbytery of Steubenville (Ohio) met in early September. When the question of voting for Vallandigham came up, the presbytery declared voting to be a great moral question; no member could vote for Vallandigham because of his principles on slavery and his encouragement of disloyalty. The United Presbyterian Church of Monroe County, Indiana, took the same radical stance toward the Democrats, but the sentiments of its members did not reach a head until after the election of 1864. At the congregation's session after the election, a ruling elder was dismissed from his office when he admitted that he supported the principles and doctrines of the Democratic platform.[41] Most of the New School Presbyterian clergy in Ohio used their pulpits to endorse the Republicans without specifically naming the party. Even the Old School Presbyterian church in which Vallandigham had once owned a pew turned its back on the Democratic candidate.[42]

The Methodist Episcopal journals took a strong stand for Brough's candidacy. The *Western Christian Advocate* openly supported the Republican candidate. Reverend Granville Moody attended a July 4 mass meeting in Dayton, in which he was asked to offer a prayer. He prayed: "Lord God Almighty bless John Brough, the candidate . . . who is called upon to bear the ark of our cause. . . . Give him favor among this people, that he may have a most unequal majority . . . , and God have mercy on poor Vallandigham and Pugh. Lord pardon their sins . . . , and if they are in reach of mercy, Lord have mercy on them." Moody toured the state, speaking against Vallandigham. He accused Vallandigham of "poisoning" the mind of the people "almost equaling the audacity of Satan himself." After the election, Moody was a guest of Eddy, the editor of the *Northwestern Christian Advocate*, who lauded him "for his superb service for Brough."[43]

The Zanesville Conference of the Methodist Wesleyan Church resolved that "when one of the political parties has the audacity to nominate for the office of Governor, a 'tried and convicted traitor' . . . , as patriots or Christians, can we doubt or hesitate" for which candidate to cast our votes? Most of the Ohio Mennonites also endorsed Brough.[44] The president of the Lutheran Synod of Ohio reported that ministers who tried to carry out the mandate to let religion guide their political action had suffered slander and defamation.[45]

As October 13 drew near, the nation watched Ohio. Calvin Fletcher noted in his diary on October 12 that he feared a mob attack when the soldiers voted. On election day he wrote: "If Ohio elects Vallandigham . . . , it is a triumph for the rebellion. May God avert it." On October 14 he added: "This I esteem a great Providential victory."[46] Archbishop Percell of Cincinnati gave great offense to the Copperheads in his diocese by voting against Vallandigham. The editor of the *Sandusky Register* wrote after the election that the hand of the Almighty had entered into the affairs of Ohio.[47]

The Democratic gubernatorial candidate in Pennsylvania was state Supreme Court justice George E. Woodward, a Copperhead sympathizer. The *New York Post* revealed that twenty-five years earlier, Charles C. Burleigh had visited Wilkes Barre, Pennsylvania, to deliver a lecture on freedom and slavery. A meeting was held to oppose the speech, and George C. Woodward had taken the lead in the meeting, after which Burleigh was escorted from the village.[48] The issue of slavery was deeply implicated in the campaign in Pennsylvania. Episcopal Bishop John Henry Hopkins of Vermont in 1851 published a tract, *Slavery: Its Religious Sanction*, which treated slavery as sinless and defended it on scriptural grounds. Early in the political campaign, the Democratic state committee republished the tract as a campaign document with Hopkins's consent. The pamphlet became one of the most frequently quoted tracts during the war years. Controversy about the book swept the state of Pennsylvania during the election. Alonzo Potter, the Episcopal bishop of Pennsylvania, opposed slavery and disputed the claim that it was justified by the Bible. Bishop Potter indignantly protested to Hopkins for having consented to the book's reprinting as a Pennsylvania election document. Hopkins replied with a bitter letter which was printed in many of the Democratic papers. The Episcopal clergy entered the controversy and called Hopkins's letter "unworthy of any servant of Christ." Eventually 167 Episcopal clergyman signed the protest.[49]

The controversy over Hopkins's tract drew the clergy into the center of the political contest. In some towns the clerical protest was printed as a handbill and was posted in the streets before the election. Reverend Van Deusen, the rector of St. Peter's Episcopal Church in Pittsburgh, refused to sign the protest because he considered it a political document. The majority of the vestrymen of his church passed resolutions deploring the failure of their rector to join the majority of the Episcopal clergymen in signing the protest. The minority of the vestrymen of St. Peter's parish published a pamphlet approving the position of their pastor and included reasons for his failure to sign the protest.[50]

The political controversy in the Episcopal Church caused other churches to take a stronger political position. The usually moderate Philadelphia Baptists were affected by the political developments. The Philadelphia Baptist Association informed members that it was the duty of Christian patriots to uphold the government with their votes as well as with their prayers. The North Philadelphia Baptist Association maintained that every Christian must cast his vote in the coming election to uphold public order and liberty.[51]

Slavery was the central issue in the Pennsylvania election as it had been in Ohio. Phillips Brooks, an Episcopal clergyman, described the Pennsylvania election to a relative: "The *radical* character of this campaign . . . has been not merely Republican, but antislavery; not merely antislavery, but abolition all the way through." The western Pennsylvania clergy were active in the election meetings and rallies. The most surprising development in the Pennsylvania election was that almost every Republican ward meeting, township political meeting, and mass meeting in western Pennsylvania had a liberal representation of clergymen who participated in the proceedings. In a Thanksgiving sermon Phillips Brooks mentioned the bishop who had upheld the Bible argument for slavery, and he rejoiced that during the canvass a protest had been made by the clergy and laymen alike. "As name after name was added to that protest," he said, "as the assent came in so unanimously from every direction," the charge that his church as a whole was in sympathy with slavery had been repelled. Judge Woodward withdrew from Brooks's Holy Trinity Church after the election.[52]

Lincoln was apprehensive about the results of the election, but he remained committed to emancipation. On August 5, he informed a correspondent: "As an anti-slavery man I have a motive to desire emancipation which pro-slavery men do not have."[53] In his concern about the election, Lincoln wrote a letter to an Illinois Union mass meeting that he had been invited to attend. He admitted that some of the organizers of the Springfield meeting were dissatisfied with him because he had used too much force. "If you are not for force, nor yet for dissolution," he reasoned, "there only remains some imaginable *compromise*. I do not believe any compromise . . . is now possible. But, to be plain, you are dissatisfied with me about the negro." Lincoln remained firmly opposed to retraction of the proclamation.[54] The letter was reprinted in the Republican press throughout the country. Charles Sumner called Lincoln's message a "true and noble" letter. The *Evangelist* recognized Lincoln's letter as a clear statement of the policy of the government which had been developed slowly. "Believing as we do that the policy of justice is always the policy of wisdom and safety," the editor reasoned, "we believe this is the true course." "We thank the President for that declaration," wrote Goodell in the *Principia*, "We thank God, and take courage."[55]

Horace Greeley felt that if a vote of the people on emancipation had been taken, the Northern people would have voted against it until July 1863, when Union military victories came. He said that the change of opinion on the slavery question since 1860 was "a great historical fact, comparable with the early progress of Christianity." The fall election advanced the cause of emancipation. Lincoln admitted that the proclamation had been followed by "dark and doubtful days," but with the fall elections "the crisis which threatened to divide the friends of the Union" was past. "We verily believe the spirit of the Lord has moved upon the hearts of many. God has averted a threatened calamity. Let His name be praised," wrote Calvin Kingsley, editor of the *Western Christian Advocate*.[56]

The antislavery Christians influenced the elections of 1863. The leaders of the Republican party were often prominent laymen in the Methodist, Presbyterian, Congregational, and Unitarian churches whose clergy advocated "pulpit politics" and prayed for the success of the Republican officeseekers and of the Northern armies. The importance of the moral issue was stressed by a Democrat of Orange County, New York, who said it was "those people who get together in Peoples' Hall who defeated me. They get together—three or four hundred of them—they sing a good deal; they pray a little; they swear them all not to vote the regular Democratic ticket—and they raise hell generally." The victories of Gettysburg and Vicksburg during the first week of July caused all grievances arising from the draft, suspension of habeas corpus, emancipation, and the use of black troops to seem more minor than they had before the victories. No longer was emancipation a political liability. Antislavery religious opinion and propaganda played an important role in the fall elections as well as in the spring contests.[57]

Seeing that public opinion supported the emancipation of slaves, Lincoln offered additional assurance in his December message: "While I remain in my present position I shall not attempt to retract or modify the emancipation proclamation." The radical clergyman Henry Wright wrote the president: "God bless thee Abraham Lincoln! With all my heart I bless thee, in the name of God and Humanity."[58] The strong pledges Lincoln had given during and after the election of 1863 were an important victory for radical religion. The president had not yielded to the conservative Republican pressure that had been exerted during the election of 1863 because of the results of the contest of 1862. Lincoln had placed himself uncompromisingly and irreversibly on the side of freedom and radical religion.[59]

The fierceness and passion of the attack on the Democrats by the radical evangelists led to a secession movement of the conservatives from these churches in the northwestern states. Conservative Methodists left their churches in the largest number, but most evangelical churches experienced some withdrawal. The intensity of the political activity of the antislavery Christians had hardly slackened after the election of 1863 in Ohio before emotions began to rise as a result of the election campaign of 1864. The reason was largely the agitation of the Democrats against the antislavery Christians and evangelical churches. The Democrats spurred the movement to organize a new church free of politics and sympathetic to the advocates of a negotiated peace. The new church movement took shape after James F. Given, a Methodist minister of the Ohio conference, stationed in Franklin County, Ohio, offended the members of the Ohio conference by making political speeches for Vallandigham. Given was a native of Princeton, Kentucky, had been educated at Marietta College, and had entered the Methodist ministry after completing his education.[60]

The Christian Union ceased to exist as an organization after the war, having no further reason for being. Given, one of its leading spirits, died shortly after the conflict. It had come into existence, according to the claims of its organizers, because ministers preached political sermons from the pulpit, but in fact the reason was that the ministers did not preach the political sentiments of the Democrats in the pulpit.[61] The Christian Union movement caused attention to focus on the role played by the church in shaping public opinion on the war issues. For this reason and others, the questions of slavery and the conditions of peace continued to be heated political issues in the church after the election of 1863.

# CHAPTER FIVE

# The Election of 1864

The Union party was seriously divided during the winter of 1863-64. To a great extent the division was caused by the dissatisfaction of the Radical Republicans with the emancipation policy and the moderate program of Reconstruction of the Lincoln administration. Chase had submitted suggestions in writing to Lincoln when the Emancipation Proclamation was being considered. In November 1863, he suggested to Lincoln that the principles of emancipation should be incorporated in the constitutions of the reconstruction states. Chase added: "Permit one again most respectfully to urge on you the expediency and duty of making the Proclamation itself complete within the States in which it operates by revoking the exceptions of certain parts of two of them from its operation." But Lincoln did not heed Chase's suggestion when he issued his "Proclamation of Amnesty and Reconstruction" on December 8, 1863. Lincoln's proclamation offered a full pardon to most Southerners if they would swear an oath of allegiance to the United States. When in any state the number of voters taking the oath reached 10 percent of the number who voted in the 1860 election, this loyal nucleus could reestablish a state government, which Lincoln promised would be recognized. Many ultraradical Christians, who were guided more by the Old Testament than by the New, opposed Lincoln's measure. They favored a Radical Reconstruction and contended that only Congress could organize the secession states. Reverend John G. Fee of Kentucky considered the amnesty proclamation "all wrong . . . and a great error." Whitelaw Reid, a radical Calvinist journalist, asserted that the proclamation of December 1863 represented a "dangerous conservatism" to which the radicals should not acquiesce.[1]

A broad group of antislavery Christians felt that the country should move quickly to abolish slavery throughout the land by civil law. They believed that emancipation was a military necessity and that abolition would permanently end sectional strife by removing slavery, the cause of the war. Some antislavery Christians believed that the nation was still suffering from divine retribution intended to punish the North for harboring slavery and that the curse would be lifted only when slavery had been completely abolished. Lincoln himself voiced this belief when he wrote to a Kentucky editor: "If God now wills the removal of a great wrong, and wills also that we of the North, as well as you of the South, shall pay fairly for our complicity in that wrong, impartial history will find therein new causes to attest and revere the justice and goodness of God."[2]

When the Thirty-eighth Congress convened in December 1863, the Radical Republicans launched a drive to secure complete abolition. The drive received new energy as a result of the president's proclamation of December 8. On December 14, Congressman Owen Lovejoy, a radical Episcopal clergyman, introduced a bill in the House of Representatives to free all of the slaves. Congressman James Ashley and James F. Wilson, a Unitarian and a Calvinist layman, respectively, introduced proposals to submit a constitutional amendment to the states that would abolish slavery throughout the whole nation. In the Senate debate on the amendment, Trumbull argued that only prohibition in the form of an amendment would ensure that no state or Congress could ever restore slavery in the future. He reported a resolution from the Senate Judiciary Committee in March 1864 to abolish slavery by amending the Constitution.[3] On March 19, Senator Wilson expressed the sentiments of the antislavery Christians when he explained in the House: "Providence has opened up the way to that higher civilization and purer Christianity which the Republic is to attain. Our Red Sea passage is to be as propitious as that of God's chosen people when the waters parted . . . for their escape from the hosts upon whom those waters closed and effected the burial appointed by Him who declared, 'Let my people go.' "[4]

In the eyes of some Radical Republicans, the road to Radical Reconstruction entailed replacing Lincoln as president in 1864. At the same time, critics of Lincoln, including Henry Winter Davis and Benjamin Wade, attacked the president's Reconstruction. The discontented radicals found a willing replacement for Lincoln in Salmon P. Chase. Chase wrote to his son-in-law on November 26, 1863: "I think a man of different qualities from those the President has will be needed for the next four years." Favored by several antislavery editors and many clergymen, Chase was truly a deeply religious man.[5] In the 1840s Chase was the superintendent of a Cincinnati Episcopal Sunday school. He would arise before six o'clock in the morning and read religious tracts and memorize pages of Bible verses.[6] Ambition and religion were the driving forces in Chase's life. In 1850 he wrote Sumner: "Sometimes, I feel as if I could give up—as if I *must* give up, and then after all I rise and press on. . . . God in heaven . . . orders all things well, and will not suffer those who trust Him through Christ to be utterly cast down."[7]

When Chase entered the cabinet, he promised himself not to let "the question of Slavery" influence his actions in one way or another.[8] Yet Chase was not neutral on the slavery question. A story made the rounds in Washington that after Lincoln's election in 1860, he expressed grave doubts about pursuing the policy of emancipation, which caused Chase to threaten to join forces with the radical leaders of Congress.[9] The core of Chase's support was a group of antislavery laymen that he had gathered in the network of the Treasury Department and his ties with the antislavery Christians from the Liberty and Free Soil days. A committee waited upon Chase and urged him to be a candidate. On February 15, 1864, Welles wrote in his diary: "There are indications that Chase intends to press his pretensions as a candidate and much of the Treasury machinery and special agencies have that end in view."[10]

Chase considered Lincoln "greatly wanting in will and decision . . . and clear well-defined purpose." Beecher agreed with Chase's view of Lincoln. He wrote to the secretary that Lincoln's mind "seldom works clearly or cleanly." John Jay, an Episcopal abolitionist, complained that the most earnest supporters of the emancipation policy were convinced that the president leaned toward an unscrupulous clique whose members were lukewarm supporters of his stand on emancipation or secretly opposed it. Cheever's opinion was that Lincoln was "the choice of war up to exhaustion and compromise in the end." Cheever counseled Tilton concerning the election of 1864: "We are bound to pray God it may not be Mr. Lincoln."[11]

After praising Lincoln early in February for a policy that was "generally right-minded and straight-forward" on the question of human freedom, two weeks later Tilton wrote an editorial calling for the nomination of Chase for president.[12] On February 26, the *Boston Commonwealth* carried an editorial entitled "Our Candidate for the Next Presidency," in which the qualifications were detailed and no choice was named. The article was a full copy of an editorial from the *Independent*: "The man . . . who comes bearing in his hand credentials for the next presidency, must demonstrate, as his first token of fitness, a sublime allegiance to God, Liberty, and Human Rights."[13] The implication was that Lincoln did not fully measure up to the standard. Goodell opposed the election of Lincoln in the pages of *Principia*. He informed his readers that Lincoln should be replaced "by a successor of radically different convictions." Garrison disagreed with Goodell. He privately wrote to James McKim near the end of February that Lincoln's renomination was in the best interests of antislavery forces because the Copperheads would urge rival Republican candidates to split the Republican vote. In March, Garrison warned in the *Liberator* against dividing the party by opposing Lincoln. He acknowledged that Lincoln was not perfect, but after all, the president had freed millions of slaves. Garrison's editorial was widely reprinted.[14]

Lincoln had the support of the majority of the Christians of the nation. Schuyler Colfax, a Reformed Church layman who kept abreast of opinion in the Christian community, wrote to Sydney Gay that the praying people considered Lincoln "the instrument with which our God intends to destroy Slavery."[15] A Presbyterian layman from Illinois advised his congressman that the administration was acting as the agent of "almighty God." In February the Allentown, New Jersey, Union League found that the struggle was in the hands of the Creator, who was guiding mankind to universal freedom with Abraham Lincoln as the chief instrument to accomplish it. The league declared, "We cannot repudiate him [Lincoln] without repudiating the great principle which he has initiated." The president and vice president of the league were prominent laymen.[16] Others made public statements or testified to their congressmen that Lincoln was the choice of Christians and the masses. The president was aware that the Christian masses considered him an agent of God, and repeated exposure to this view had led him to believe it himself. Professor Jonathan Turner, a Calvinist layman, had observed as early as 1863 that Lincoln "seems to imagine that he is a sort of half way clergyman; and even our people . . . have the same confused and paralysing ideas." Several religious associations and conferences, in their state-of-the-country reports, were convinced that the president had been chosen by God as His special agent. The American Baptist Home Mission Society met in Philadelphia in the spring, passed resolutions in support of Lincoln, and endorsed his administration on the slavery policy. Almost a hundred delegates went to Washington to hear the chairman read the report to the president. The chairman addressed Lincoln as the representative of a million Baptists who "believed fully that God had raised up His Excellency for such a time as this."[17]

Alfred Gilbert, a Disciple clergyman serving in the legislature of

Connecticut, told his colleagues in January that he would "rather lie down and die" in his tracks that day than see any restoration of the Union as it was. He insisted that Lincoln should be retained. Samuel Plumb, an Oberlin antislavery Calvinist layman, was also sure Lincoln "had been converted to the doctrine of Equality." Joseph R. Hawley, the son of an abolitionist Congregational preacher and an antislavery layman who edited the *Hartford Evening Press*, advised a friend, " 'Uncle Abe' must be our next President."[18] William M. Dickson, an antislavery Episcopalian, assured a correspondent that Lincoln had the inside track. Dickson added: "He is my choice."[19]

In February, Senator Samuel C. Pomeroy, chairman of the National Executive Committee of the Republican party and supporter of Chase, brought out the so-called Pomeroy Circular, a document opposing Lincoln's reelection and declaring for Chase. The circular, which was mailed to Republicans, was franked by John Sherman, and the Senator and Chase were censured by many Republicans.[20] Although Pomeroy explained to the Senate that Chase had not participated in writing the circular, many Republicans believed that Chase had made an unfair and base attack on Lincoln. Welles confided to his diary: "The circular will damage Chase more than Lincoln." The editor of the *Pittsburgh Gazette* declared that the circular would "make no friends for Mr. Chase among honorable men."[21] R.C. Parsons, a Western Reserve Presbyterian layman who had been one of the early leaders in the drive to draft Chase, informed Chase that he was strong enough to defeat Lincoln but that Lincoln's supporters would challenge Chase in the end and a contest between Lincoln and Chase would be fatal to both.[22]

A Cincinnati supporter warned Chase that more than one Republican candidate would "be a public disaster."[23] Chase's old friend James Freeman Clarke, a Boston Unitarian clergyman, dashed off a letter to the secretary. "Your friends who are bringing you forward for the President at this time are not doing you any service. Unless some change takes place, . . . Lincoln is sure to be re-elected . . . ; if I were to vote tomorrow, I should vote for Lincoln. Why? Because we cannot afford to . . . experiment, to run any risks. . . . This is the feeling of seven-tenths of the people." He urged Chase to "come out and decline to be a candidate."[24] The Unitarian layman George L. Stearns believed that the impending contest damaged the great cause. "We must trust in God, and the great heart of our people that never goes far wrong," he wrote to his wife. Stearns considered Lincoln "unfit by nature and education to carry on the government for the next four years," but he took no active part in publicly advocating Chase or Frémont. The radical Quaker abolitionist Miller McKim informed John Hay, the president's private secretary, that he and other abolitionists were entirely satisfied with Lincoln.[25]

Late in February a Union caucus of both houses of the Ohio legislature voted to favor the renomination of Lincoln. Many of the Radical Republicans were satisfied with the president's antislavery progress and considered opposition to his reconstruction steps premature. They agreed with Giddings that Lincoln's "worst sins" were keeping Seward and Blair in office and that Lincoln could be attacked effectively only on this ground.[26] Seeing that a contest to unseat the president might mean losing the election to the Democrats, Chase asked Ohio state senator James C. Hall to withdraw his name from the contest before the state legislature. "All our efforts and energies should be devoted to the suppression of the rebellion," Chase urged. "Allow nothing to divide" the Republican counsels "while this great work . . . remains unaccomplished."[27]

Newspapers throughout the country carried Chase's letter asking that his name be withdrawn. Thereafter Chase was no longer considered an active candidate, and this fact was reflected in the communications of leading radicals. In April, Lydia Maria Child, a Unitarian abolitionist, wrote Gerrit Smith: "God is doing a great work in this nation, but the agents by which He is accomplishing it are so narrow, so cold! The ruling motive of this administration, from the beginning to the present time, seems to have been how to conciliate the Democratic party." A month later Tilton also expressed the belief that the developing events were being shaped by Providence. He informed Parker Pillsbury, an abolitionist clergyman who opposed Lincoln, that, in his opinion, God meant Lincoln to be president. Beecher spoke out for Lincoln. In a letter to a distinguished Indiana politician that was made public, Beecher insisted that Lincoln should be the next president because of "his moral purity" and because of the past record of his administration. Failure to nominate him, Beecher concluded, would be interpreted as a "rebuke of his policy." Pillsbury, Cheever, and Goodell remained unconvinced. The irreconcilable ultraabolitionists, however, did not constitute a significant number of Christian antislavery men. John Hay recorded in his diary on May 14 that Ashley had reported having written to all Ohio counties urging the endorsement of Lincoln. On June 1, William D. Kelley, the radical Unitarian Congressman from Pennsylvania, informed Hay that he and other radical abolitionists were completely satisfied with Lincoln. Since some observers still had a question in their minds concerning Chase's status, the secretary of the treasury addressed a letter to Governor William Buckingham of Connecticut, a leading Congregational layman and vice president of the AHMS, affirming that Chase had withdrawn his name because leading men had attacked him and that he would have divided the party if Lincoln did not withdraw.[28]

To many antislavery Christians, the emancipation of all slaves was more important than the controversy about the nomination of a Republican presidential candidate. Joseph Hawley informed Sherman that Chase was his first choice, but he was willing to submit to the will of the majority. "One thing that is more precious . . . than making Presidents is the alteration of the Constitution to make this country forever free. Don't let Congress adjourn until you make a law giving the people the privilege to act. . . . Let us associate this with the Presidential canvass."[29] An Illinois antislavery man explained to his congressman: "What we in northern Illinois deem of vast importance to our distracted country [is] the passage of a law by Congress of universal emancipation."[30]

Some of the Methodist Episcopal annual conferences met in April 1864, and the congressional debate on the constitutional amendment was the focus of their attention. The New York east conference considered it the duty of Congress to pass the amendment abolishing all slavery. A resolution proclaimed: "We trust that our entire Church, ministry and laity with all the organs and representatives of her opinions, will throw her whole moral force upon the side of truth and freedom until the victory is won and not a slave treads the soil of our United Republic." A petition signed by all the members was sent to both houses of Congress urging that the amendment be speedily adopted. Three other Methodist Episcopal conferences met in the spring and early summer and adopted similar state-of-the-country reports. The General Conference of the Methodist Episcopal Church met in May and quickly adopted measures favoring the passage of the amendment.[31]

The Tri-Annual Convention of Congregational Churches of the North-West, which represented all of the Congregational churches in the northwestern states, met in Chicago in April and adopted strong measures in favor of an amendment. Three state Congregational associations met in the spring and early summer and approved the amendment before Congress.[32] The Progressive Friends of Chester County, Pennsylvania, met in yearly meeting and sent a memorial to Congress in support of the amendment. The Central Association of Seventh Day Baptists declared it the duty of the people to see that

Congress adopted the amendment. Even in the border states, the General Assembly of the Cumberland Presbyterian Church recommended that Cumberland Presbyterians, both North and South, "give countenance and support to all constitutional efforts . . . to rid the country" of slavery. The Rock River (Illinois) Baptist Association and the General Reformed Presbyterian Synod were decidedly in favor of the amendment. Although the Church Anti-Slavery Society insisted that the spirit of the Constitution already prohibited slavery, the society urged that a declaratory amendment be adopted.[33]

Even with Congress debating the question of an amendment to the Constitution, a few religious bodies preferred to address their appeals for universal emancipation to the president. The Primitive Methodist Conference of Wisconsin addressed a memorial to the chief executive earnestly praying that the time would soon come when universal emancipation would be adopted. The Reformed Presbyterian Synod of New York "demanded in the great name of . . . God" the immediate emancipation of all slaves in the United States. The antislavery delegates of the Protestant Episcopal Convention of Pennsylvania tried to put their church on antislavery grounds by resolving that "the National Government, whether executive, legislative or judicial is, in our judgment, solemnly bound to use all its power and employ every authorized Constitutional means for the speedy and total abolition of slavery throughout the land." The majority rejected the measure for a substitute that expressed "unfaltering allegiance to the Government."[34]

In spite of all efforts, the constitutional amendment was voted down. Although the Senate passed the amendment resolution on April 8, the lower house did not bring the resolution to a final vote until the middle of June. Congressman Thomas Williams, a Presbyterian layman from Pennsylvania, in a speech in the House on the amendment, told his colleagues that "God's justice demands it, and the heart and conscience of the American people will say, Amen." Congressman Isaac N. Arnold, an antislavery Episcopal layman from Illinois, in a speech on the amendment pleaded with the House on June 15: "Let the lightnings of God transmit to the toiling and struggling soldiers of Sherman, and Hunter, and Butler and Grant the thrilling words, 'slavery abolished forever,' and their joyous shouts will strike terror into the ranks of the rebels and traitors fighting for tyranny and bondage."[35] The next day the House voted down the amendment resolution. The antislavery Christians were disappointed but did not admit defeat. The presidential convention would soon select a candidate and draw up a platform that they intended to try to make antislavery in character.

Some antislavery Christians were occupied solely with efforts to secure an amendment prohibiting all slavery. When Senator Sherman informed Francis D. Parish, an elder in a Congregational church and vice president of the antislavery AMA, that he planned to amend the Fugitive Slave Law of 1850 by reenacting the law of 1793, Parish opposed Sherman's plan because it was "inconsistent" with the objective of the proposed constitutional amendment. An antislavery constituent informed his congressman that he was astonished that men could be found to vote down an amendment abolishing slavery at such a late date, but he was consoled by the repeal of the odious Fugitive Slave Law.[36]

By March, public attention was being focused more on the presidential election of 1864, and some of the religious conferences were concentrating on instructing their members concerning the election. The Methodist Episcopal Conference of Pittsburgh pledged to condemn emphatically any ministers or members of the church who gave or may give "just cause of suspicion as to their loyalty" to the federal government. The Methodist Episcopal Conference of Troy considered members who embarrassed the government in the conduct of the war "as in the last degree criminal."[37] The Brownmansville (New York) Conference of the United Brethren in Christ declared it was "unitedly opposed by our words, our prayers, and our votes to the disloyal spirit manifested here in the North."[38]

Anna Dickinson and Theodore Weld played important parts in the election of 1864, as they had in 1863. In Lynn, Massachusetts, and at the Cooper Institute in New York, under the auspices of the Loyal Women's League, Weld gave a lecture entitled "The Work, the Times, and the War" and took a radical stance. Dickinson spoke on January 16, 1864, in the U.S. House of Representatives at the invitation of the vice president and the Speaker. Her lecture was full of patriotic sentiment, and she was sharply critical of the president's Proclamation of Amnesty and Reconstruction, but her attack focused sharply on the Democrats. Dickinson's criticism of Lincoln appeared to be less harsh when she called the president his own successor and boldly declared that the people would insist on Lincoln for a second term.[39] In Washington, Dickinson spoke in Grover's theater and bore down hard on the administration, on Lincoln, and on General Banks while praising General Butler and Frémont.[40] Radicals Whitelaw Reid, Kelley, Tilton, and B.F. Prescott, chairman of the Republican party of New Hampshire, tried to persuade Dickinson to refrain from favoring personal political choices, but she persisted, lacking faith in Lincoln's ability and integrity.[41]

After the collapse of the Chase nomination, the hopes of the anti-Lincoln radicals focused on John Frémont. A Frémont convention met in Cleveland on May 31 and nominated Frémont for president on a platform calling for a constitutional amendment to "secure to all men absolute equality before the law."[42] Only a few ultraradical ministers represented the clergy at the convention. *Harper's Weekly* reported that the convention represented the feeling of Pillsbury and Stephen S. Foster. The Anti-Slavery Church Society was represented by two clergymen and a layman. The majority of the delegates were war Democrats and radical German-Americans.[43]

Elizabeth C. Stanton, a social and religious reformer, publicly announced that she was supporting the Radical Republican party (Frémont) because it had "lifted politics into the sphere of morals and religion," but Edwin Cowles, a Presbyterian antislavery editor of the *Cleveland Leader*, a Radical Republican organ, told a correspondent that the Cleveland convention consisted of "sore-heads, Garrisonians and Copperheads." No prominent Republican endorsed Frémont. Referring to the convention, Tilton informed Anna Dickinson that he would "not be a party to any alliance with Copperheads—they are not to be trusted." Prescott wrote to her that he had lost all confidence in Frémont because the men supporting the Pathfinder were among "the vilest Copperheads." In his letter of acceptance, Frémont violently criticized the Lincoln government and offended many antislavery Christians, who associated such bitter denunciation with Democrats.[44]

The Republican convention met in Baltimore on June 7. Robert Breckinridge, an Old School Presbyterian clergyman and unconditional Republican, was selected to be the temporary chairman. In naming Breckinridge, the convention departed from tradition in choosing a clergyman and "one of the most eminent divines in the union." The choice reflected the supremacy of the moral issue in the mind of the Republican party. The convention drew up a platform calling for unconditional surrender, no compromise with the Rebels, and an amendment to the Constitution abolishing slavery forever. In his speech nominating Lincoln, Robert Breckinridge declared slavery contrary to the spirit of the Christian religion and incompatible with the natural rights of man. "I join with those who say, 'away with it forever,' " he thundered.[45]

Before the Republican convention, Samuel Aaron, an abolitionist

Baptist minister, wrote with some truth to a friend, "Fremont's progressive platform . . . will compel the adoption of an advanced position at Baltimore," but one of the reasons for offering a plank abolishing slavery by amending the Constitution was the persistent demands of the antislavery Christians.[46]

In April, Susan B. Anthony, the Quaker reformer, had labeled Lincoln's communication of April 4 that he could not immediately free all the slaves a "canting lie." Five days after the Republican convention, Anthony wrote to Elizabeth C. Stanton: "I hope Fremont will just hold on in patience to the day of election. Already the desired effect is apparent. Baltimore gave us a better platform and old Abe a more explicit letter of acceptance." Six days later Oliver Johnson, the Quaker editor of the *Anti-Slavery Standard*, sharply attacked the Frémont movement and put the organ of the American Anti-Slavery Society on the side of Lincoln. The liberal Christian Giles B. Stebbins echoed Johnson's sentiments. He insisted that "the resolve of the Cleveland Convention for 'equal rights for *all*' is looked upon as vague, and of no meaning. *That Convention has no moral power.*" Gerrit Smith, a cousin, disagreed with Elizabeth C. Stanton's letter of May 14. He had no favorite and would postpone a choice until September, when events and time would determine his vote. Above all, he stressed, the party should not divide. By the middle of September, Smith and the old Congregational abolitionist Reverend John Keep decided to sustain Lincoln; doing so seemed the only way to "save the nation." Early in October, Smith wrote to Elizabeth C. Stanton again, regretting that "neither Wendell Phillips nor you cañ favor Lincoln's re-election. I am spending a great deal for the election of Lincoln," he wrote, "I see safety in *his* election." Lydia Maria Child in turn disagreed with Smith about the wisdom of waiting to decide whom he would support. Lincoln "is an honest man, conscientiously hates Slavery. Fremont . . . is a selfish unprincipled adventurer," she argued in July. After Lincoln was elected, Child confided to a friend that Lincoln "has his faults . . . but . . . I have constantly gone on liking him better." Speaking at the annual meeting of the American Anti-Slavery Society, Lucretia Mott, a Quaker member of the society, also had mixed feelings. "I wish we could hold up Fremont a little more for the act he did," she reasoned, "but I am glad to hear Abraham Lincoln held up . . . for the many things he has done."[47]

The summer of 1864 was a critical and depressing time for conscientious antislavery religious radicals. George Tuthill, an antislavery Congregational minister, in his diary on June 30 registered uncertainty that many shared: "Sec. Chase . . . resigns. . . . July 7 has seen President Lincoln renominated. . . . While Fremont and John Cochran[e] head another ticket. The fearful fighting before Petersburg makes the nation feel sober and the party spirit is in full blast. Copperheads hiss and bite and spit out the venom. God is trying us sorely."[48]

On July 2, 1864, Congress passed the Wade-Davis Bill, which provided for Radical Reconstruction, and Lincoln issued a statement on July 8 that he intended to pocket veto the bill because he wanted to be committed to no single plan of Reconstruction.[49] The ultraradicals responded to the veto with increased hope and vigor. Henry Cheever, brother of George Cheever and a clerical member of the Church Anti-Slavery Society of Worcester, Massachusetts, formed the Freedom Club to give "tone to public opinion." Although Senator Henry Wilson, who had recently joined the Congregational church, "deeply regretted" the veto of the Wade-Davis bill, he refused to address the Freedom Club because he could not endanger the cause "by participating in any movement that tends to bring back to power the 'Slave Democracy.' " Henry W. Davis was sure the veto would "destroy what little confidence" remained in the president's "good sense and good faith." Amasa Walker, a former professor at Oberlin College, maintained that the nation must have "a change of management of national affairs or face utter ruin."[50] The *Principia* became one of the chief organs for the Frémont party. George Cheever became the most important clerical spokesman writing in its pages. Cheever argued that the country could not wait for an amendment because "God's command was not amend your constitution! but 'amend your morals.' " William Goodell's three long letters to Lincoln, published in the *Principia*, argued that the administration did not measure up to the antislavery standard.[51]

Early in 1864 George Julian was firmly identified with the Chase movement because he opposed the moderation of Lincoln's reconstruction program, but when Chase withdrew from the contest, Julian decided to "let the presidential matter drift" for a while. Shortly after Lincoln's nomination, Julian repudiated Frémont and came out for Lincoln.[52] Nathan Brown, editor of the abolitionist *American Baptist*, came out for the Cleveland convention because "the platform offered something more than accidental freedom and partial liberty." After much hesitation he announced for Lincoln.[53] The majority of antislavery religious people favored Lincoln. They were in harmony with an Episcopal layman who informed his senator: "We can unite more strength on Lincoln" than anyone else. Giles Stebbins wrote to the *Anti-Slavery Standard* from the West, where he had been lecturing for more than a month: "I have not seen an abolitionist, or heard of one, who is satisfied, or feels any earnest zeal to support the Fremont Movement." The movement "has no moral power," he added.[54]

The Democratic party had been holding local peace conventions for several weeks, some under the Democratic label and others advertised as nonpartisan citizens mass meetings. Democratic district conventions in the Midwest adopted resolutions calling for an armistice and a negotiated peace. Democratic Congressmen also introduced resolutions favoring a negotiated peace which Republicans voted down. Many religious conferences and associations held annual meetings during the summer and condemned any peace without the abolition of slavery, urging unconditional surrender.[55]

As public opinion began to register war weariness, some Republicans despaired of victory for the party in the election. Horace Greeley reflected the prevailing mood when he wrote the president on July 7: "Our bleeding, bankrupt . . . country . . . longs for peace." There was a widespread conviction that the government was not anxious for peace. "It is doing great harm now," he added, "and is morally certain, unless removed, to do far greater harm in the approaching election." A month later he warned the president that if something was not done to meet the yearning for peace, "We shall be beaten . . . next November." Lincoln assured Greeley that he would consider any negotiated peace that embraced the restoration of the Union and the abandonment of slavery. Greeley arranged a Niagara conference with unofficial representatives after Lincoln, in a letter dated July 18, stated that peace could be restored on terms embracing "the integrity of the whole Union, and the abandonment of slavery." The conference came to nothing. On August 5, after the Democratic convention, Greeley published Lincoln's July 18 letter and other correspondence at the suggestion of the *New York Times*.[56] Rumors had been spreading about secret peace negotiations before the letters were made public. The antislavery religious men were depressed about the developments. When Lincoln's July 18 letter, addressed "To Whom It May Concern," was published, Lincoln's position among the antislavery religious forces was strengthened, but extremists distrusted him more than ever. The *Christian Advocate and Journal* printed the letter and called it "one of the most dignified and appropriate acts in the records of the war."[57]

Lincoln had called for a day of Thanksgiving and prayer on August 4. The fast day coincided with the publication of Lincoln's letter. All over the country pulpits rang with sermons proclaiming "Purity must go before peace." Dr. Tyng told the members of St. George Church that "if a compromise was effected every death in our armies has been an unprincipled murder." Jacob Manning assured the congregation of Old South Church in Boston that "Lincoln had exactly struck the pulse-beat of the nation in his note 'to whom it may concern' which so effectually demolished some would-be negotiators." Other ministers throughout the North preached against a compromise peace and supported the Republican position. Lincoln's position was made more secure with antislavery Christians. Harriet Beecher Stowe, the sister of Henry Ward Beecher, fully supported the president in an article in the Baptist *Watchman and Reflector* of Boston. "When we were troubled, and sat in darkness, and looked doubtfully toward the Presidential Chair, it was never that we doubted the good will of our pilot," she explained; "Almighty God has granted to him that clearness of vision which he gives to the true-hearted . . . to set his honest foot in that promised land of freedom which is to be the patrimony of all men, black and white."[58]

The editor of the *Christian Advocate and Journal* observed that it was one of the remarkable facts of the campaign that while "nearly every pulpit gives its utterances in favor of war, the cry from the dram shops and all the purlieus of vice is peace! peace!" The *Pittsburgh Christian Advocate* informed its readers that in almost all denominations the clergy were unanimous in urging the suppression of the rebellion by military power and opposing a compromise peace. "Let us, then, by our vote, place men in office who . . . will vigorously prosecute the war." The editor of the *American Presbyterian* called the idea, advanced by Lincoln's supporters, of a peace without abolition weak and shortsighted. The truce, he said, would be short-lived.[59]

The Democratic party met in Chicago, August 29, and nominated George McClellan. The peace platform drawn up demanded the immediate restoration of the Union and called for a peace convention at which negotiations could begin in "a spirit of conciliation and compromise." After the Democratic National Convention met, religious conferences and associations attacked the Democratic platform in strong language for proposing a compromise peace and peace before slavery had been completely abolished. Seven Methodist Episcopal annual conferences and the general conference condemned a compromise peace as unchristian and sinful.[60] Eleven Baptist associations remained determined opponents of a compromised peace or of peace before slavery had been completely abolished.[61] The Free Methodist Church, some Wesleyan Methodist conferences, the Seventh Day Baptist Church, and the Universalist Church went on record in favor of an unconditional peace after emancipation throughout the country.[62]

The editor of the *Christian Advocate and Journal* informed readers in September that "the highest moral and religious interests . . . demand the prosecution of the war to the extinction of the rebellion and the extirpation of slavery." J.M. Reid, the new editor of the *Western Christian Advocate*, insisted that "we must conquer peace." The editor of the *Zion's Herald* wrote, "Our voice is still for war; not for the sake of war, but for the sake of peace." I.W. Wiley, editor of the Methodist *Ladies' Repository*, told readers that the Union party motto was "To conquer a peace," while the Democratic motto was "Peace by compromise."[63]

The Methodist and the Baptist conferences and associations were more prone to instruct their members to vote for the administration. Some pronounced it a religious duty to vote for the party waging the war. Congregational associations, Presbyterian synods, and the New School and Old School Presbyterian general assemblies instructed their members to support the government. Stanley Matthews, a Cincinnati abolitionist, drew up the Old School General Assembly report on the state of the country. Some of the smaller church bodies also instructed their members to vote for the Republicans as a patriotic and religious duty.[64] The Seneca (Ohio) and the French Creek (Pennsylvania) Baptist associations unanimously agreed that any minister who passed a Sunday service without reference to the perils of the crisis was too disloyal or indifferent "to be tolerated in a Christian pulpit."[65]

The *Western Christian Advocate* bitterly condemned the Democratic platform and urged each voter to ask which side God was on before casting his ballot. The Methodist *Repository* reminded Christians of their solemn duty to vote in the fear of God, with a pure conscience, and "in the spirit of true and honest loyalty to our government. "The New School *American Presbyterian* fully supported the administration. "To embarrass and seek to overthrow the Government in the very crisis of the awful struggle . . . , to seek to baffle and confound it by sowing discord, discontent and despondency among the people," explained the editor, "—What is this but *Disloyalty?*" As late as October the Old School Presbyterian *New York Observer* commended a New York Episcopal clergyman who, when asked by some parish members to deliver a political sermon, had preached against political preaching. The Old School *Presbyter* of Cincinnati took the opposite stance. When the Old School Presbytery of Cincinnati voted "that any person teaching and maintaining that American slavery is not a sin, and is justified by the word of God, is justly liable to censure," the *Presbyter* defended the position and urged support of the Republican party.[66]

As the weeks dragged on, the war took on the character of a stalemate. Deep depression and defeatism led a group of Republican statesmen to oppose Lincoln politically. They planned to persuade Lincoln and Frémont to withdraw and to call a convention that would choose another candidate on whom all could unite. Greeley had reversed himself and had joined in the opposition to Lincoln. When he listed for James Gilmore, an antislavery journalist, the statesmen who opposed Lincoln, it was "a fearful revelation," Gilmore remembered later, and he "went away with a heavy heart forgetting that 'one with God is a majority.' " The faction that wanted a new candidate included David D. Field, H.W. Davis, George Opdyke, John A. Stevens and Greeley. A new convention was scheduled for September 28 in Cincinnati.[67]

On September 2, three important New York editors—Greeley, Tilton, and Parke Goodwin, representing the *Tribune, the Independent*, and the *Evening Post*—wrote joint letters to Northern governors, seeking to promote the movement to discard Lincoln for a new candidate. On the same day the whole political spectrum suddenly changed. The military defeats and stalemate ended with the capture of Atlanta. By the beginning of September the Republicans were exposing and attacking the Copperhead peace platform. The views of the journalists began to change. The religious support for the Republicans became stronger. The liberal lawyer George T. Strong, a vestryman of the Trinity Episcopal Church in New York, anticipated the changes that would result from the military victories and from the publication of the Democratic platform. On September 5, he wrote in his diary: "Thank God the fall of Atlanta is fully confirmed. . . . The general howl against the base policy offered . . . at Chicago is refreshing. Bitter opponents of Lincoln join in it heartily, and denounce the proposition that the country should take its hands off the throat of half-strangled treason."[68]

George Stearns informed Garrison in a letter published September 12 that the plot to induce Lincoln to withdraw had been brought to a halt by the victory of Atlanta and the "traitorous character of the Chicago platform." On the same day, John Gulliver, the pastor of the Congregational church in which Governor Buckingham of Connecticut was a deacon, wrote to Lincoln: "A most healthy reaction is now taking place in the public mind in regard to the coming election."[69] The military and naval successes won by William T. Sherman, Philip Sheri-

dan, and David Farragut ended the dilemma in the minds of many
radical Christians and forced Lincoln's opponents to unite in support
of the choice of the Baltimore convention. The victories of Atlanta
and Mobile Bay encouraged people to believe that God had chosen
Lincoln to carry out His purpose. The journalist Gilmore, after a conversation with Lincoln, concluded that the president had been imbued
with the idea that he was an agent of God and was being "led infallibly
in the right direction." More and more the religious people believed
that the hand of God was directing the war and that Lincoln was "His
selected leader."[70] Zachariah Chandler had become thoroughly convinced that he should help win radical support for Lincoln by urging
the withdrawal of Frémont and securing the removal of Blair from the
cabinet. After much effort Chandler saw both objects accomplished,
and the radicals worked harmoniously to secure the election of Lincoln.[71]

Meeting the day after the fall of Atlanta, the Mad River (Ohio)
Baptist Association urged the administration to accept no compromise
with traitors because "we recognize the hand of God in the success of
our arms . . . around Richmond and Atlanta." The Congregational associations of New York and New Jersey called for "fervent gratitude
to Almighty God" for the signal victories coming after "a season of
darkness and humiliation."[72] The New School Presbyterian Synod of
Peoria regarded the victories of the army and navy as increased evidence
that Providence was directing the country in the "only path that leads
to a righteous and lasting peace."[73] The Michigan Conference of the
Methodist Episcopal Church also recognized "the hand of God in the
recent military victories," and its members promised to support Lincoln. The National Universalist Convention felt duty bound to express
gratitude to God for victories at Mobile Bay and Atlanta and urged
people of all parties to support the administration.[74]

Lincoln did not fail to see the political value of an official day of
Thanksgiving and prayer for the military victories when he issued a
proclamation on September 3 for a fast day on the next Sunday.[75] The
Republican press praised Lincoln's proclamation as evidence of a firm
trust that God was the arbiter of all human events. Lincoln's trust
cheered "the heart of every Christian," wrote one editor. The *New
York Tribune* urged every minister to read the proclamation from the
pulpit, calling a prayer for a righteous peace a "Christian duty." The
Democratic press considered the proclamation a cheap political effort
to excite the clergy to more pulpit politics.[76]

A Methodist minister in Pittsburgh preached a fast day sermon in which he averred that the nation was entering upon a stage of the struggle in which God approved the new objectives and the victories achieved came not from human ability "but by the great strong right arm of Him who brought Israel out of Egypt." The antislavery Methodist minister Gilbert Haven preached a fast day sermon in Boston in which he interpreted the military victories as evidence that the nation's principles were at last in harmony with God. "The Church should unite as one man in this exigency," he urged. "Let her . . . march to the ballot-box as an army of Christ." A Presbyterian clergyman told his congregation that God had so ordered events that they thundered in the ears of the nation: "It is vain to trust in wrong: without justice there is no power!"[77]

Joseph P. Thompson, a New York Congregational minister, delivered a speech entitled "Peace through Victory." He carried his message to common people and rural areas of eastern New York and printed a campaign tract so that he could influence voters even when he could not appear in person. The military victories had such effect on Roswell Hitchcock, a professor at the Presbyterian Union Theological Seminary, that he wrote to Gerrit Smith: "The hand of God is to me so conspicuous in this struggle, that I should almost as soon expect the Almighty to turn slaveholder, as to see this war end without the extinction of its guilty cause."[78]

Reaction to the Democratic platform and the military victories led to a truce during the last three months of the political campaign between the conservatives and Radical Republicans. A few ultraradical Christians withheld any endorsement of Lincoln because of his veto of the Wade-Davis bill and because of the fear that conservatives in the cabinet would dominate the executive department. The difficulty became more acute when Secretary of State William Seward, on September 3, 1864, in a speech at Auburn, New York, claimed that when peace came "all the war measures then existing, including those which affect slavery," would cease. The antislavery Christians insisted that Seward could not speak for the president. They cited Lincoln's letter "To Whom It May Concern" against Seward's position. But Henry Cheever, secretary of the Church Anti-Slavery Society and the Worcester Freedom Club, was not satisfied to let the matter rest with Lincoln's letter. Cheever asked John D. Baldwin, a Congregational minister and editor of the *Worcester Spy*, to publish a letter to Seward from the Freedom Club asking specifically whether emancipation would cease after peace had been restored. It was later decided to send the letter directly to Seward. The secretary of state refused to clarify his position, and a few ultraradicals maintained their neutrality.[79] The great majority of antislavery Christians continued to support Lincoln because, in his reply to the convention in which he accepted the nomination, he had endorsed the amendment abolishing slavery, and he insisted on making the amendment a campaign issue.[80]

Anna Dickinson, who had been silent since Lincoln's nomination, was urged by many antislavery Christians to lecture in support of Lincoln. Most of the people who urged her to back Lincoln assumed that she was for Frémont, but on August 29 in a letter to a correspondent she denied that she had ever been for Frémont; she had, she said, never uttered a word in public that would have permitted anyone to draw that conclusion.[81] On September 3, Dickinson wrote to the *Independent* that she would lecture for the Republican party. She explained that she had tried to influence the party to select a better man than Lincoln, but she denied that she had favored the Cleveland nominee. Dickinson's letter was printed in almost all antislavery newspapers, and she was soon touring the country lecturing for the Republican candidates.[82]

The radical movement to replace Lincoln as the 1864 Republican party presidential nominee was endorsed by Dickinson, Tilton, and other radicals, but the September march of the radicals back to the Lincoln banner carried almost all of the radicals into the Lincoln camp. Oliver Johnson, who had never taken a part in any anti-Lincoln movement, wrote to a friend that of all the political abortions the opposition to Lincoln had produced, "the Fremont movement has been the worst." The antislavery Christians threw themselves into the campaign and mounted the stump to ensure that no radical stayed away from the polls. Tilton spoke in the East, Henry Wright campaigned in Illinois and Michigan, and Giles Stebbins lectured in Michigan and Ohio for Lincoln. The New Hampshire Methodist abolitionist Reverend Andrew T. Foss was recruited by the National Republican Committee to campaign for Lincoln and delivered some forty addresses. Gerrit Smith covered upstate New York in a speaking tour that lasted more than a month. Marius R. Robinson, former editor of the *Anti-Slavery Bugle*, Theodore Weld, and Ichabod Codding—all Lane Rebels of the 1830s— hit the campaign trail for Lincoln.[83] Calvin Fairbank, the Presbyterian minister who had been imprisoned for aiding fugitive slaves, Sallie Holley, the daughter of one of the founders of the Liberty party, and Reverend John A. Rogers, an Oberlin College graduate, spoke for the Republican party at every opportunity.[84]

Early in September, the *Independent* appealed to the clergy to counsel citizens from the pulpit whenever possible on the duty of Christians to vote against the Chicago platform: "If pew-holders refrained from attending church, the pastor should immediately visit them at home, in their stores or work-places." The editorial was reprinted widely in the Republican press.[85] The Republican secular press took the cue. Many writers reminded the ministers of the gospel that it was their highest duty to instruct, counsel, persuade, advise, and command their flock to vote for Union candidates. Sydney H. Gay unequivocally endorsed Lincoln's reelection on September 6 in an editorial in the *New York Tribune.* Clergymen responded to the appeals of the religious and secular press, and many wrote to the president. One clergyman wrote Lincoln: "We . . . are doing what we can for you and the country." He reminded the president that he had been put in office "by the Providence of God."[86]

During the last two months of the canvass, many clergymen were active participants and speakers at ward political meetings, Republican rallies, and mass meetings. Clergymen took the most active part in Republican meetings in the Boston area[87] and were influential and active members of almost every Republican gathering in the last few weeks of the canvass in the Pittsburgh area.[88] The Ohio clergy were probably the most active in politics of any state in the North. Granville Moody, a Methodist preacher, gave political lectures throughout Ohio and western Pennsylvania that were skillfully interlaced with religion. James A. Garfield and J.H. Jones, Disciples of Christ ministers, covered the Western Reserve with political addresses for the Republican party.[89]

Henry Ward Beecher was engaged by the National Republican Committee to speak on behalf of the party during the last weeks of the campaign. The *New York Journal of Commerce* condemned him at length because he rendered greater service to the Republican party than did any other clergyman.[90] Bishop Matthew Simpson spoke widely throughout the North in addresses that revealed more patriotism than radicalism.[91] Robert Breckinridge influenced many along the borderlands with a radicalism that promised to accomplish the will of God without revolutionary effects.[92] Ministers in Chicago, New York, Detroit, and hundreds of other communities were more active in politics than they had been in any other political campaign.[93]

The AMA missionaries and colporteurs distributed tracts by the thousands as campaign literature. Lewis Tappan's *The War: Its Cause and Remedy* and *Immediate Emancipation: The Only Wise and Safe Mode* were probably the most effective. Not all the religiously oriented political literature circulated on the Republican side. The more than three dozen campaign tracts that the Democratic National Committee circulated included three religious pamphlets: Bishop John H. Hopkins's *Scriptural, Ecclesiastical, and Historical Views of Slavery*, Sidney E. Morse's *Ethical View of the American Slave-holders' Rebellion*, David Christy's *Pulpit Politics,* and an anonymous tract arguing that emancipation everywhere had been a failure. Hopkins was an Episcopalian, and Morse and Christy were Old School Presbyterians.[94] The antislavery clergy made extensive use of agricultural fairs and festivals as an institution to draw potential voters who might not frequent churches. At one fair during the fall of 1864 at least four preachers gave political addresses.[95]

The clergy and the churches were indisputably important in influencing the election of 1864. James Moorhead concludes in his study that the churches, for the most part, "contributed to the blurring of lines between dissent and disloyalty." There is some truth to the charge that the clergy oversimplified the problem of disloyalty, but all efforts to shape public opinion reflect oversimplification. Count Gurowski expressed confidence in the political insight of the clergy. He wrote in his diary during the campaign that the religious press "at times appreciate the events and men from a standpoint by far higher and clearer than that of the common press; . . . these preaching and writing divines . . . are the genuine apostles of the spirit of our age"; and "generally the immense majority of reverends from all Christian denominations are patriots, and . . . enlighten the people about its duties in the struggle." Count Gurowski evaluated the clergy realistically. Many of them, for example Beecher, drew on informed scholars and documents for their sermons.[96]

The editor of the *Elmira Advertiser* the week before the election correctly observed: "If McClellan is elected he must breast and overcome almost the entire ecclesiastical and ministerial force of the land. . . . These are the men, together with those who are found in the house of God on the Sabbath and who countenance the spiritual gatherings of the week time." It did not go unnoticed that McClellan joined the Episcopal Church before the Democratic convention of 1864. As the election results began to come in, the *New York Express* ascribed the Republican victory in Maine to the electioneering of the clergy on Sunday and declared Maine "hopelessly priest-ridden."[97]

The Republicans carried the election of 1864 because the tide of the military conflict had turned in favor of the North. The soldiers' votes in certain states were crucial. Lincoln carried the vote of the soldiers by a large majority, and the chaplains were probably as influential as the clergy back home. "I . . . watch and pray for the Union cause in the interest of . . . the reelection of our God given President," wrote one soldier who was reasonably representative. The Republicans carried almost all of the evangelical votes. The great majority of Baptist, Methodist, Congregational, Presbyterian, Quaker, and pietist votes went for Lincoln, and there was a substantial increase in Unitarian and Universalist support for Lincoln in 1864. While Dale Baum found that the Republicans in Massachusetts did not run particularly well in areas where the antiforeign, anti-Catholic Know-Nothing party received disproportionately high levels of support in the 1850s, the Republicans carried a portion of the Episcopal and Old School Presbyterian votes. The Old School Presbyterian General Assembly in 1864 had abandoned its silence on slavery and expressed full and frank opposition to the institution of slavery and all that it stood for. A large majority of the Old School Presbyterian votes going for Lincoln were from the Northwest.[98] The clergy and the religious press were important in the conspiracy issue. They drew attention to the dangers of conspiracies, assassinations, and the burning of cities and aroused the electorate.[99]

The election of 1864 was a referendum on the war and emancipation, and the antislavery religious people kept the issue before the public even though many moderate Republicans were silent on the slavery question. Theodore Tilton and other antislavery Christians noted in public addresses that the constitutional amendment had not received due attention in public meetings of Republicans. Lincoln and the Republican party, however, had gradually been persuaded to accept the radical Christian views. The election victory sealed the commitment to emancipation.[100]

In his annual message to Congress in December 1864, Lincoln recommended a constitutional amendment abolishing slavery because "it is the voice of the people now." He reaffirmed that the Emancipation Proclamation would stand. "If the people should . . . make it an Executive duty to re-enslave such persons," he warned, "another, and not I must be their instrument to perform it."[101]

# CHAPTER SIX

# The Churches and Presidential Reconstruction

While the Confederacy disintegrated during the winter of 1864-65, the unionists made new efforts to define the conditions of Reconstruction. Republican harmony in the wake of the 1864 election augured well for a compromise between the reconstruction plans of the president and those of Congress. The editor of the *Universalist Quarterly and General Review* informed his readers that he "solemnly believed that . . . if the factious spirit of the North can be held in subjection," and if Lincoln could be given a fair chance to finish the work entrusted to his care, a just and humane Reconstruction would result. Writing in the same vein, Unitarian William Henry Channing commended Garrison for his support of Lincoln. Although he did not fully accept the president's policy, Channing was sure Lincoln would keep his pledge of universal freedom and "never go back a hair's breadth."[1]

Meetings were called by patriotic and Christian men in Detroit and Chicago to exchange views and "to secure more harmonious action among loyal men." At the suggestion of M.P. Gaddis, a Methodist clergyman, the secretary of the Michigan Union League organized a committee to issue a call for a grand mass convention to unite Republicans behind a program of action. To the evangelical Christians, the events of the last half of 1864 seemed to confirm that God approved of the policy of the administration, but many radicals were not inclined to trust Lincoln. The radical Episcopal layman Preston King wrote to James Doolittle that "the Lord of Hosts" had shielded the Union army and had guided the administration in the recent election. John Andrew informed a black friend that the slaves had been delivered from bondage by "the hand of God," and a Free Will Baptist clergyman explained at length in the *Free Will Baptist Quarterly* that the election furnished evidence that God approved of the administration's program to overthrow slavery.[2] The *Presbyterian Witness* of Cincinnati used the same events to show that many who had refused to recognize God as an element of power in political questions in 1860 were now willing to acknowledge His overruling providence in the affairs of men and nations. The Thanksgiving sermons and the New Year addresses of ministers reached a new high point as political statements favorable to the administration. The Democratic press complained that the evangelical churches had been abolitionized, but the *Religious Herald* of Hartford insisted that abolitionism was nothing more or less than the religious reverence for man and his natural rights.[3]

Some radical Christians were not reconciled to the president's reconstruction plan or even to a modified plan that would include token concessions to the radicals. The Free Will Baptist *Morning Star* complained that Lincoln's plan ignored the black man. "If we follow the plain dictates of duty," and accept the guidance and work offered by God's providence, added the editor, "we shall not be allowed to stop at any half-way measure in the work of repentance and righteousness." A correspondent to the *American Presbyterian* warned the Christian public that it would be disastrous "for the blacks to again fall into the hands of their merciless oppressors," but the Baptist *Examiner* was of the opinion that a backward step was not likely because the Christian public was almost unanimous in opposing any peace before the unconditional submission of the secession states. A Congregational missionary of the AHMS also expressed faith and hope that the peace would be "untarnished by the foul blot of Compromise with Slavery."[4]

Some observers demanded that Congress intervene in Reconstruction and that the Christian public let its progressive position be known. *Zion's Herald* demanded that Congress have a voice in peace when it was made. "Let us not forget that righteousness and humanity have other claims that in this hour must not be ignored or forgotten," the editor reminded his readers. Two weeks later he informed them that it would be "morally and politically" wrong to pardon the leaders of the rebellion. A correspondent to the *Christian Herald and Presbyterian Recorder* was also dissatisfied with the direction Reconstruction had taken. He was convinced that the time had come for "the Church and her ministers to take the high ground that belonged to them." Gerrit Smith alerted James Ashley to the discontent with Reconstruction that existed in some radical circles and warned him that God would not be pacified by such a course. "He requires us to cut down the tree," Smith said in explaining his dissatisfaction, as a radical Christian, with the reconstruction bill before Congress.[5] But no one did more to stir the public to an awareness of the need for radical measures than Theodore Tilton. At the end of 1864 he set out on a speaking tour in the West to be sure that this section continued to support Radical Reconstruction. He traveled almost three thousand miles and spoke in about a dozen cities.[6]

Lincoln had shown a tendency to make concessions to the radicals. The president's annual message expressed his willingness to support "more rigorous measures than heretofore" toward the South. As late as April 11, he said in a speech that the Louisiana precedent of denying blacks suffrage would not necessarily be followed in other states. Lincoln's appointment of Chase to the Supreme Court was pleasing to the radicals, who were working to have John Andrew added to the cabinet. The president and House leaders evolved a compromise by which Congress would recognize Lincoln's governments in Arkansas and Louisiana in turn for presidential approval of legislation for the rest of the Confederacy similar to the Wade-Davis Bill vetoed in July 1864, but a series of committee and floor votes defeated the stronger versions of a reconstruction bill. As a result no bill passed in the session of 1864.[7]

Some radical Christians were despondent, but most remained optimistic. They knew that the Republican party had accumulated a tremendous fund of moral capital. The war principles were their own. Never was a party more fully and automatically identified as reflecting the public consensus on matters of public morality. Reformers were ready to regroup to shape public opinion and to lobby for their program. George Stearns wrote to Sumner, "You, I understood are to have a 'fight' with Trumbull and Co. next winter. Today when the events of the past month have softened mens [sic] hearts and disposed them to listen to the voice of God, is the time to prepare the public mind for it."[8]

The radicals had greater success in carrying out other parts of their program. When the Thirteenth Amendment abolishing slavery throughout the nation failed to pass the House of Representatives in June 1864, religious reformers did not abandon their effort to secure passage in the next Congress. In December 1864, Lincoln called for the passage of the amendment as a commitment to carry out the platform of 1864. George Cheever and other radical Christians completed their labors to send petitions to the new Congress to "remove the great curse" from the land. The measure passed the Senate, and the administration lobbied earnestly to persuade the Democrats as well as the Republicans and border state men to support the Thirteenth Amendment.[9]

The Congregational *Boston Recorder* expressed gratitude that the

Thirteenth Amendment had passed the Senate and predicted that passage by the House would avoid many troublesome questions in the future. When the amendment passed the House on January 31, the radical Congregational minister George Tuthill expressed the sentiment of many evangelical Christians in his diary. "Slavery . . . shall exist no more. Will say *Amen*. This war is proving a blessing." The *Christian Intelligencer*, an organ of the Dutch Reformed Church, optimistically predicted that the passage of the Thirteenth Amendment would establish the righteousness of God and the rectitude of Providence and would impress upon the nation the sacredness of the human soul. To the Unitarian *Christian Register*, passage of the amendment represented the beginning of regeneration, and a Unitarian minister saw the amendment as signaling the end of an era. He assured his Brooklyn congregation that now their "new-born hope would stand no chance of being snatched away." The Baptist *Christian Watchman and Reflector* informed its readers that if the nation had been born on July 4, 1776, it had been "born again" on January 31, 1865.[10] Some radical religious journals attempted to analyze the forces that contributed to enactment of the Thirteenth Amendment. The *Zion's Herald* spoke of the wholesome outside pressure brought to bear upon reluctant representatives by zealous constituents. "We can but recognize the hand of an overruling Providence," explained the *Morning Star*.[11]

Several Methodist Episcopal conferences urged support of the amendment in 1865. The Conference of New Hampshire found evidence of the hand of God in the affairs of the nation manifested in the passage of the amendment. When the New Jersey legislature failed to ratify the amendment, the New Jersey Conference of Methodist Episcopal Churches expressed mortification. In the eyes of the New Jersey Baptist Convention, the legislature had stigmatized the whole state by its failure to act.[12]

The failure to secure a Radical Reconstruction law and the hopes of avoiding a conflict with the president prompted Christian reformers to renew their efforts to secure the passage of a law creating an agency to protect the rights of the freedmen and to serve as a barrier against the Southern governments created by presidential Reconstruction. A Freedmen's Bureau was first proposed in 1863, but there was very little lobbying at that time. The AMA took the lead in efforts to create the Bureau. The association worked primarily through Grinnell, Garfield, and Schenck—all committed laymen in Congress. The editor of the Baptist *Examiner and Chronicle* agreed with the *Independent* that no one could deny that the freedmen required protection. The persistent efforts of the reformers contributed significantly to the passage of the Freedmen's Bureau Bill in 1865.[13]

Evangelical Christians had put much effort into securing the repeal of the black laws in the Northwest. They began to succeed after 1862. Illinois, in 1865, remained one of the most backward states in granting black rights. The missionaries of the AMA in that state worked tirelessly, supported by the secretaries in New York and by the church associations in Illinois. Reverend R.C. Dunn of the Congregational Church of Toulon, Illinois, who was a missionary for the AHMS, was sent to the Illinois House of Representatives to represent Peoria and Stark counties and to strengthen the forces for repeal of the black laws. A bill to repeal them passed the Senate. When it was reported to the House, the chairman of the Committee, Washington Bushnell, a Christian layman, lamented that Illinois should be "the last to enforce the decrees of God, reechoed in the demands of the people to enact 'equal laws' and 'let the oppressed go free.' " Illinois repealed the black laws in February 1865.[14]

When Lincoln was assassinated on April 14, 1865, many radical Christians believed that the hand of Providence had permitted the assassination. Sumner thought that the murder of Lincoln was "a judgment of the Lord . . . to lift the country into a more perfect justice." According to Chandler, "the Almighty continued Mr. Lincoln in office as long as he was useful and then substituted a better man to finish the work." Funeral sermons depicted not the Christ of sacrifice and forgiveness but the God of righteousness and vengeance. George Cheever was convinced that Lincoln "was too gentle, too lenient to deal justice to traitors"; another "of sterner mold" was needed to "carry out justice and the will of God."[15] In many commemorative sermons Lincoln was compared to Moses, and Johnson was a new Joshua. It was believed that Lincoln had been removed when mercy seemed to interfere with the claims of justice.[16]

Radical Christians interpreted Lincoln's murder as a warning against leniency in Reconstruction. Reverend George Candee, a radical Congregational minister, told his Ohio congregation that "God seemed to say to us . . . , punish rebels or you must be scourged." "We were just about to 'reconstruct' our Government with traitors in power," O.A. Burgess of Indiana informed his Christian Church congregation, and that the removal of Lincoln was a last warning blow "to show us how near the precipice we stood." The radical Unitarian layman Dr. George Loring advised an audience at the Lyceum Hall in Salem, Massachusetts, that in all questions of Reconstruction, Congress should hold the power. The assassination of Lincoln greatly contributed to the radicals' power to shape Reconstruction.[17]

On May 29, 1865, President Andrew Johnson issued two significant proclamations. The first offered amnesty to all except certain categories of Southerners who would take an oath of allegiance. Those who were not offered amnesty could apply for individual pardons. Johnson's second proclamation named a provisional governor for North Carolina and provided for a constitutional convention in which only whites who had taken an oath of allegiance could participate in organizing the government. In subsequent weeks, Johnson issued similar proclamations for six Southern states. Radical Christians protested to Johnson about his mild reconstruction plan. A Connecticut radical complained: "Justice needs attention paid to it, as well as mercy. When I read the Bible . . . , I find that thine eye must not pity, nor thine hand must not spare the guilty." The clergy were very critical of the provisional government of North Carolina for excluding the blacks from the organization of government. Ministers of the Black River Baptist Association called upon Johnson in the name of the government to recognize the freedmen as citizens and protect them from their late masters. "You are committing the blackest crime of the ages," an angry radical wrote to Johnson because he had given the ballot to Rebels stained with the blood of loyal men while he denied it to loyal men who had fought for the Union. An active Methodist layman urged Johnson to become the freedmen's Joshua and see that loyal blacks enjoyed the same rights as naturalized citizens. George Stearns earnestly entreated the president to lose no time in recognizing blacks as equal in the sight of God. The radicals saw the victories of war fast slipping away. Horace Greeley urged Gerrit Smith and other abolitionists to hasten to Washington and stay there three or four weeks to persuade Johnson to favor Radical Reconstruction and universal suffrage.[18]

Radical Christians made determined efforts to alert radical lawmakers to the dangers of presidential Reconstruction. A Boston minister warned Sumner that the president was not sympathetic to the reconstruction sentiments of the majority in the free states; whatever was to be done must be done before the rebellious states were readmitted. "My hope is in God"—and in you, he added. A Universalist minister complained to Sumner that Johnson's policy was "all wrong." J.W. Alden, editor of the *Principia*, was alarmed at Johnson's actions, which he interpreted as reflecting a desire to create a party for his reelection, but Edgar Ketchum, treasurer of the AMA, did not see how the president could hold to his policy in view of developments in the South. "It is a defiance to God and truth," wrote Sumner. His words echoed the sentiments of his correspondents on presidential policy.[19]

The Presbyterian president of Miami University wrote Sumner of his conviction that the president had made "a great mistake in refusing to recognize the colored citizens as a part of the people" of the Southern states. In June 1865 the Progressive Friends met in Boston and petitioned the next Congress to pass an amendment to the Constitution prohibiting legislation that would discriminate on the basis of race or color. The radical lawmakers responded to progressive public opinion and in some cases were chiefly responsible for shaping radical public opinion among their constituents. Congressman James Harlan, a Methodist layman, maintained that Congress should refuse to admit the South "until their constitutions provide a just rule for the exercise of the elective franchise." The Unitarian radical senator J.M. Howard believed that the policy of proclamation would have, "in the end, to be abandoned." Sumner was astonished to see the president begin Reconstruction by discriminating against the blacks—a course which Sumner considered illegal.[20]

The evangelical religious journals were in the vanguard in support of Radical Reconstruction. Thomas Eddy, editor of the *Northwestern Christian Advocate*, urged the perpetual disfranchisement of all who had voluntarily borne arms for the Confederacy. The *Western Christian Advocate* termed restoration of citizenship to Confederates "a dangerous experiment." The *Christian Advocate and Journal* viewed the exclusion of blacks from participation in the reorganization of the government of the South as "a blunder in policy" and "a violation of political rights." *Zion's Herald* agreed that Johnson was proceeding too fast with Reconstruction. The editor favored military government until the situation became more settled, and the *Independent* was appalled at "the haste" with which the rebel states were being brought back into the Union. The editor found the president's North Carolina measures unacceptable.[21]

When the religious conventions met in May and June 1865, the evangelical churches took a progressive stance. The New School Presbyterian General Assembly was "vigorously radical" and insisted upon the punishment of the Rebels. The Conference of the Methodist Episcopal Bishops declared its support for the administration as long as the administration acted with equity and rendered "justice to all." The National Congregational Council met in Boston in June and resolved that the rights of the blacks should be secured as a religious duty and because security demanded it.[22]

The Baptist associations took the most radical position on presidential Reconstruction. Almost all associations favored granting suffrage to the freedman. According to the Sussex association, for example, events showed that God was on the side of equity, and the American system of government guaranteed protection without respect to color. The North-Western Seventh Day Baptist demanded, in the name of divine rights and the Constitution, full recognition and guarantee of inalienable rights to liberty for all people.[23] The Genesee (New York) Baptist Association rejected presidential Reconstruction. It urged Congress to take charge of Reconstruction to prevent the victories gained in the field from being neutralized by the peace. The East New Jersey Association and the Niagara (New York) Association went even farther. They maintained that the rebel leaders should be punished. The Central Union Association of Pennsylvania, still more radical, called for the confiscation of rebel property, to be given to the freedman as necessary. Since 1864 the Baptists had taken a more radical stance. Senator Ira Harris of New York had been president of the Baptist Missionary Union, but in 1864 he had opposed the repeal of the Fugitive Slave Law of 1793 and had been generally averse to the enlargement of black rights. When the Missionary Union was preparing to meet in 1864, the antislavery Baptists opposed Harris's reelection as president of the Missionary Union because of his voting record. Harris's friends vehemently denied the aspersion as a calumny, and the antislavery men produced the *Congressional Globe* to show that he had voted against a bill to prohibit discrimination against blacks on streetcars in the District of Columbia, against an amendment to an appropriation bill providing that no witness should be excluded on account of color, and against a proposition to prohibit the coastwise slave trade in the United States. The *American Baptist* took Harris to task for his votes, and a letter from Harris failed to improve his image. The senator was removed as president of the Union and was not returned to the Senate when his term expired in 1867.[24]

When Johnson followed his plan of reconstructing North Carolina with similar plans for other Confederate states, the anxiety of radical Christians increased. On June 21, 1865, a large meeting was held in Faneuil Hall, Boston, to arouse and influence public opinion against conservative Reconstruction. In order to define the objectives of the meeting, John A. Andrew advised the organizers that they should oppose Reconstruction of the South at the present time, for it could not be done with safety and security. The North should keep the power and "use it in the fear of God."[25] Stearns engineered the Faneuil Hall meeting of patriotic men and liberals and evangelical Christians as a way of putting pressure on Johnson to modify presidential Reconstruction. Henry W. Beecher and Richard Henry Dana, an antislavery Episcopal layman, gave the main addresses. Dana emphasized the need for black suffrage to ensure the success of Reconstruction. Beecher spoke on behalf of universal suffrage as a natural, inalienable right. Pomeroy asserted, "We must secure to the Negro the homestead, . . . and the ballot." A committee chaired by Dana prepared an address to the public. The entire committee consisted of outstanding church members and clergy. The address demanded that freedmen be given the power to defend the rights of blacks. "Political justice and safety" demanded nothing less. The address was sent to Johnson with the warning that the opinions expressed in it were "rapidly spreading all over the country." The Faneuil Hall meeting attracted nationwide attention and inspired similar meetings in other cities.[26]

Chase was one of the most active Christian laymen in trying to secure the modification of Reconstruction. He was in touch with a wide range of radicals and spoke in many places during 1865 in favor of black suffrage. In July he wrote a friend that impartial justice and sound policy required the recognition of equal rights for all loyal citizens, and he declared that nothing would secure it as certainly as universal suffrage.[27]

By July the religious journals were more pronounced in their opposition to presidential Reconstruction. Alfred Brunson, editor of the *Christian Advocate and Journal*, denied that the Southern states reconstructed by Johnson were legal entities or could be admitted to seats in Congress. The Boston *Congregationalist* maintained that the president's plan of restoration "awakened deep solicitude among the people because the exclusion of the blacks from a voice in the reorganization of the government leaves the South in the control of traitors." The *New York Christian Advocate* expressed the same sentiments. The *Independent* urged the people to inform their congressmen that they wanted the ballot to be given to blacks so that presidential Reconstruction could not be founded on injustice.[28]

As late as the summer and autumn of 1865, some of the moderate and radical clergy believed Johnson could be influenced to change his course. The radical Episcopal clergyman Charles Brooks urged Johnson to secure the rights of every person because only in this way could the nation fulfill its divine mission. A Baptist layman advised the president to disfranchise every civil and military leader of the Confederacy and grant suffrage to the blacks. The Confederate states could demonstrate their repentance by shaping constitutions that recognized the rights of every man. Radical Reverend Granville Moody wrote to Johnson that God "spoke from the *burning* bush as in the days of Moses saying to America as he said to Egypt and Pharoh, 'Let *my people go that they may serve me.*' " A Congregational clergyman addressed Johnson more humbly: "I am sure it cannot be just to deny to any man the rights and privileges" because of his color. Joseph Medill, editor of the *Chicago Tribune*, wrote Johnson an epistle that combined advice with a warning. "No scheme of reconstruction will ever again include the vassalage of the North to the Southern aristocracy. . . . You may affect to despise the Radicals but their votes made you President. . . . You cannot break up the great Republican anti-slavery party, which will follow in the footsteps of the martyr Lincoln. . . . For God sake move cautiously and carefully. . . . The great doctrine of *Equal Rights* is bound to prevail."[29]

In July, as the Southern and Northern Democratic praise and flattery of Johnson increased, powerful Christian laymen and clergy mounted new attacks on Johnson and urged Congressmen to more radical action. John Covode, a former congressman and a Methodist layman, warned Wade that the slaveholders would have slavery in some form if they gained control. Charles Norton, president of Harvard, wrote Sumner that a hard struggle would plainly be required to maintain the principles of liberty. Reverend A.L. Stone, a Congregational clergyman, expressed fear to a July 4 audience in Providence, Rhode Island, that the old conservatives and aristocrats of the South would now creep out of their holes and hiding places to reenact state laws that would imperil the gains made in four years of war. The Christians were apprehensive as to how Southerners might behave when they were fully in control of their states and back in the Union because the Christians saw no evidence of repentance, which they considered necessary when a sinner or wrongdoer asks for forgiveness or a pardon. According to Edward Mansfield, who wrote under the pen name "Veteran Observer," eminent lawyers had always taught that political oaths of the kind Johnson required Southerners to take meant nothing; the whole rebel population would vote under Johnson's proclamations. The Rebels would come back stronger than before. Bland Ballard, a Unitarian federal judge, asked Sumner: "Can it be possible" that the president "really believed in the sincerity and repentance of the rebel devils?"[30]

The situation was so critical that Charles Sumner remained in Washington during the summer of 1865 in a futile effort to keep Johnson persuaded of the radical position. His fellow senators brought him gloomy reports from the countryside. Near the end of July, Wade was convinced that the president's policy was "nothing less than political suicide." Senator Howard wrote from Detroit that public safety demanded Negro suffrage. He held that Congress had the power to reorganize the states and to secure them. Sumner was distressed by the course of events in Washington. He wrote to Senator Edwin Morgan of New York that, to his mind, the president's reorganization of the Southern states was illegal and unconstitutional. Sumner wrote to Wade that the salvation of the country depended upon Congress. To accept Johnson's plan was to deliver the country into the hands of the traitors who had just been conquered in the field.[31]

When the evangelical church conferences and associations met in the late summer and fall of 1865, they were more forthright in their demands for Radical Reconstruction. For example the Erie and the Iowa conferences of the Methodist Episcopal Church and the Illinois Conference of the Free Methodist Church resolved that justice and public safety demanded giving the freedmen the ballot.[32] The Chemung River Baptist Association in New York promised only to support the president in "all equitable and constitutional measures." The strongest position was taken by the New Jersey State Baptist Convention. It called for a harsh Reconstruction of the Confederate states.[33]

Individual clergymen were in the field in great numbers in the autumn of 1865.[34] They demanded equal rights for blacks and modification of presidential Reconstruction. "I have again and again, in sermon, speech and conversation urged the necessity of universal suffrage and emphatically of black suffrage—on grounds of humanity, justice, equity and safety," the Universalist clergyman O.B. Frothingham informed Sumner. James R. Gilmore, an influential writer and Methodist clergyman, reported to Garfield that he found his preaching running "into politics insensibly and necessarily." Gilmore was convinced that Johnson was not worthy, and he insisted that blacks had the same natural rights as whites and must be endowed with political rights to protect their natural rights.[35] The Democratic press raged against what it called political preaching when the clergy spoke out in support of Radical Reconstruction or opposed presidential Reconstruction.[36]

As the first session of the Thirty-ninth Congress approached, S.G. Arnold, an auditor in the government and a radical Methodist layman, sent two letters to the *Toledo Blade* outlining a practical program that would prevent insurrection in the South by purging the Constitution of all inequalities. The answer, Arnold said, was to give the blacks suffrage. He followed the letters with an article on suffrage in the *Methodist Quarterly Review*. Arnold expressed grave doubts as to whether a democratic republic could long endure without the support of Christianity. Christian teachings, he believed, were particularly calculated to make for a strong, self-reliant, and self-governed electorate, and an elevating influence was necessary in a democratic Christian republic, where the political franchise should not depend on complexion. He suggested an amendment to the Constitution that would base representation in Congress on the number of actual votes. In this way, he believed, the South could be induced to enfranchise its people without regard to color. Arnold sent a copy of the article to Johnson for his consideration.[37]

On November 17, the radical Unitarian congressman George Julian addressed the people of Indiana from the state House of Representatives in Indianapolis. He told his audience that if they wanted to prepare the black for suffrage, they must take off his chains and give him equal rights. "It is ordained by Providence that retribution shall follow wrong doing," Julian explained. "Thunder in the ears of your President and Congress that you demand the hanging, certainly the exile of the great rebel leaders, the confiscation and distribution of their great landed estates."[38]

The fact that Johnson pardoned several former Confederates after it appeared that they would win political office caused radical Christians to doubt the Southerners' repentance at the time of amnesty. Republicans insisted more firmly that national law should replace executive proclamation as the basis of state restoration; in the autumn the Southern states had begun to define the status and rights of the blacks with laws that regulated almost all aspects of the life of the freed people. These laws, known as Black Codes, created a quasi-slavery, or serfdom, which was offensive to the humanitarian sentiments of many Christians.[39]

As the important Thirty-ninth Congress of December 1865 approached, the radical Christians made efforts to influence Congress and the electorate. In November, Garrison embarked on a six-week lecture tour that took him as far west as Chicago, Quincy, and Springfield, Illinois. Everywhere he urged the members of his audience to use their influence to have Southern representatives excluded from Congress until the freedmen had been granted equal rights. Everywhere

Garrison found the people to be of one opinion that not a single Confederate state "should be admitted into the Union without being put under a long probation."[40]

Throughout his western tour, Garrison spoke before audiences composed of select, respectable, and intelligent people. A significant number were active laymen and clergymen. At Erie, Pennsylvania, the arrangements for his lecture were handled by a Presbyterian minister. He spoke in a Universalist church. In Cleveland, layman Rufus Spalding and Reverend James Thome, pastor of the First Congregational Church of Cleveland, were representative auditors. In Detroit, Jacob M. Howard, Giles B. Stebbins, Reverend George Duffield, and the Congregational minister Calvin Dufree were present in a highly appreciative audience. Garrison addressed a large congregation in Reverend Edwin P. Powell's Plymouth Congregational Church in Adrian, Michigan. The intellectual and moral leaders of the city and its surroundings were present to hear him in the spacious and beautiful church. At Hillsdale, Michigan, the Free Will Baptists composed the greater part of his audience. In LaPorte, Indiana, the arrangement committee of three that greeted his arrival consisted of a Presbyterian, a Baptist, and a Unitarian minister. In Chicago, Garrison was introduced by the radical Unitarian clergyman Robert Collyer. After Garrison completed his lecture, listeners, including many clergymen, crowded the platform. The renowned abolitionist dined with Collyer that day, and the next evening had tea with him and compared notes. Garrison lectured in Strawn's Opera House in Jacksonville, Illinois, where the audience was largely clergymen and laymen, including Reverend Julian M. Sturtevant, president of Illinois College, and his professors. In Springfield, Illinois, Garrison spoke in the chamber of the House of Representatives to the governor, state officers, lawyers, merchants, and clergy. The most renowned clergyman present was Albert Hale, pastor of the Second Presbyterian Church and agent of the AHMS. Garrison dined with him and listened to him preach the next day. Later in Cincinnati, Garrison was met at the depot by a prominent Quaker. Quakers were the most numerous group attending his lecture.[41]

Garrison returned east on a train carrying several Republican congressmen on their way to Washington. He found that most of them felt that the South should not be readmitted to the Union until the problems had received further examination and safeguards had been established for the freedmen. Garrison's impression of Congress's probable stance was like that of other informed people. The *Cincinnati Commercial* reported that the radical Congressmen were "unreserved in their expression that not a single representative from the rebellious states" should be admitted to a seat in the House of Representatives.[42]

The setbacks that the radicals suffered in the Northern states in their drive to secure black suffrage at the state level caused the moderates and some radicals to rethink their plans to secure national legislation for black suffrage and to change their tactics and strategy. Radicals became more determined than ever to keep the South out of the Union until a radical program had been set in place. Seeing that admission of the Southern states must be greatly delayed, Garfield wrote to Chase, "If we shall not be able to maintain the fight on the suffrage question alone, should we not make a preliminary resistance to immediate restoration and thereby gain time?" William M. Grosvenor, a Congregational layman, expressed the same sentiments. He suggested to Sumner, "If we cannot yet control public opinion on the direct suffrage issue, or hold a sure majority in Congress on that, perhaps other topics, nearer to the popular appreciation, may serve to unite enough to prevent final action for the present."[43]

Radical Christians were still determined to settle for nothing less than equality before the law. The annual meeting of the AMA summed up the feelings of its members by declaring, "In this age, and in this nation, there can be no meaning to liberty which leaves a man stripped of all civil rights, and free only as the beasts of the forest are free. Emancipation and liberty are but empty and mocking words if they do not convey the idea and rights of citizenship." After a trip to the South in the winter of 1865, the Boston Congregational clergyman Edward N. Kirk identified the direction he thought congressional Reconstruction should take. "The reconstruction we want," Kirk declared, "is . . . that rebellion against the federal government shall be demonstrated to be so costly, so despicable, so hopeless, that a thousand Calhouns, Macons, Ruffins, and Davises, can never again 'fire the Southern heart' to undertake it." Kirk also mentioned the need to guarantee "that the black man shall be a citizen, fully and everywhere protected, as every white child is, by the whole military power of the country, and in full possession of his rights of manhood."[44]

By November 1865, discontent with Johnson's Reconstruction had taken hold in the minds of radical Christians. They believed that Johnson's policy was a failure and that the fruits of victory were being lost. Radical Christians wanted justice done and repentance shown. Colfax expressed the sentiments of the radical Christians in November when he spoke on Reconstruction. He believed that the ideas of the Declaration of Independence should be expressed in the law of the land, and both blacks and white should have equal protection of life and property. A radical Christian of Ohio wrote to Senator Sherman, "I have read with unqualified approval Colfax's speech. . . . He is right and Congress should not be lenient, nor harsh beyond what he intimates. We beg of you to be content with nothing less. Your constituents expect you to occupy ground not less radical than this." Another radical wrote to Stevens, "Justice is what the colored man asks. It is what the white disloyalist does not want. In both instances it is in my opinion what the nation cannot in safety refuse to give to both."[45]

Radicalism had gained substantial grounds during the year of 1865. A considerable part of this gain reflected radical Christian agitation and propaganda. The assassination of Lincoln was a powerful force that religious leaders used to push the Republican party to a position of Radical Reconstruction. The mild restoration that Johnson set in motion, together with the praise and vigorous support he received from the Southerners and Northern Democrats, aroused suspicion in the minds of reformers. Johnson's liberal pardon policy, which reached an average of a hundred pardons a day in September 1865, offended many Christians who felt that the justice of God meant that retribution must be allowed to run its course.[46] They saw no repentance on the part of the South, and most Christians believed that without repentance there should be no forgiveness. According to the *Presbyterian,* a Reconstruction that offered a ready pardon would "make the forms of criminal law a mockery."[47] When the South honored and glorified its leaders and military officers, some Christians felt that criminals were being made into martyrs. Many Christians wanted, more than anything, a symbolic gesture vindicating the Union position with some concrete action that would place the moral onus on the South and elicit repentance. The South failed to meet these "symbolic requirements."[48]

When Congress met in December 1865, Northern Christians showed a great degree of unity on Reconstruction. Radical Christianity became more significant in the last year and a half of the war because many moderate Christians had adopted a radical position on Reconstruction. The clear-cut issues in the election of 1864 and the assassination of Lincoln had been the most significant factors in making religious opinion more radical. A generous peace, mercy, conciliation, and the sentiment of the New Testament were put away and were replaced by loud demands for punishment, vengeance, and concern for the fruits of victory. It was felt that divine intervention had strengthened religious feeling in the North, and concern with the workings of

Providence replaced thoughts of a pragmatic and magnanimous peace. Radical Christians called for justice, retribution, and repentance in the name of the Old Testament. They focused their attention on Congress and thought Radical Reconstruction would bring the promised land within sight.[49]

# CHAPTER SEVEN

# The Christian Opposition to Johnson

On December 4, 1865, when the Thirty-ninth Congress convened, almost all Republicans were united in a determination not to admit Southern representatives to Congress. Moderate Republicans agreed with radicals that the president's policy did not go far enough to safeguard the fruits of the Union victory. Moderates, however, believed Northern voters would not support the radical policy of black suffrage as a minimum condition of restoration. In his message to Congress, Johnson restated his objection to prescribing suffrage qualification in the Southern states. Many moderates went along with him because they wanted to prevent a break with Johnson. Charles Sumner moved that the president be asked to report on the conditions of the states lately in rebellion. When the president's message and report came in on December 19, Sumner found occasion to take the floor on Henry Wilson's bill for the protection of freedmen. After showing that a hostile spirit existed in the Southern states, he made a dramatic appeal. "Insist upon guaranties. Pass the bill under consideration,—pass any bill,—but do not let this crying injustice rage any longer. An avenging God cannot sleep while such things find countenance." He directed his final remarks to Johnson. "If you are not ready to be the Moses of an oppressed people do not become its Pharaoh."[1]

Sumner had acted partly in response to radical clergy and religious laymen. Reverend W.E. Walker, who had formerly served among blacks in the South, only a week before Sumner's speech had urged him to secure radical measures. Walker told Sumner that the Southerners bragged that "they will give the colored people *Hell* as soon as the troops are withdrawn." Other radical clergy were sure that Johnson could be won over after Sumner's speech. Justin D. Fulton, the radical Baptist antislavery pastor of Tremont Temple in Boston, advised Sumner, "Johnson belongs to the Strata of Society from which Southern Serfs were reared. . . . It is on this rock, if any, he will flounder. Let him know that the Southern Aristocrat is unchanged since his wife was insulted and his life was endangered and he will come to the help of the loyal and the true."[2]

The retiring radical governor of Massachusetts, John A. Andrew, informed a member of Congress that the South "must clearly and completely cede to the freedman *the same civil rights enjoyed by the whites.*" In Andrew's opinion, the administration had made a grievous blunder in neglecting the enfranchisement of the freedmen as an essential element of Reconstruction. He proposed an amendment enfranchising the blacks on the same basis as whites throughout the whole country, but in order to promote harmony he asked that the law take effect after a twenty-five-year delay. The moderate John Binney, an Episcopal layman, also suggested a delay of twenty-five years to Thaddeus Stevens as a compromise measure to secure the approval of the president.[3]

Most radical Christians believed it imperative that Congress should immediately legislate equality before the law. The New York Presbyterian clergyman Samuel Burchard advised his congregation on its Christian responsibility in connection with Reconstruction. "Let us be true to our duties and honor humanity, and God will take care of us and them. The qualification for voting should be *uniform, universal and irrespective of color.*" The next day, on January 1, in Tremont Temple, Reverend E.N. Kirk told an emancipation anniversary observance audience that the blacks' citizenship must be acknowledged. The speaker emphasized that Congress was bound to secure to humanity and the country the fruits of the war. The radical Christians believed that unless the nation conformed to God's law, retribution would again be visited upon it. A Christian layman wrote to Sumner that "as soon as the colored men are allowed the same and equal rights with the white men all these troubles will soon fade away and never before because God will accept nothing else."[4]

Some radical Christians looked beyond black rights as a Christian duty. They saw the blacks as a necessary ally against the Southern aristocracy and Johnson. On January 14, Theodore Tilton terminated his western speaking tour on Reconstruction with a speech in Cleveland. "We must strike an alliance with the negro race arming them with the musket and with the ballot," Tilton told his audience. A radical Ohio Quaker agreed about the need to reconstruct the South regardless of the Southern aristocracy or Johnson. He wrote to Congressman Samuel Shellabarger that the way to handle the crisis was to ignore Johnson and proceed with congressional Reconstruction.[5]

John Binney suggested to Stevens that the radicals ought to support a measure for suffrage for the freedmen in the District of Columbia. "Logically this should be taken up before the proposed Amendment enfranchising the blacks over the whole of the states in the Union, as the former is the centre and the latter the radii around it," Binney reasoned. Many radicals were already thinking along the same lines. The bill for black suffrage in the District of Columbia was introduced by William D. Kelley. In explaining his reason for proposing the bill Kelley said, "I am . . . a radical who stands by the eternal principles which God ordained, and one such, having the Almighty with him is ever in the majority."[6] On January 16, George Julian spoke in defense of the black suffrage bill in the District of Columbia. To Julian, the debate on the bill was a moral issue. "On this broad ground, co-incidental with Christianity itself," Julian informed his colleagues, "I plant my feet . . . in demanding the ballot in this District for the despised and defenseless, I simply demand the national recognition of Christianity, which is 'the root of all democracy, the highest fact in the rights of man.' " Garrison expressed his gratitude to the determined band of radicals after the bill was introduced in the House. "All honor to you," he wrote to Julian, "and the noble band in both Houses, who are resolved to make no compromise that shall leave the colored population of the District . . . without the possession of all those rights and immunities which belong to citizenship."[7]

The House of Representatives passed the black suffrage bill for the District of Columbia on January 18, 1866, after receiving petitions from blacks and radical Christians. The Washington correspondent to the *Independent* informed the editor: "Radicalism is still popular in the House and Conservatism hides its head." It was rumored in the city that many members of the House who had voted for the suffrage bill would have liked to vote against it but were afraid of their radical constituents. The Washington correspondent for the *Independent* thought that this rumor was quite likely true.[8] Assuming the Senate would concur, the *Congregationalist* urged every Congressional district to rally in support of Congress in case of a presidential veto. "Let the people speak, by letters, by memorials, by the press, by deputations, by public meetings, and uphold Congress in the great act of justice which it has not adopted," the editor counseled.[9] The editor of the *Zion's Herald* warned his readers, "We believe the God of nations requires, demands this at our hands, holds the Church and the nation responsible, and will in due time punish both should they prove false to this important duty."[10]

Although the radical Christians wanted black suffrage in the District of Columbia to be the entering wedge for suffrage throughout the country, the Republican majority in the Senate, under the control of the moderates, decided to play down the suffrage issue. They quietly shelved the bill granting black suffrage in the District of Columbia. The *National Anti-Slavery Standard* was disgusted with the cowardice of the Republicans. "We agree with Mr. Thaddeus Stevens in holding President Johnson responsible for the fearful guilt in obstructing the path of justice," Parker Pillsbury, the editor, charged, but he was convinced that there was a broad responsibility for the bad faith and broken promises to the blacks. "With the single honorable exception of the *New York Independent*, we do not know of a journal of influence, from Boston to St. Louis, which has given an earnest protest against this proposed surrender of the political rights of the negro into the hands of his rebel master," he complained.[11]

The shelving of the District of Columbia bill caused the radicals to become more vocal in their opposition to presidential Reconstruction and more outspoken concerning Johnson. Sumner and Stevens were the nucleus of the attack. Already Sumner had compared Johnson's message of January 19 with the "whitewashing message of Franklin Pierce in regard to the enormities in Kansas." Five clergymen of different denominations wrote to Sumner thanking him for his faithful and stern challenge to the conservative forces in the government.[12] Sumner hesitated to advocate the enfranchisement of the large numbers of Southern blacks, but in common with many others, he soon reached the conclusion that there was "no substantial protection for the freedman except in the franchise." Sumner argued, "We put the musket in his hands because it was necessary; for the same reason we must give him the franchise."[13] He took the initiative and proceeded to write bills and resolutions for equal rights for blacks. Radical Christians responded with approval and support. A Connecticut girl wrote to Sumner, "I thank God that I live in an age in which He speaks" with Sumner as an agent.[14]

Many applauded Sumner for daring to do right. A minister from Michigan commended Sumner for having "the true independence" to stand up for equal rights without party support. "I *am glad especially,*" he added, "that in your great work you dare rebuke the President."[15] An unidentified correspondent expressed approval of Sumner's moral courage. "It seems to me," he wrote, "that God has raised you up as a special agent in our nation." A Unitarian minister informed Sumner that it was "good to know that there are those whom no threat of personal violence, no bloody fingers—hideous proof of unsuppressed barbarism can make flinch." One of the most respected Congregational clergymen assured Sumner that he had "the approval of all loyal men and angels, while struggling against the devices of the arch-enemy of God and man."[16]

Thaddeus Stevens occupied a position in the House of Representatives similar to that held by Sumner in the Senate. Stevens was not an advocate of black suffrage. He concentrated on destroying the political power of the Southern aristocracy. Stevens regarded franchisement of the freedmen as rather inefficient. Radical religious men tried to persuade Stevens of the need for black suffrage. For example, Amos Tuck, a New Hampshire radical Congregationalist who served as a superintendent of the Sunday school in the First Church of Exeter, New Hampshire, wrote to Stevens, "I wish you would give the idea consideration: the importance of the ballot, as well as the right of suffrage to the freedmen."[17]

Meanwhile Lyman Trumbull, chairman of the Senate Judiciary Committee and an influential moderate, drafted a Freedmen's Bureau bill to strengthen the organization so that it could properly deal with the black codes that the Southern legislatures had passed. The bill would permit the Bureau to offer more aid to the freedmen. Trumbull also drafted a civil rights bill which gave federal courts appellate jurisdiction in cases concerning black rights. On January 12, Trumbull reported both bills. He hoped the president would support them and thereby check Sumner and his radical supporters. The radicals quickly accepted the Bureau bill and joined the moderates in backing it. The radical Ignatius Donnelly and others spoke in support of the bill. He was congratulated by an old Philadelphia classmate for taking a noble stand on the side of "advancing civilization and Christianity."[18]

The editors of the religious journals focused their attention on the action of Congress and let their readers know how they felt about the developments in the legislative branch of the government. On January 19, the editor of the *Congregationalist* declared that "Congress, as its first duty, must see that whatever safeguards are necessary to give effect to the constitutional prohibition of slavery are established and maintained." The editor of the *Presbyterian Witness* was exasperated by the delay in granting the Negro his rights. "It is time we would away with our squeamish objections to the exercise of justice toward the African race." The Unitarian *Christian Examiner* wanted Trumbull's bill passed so Congress could move to assume power and reestablish republican government in the South. The editor insisted that the first condition for the reestablishment of government was manhood suffrage because "the existence of Christianity . . . necessitates. . . political equality."[19]

The Joint Committee on Reconstruction, created by Congress in December 1865 and controlled by moderates, reported a constitutional amendment early in February 1866. The amendment gave the states power to determine who was eligible for suffrage but provided for a reduction in representation if they did not grant blacks the right to vote. The proposed constitutional amendment met a hail of radical criticism in both houses of Congress and from the radical Christian public. The *Christian Advocate* and the *Independent* condemned the amendment for leaving the fate of the oppressed to the discretion of the oppressors, and the conservative Presbyterian *New York Observer* and *Christian Intelligencer* criticized Congress for interfering with the rights of the states.[20]

Theodore Tilton, editor of the *Independent*, demanded personal liberty, security, and all the rights of American citizenship for the blacks. "God himself made these demands of this nation," Tilton wrote. "Woe be the nation if these be unheeded!" Tilton's letter to Sumner read: "I protested with all my heart against the Amendment" because it left the blacks at the mercy of the Rebels. The next day he told a mass meeting in New York that the amendment was "practically subversive of human freedom."[21] Religious journals in Chicago and Boston were also critical of the amendment. If the amendment passed, the editor of the *Boston Recorder* declared, it would "inflict upon our free institutions greater infamy" than anything written in our body of laws. The editor of the Baptist *Christian Times and Witness* was just as uncompromising concerning the amendment as the Congregational journal in Boston. "Citizenship for the emancipated black man has to be met, cannot be met too soon, and *can only* be met adequately by defining his position, in this regard in the organic law," warned the editor.[22]

The clergy and Christian laymen lost no time in informing their Congressmen how they felt about the amendment. The Baptist clergyman William C. Child, secretary of the American Tract Society, informed E.B. Washburne that he wished Congress would amend the Constitution in such a way as to remove the suffrage question altogether from the purview of the states. A Presbyterian layman suggested to Senator Sherman that martial law was needed to protect the freedmen in the South if they were not given the means to protect themselves.[23] A Congregational layman and the renowned Baptist minister

Richard S. Malcom both commended Richard Yates for joining the
forces against the amendment by taking the floor against the measure.
A well-known Rhode Island Quaker spoke out against the amendment.
He protested to Congressman Thomas Jenckes that the amendment
failed to protect the blacks, and the Wisconsin Methodist abolitionist
Charles Durkee thanked Thaddeus Stevens for resisting measures that
left the fate of the blacks in the hands of the Rebels.[24]

Sumner received by far the largest amount of protest mail against
the action of the joint committee. He had publicly stated that Christian
citizens should write to their lawmakers at least twice a month. An
abolitionist wrote to Sumner that when the amendment was reported,
he had prayed fervently that the country "be saved from the intolerable
infamy." Gerrit Smith wrote that the passage of the amendment
"would not only be disgraceful, but . . . might prove fatal."[25] The Presbyterian clergyman George Duffield revealed to Sumner that he considered the Massachusetts senator's principles "identical with the
teachings of 'the ever lasting gospel of the Grace of God.' " Other clergy
addressed Sumner in the same vein.[26]

On February 19, 1866, Johnson vetoed the Freedmen's Bureau bill
in part because Congress could not legislate for states that were being
kept out of the Union by Congress.[27] The radical Christians were
apalled and mortified. There had been rumors in Democratic circles
that the president would veto the bill, but the Republicans had expected
him to sign it. James M. McKim wrote to a friend three days before
the veto, "I can hardly think he will be so unwise. . . . To veto
it . . . would be to fly in the face of the whole people." On February
19, McKim received a telegram from a friend in Washington, "Bureau
bill vetoed at one-thirty this afternoon."[28] McKim reacted to the veto
with disgust, "He is a man of . . . strong prejudice with antecedents
and habits which forbid the hope that he will be the willing instrument
of Providence." He hurried to Washington to determine how the radical
forces could meet the crisis. From Washington McKim reported, "Loyal
and virtuous men here, who are well informed, as a general thing have
no confidence in and no sanguine hope of much good from President
Johnson."[29]

The radical Congregationalist minister George M. Tuthill vented
his feelings in his diary. "Our President has disgusted and angered the
nation. . . . We have not a worthy successor of Lincoln." The alarm
was greater, Calvin Fletcher wrote in his diary, because Johnson had
intimated that the leaders of the rebellion would have to be returned

to Congress before legislation for the secession states could be passed without a veto.[30]

Samuel May, Jr., felt the cause of freedom had been betrayed by Johnson, and Tilton concluded that all disguise had been torn off the president. "As God lives, what the veto intends to put down, it will in essence and substance put up," Garrison observed in a letter to Tilton. A citizen of Chicago wrote to Senator Sherman that Johnson should be resisted. "Compromises have had their day, *absolute right* must prevail, 'tis demanded by God, and the spirit of the people," he added.[31] A Presbyterian physician from Ohio wrote John Sherman: "Cannot the traitor be driven from his place?" Congressman William Kelley believed that the people should be aroused still more. He wrote a radical friend a letter, which was made public, stating, "Every school district in the country should be canvassed in the cause of justice and equality."[32]

Congressman F.C. Beaman, who regularly took his place in the Congregational church of Adrian, Michigan, spoke in the House on February 24. He promised that he would listen to the prayers of the blacks. "No earthly power shall induce me to consent to the terrible wrong of turning over to those traitors" the government of the country and the lives of patriotic men, he promised his radical Republican colleagues. Clark Waggoner, editor of the *Toledo Blade* and a Presbyterian layman, like Beaman was consoled because he believed that a merciful Providence would overrule the president.[33]

Many radical Christians were as optimistic about the crisis as Waggoner was because they believed Providence would lift the dark clouds.[34] Henry Ward Beecher, however, did not believe that there was a crisis, and he supported the veto. His action came as no surprise to many Christians, for he had found good things to say about presidential Reconstruction from the beginning. In December 1865, a radical Wisconsin minister informed Beecher that he and many other Christians were deeply aggrieved by Beecher's support of presidential Reconstruction. "We trust and pray that you may yet redeem yourself," he wrote, "and stand unerringly to defend the principles of eternal right and justice." Beecher continued to support the measures taken in the South in his addresses during January 1866.[35]

On February 20, Beecher spoke at the Academy of Music in Brooklyn and approved the president's veto. He rebuked the zealous radicals, whom he accused of ignoring the operation of social and economic laws. There were rumors that Leonard Bacon also supported the president's veto. On February 28, Bacon took part in a meeting in New Haven with James Doolittle and others who were supporting Johnson. Bacon did not go so far as to endorse the president's veto. He said he was a believer in states' rights but not in state sovereignty. Bacon favored admitting the South to Congress as soon as the president announced that the South was restored.[36]

Johnson followed his veto with a speech from the White House on February 22 to a group of Democrats celebrating Washington's birthday. He lashed out at the Radical Republicans in an attack that appalled and dismayed even his best friends. The speech mortified Republicans everywhere and called forth irate responses from the religious press and radical citizens.[37] The veto and the February 22 speech provoked mass meetings throughout the North in support of Congress.[38] The clergy and lay officers in religious bodies took a noticeable part in the spontaneous gatherings.

Almost all the religious press denounced the veto. For example, the *Congregationalist* insisted that the freedmen must have security. Since the president had vetoed the Bureau bill, "let them have the power of protecting themselves through the ballot box." The *New York Evangelist* called the issue involved "the underlying *moral question* in the whole matter of reconstruction, it defines the work which the Providence of God calls us as a nation to perform." Tilton's *Independent* was equally direct. The editor called presidential Reconstruction a failure and declared that Johnson had "become the supporter of a form of slavery identical in spirit with that existing before the war."[39]

The *Independent* was so devastating in its attacks on Johnson that the secretary of the treasury had an agent intimate to Henry C. Bowen, the publisher, that he would be removed from his Treasury Department position if the criticism of the president did not stop. It was claimed that Bowen was no longer connected with the paper and had no control over its contents. Efforts were made to rally support for Bowen without much success. Lewis D. Campbell, a conservative and a supporter of Johnson, wrote to the president, "Your most bitter foes are readers of the 'New York Independent,' General Howard's paper, 'The Right Way,' and similar sheets of the same stripe that are being circulated by your post masters and revenue officers all over the country." A supporter of Johnson from Connecticut informed Secretary Gideon Welles, "Our people are very much governed by the papers they read. Those who read the New York *Independent*, *Tribune*, and Philadelphia *Press*, are the most violent and radical." In August, Bowen was relieved of his duties in the Treasury Department.[40]

Congress attempted to override the president's veto before the full effects of public opinion had been felt in Washington. The Senate was two votes short of overriding the veto.[41] "Philanthropy and religion must forbid such injustice," wrote the editor of the *Western Christian Advocate*. "As Christians we have a right to demand that humanity shall not be sacrificed to party."[42]

By March 13, 1866, when the civil rights bill passed Congress by an almost unanimous Republican vote, radical Christian sentiment and pressure again focused on urging Congress to pass a new Freedmen's Bureau bill. On March 16, almost a month after Congress's failure to override Johnson's veto of the Freedmen's Bureau bill, Samuel Burnham, the editor of the *Congregationalist*, wrote an editorial urging Congress to stand firm and advising his readers to assure Congress that the "moral and political sentiment of the country" would sustain Congress. The next day the *Christian Register*, in an editorial on the nation's duty to protect the freedmen, warned that this work could not "be evaded nor postponed."[43]

Sumner continued to suggest that citizens should communicate with their lawmakers at least twice a month, and radical Christians persisted in bombarding Congress with letters of encouragement and messages on the moral responsibility of Congress. "Stand for God and humanity," John Longyear was told by a Michigan constituent. Trumbull was complimented on his speech reviewing the presidential veto by a liberal Episcopal layman, who was convinced Johnson had gone over to the Copperheads. At the same time that members of the clergy were sending messages to Congress, they were issuing warnings from the pulpit and summoning their congregations to appeal to Congress. David A. Wasson spoke in the Melodeon in Boston late in February. He sounded a call to the Christian public. "The President's intentions must be thwarted, or the people must surrender. God help us to do our duty! Let us entreat Congress to get God on its side by going straight to the simple right of the case," he pleaded.[44]

In March 1866, Austin Blair, the previous governor of Michigan, became an anonymous correspondent for the *Detroit Advertiser and Tribune* under the pen name of "Walsingham." In his first article, he wrote on the presidential veto of the Freedmen's Bureau bill. "Moses has deserted to the Egyptians, and will perish with them as he ought," he prophesied.[45] The radical Christian Ralph Plumb wrote to Garfield and reminded him that if the veto and the schemes of Johnson and Seward prevailed, the nation could not "escape the vengeance of Almighty God." The radical stance of Richard Yates was encouraged by his constituents. Two powerful radical Christians thanked Yates for his righteous speech for black freedom. One of them was an old Free Soil Baptist minister who recalled that "God and Liberty" had been the motto of moral men in 1848. "We must prove faithful, though compelled to forsake Father-Mother, President and patronage," he counseled Yates. The second was J.B. Turner, a Presbyterian professor at Illinois College, who urged Yates to persist in his efforts and assured him that "Divine Providence" would bring success to his efforts.[46]

Sumner continued to be the principal recipient of communications from anxious Christians. He received an appeal and a petition from Moses Thatcher, a radical Congregational clergyman, urging that blacks be given full rights, and he received several petitions and memorials from various church groups. A Methodist minister encouraged Sumner with the assurance that God's good Providence was on their side.[47] A radical Christian who had been an advocate of moral politics since the Free Soil days thought the very idea of "a compromise was an insult and outrage upon decency. . . . Let thou willing spirit kindle the fires of Evangelism," he exhorted Sumner. Amos Dresser, one of the Lane Rebels, who was pastor of a Congregational church in Michigan, placed himself with Sumner against compromising with evil. "How long ere we learn that we never can compromise with wrong without loss. That God is with us only in the right," he wrote encouragingly to Sumner.[48]

The pulpit rang with political sermons against the stand that Johnson had taken. In March Reverend George H. Hepworth spoke before the Washington Unitarian Association. "New England speaks to you, to our national Congress, and even to the occupant of the White House, and desires that the boon of representation may not be granted the late rebellious states . . . until they prove, beyond the shadow of a doubt, that they are truly repentant and thoroughly loyal," admonished the Boston Unitarian minister.[49] More than a week after the passage of the civil rights bill, most radical Christians became convinced that Johnson would veto it. R.M. Pearson, one of the founders of an independent antislavery Presbyterian church, advised Congressman E.B. Washburne that after the "monstrous policy" the president had undertaken, it was "time for us to stop legislating for white men and legislate for freedom and equal rights." A Methodist minister appealed directly to Johnson to avoid supporting a policy of conservative restoration. He was importuning the president, he said, "from the clearest and highest convictions of Christian duty."[50]

Theodore Tilton worked more diligently than any other man to shore up the radical forces for the conflict he was sure would soon develop. He rushed off to Washington after the civil rights bill had passed Congress and contacted the leading radicals. On March 19, he wrote to the *Independent*, "I cannot say that the expectation of a reconciliation between the President and Congress is to be finally disappointing. But I can say that this reconciliation will not be purchased at the price of a surrender by Congress to the President."[51]

As the rising tide of moral feeling became more turbulent, ten days before Johnson made his position known on the civil rights bill, Henry Ward Beecher wrote the president that his signature on the bill would be exceedingly expedient. "The *thing itself* is desirable," he asserted, "and the approval of the bill would frustrate the purpose of those that sought to produce the impression that the President was untrue to the cause of liberty and loyalty." Beecher was correct in his evaluation of the bill's importance in the eyes of radical Christians. The editor of the *Examiner and Chronicle* declared that the civil rights bill was the most important measure passed by Congress during the current session. He optimistically felt that the president would sign it, but on March 27, Johnson sent a veto message to Congress, once again asserting that the bill was illegal because it had been passed in the absence of Southern congressmen.[52]

William Coggeshall, the private secretary to Governor Jacob Cox of Ohio, was alert for news from Washington. He had extensive experience as a temperance lecturer, journalist, and moralist. When he received the news of the veto message, he wrote in his diary: "The President, I am confident, made a mistake." But for the majority of Republicans the veto was the last straw. Reverend R.S. Storrs wrote Sumner, "The very tho't of Johnson makes me heartsick; a perfect Judas in character." The only hope was that "he may either come to repentance before 'tis too late, or meet the fate of him who betrayed his Lord." Storrs believed that his sentiments were shared by the masses of people. The majority of Republicans had come to agree with them. Warner Bateman, a Quaker senator from Ohio, sensed the changes in public opinion. He wrote to Senator Sherman, "I have lost faith entirely in the President. . . . His last message hands the Freedman over helplessly to the tender mercies of state legislation and his exasperated master." Sumner also thought only of the defenseless condition of the freedmen in the hands of their former masters. He wrote to the Duchess of Argyle, "I see no substantial protection for the freedman except in the franchise."[53]

When Johnson's veto of the civil rights bill was addressed by Congress, Benjamin Wade attacked the president's action. "I feel myself justified in taking every advantage which the Almighty has put into my hands to defend the power and authority of this body. . . . I will tell the President and everybody else, that if God Almighty has stricken one member so that he cannot be here to uphold the dictation of a despot, I thank Him for His interposition, and I will take advantage of it if I can." While Congress was considering the civil rights bill, radical Christians and benevolent men were working to shape public opinion. Oliver O. Howard, the Congregational commissioner of the Freedmen's Bureau, spoke to church groups about the great value of the Bureau. He addressed the African Methodist Conference and compared the Bureau bill to the Magna Charta. He informed the conference that when the bill was fully executed not only the secession states but also Kentucky and Maryland would be free.[54]

The greatest reaction to the veto occurred in the pulpit. In the New England fast day sermons delivered April 5, emotions soared to unexpected heights. Jacob Manning, the radical Congregational clergyman, informed his congregation that the betrayal of the civil rights bill reflected cowardice. He condemned the president for having abused both the appointive and the pardon powers. In his Church of the Unity, George Hepworth informed his congregation that "the man who would veto that bill would veto the sermon on the Mount," and he called for the impeachment of Johnson. In his fast day sermon, James Freeman Clarke warned his congregation that if the country was not faithful to the blacks, God would "do with us as he did with his other chosen people."[55]

Aware of the effects on public opinion of the New England fast day sermons and of the fast days Lincoln had called in 1864, Henry H. Crapo, governor of Michigan, proclaimed a fast day in Michigan. Although Crapo denied any purpose relating to politics, he wrote to his son, "I wrote it with no political thought or purpose . . . but with a view to counteract the influence of the Johnson-Copperhead party here and to keep the Republicans true to the great work of maintaining their principles." He informed his son that the publication of the fast day proclamation was received by the Democrats "like firing a whole battery of grape into the bushes where a thousand rebels lay concealed." Before a week had passed, former governor Blair published one of his "Walsingham" articles, in which he denounced Johnson for "not trying to restore the Union but the rebels."[56]

Since the election in Connecticut took place on April 3, shortly after the president's veto, efforts were made on both sides of the veto issue to influence the election by exploiting the rift between Johnson and Congress. Tilton addressed an editorial to the people of Connecticut. "Men of Connecticut! sharers of the great struggle which has delivered our land from the curse and shame of Slavery! . . . Let us trust that no one of you will relax a muscle . . . until you have made it certain that the very last vote attainable . . . has been secured to the cause of . . . universal freedom." Joseph Hawley, the radical candidate for governor, took a strict moral position on black rights and suffrage. He won the election, but some radical legislative candidates lost. The election's significance extended beyond state politics; there were strong indications that the fall election would be a clear-cut struggle between the radicals and the supporters of Johnson.[57]

Senator Edwin D. Morgan, a Presbyterian trustee of Brick Church in New York, tried desperately to find a compromise between Congress and the president which would stave off a veto. Failing to accomplish that, he voted for the bill, since he believed some measure should be passed.[58] Morgan's vote on the bill was everywhere popular among the clergy. Reverend Francis Vinton, an Episcopal clergyman who was by no means a radical, applauded Morgan's vote because the civil rights bill gave vitality to the amendment abolishing slavery. "My voice is the echo of . . . a majority of the clergy and members of the Episcopal Church," he informed Morgan. Samuel Osgood, a Unitarian clergyman of the same mold as Vinton, expressed satisfaction with Morgan's vote because the loyal heart would be contented "with nothing less than the essential principle of that bill."[59]

The Senate overrode the president's veto of the civil rights bill on April 6 by a margin of a single vote. Edgar Ketchum, an executive officer of the AMA, reported to Sumner that, at family altars all over the country, prayers of thanksgiving were offered because the civil rights bill had passed the Senate over the president's veto. A large number of people obviously considered the crisis surrounding the civil rights bill a critical moral issue.[60] The House overrode the president's veto of the civil rights bill on April 9, and the radical Christians responded with approval to Congress's action. A class leader of a Methodist Episcopal church congratulated Congressman E.B. Washburne on the firm action Congress had taken in overriding the veto. "I have great confidence in the power of truth and the integrity of the people," he added. A Methodist minister commended Richard Yates for his stand on the civil rights bill. "God bless you for your noble words," he wrote, "in behalf of *Truth* and *Right* and *Humanity*." A Baptist deacon expressed his approval of the part Trumbull had taken in the passage of the civil rights bill. "I congratulate you upon the position which you have taken in relation to perpetuating the great principle of the Declaration of Independence," he wrote to Trumbull. By April 1866, most ministers favored a harsher readmission policy for the secession states.[61]

The overriding of the president's veto of the civil rights bill came in response to the great outpouring of sentiment from the public. The religious journals contributed powerfully to the rise of radical sentiment after the president's veto. Two days following the veto, Daniel Curry, editor of the *Christian Advocate*, vented his wrath at Johnson for trying to take control of Reconstruction. The next day Samuel Burnham, editor of the *Congregationalist*, published an editorial entitled "Make a Stand Now," in which he warned the Christian public that "all we have struggled for . . . will be in jeopardy if not fatally lost" unless moral men take "a stand upon the principles embodied in the Civil Rights bill." "Let us appeal from him to Congress, to the people and to God," advised John Chadwick, writing for the *Christian Inquirer*.[62]

The religious journals had put great pressure on Congress. Many of them treated the congressional passage of the bill over the veto as a great victory and glorious triumph of principle over policy.[63] Some religious journals sensed that the conflict was not over and feared that the president might try to force his views on the country by refusing to enforce the reconstruction measures or that he might try to use his recent proclamation that peace had officially been established to force Southern representatives on Congress.[64] But the editor of the *Christian Herald* hoped the president would wisely discern the signs of the times. Samuel Burnham, editor of the *Congregationalist*, who had conferred with Sumner during the crisis, trusted that Johnson would heed the warning given by the people. Burnham assured Congress that the American people were behind it. He wrote to Sumner, "The hearts of the true and the faithful are with you until the end."[65] The Congregational *New Englander* also wanted drastic measures taken. Although Congress had been vindicated by passing the civil rights bill over the veto, the editor saw no means of accomplishing the end desired except by putting "quasi-military magistrates in districts where the blacks are exposed to peril."[66]

Many church associations and conferences were scheduled to meet shortly thereafter. The New England, New York, East New York, Troy, and Maine conferences of the Methodist Episcopal Church heartily endorsed the action of Congress in passing the civil rights bill over the veto and viewed with alarm the attempt of the chief executive to frustrate the benign and just legislation.[67] The Burlington (Iowa) and the Northumberland (Pennsylvania) Baptist associations took a stronger stand against the president than other Baptist associations.[68] The Universalists took a more radical position on the dispute over the civil rights bill. The Maine Convention of Universalists refused a vote of confidence in the president, and the General Convention of Universalists criticized Johnson for not taking a hard line on the treatment of blacks in the South and for failing to give the freemen security. The general convention gave its political measures more weight by electing the radical Universalist Congressman Sidney Perham president of the convention.[69]

The Freedmen's Bureau bill passed over Johnson's veto on July 16, 1866. Congress had failed to override Johnson's first veto of the Bureau bill because the attempt came only a few days after the veto and public opinion had not had time to develop fully. Many citizens were aware that a weak Bureau would be in place for a year after the presidential proclamation officially declared an end to the war. The civil rights bill concerned liberty and the rights of Americans, while the Freedmen's Bureau bill dealt primarily with benevolence. The commitment to the latter was less strong. A Presbyterian banker described the difference in the Christian mind when he wrote his senator, "The Freedmen's Bureau bill involved a question of expediency about which earnest union men might differ—the Civil Rights Bill however stood upon a different basis. The people whose rights as citizens are sought to be protected by the Bill, were entitled to receive from the Government a law that would secure to them the practical enjoyment of those rights."[70] The radical Christians had shown a far greater concern about the Freedmen's Bureau bill than had the average citizen.

The Memphis riot, in which forty-six blacks were murdered, contributed to the final passage of the Freedmen's Bureau bill. The editor of the *New York Tribune* scoffed at those who insisted that the former masters would protect the blacks and favored abolishing the Bureau forthwith and remitting the blacks to the care of their old masters. According to the *Independent*, the Memphis riot showed that some way must be found to restrict such lawless men unless the blacks had suffrage to counteract violence against them. The editor of the Baptist *Christian Watchman and Reflector* declared that people must be prepared to see the events of Memphis occur throughout the South. "Nothing but the government's course has thus far prevented wholesale massacres of freedmen; and when federal troops shall be dismissed

from the South, atrocities . . . will bring permanent disgrace," he insisted. William W. Thayer, editor of the *Right Way*, was convinced
that the riot heralded the beginning of a reign of terror in the South.
"Just as sure as God reigns, as sure as Hell is let loose in the person
of Andrew Johnson, so sure will blood flow before our material diffi-
culties are settled," he wrote to Sumner. A founding member of the
Keene, New Hampshire, Unitarian Church shared Thayer's views. He
informed his congressman, after the Memphis riot, that hopes for Reconstruction with cordial relations between Congress and the president
had given way to the belief that there will be "an irrepressible conflict
between them."[71] Tilton criticized the president for leaving the freedmen defenseless by refusing to sign the Freedmen's Bureau bill. He
also accused Johnson of destroying the weak Freedmen's Bureau then
in place by making its operations incidental to the operations of the
military department in the Southern states so that no protective arm
was available.[72]

During March and early April, Congress had given little attention
to the suffrage provisions and had concentrated on the Freedmen's
Bureau and the civil rights bill. But suffrage for the freedmen had not
been forgotten. Charles Slack, the radical Unitarian editor of the *Commonwealth* and former editor of a temperance journal, wrote to Sumner
at the end of February that "the idea of negro suffrage grows daily in
favor and advocacy among businessmen" of Boston. Early in March
while attention was still focused on the Freedmen's Bureau and the
civil rights bills, the Pittsburgh Conference of the Methodist Episcopal
Church recognized "it as a Christian duty to employ the right of suffrage" to elevate the blacks to full status as citizens. Delegates to the
East Maine Conference of the Methodist Episcopal Church solemnly
pledged to each other and to God "that while life shall last," they
would "never cease" their efforts until civil and political rights had
been secured for all people. These sentiments were accepted by many
religious men of various denominations.[73]

Many radical Christians considered the Freedmen's Bureau and the
civil rights bills secondary issues in the fight for black rights. The main
battle would be fought over black suffrage. When the civil rights bill
passed over the president's veto, David Plumb wrote to Sumner, "Now
for the '*Main Question*'—the Suffrage of the Negro, I do not expect
great things from the 'Civil Rights Bill,' unless backed by Negro Suffrage. . . . Since half-measures cannot win the President, now, why not
go for a whole one?" Parker Pillsbury, the independent Congregationalist editor of the *National Anti-Slavery Standard*, registered the same

sentiment in his paper: "What are civil rights worth that do not include suffrage?"[74] Salmon Chase agreed with Pillsbury. He wrote to the American Anti-Slavery Society about the importance of suffrage for the blacks and spoke before the Methodist Ladies Association on the subject. "Among the most urgent duties of the hour," he said, was that those to whom we gave freedom "be permitted to defend it by the ballot."[75]

On April 28, the Washington correspondent to the *Independent* reported that the issue was already decided. "The President demands the instant admission of the rebel states to representation, and Congress asks further guaranties," he wrote. Tilton's response was: "A Christian government must not trifle with sacred rights. . . . We believe that if Congress shall make justice to the negro a condition of reconstruction, its action will be triumphantly sustained."[76] Two days later the joint committee submitted its report to Congress for debate. The Fourteenth Amendment permitted the Confederate states to deny suffrage to blacks but penalized them with a loss of seats in the House of Representatives and a loss of electoral votes.

George Stearns wrote to Sumner the next day that he was not willing to accept a finality of anything less than impartial suffrage. But he pragmatically accepted the fact that it might be the best that Congress could secure. William Claflin, a prominent antislavery Methodist, reported to Sumner that the suffrage provision had been received with considerable favor in Boston as the only measure that could pass in 1866. "The people desire to have some position on which they can stand in opposition to the Copperheads," he informed Sumner. A trustee of a Methodist church wanted more for the blacks than the Fourteenth Amendment offered. He encouraged Senator Yates to continue on his radical course. "Fear not to tread the path you have so nobly entered," he urged, "the ballot *will* lead the freedmen over the Red Sea of our troubles." A Chicago citizen advised Trumbull, "God demands truth and justice of this nation. Nor will He accept anything less. . . . There is no security but the ballot in freedmen's hands."[77]

The suffrage amendment was the principal topic at the special meeting of the American Anti-Slavery Society on January 24. Most of the committee on resolutions consisted of clergymen. The resolutions condemned the amendment for leaving the freedman "to his own fate" and concluded that such half measures should be defeated. George Cheever took the lead in criticizing the amendment when the Church Anti-Slavery Society met. Cheever believed God would overrule Congress because "the right to vote was a natural right."[78] When the contents of the committee's report were first made public, Theodore Tilton expressed opposition to the amendment in a letter to Sumner. "It leaves the Negro to the decision of the Rebels," he complained. In an editorial in the *Independent*, Tilton condemned the joint committee for reporting an amendment that left the blacks without suffrage: "We believe there is a party in this country, strong enough to control its legislation, who will never be content with any other readjustment of the union than on the basis of Equal Rights." Tilton visited Washington to confer with the radicals. On June 15 he spoke there, saying, "Let both ends of the avenue take heed that the party of justice, the party that controls the conscience of the nation . . . will sooner or later" control policy in Washington.[79]

The next day Julian explained the principles of radicalism to his colleagues in the House. "It did not believe in conciliation and compromise. . . . It understood the conflict as not simply a struggle to save the union, but a grand and final battle for the rights of man now and hereafter; and it believed that God would never smile upon our endeavors till we accept it as such. . . . Its trust was in the justice of our cause and the favor of the Almighty." Later Tilton refrained from attacking the Fourteenth Amendment in the expectation that supplementary legislation would remedy its shortcomings, and Julian voted for the Fourteenth Amendment.[80]

Stearns organized a mass meeting at Faneuil Hall on May 31 under the auspices of the Impartial Suffrage Association. The association included antislavery politicians, clergymen, and reformers. Governor Alexander Bullock of Massachusetts, a Baptist layman, presided over the meeting. In a keynote speech Bullock asserted that he believed in national and impartial suffrage. The convention endorsed the Fourteenth Amendment and asked Congress to pass an act requiring the Southern states to enact impartial suffrage before they were returned to the Union.[81]

Radical Christians increasingly tended to view the granting of suffrage to blacks as a matter of security. In January 1866, Alexander C. Twining, a Presbyterian layman who was trained in theology, and five prestigious doctors of divinity and others from New Haven sent Johnson a memorial advocating universal suffrage as a measure to protect the blacks' civil rights. On June 1, at the suggestion of Reverend Theodore Woolsey and others, Twining sent a copy of the memorial to Trumbull with the suggestion that it be published. Others looked to a suffrage measure to provide security for the blacks. Judge Samuel

Sewall, a Unitarian, sent a suffrage bill to Sumner with this objective in mind. Sumner drew up a refined bill with the same purpose that Congress did not consider. William Burr, editor of the *Morning Star*, was sure that equal suffrage for the freedmen would be enough to place the country at peace.[82] The *American Presbyterian* informed its readers on June 21 that the sentiments of the Christian people of the North were fixed and nearly unanimous. "In short," he continued, "the position of the entire body of evangelical Christians in the North may be described as substantially that of advanced radicalism, and such it will be found in the position of the country too."[83]

On June 22, 1866, before the amendment had passed, Johnson sent a message to Congress condemning it and repeating his objection to any amendment until after the Southern states had been admitted to the Union. "This action on the part of the President shows we are to have no peace with him," Trumbull wrote his wife. In the second week of June, the Fourteenth Amendment passed Congress, with only four Republicans voting against it. The radicals had not effected equal suffrage, but they had attained a firm alliance with the moderates under the leadership of the radicals in the continuing struggle with the president.[84]

On July 4 the radical Christians renewed the attack on the president with fresh vigor. Henry Crapo warned a Flint, Michigan, audience that although slavery was gone, the spirit of slavery still sought to establish itself as the cornerstone of an empire by its insidious attacks. D.F. Reid, an associate Reformed Presbyterian clergyman, wanted to destroy all vestiges of the slave power. In his determination to discourage Democratic sympathy, he announced to the elders of his congregation that he intended to preach them "out of the filthy Democratic party or out of the Church."[85]

The radical clergyman Granville Moody had not given up on Johnson. He had had a close relationship with Johnson in Tennessee in 1864 and believed he could influence the president concerning the South. Moody wrote Johnson in July, "To restore those rebel states to power without at least the condition . . . presented by Congress, would be the blunder and crime of taking in the wooden horse, within the walls of our Troy." The president, however, was beyond appeal. On July 16, Johnson vetoed the Freedmen's Bureau bill and Congress overrode the veto.[86]

Many radical Christians welcomed the final break between the president and Congress. In the opinion of the radical Reverend E.P.

Tenney, a Congregationalist, an open fight permitted people to know where everyone stood. He was glad the compromising days of Congress were over and urged Congress to pass an impartial suffrage bill in the next session because the people demanded it.[87] Henry Snapp, an Illinois Baptist deacon, thought that Johnson should be impeached to avoid the terrible violence that was sure to come. A radical clergyman from Wisconsin informed Benjamin Butler that he did not believe the country would be safe for an hour after Congress adjourned. He suggested that Congress impeach the president and "nail him to the wall."[88] Joseph Medill, editor of the *Chicago Tribune*, warned Trumbull, early in May, that the plan for the amendment was being received with hostility in Illinois. He looked on the amendment as the "offspring of cowardice." As the weeks passed, Medill expressed to Washburne his concern that Congress might adjourn without giving the country a reconstruction plan.[89] William M. Dickson, a liberal Episcopal layman of Cincinnati, wanted Congress to remain in session. Others were of the same mind.[90] When Congress adjourned, the *Northwestern Christian Advocate* lamented that the gains made in the great war had been lost by the failure of Congress to remain in session.[91]

All of the religious bodies that met from May to July took a position that was favorable to Congress. For example the General Synod of the Reformed Presbyterian Church condemned the president's policy in detail, with specific charges. The Congregational Associations of Iowa and Ohio favored equal suffrage. In the eyes of the Central Union Baptist Association, justice and safety dictated that suffrage should be given to all loyal people. The Michigan Free Will Baptists as well as the Eastern Association of Seventh Day Baptists held that no distinction should be made in distributing suffrage on account of color. The Erie and New England conferences of the Methodist Episcopal Church favored black suffrage.[92]

The radical Christian response to the Fourteenth Amendment was lukewarm at best. Julian called the adoption of the Fourteenth Amendment "a wanton betrayal of justice and humanity." Helpless millions would be turned over to "unhindered tyranny and misrule of their enemies" who would make "the condition of the freedmen more intolerable than slavery itself, through local laws and police regulations."[93] The amendment was generally recognized as a compromise that would become a platform for the fall election. Some radicals preferred to postpone the decision on the amendment until the next session of Congress in the hope that the new Congress would be more radical. But in the last analysis the radicals accepted the amendment as the best they could get and hoped to secure black suffrage in the future. Expediency was so much the watchword of the framers of the amendment that they avoided any unnecessary challenge that could be used by their opponents in the fall election.[94]

# CHAPTER EIGHT

# The Fourteenth Amendment
# and the Election of 1866

Congress did not pass a reconstruction bill in 1866. The lawmakers preferred to campaign on the basis of the Fourteenth Amendment and to work out a reconstruction bill in the next session of Congress after the election. Stephen Field, a Supreme Court justice, believed that the Amendment would unite the Republican party. He wrote to Chase: "If the President withholds his approval he will sever all connection with the Union Party." Warner Bateman informed Senator Sherman that he thought that all factions of the Republican party could unite on the Fourteenth Amendment. The radical Unitarian Attorney General James Speed wrote to Dr. Francis Lieber, "Let me say in your ear and for you only, that to me the prospect of harmony is brightening." But Trumbull had "no faith" in Johnson's "good intentions. How could I after he so deceived me about the Civil Rights bill and the Freedmen Bureau bill?"[1]

Johnson had registered his opposition to the joint committee's report on May 1. He called a meeting of the cabinet to denounce the amendment and asked the cabinet members to oppose it. The president's press release expressing his objection was circulated to the newspapers. The joint committee bill was changed to accommodate some of Johnson's criticism, and many believed that it would meet with his approval, but on June 22, Congress received a message from the president objecting to any amendment as long as the Southern states were not in the Union. All hopes faded that the Union party would be unified.[2]

Early in the summer of 1866 the Republican state executive committees prepared for the fall elections. No state organization was more uneasy about securing unity than the Ohio Republicans. Governor Jacob Cox had worked harmoniously with the Johnson administration during his term, but there was concern about impending conflict between the Western Reserve Republicans and the conservatives of

southern Ohio regarding black suffrage and between the defenders of
Johnson and the supporters of Congress. M.C. Canfield, a radical Christian of Geauga County, Ohio, worried that the Western Reserve Republicans would be unable to sustain politically pure radicalism in the
state convention that was to meet at Columbus on June 20. "Columbus
will swarm with Copperheads, administration partisans and place seek-
ers and a three day commingling with such elements would lead a
man to despise humanity, detest democracy and doubt the wisdom of
Deity." The convention proved to be united in its support for the action of Congress. Peter Hitchcock, a Presbyterian layman, reported to
Garfield that the convention was united in spirit. " 'Andy' was not
in the convention and nothing but the sense of propriety prevented
shouts of applause when Granville Moody prayed '*God bless our noble
Congress.*' " Wendell Phillips felt that it was dangerous to leave the
crisis in the hands of politicians. In an editorial in the *National Anti-
Slavery Standard*, Phillips appealed to the clergy of the loyal states.
"Clergymen of the North, I beg you to realize that the nation's opportunity still continues," he wrote, "God thunders from a hundred
battle-fields, 'Be *just* and fear not.' Deliver his message; strengthen
the people to heed it; rally the national conscience as you did in
1861."[3]

One of the features of the political campaign of 1866 was the effort
to create a new political party which would back presidential Reconstruction. The radical Christians vigorously attacked Johnson when
his supporters announced that the National Union Convention would
be held in Philadelphia to create a new party. Sidney Gay, the editor
of the *New York Tribune*, declared that the movement was a plot to
restore Rebels and Copperheads to power. Others echoed his charge.
To make matters worse, Henry Raymond, the chairman of the Republican National Committee and one of the organizers of the meeting,
conceded to Ransom Balcom, a radical Republican lawyer, that it
looked as though the convention might be "mainly in the hands of the
Copperheads." In the heat of the campaign, after Raymond had deserted
the movement, the letter was published in the *New York Times*. When
the National Union Convention convened, the religious press denounced the movement in harsh terms. The editor of the *Baptist Christian Watchman and Reflector* claimed that the men who rallied around
the president were those who had tried to overthrow the government
in the recent war. Other radical religious journals attacked the convention in equally bitter language.[4] By the time the convention met,
few Republicans of standing had endorsed the movement. Failing to

create a viable alternative party, the National Union movement crumbled.[5]

To counter the National Union movement, a convention of Southern Loyalists met in Philadelphia early in September. Northern radicals were there to lend a hand. James Speed presided, and the radical clergy made its presence felt. Reverend J.W. Jackson delivered the opening prayer. He asked God to teach the people "to whom thou hast committed the reins of civil government . . . and by righteous legislation to secure to all people . . . the blessings of equal rights before the law." The radical Reverend John B. Newmann, residing at that time in Louisiana, was elected chaplain. On the second day, in the opening prayer, he beseeched God to "deliver us from the rule of bad men, especially from him who through satanic agency has been . . . a weak and wicked President." As the speaker prayed for Congress in its determined resistance to the power set in place by a satanic agency, the audience and the convention murmured fervent amens. He ended his prayer by calling on divine aid: "Great God, interpose, and in making bare Thine arm for vengeance, save us from his infamous and ruinous policy." The delegates from the Deep South wanted the convention to endorse black suffrage; without black suffrage they were powerless. The New York delegation, influenced by Tilton, offered a resolution in support of the reform. Even though the committee on unreconstructed states reported a resolution endorsing black suffrage, the convention passed only watered-down conservative resolutions. After the convention had adjourned, the radicals, led by Tilton, Anna Dickinson, and Frederick Douglass, remained at the convention and organized a mass meeting to pass a resolution endorsing the enfranchisement of the freedmen.[6]

One of the main issues in the election of 1866 was violence against the Union men in the South and security for the freedmen. The May riot in Memphis was followed by one on July 30 in New Orleans in which two hundred black and white Unionists were killed or wounded. General Phillip Sheridan investigated the riot two days after it occurred and sent a report to Washington. A *New York Times* correspondent forwarded to his newspaper a dispatch that had been prepared by the executive department. The chief executive's office had suppressed key passages of Sheridan's report, so that blame for the riot was fixed on the victims of the riot, although Sheridan had blamed the conservatives who controlled New Orleans. The general was incensed that his report had been tampered with. Shortly after the riot, Sumner wrote to a friend in England that the president was "perverse, distempered, ignorant, and thoroughly wrong. You may judge him by the terrible massacre at New Orleans. Stanton confessed to me that he [the President] was its [the dispatch's] author." That Johnson was the culprit few radicals doubted. The president did little to prevent further occurrences of mob violence, and the issue of security became more prominent as a result of a speech Johnson made on September 8 in St. Louis in which he expressed no regret over the bloodshed and launched a tirade against the New Orleans radicals and the radical members of Congress.[7]

The National Union Convention adopted a resolution claiming that in no section of the country had the Constitution and laws been more promptly and entirely obeyed than in the South. Gerrit Smith was astonished that such a statement could be made "of the half of our country in every part of which it is unsafe to be a black man, and in every part of which crime goes unpunished and murder is a pastime!" The radical Methodist clergyman Mansfield French, writing from Washington, identified the riot's probable effects on the election. "The New Orleans tragedy is costly seed for the cause, but God will bring in a good harvest," he wrote to George Whipple, secretary of the AMA. Elizur Wright, a radical Congregational layman, hoped that the riot would arouse people to "acknowledge the dangers to which the national cause is exposed, and lead them to see the necessity of passing a suffrage bill" that would give the freedmen security. Gerrit Smith saw the riot in the same light. "It was very wrong in Congress to adjourn and thus to increase the liberty of the President to work iniquity," he wrote Garrison. "Moreover, I think the New Orleans murders would have opened the eyes of Congress to its folly in restoring Tennessee, and to the folly of restoring any other Rebel States whilst such States was [sic] continuing to oppress the negro." Senator Henry S. Lane, a Methodist layman, while presiding over a Republican convention in Indiana, addressed the gathering and said that he regarded the Memphis and New Orleans riots as "the legitimate results of Johnson's policy." In a sermon to his Unitarian congregation in Chicago, R.L. Collier asserted that "one word from the President" would have prevented the wicked slaughter at New Orleans. Reverend L.N. Breakman, the former chaplain of the Twenty-first Indiana Volunteers, who took up residence in Louisiana, lectured in Kalamazoo, Michigan, early in the political campaign. In his lecture, "The Past and Present Condition of the South," he described the horrors of the massacres at both Memphis and New Orleans and maintained "that the New Orleans riot was a premeditated affair." The radicals kept the violence before the public throughout the political campaign. As late as August 13, a mass meeting on the New Orleans massacre was held in Cooper Institute in New York. The radical clergymen and Freedmen's Bureau officers attended the meeting to give a firsthand report. Northern clergy and Republicans had organized the meeting to exploit the full political benefit of the New Orleans riot.[8]

The radical religious journals used the issue to whip their readers into early action. The *Christian Instructor and Western United Presbyterian* called on the authorities to visit retribution on the offenders so that "a righteous God" would not bring retribution on the whole country.[9] The Baptist *Examiner and Chronicle* accused Johnson of gravely offending the loyal people of the country by throwing "the whole weight of his influence in favor" of the rebellious and disloyal class in New Orleans. The editor of the *Morning Star* identified Andrew Johnson as "a prominent actor in the bloody drama who could have thrown a protection around the loyal men in New Orleans" but instead "chose to aid and abet their enemies." He was convinced that this action was proof enough that the blacks should have equal suffrage. "Justice demands it . . . , and security demands it," he insisted. Samuel Nesbit, editor of the *Pittsburgh Christian Advocate*, condemned the executive department for suppressing information contained in General Sheridan's report and expressed extreme regret that the president had put himself in "sympathy with the leaders of the riot." The editor of the Baptist *Christian Watchman and Reflector* was particularly bitter because a Baptist minister had been killed in the riot. "Unless the American people shall rebuke at the ballot-box the outrage which the President has abetted in New Orleans, anarchy will become the common law of the South—nay, of the North," Tilton warned. Samuel Burnham, the editor of the *Congregationalist*, reminded his readers that the country had not yet cleansed itself of the sins of failing to render justice to the oppressed and the oppressors. Burnham returned to the subject of the New Orleans riot again after the National Union Convention met. The men who attended the Philadelphia convention, he charged, were the same men who had shot and stabbed defenseless Union men in the streets of New Orleans.[10]

Some of the religious journals accused the administration of denying freedom of speech and religion after the New Orleans riot. The editor of the *Examiner and Chronicle* called it sad and humiliating that the president sided "with rioters and murderers in the suppression of free speech and individual liberty."[11] For more than a week following the riot, excitement was very intense in Washington. Many people expected riots to break out through the South. In the other parts of the country, the tension also remained great. The editors of the Methodist journals exhorted the faithful to pray and to send letters and petitions to the leaders of Congress. The editor of the *Christian Advocate* admonished his readers "to pray for the gracious interposition of the Divine power to save the nation." Wendell Phillips called again on the clergy to preach another crusade against the enemy of the nation.[12]

When the religious associations and conferences met in the autumn of 1866, many of them denounced the riots in the Southern states and were critical of Johnson's handling of the crisis. The Wesleyan Methodist Conference of central Ohio expressed alarm that the president had connived with the persecutors of loyal men. The Cincinnati Conference of the Methodist Episcopal Church deprecated the lawless violence and semiofficial sanction that had been given to these mobs. The Rock River (Illinois) Methodist Episcopal Conference solemnly protested against the policy of Reconstruction which had "disarmed the friends and armed the foes of the nation" and had culminated "in the atrocious massacres of Memphis and New Orleans." The Huron (Ohio) Baptist Association warned that if the Southern whites who committed violence against Union men were not restrained by civil authorities, a terrible judgment of God would be visited on the whole country. The New London (Connecticut) Baptist Association believed that loyal men should administer all departments of the government, or the revolting scenes inaugurated in Memphis and New Orleans might be duplicated throughout the South. The General Conference of Congregational Churches of Maine doubtless had the Memphis riot in mind, among other things, when it resolved that, "as a security for the future, we desire the adoption of the proposed constitution amendment."[13]

Some religious associations criticized the president more than the rioters. The Oswego (New York) Baptist Association sincerely deplored the defection of the president, the "atrocious scenes of Memphis," and "the cold-blooded murders of New Orleans." The Bridgewater (Pennsylvania) Baptist Association condemned the president, who had "sworn to faithfully enforce the laws" but had "so used the power as to encourage lawless traitors in the slaughter of innocent loyal men. . . . The blood of the martyred dead of the massacre at New Orleans cries for vengeance." A copy of its report went to the president.[14] The Methodist Episcopal Conference of Wisconsin unanimously resolved that it was a matter of deep regret that the chief executive had deserted the national cause, betrayed its interest, and encouraged wholesale massacre of the nation's friends. Moved by the brutality of the Memphis and New Orleans riots, the White River Conference of the United Brethren of Indiana urged Johnson to adopt measures that would give "legal security to all citizens everywhere and of all classes and colors."[15]

The president made a speaking tour between Washington and Chicago in late August and early September to defend his Southern policy and to oppose congressional Reconstruction. Johnson's "swing around the circle," as it was called, drew the fire of radical Christians. Austin Blair prophesied in one of his "Walsingham" articles that the "stern determination of the people to stand by Congress and uphold the loyal men and not the rebels" would show itself even to the president. A Congregational layman informed the AMA that Johnson had spoken in Buffalo. "We simply looked at the President . . . in respectful silence, and cheered loudly for Grant whom it was such a pleasure to see," he reported to the officers of the association. A Congregational layman and executive secretary of Olivet College in Michigan wrote to Austin Blair about the president's visit to Michigan: "I am sure his visit to Michigan will help our majority largely. Who ever heard of such a Presidential ass?"[16] In reference to Johnson's remarks about what he wanted from the electorate, the editor of the *Independent* advised, "Let the people give him a Congress that cannot be conquered. . . . Question every candidate before nomination whether or not, after election, he will oppose all compromises of Equal Rights: and if he hesitates in his answer, let him stay at home."[17]

The *Christian Register* reported that not a single Protestant journal among its exchanges supported Johnson's policy. The religious press instructed the clergy on its duties as leaders of its congregations in the critical election that would soon follow. The editors were no less earnest in advising members of their denomination on the seriousness of the way they cast their votes. The *American Presbyterian* counseled Christians that they must declare that "mere self-seeking politicians who have no thought of reverence toward the Ruler of all and no concern for the principles of righteousness, justice and humanity, shall not rule this country." "We deem it our duty, and the duty of all who have any influence they can use to that end, to urge that in the coming elections each man remembering that country is more than party, and that right is always the expedient, shall cast his vote so as to sustain Congress, and thus preserve the nation," urged J.A. Smith, editor of the *Christian Times and Witness*. The editor of the *Morning Star* urged that all Christians should attend primary political meetings to root evil out of politics. The editor of the *Western Christian Advocate* insisted that Congress must be sustained. "Our Christianity demands that we should stand by the nation," he exhorted. The editors of the *Central Advocate* and the *Christian Herald and Presbyterian Record* saw correct political teaching and education of the voters as the most critical and pressing duties of the hour.[18]

The religious associations and conferences were very specific in counseling their members of political duties. The Michigan Conference of the Methodist Episcopal Church appealed to the electorate to "bear a clear emphatic and unmistakable testimony for Liberty and Loyalty. We earnestly exhort all our people, insomuch as in them lies, to see to it that the men returned to our National Congress shall be men of undoubted loyalty." The Wisconsin Methodist Episcopal Conference insisted that religious men should not refrain from politics but should assist "God and their country with their suffrage as an important part of the Christian work." The Cincinnati Conference of the Methodist Episcopal Church resolved that it was "the duty of Christian men to make their influence felt in our primary political meetings and at the polls, so as to secure the nomination and election of men of high moral character . . . who 'fear God' and work righteousness." The Illinois Conference put the burden of influencing the election of the right kind of men almost entirely on the clergy, but the Genesee Conference of the Free Methodist Church was more precise in instructing its members on voting. The conference announced that the faithful should support for office only individuals who were heartily and unequivocally in favor of giving blacks the same political rights as whites.[19] The Central Iowa Baptist Association called attention to the New Orleans riot when it advised its members on the election. The association regarded the course of the president in relation to the New Orleans riot as meriting censure. The Ohio State Baptist Convention admonished the Christian people to take a high moral stand in choosing men for elective office.[20]

The conservative Republicans controlled the congressional election organizations and were determined to take a safe conservative position throughout the campaign of 1866. They noted the inability of the extremists in Congress to rule the majority on the question of Reconstruction. They concentrated on the proposed Fourteenth Amendment as the platform for their campaign and denied any intention of imposing black suffrage on the South. The Democrats sought to brand the Republicans as radicals and announced that the Fourteenth Amendment would lead to black suffrage.[21] The conservative Republicans maintained that Reconstruction would reach an end when the

Southern states ratified the Fourteenth Amendment. Theodore Tilton did not accept the conservative position and encouraged the radical religious men to take a strong stance. He charged that "the Republican majority . . . [had] abandoned for the sake of party a principle which they ought to have maintained for the sake of mankind." Tilton lamented the failure of the Republicans to place themselves in the vanguard of liberty and justice. In another issue in August, Tilton asked, "How long a time is it necessary to continue an experiment which is already ripe and rotten with failure . . . ? The remedy is in a *more radical, not a less radical*, policy of the Government."[22] The editor of the *Christian Advocate* also encouraged a radical stand on the part of the Republican party. The editor expressed "confidence in the great heart of the nation, in the public conscience, in the power of our holy religion, in the public intelligence that will not be hood-winked, and the public fidelity that cannot be corrupted."[23]

The radical Christians followed Tilton's lead. In religious circles the conservative position did not get much of a hearing. A conservative from Boston wrote to Johnson that on Sunday, July 1, 1866, "the Presidential campaign of 1868 was opened by several of the clergy of the city . . . , by the most low and vulgar abuse of *Yourself* and your policy. The campaign of 1860 was opened in the same disgraceful manner— nearly every pulpit in the State being desecrated by vile political harangues on the Sabbath. Mr. Lincoln owed his election more to these 'Men of God' (or the D . . . l) than to any other single cause." On August 18, Senator Henry S. Lane of Indiana spoke at a political rally in Indianapolis. Lane was a member of a local Bible society and a trustee of a Methodist church. He expressed the views that the radical Christians held of themselves. "Any man who has honest convictions, who listens to his own conscience and the teachings of Providence," he asserted, "if he is worth a single cent for any human purpose, he is a radical."[24] The radical Unitarian Samuel Johnson declared before his Lynn, Massachusetts, congregation that the nation had dangers more pressing than the plot of Andrew Johnson. "We are imperilled by well-meaning politicians, who perpetually stave off impartial suffrage to a safer opportunity. . . . Do not be blinded to the fact that this Amendment is a substitute for impartial suffrage. . . . Your Congress would never have proposed a measure so inadequate and perilous had they dreamed of the popular uprising for liberty which the hour promises now."[25]

When the campaign reached its midpoint, the usually conservative Leonard Bacon took a radical position in a series of articles in the

*Independent.* "If we now permit those men [freedmen] to fall unde-fended into the power of their relentless enemies, . . . we shall bring perpetual shame upon our country," he warned his readers.[26] Reverend R.L. Collier expressed the same sentiments to his congregation. He asserted that he was making a plea not for party but for God and for downtrodden humanity. He predicted that if there should be a majority for the president in the next Congress, the freedmen "would be at the mercy of their late masters and, to all intents and purposes, would be remanded back to slavery."[27] Henry Day, pastor of the First Baptist Church in Indianapolis, reiterated the commitment to duty. "When . . . politics . . . involves questions of morals, of social improvement, the Christian minister may not be silent without being derelict to his duty, his people and his God. . . . If we are untrue to the interest of humanity, we commit treason against God."[28] Several clergyman fo-cused their attacks on the president rather than on the Democrats. O.B. Frothingham informed his Third Unitarian Congrégation in New York that Johnson's influence was to be deplored. Augustus Woodbury, a Congregational clergyman of Providence, Rhode Island, discussed the conflict between Congress and the president and concluded that the split between them was of the president's "own making"—he must bear the responsibility and consequences of his folly.[29]

The radical clergy discussed at length the circumstances under which the Southern states should be readmitted to the Union. No radical clergyman wanted to readmit them after the ratification of the Fourteenth Amendment. All wanted some further guarantees. Equal suffrage was the most common requirement. Samuel Spear demanded "something safer and stronger, . . . something more radical than what seems to me a mere system of patchwork." In addition to guarantees, some clergy demanded genuine repentance. Woodbury said the South "must show some signs of genuine repentance before we consent to kill for them the fatted calf."[30]

When J.W. Cracraft delivered a political sermon on the claims of humanity in his Episcopal church in Galesburg, Illinois, the bishop of Illinois stopped preaching in his church. Cracraft belonged to the dio-cese of Ohio and was upheld by the more liberal Bishop McIlvaine of Ohio. Since his congregation was largely antislavery, he was also up-held by the Galesburg vestry, but he eventually chose to return to Ohio.[31] The Democratic *Chicago Times* claimed that more than half the Protestant churches were being used simply as institutions for the propagation of political fanaticism. Not all clergymen opposed John-son, but probably fewer than a dozen publicly spoke in favor of his

policy. When Congressman R.W. Clarke campaigned in the Sixth
Congressional District for black suffrage, the Reverend M.P. Gaddis,
Jr., who supported Johnson, answered Clarke's speeches in Clermont
County, Ohio, and announced that he would rather vote for Jeff Davis
than for Clarke. The Ohio Methodist Protestant Conference charged
Gaddis with treason.[32]

In late August plans were made to hold a convention of soldiers
and sailors in support of Johnson in Cleveland. The executive committee of the convention asked Henry Ward Beecher to serve as chaplain. Beecher did not accept the invitation because of previous
engagements but used the occasion to express his views on Reconstruction in a letter made public at the convention. Beecher opposed
federal intervention in the affairs of the Southern states because he
considered the federal government unfit to exercise authority over
remote affairs of state and local governments. He criticized the refusal
to admit the Southern states to Congress because it hampered the
freedmen in their efforts to establish a new relation with the whites
of the South and only increased the dangers confronting blacks in the
South. Beecher believed that suffrage was a natural right, and he had
strongly supported Negro suffrage in 1865. While the radical clergy
emphasized the principle of biblical justice, Beecher looked to the law
of love to establish a Christian relation among people within the South
and between the sections. Beecher's letter raised an uproar in religious
circles. A second letter that the minister intended to calm tempers
only fueled the controversy. Beecher suggested that the freedman
should look to the South for suffrage and all other rights and that the
South should be trusted to grant these rights after the section had
reentered the Union. Even after the usually liberal Episcopal clergyman
Stephen H. Tyng and Leonard Bacon had published letters to Beecher
in newspapers defending his position, the great masses of the radical
clergy and religious people felt themselves betrayed by Beecher and
refused to listen as he sought to justify his position. The radicals of
Beecher's church held a meeting and condemned their pastor. Beecher's
brother, Reverend Edward Beecher, in a public letter, opposed his position and advocated Radical Reconstruction and black suffrage.[33]

Beecher was severely attacked by the radical religious press, but
Tilton's criticism was the most relentless. The editor of the *Indepen-
dent* wrote of Beecher, "under the spell of an unhappy blindness which
rested on his eyes for a year past, he has done more injury to the
American republic than has been done by any other citizen except
Andrew Johnson."[34] The clergyman was also criticized from the pulpit.

W.H. Daniel, pastor of the Congregational church at Normal, Illinois, for example, discussed the national political question in relation to religion on a Sunday early in October. He took a radical position and rejected the policy of Johnson and Beecher and advocated a bold stand for impartial law. The reading of Beecher's second letter prompted the Presbyterian layman Edward Mansfield to write another of his "Veteran Observer" letters. Every minister should adhere to the great social principle of working to elevate the welfare and advancement of all classes of people, the Veteran Observer explained. He disagreed with Beecher's position and considered the great social principle of Christianity a radical doctrine.[35]

N.F. Raven, minister of the Racine (Wisconsin) Baptist Church, the church attended by Senator James Doolittle, delivered a sermon to his congregation entitled "Congress vs. the President and Their Respective Supporters," in which he informed his congregation that 100 percent of all religious journals opposed Johnson. "I have yet to learn of an ecclesiastical assembly, convention, association, bishoprick, synod, presbytery or conference, that has endorsed him by a single resolution. . . . The Christian ministry are universally opposed to Andrew Johnson's administration." Since Senator Doolittle identified himself with presidential Reconstruction, he had lost standing in his Racine Baptist Church and the local Wisconsin Baptist Association. Doolittle left the Baptist Church and connected himself with the Episcopal Church because the Baptist pastor preached against presidential Reconstruction.[36]

In the Grand Rapids, Michigan, area, approximately twenty Republican rallies were planned for the last six weeks of the campaign, with four or five ministers committed to sharing the duties of addressing the meetings.[37] The Reverend B.I. Ives of Auburn, New York, was regularly occupied as a political speaker for the Radical Republicans. On September 18, Ives made the welcoming speech for the Southern loyalists visiting Auburn. Addresses were given in the Presbyterian and Methodist churches by the Presbyterian clergyman Dr. H.A. Nelson of St. Louis, formerly of Auburn, and William G. Brownlow, a radical Methodist and governor of Tennessee.[38]

Tilton wrote in the *Independent* in September that the Republican party seemed to owe all of its past victories "to a moral idea." Most radical Christians were of the same opinion. While the moderate Republicans desperately tried to avoid being labeled radicals, most progressive Christians equated radicalism with the essential elements of Christianity. The liberal Episcopal clergyman Phillips Brooks spoke to an audience of benevolent leaders just before the election and observed that "radicalism" did indeed seem the best description of the action of the clergy, but he added that Christianity itself was radicalism. M.J. Miller, pastor of the Christian Church in Troy, Ohio, instructed his congregation that the people who believed that all men were brothers and equally entitled to partake of God's gifts of freedom and happiness were the people who had given direction to the power that saved the nation. "The principles they advocate strike more or less near the root of evil and plough up the foundation of injustice. . . . Radicals they are called and they are not ashamed of the word."[39] Samuel Galloway, a ruling elder in the Presbyterian church, had taken an active part in political campaigns since the conflict arising out of the Kansas question. Galloway, whom the Democratic *Ohio Statesmen* called an "unsufferable radical," believed that the radicals were promoting the purpose of God. At the height of the campaign of 1866, he publicly defended the position of Congress. In Medina County, Ohio, he spoke at a Union meeting and insisted that the Union belonged in the care of "the patriots who redeemed it from treason and rebellion"; the Union organization embraced the patriots who, in the providence of God, had won the redemption of the country.[40]

Almost all religious conferences and associations expressed their convictions about Reconstruction, but no religious body supported the president in the controversy with Congress. The pulpit, religious journals, and church conferences pictured the Radical Republicans as the political group of respectability and piety. The editor of the *Examiner and Chronicle* observed that the salient mark of the times seemed to be a fondness for politics. He wrote, "The pulpit feels the pervading influence and scarcely any ecclesiastical body now holds a meeting without adopting resolutions of one sort or another, about the President and Congress." The editor of the *Christian Examiner* spoke of the opponents of the radicals. "There are always in this country powerful elements to which such a party as the President has started may effectively appeal. The 'unwashed' democracy, who hate Godliness and cleanliness with equal cordiality . . . are ready for any measure which they instinctively know to be offensive to high-toned, moral, and philanthropic men. They properly regard the Republican party as led by the piety and worth of this nation."[41]

As the election campaign approached the final stage, the contest centered more and more on the suffrage issue. The Johnson supporters and the Democrats tainted the Republicans with the label of radicalism and black suffrage. The moderate Republicans made the Fourteenth

Amendment the leading feature of their campaign and stoutly maintained that it was the final stage of Reconstruction. The radical religious wing of the Republican party accepted the Fourteenth Amendment but insisted that the Southern states should not be admitted until the blacks had security, which they equated with suffrage. A few religious bodies still insisted on universal suffrage. For example, the Woodstock (Vermont) Baptist Association held that the true principles of republicanism demanded "that the nation should plant itself on the broad principles of universal rights and suffrage."[42] The Massachusetts Universalist Convention endorsed the course of Congress and set forth the belief that the cause of Christian civilization would be advanced by universal suffrage, but the General Convention of Universal Churches, meeting in radical Galesburg, Illinois, would go no farther than impartial suffrage. The National Conference of Unitarian Churches also pledged itself to work without rest for suffrage for blacks and whites alike because of the persecution the freedmen had endured in the South.[43]

The Calvinist churches generally approved equal suffrage on the grounds that it was a religious duty to grant the blacks the ballot. The Fox River Union of Congregational Churches declared it their conviction that "the election franchise should be extended to all, irrespective of color or caste." The New York Congregational Association regarded impartial suffrage for blacks as the only means of securing peace for the nation. The Congregational and Presbyterian Convention felt that no sound and enduring system of reconstruction would be established in the South until blacks had suffrage on the same terms as white citizens.[44] The Iowa Congregationalists were so concerned about the issue that they called a statewide convention late in October and registered their convictions that "the laws of God require that impartial suffrage be bestowed on all classes of men."[45] The Presbyterian Synod of Peoria met in October and concluded that the declaration of the General Assembly in 1866 encompassed the duty of equal suffrage for blacks, a position the synod reaffirmed. The General Assembly of 1866 had resolved that, "Even if suffrage may not be universal, let it at least be impartial."[46] The United Presbyterian Synod of Iowa asserted that the support of the Reconstruction was incumbent on all the faithful. "The voice of justice in the Government and the word of God vests the perfected political redemption of our country alone in impartial suffrage," asserted the United Presbyterian Synod of Iowa.[47]

In the last five or six weeks of the campaign, the question of whether the Fourteenth Amendment constituted Congress's last word on Reconstruction emerged as a key issue of the campaign. The *New York Tribune* insisted that the majority favored the readmission of the Southern states immediately after their ratification of the Fourteenth Amendment. Once the amendment had been ratified, in the words of the editor of the *New York Times*, "the Southern states would at once be readmitted to the right representation and restoration of the Union would be completed." On September 16, the Republican National Committee issued an address proclaiming that when the Fourteenth Amendment had been ratified by the Southern states, they would be readmitted to the Union.[48]

Theodore Tilton disagreed with the national committee regarding reconstruction. "We repudiate the Committee's pledge to the rebels as wholly unauthorized, invalid, and void." He charged that the committee's address amounted to "the white feather of surrender" on principles of political equality that the majority of Republicans shared. "God grant that the great party of Liberty shall prove braver than its half-hearted leaders! . . . The radical party . . . can assent to no reconstruction short of Impartial Suffrage."[49] The *Christian Advocate* opposed a "speedy" Reconstruction because the editor believed no interest would suffer if no rebel state was reconstructed for the next ten years. Charles Slack, the radical Christian editor of the *Commonwealth*, viewed the suggested terms of the national committee as "wholly inadmissible if we desire permanent peace and security in the Southern states." "The people are rapidly coming to the conclusion that impartial suffrage is the only guarantee of safety for the future," he informed his readers.[50]

Oliver O. Howard, the commissioner of the Freedmen's Bureau and a Congregational layman, spoke at the Academy of Music in Pittsburgh in mid-October. His speech, entitled "Our Christian Duty toward the South," expressed doubts that Reconstruction would end with the passage of the Fourteenth Amendment. He asserted that the fruits of victory were manhood developed, strengthened, and ennobled and liberty enlarged and made universal. "God has given us these fruits, and He would hold us responsible for their proper use and for their preservation," he warned. On October 2, Sumner delivered a lecture in the Boston Music Hall. He insisted that Congress must dictate the terms of admission that should include impartial suffrage as a guarantee of security for the blacks. Thaddeus Stevens expressed the same sentiment as Sumner in a speech to his constituents at Lancaster, Pennsylvania. "Remember that I do not say, and never mean to, that when these amendments . . . are adopted the rebel states shall be allowed to come in until they present constitutions containing the essence of liberty."[51] Tilton wrote an editorial entitled "Courage Cuts All Knots," in which he informed his readers that "political training unfits most men for moral emergencies of statesmanship. Such an emergency is now at hand—shove the halfway men aside! All hail to a reconstructed union on the granite of Impartial Suffrage!"[52]

In the agitated atmosphere of the last six weeks of the campaign, rumors were rife that the president might resist Congress by force or might refuse to enforce the laws. The editor of the *Northwestern Christian Advocate* warned that "no course . . . could be more dangerous, more menacing of evil results." Zachariah Chandler had earlier told the Philadelphia Union convention that if Johnson refused to execute the laws, he would be impeached. The *Independent* favored impeachment if the laws were not enforced.[53] With election only four days away, the *Congregationalist* urged all loyal voters to exercise their right of suffrage and see that their neighbors voted. The editor deemed it important to return such a large majority to Congress that Johnson and his supporters would be overwhelmed.[54]

In a letter written the day before the election, the Unitarian clergyman Samuel May, Jr., probably expressed the sentiments of many. He told a friend, "I devoutly pray the great and mighty God . . . give our land a good deliverance from all her enemies tomorrow, turn the heart of many to justice and righteousness."[55] The Republicans won by as large a margin as in 1864, retained a three-to-one majority in both houses of Congress, and gained control of all Northern states. The radical Christians were overjoyed by the defeat of Johnson and the Democrats. "The House of Representatives can send a dozen members off to a picnic," rejoiced Tilton, "and yet leave a majority large enough to pass a radical measure over the President's veto." The country had been given a golden opportunity to rebuild the nation's walls "upon the corner stone of Equal Rights."[56]

The radicals interpreted the election as a repudiation of Johnson. According to the *Zion's Herald*, the election showed that the people had rejected the president's policy and were ready to follow Congress even to impartial suffrage. The *Evangelist* asserted that the election showed that the people did not want the Southern states to come back in the government "with no security against a recurrence of the same trouble." "The Party of Justice demands a policy of equal rights," Tilton reminded his readers; "the demand is based, not only on political expediency, but on a more sacred foundation in human nature."[57]

The Republicans won in part because of the mobilization of the churchgoing people. They believed that the country faced a crisis as great as that of the war. To the radical Christians the significant controversies that divided the parties were moral issues. Johnson's activities in the New Orleans affair caused most states' rights Republicans to desert him. Both the Democrats and Johnson promised to restore peace immediately, but Johnson's refusal to accept the Fourteenth Amendment and the violence in the South caused him to be viewed as the threat to the peace. Although the efforts of Johnson and the Democrats to taint the Republicans with radicalism met with some success, many Americans began to view the president as the real threat to peace and national stability.[58]

The radicals succeeded in controlling almost the entire Republican press, and the religious journals were among the most forceful segment of the media. The sectarian journals exercised a greater moral power over their denominational following than the secular press, and they set the moral tone for all the Republican press. The pulpit was almost in complete unity in support of Congress. According to the clergymen, God had sent the nation a loyal Congress to protect the blacks and the Union. They appealed to the people in the fear and authority of God. The Northern pulpit and press were two of the most influential forces in shaping public opinion at this time. The public had a genuine fear that the president, through his policy in the Southern states, was going to lose the peace and that unrepentant rebels would gain control of the South and the nation and would probably reestablish slavery.[59]

The people had spoken in the election and the primary decision on Reconstruction had thus been placed beyond dispute for the first time since the end of the war. The election of 1866 was "a final mandate for unfettered radicalism."[60] At the end of 1865, Congress was willing to see Reconstruction terminated by guarantees. The majority of Congress was prepared to accept the guarantees written into the Fourteenth Amendment; after the election the idea of guarantees was replaced by the notion that the nation would not be safe without drastic modification of Southern society.[61] The demand for black suffrage gained ground during the campaign. George Julian later wrote that "the suffrage question was constantly gaining in significance, and demanding a settlement. It was neither morally nor logically possible to escape it."[62] A great national crisis demanded that the rights of the freedmen be granted on moral and religious grounds and considerations of national welfare. The Republicans were swept away by the conviction that they could right the situation only by drastic action and that they basically had no choice but to vote Republican or support Johnson's policy by voting the Democratic ticket.[63]

The Fourteenth Amendment was not fully ratified until July 1868, but the Republican lawmakers showed in their voting behavior between 1865 and 1868 that they saw the black man, and not their party, as the main beneficiary of the Fourteenth Amendment.[64]

CHAPTER NINE
# Impeachment and the Churches

The election of 1866 was a complete repudiation of presidential Reconstruction, and the Republican party won a decisive mandate in the congressional election. Since Republicans disagreed among themselves as to whether the Fourteenth Amendment constituted the final terms of Reconstruction and the Republican platform had proposed no program beyond the amendment, radicals were encouraged to speculate on what kind of measures Congress should put in place. Reverend Edward P. Tenney, a New England Congregationalist, sympathized with the views of most of the radical Christians when he wrote to Congressman Morrill during the canvass of the election in 1866, "But can we not 'manage' so as to get the negro ballot, which the North demands, next Congress? Keep the Rebs out till we get it." Some of the moderates were willing to offer universal amnesty to soften the blow of universal suffrage in the South, but many radical Christians were unwilling to make concessions to the Southern aristocracy. James Speed wrote Sumner after the election, "Universal suffrage with universal amnesty won't do. The disqualifying clause must be retained."[1]

The Thanksgiving Day and New Year sermons gave the clergymen an opportunity to evaluate the results of the election and outline suggestions for a reconstruction program. E.H. Chapin, a Universalist clergyman of New York City, spoke at Cooper Institute on November 29 and advised his audience that the work of Reconstruction would "not be accomplished by compromising good or waving it aside." He viewed the Fourteenth Amendment as a gateway to other necessary measures. Impartial suffrage was necessary as a means to the end.[2] Reverend O.B. Frothingham considered suffrage essential for the freedmen's protection. The Methodist clergyman LaRoy Sunderland wanted the blacks to have the ballot because it was the free citizen's "mightiest weapon" for guarding his freedom and rights.[3]

Lyman Abbott explained to a member of the New England Congregational Church that the easiest way to guarantee the Negro freedom was to give him suffrage, but the South should not be bribed to grant impartial suffrage; instead, he asserted, it should be decreed.[4] Reverend Edward Kirk explained to his Mount Vernon Congregational Church that the blacks needed something more than suffrage. God had opened the eyes of the people to the dictatorship of Johnson, and the movements of the president had to be checked. W.S. Studley, a Methodist clergyman, expressed similar views to his Cincinnati congregation: "The rebellious states are to be reconstructed, and this reconstruction ought to be radical reconstruction."[5]

Some clergymen focused their attack principally on the president. For example, James Cruickshank, a Congregational clergyman in Spencer, Massachusetts, accused Johnson of winking at "the low rebel mobs organized for the prosecution and murder of the unprotected freedmen." Radical Reconstruction would prevent executive incitement, he assured his congregation. In an article in the *Boston Review*, Reverend George Magoun, the Calvinist President of Grinnell College, urged Congress to adopt stern measures and demanded retribution.[6] One of the most radical sermons was delivered by George Cheever in the Church of the Puritans. He made a violent attack on moderate Reconstruction and warned that if the Fourteenth Amendment was adopted, the freedman would be delivered into the hands of his enemy and returned to slavery from which God had delivered him. Congress should "reconstruct the nation in righteousness and justice," he asserted.[7]

The conservative Republicans and Democrats were aware that they were practically powerless. Gideon Welles recorded in his diary on November 17, 1866: "Senator Grimes writes me that if the President does not take the present terms, harder ones will be proposed—that never was more leniency shown to conquered by conquerors. These are the sentiments and views of our prominent legislators and statesmen." But the conservatives did not lose hope. James Doolittle, a supporter of Johnson, wrote to a friend that he was sure the South would reject the Fourteenth Amendment and Congress would impose radical measures "based on negro suffrage." Radical Reconstruction and black suffrage would become a national issue in the presidential election of 1868, he informed his conservative friend, and on that issue, "we will whale them." Doolittle did not want the conservatives to become disheartened. He wrote to Orville Browning, a Johnson supporter, three days later, "The elections are over and we are beaten for the present. But our cause will live. If all the states not represented refuse to ratify the Amendment . . . , the extreme Rads will go for Stevens [sic] Bill, for reorganizing the southern states on negro suffrage. . . . That will present the issue squarely . . . , and on that we can beat them at the next Presidential election."[8]

A few church bodies did not hold their yearly meetings until after the election. The meetings following the election reflected the progress made by antislavery sentiment during the year. The Chicago Presbytery of the Reformed Presbyterian Church condemned the attempt to degrade the freedmen by depriving them of equal political rights, which was "unjust in the eyes of God." The AMA met in the last days of October after the election had taken place in some parts of the North. Edward Beecher, as chairman of the resolution committee, brought in resolutions asserting that God in his providence had committed the nation to enfranchise and uplift the freedmen: "we cannot be free . . . except in the fulfillment of our duties to them." The National Unitarian Convention met in November and passed its strongest measures to date. It vowed that it would not lose the fruits of victory and its members would not rest until the freedmen enjoyed the rights of suffrage.[9]

The religious journals believed that the election results had mandated Radical Reconstruction. The Baptist *Examiner and Chronicle* felt that the election furnished proof that the people were far in advance of Congress and the executive department in being free of prejudice. Tilton informed the people in an editorial that the chief lesson of the election was that the Republican party everywhere must maintain its virtue if it hoped to retain its ascendancy. "The Radical men of the North are neither to be conquered by the Democratic, nor trifled with by the Republican Party," he explained. The *Christian Examiner* informed its readers that "the loyal people mean to keep the power of this Government in their own hands, until they can trust it to a wiser administration. They intend to defend the freedmen, and see them in full possession of civil and political rights."[10]

In an editorial in the *Commonwealth*, Charles Slack expected Congress to adopt radical measures in 1867. He believed Congress had the power to promote the welfare of the South and he urged Congress "to cut the Gordian-knot" and give the freedmen land as well as the ballot. As a guest editor of the *Independent*, Garrison wrote that the power of Congress was absolute, and if Congress did two things, the Negro question would solve itself. Land and the ballot were necessary, he explained—"Land, that he may support his family; the ballot, that he may support the state." Tilton added that the South should remain conquered territory until the Southern people "acknowledge the claims of justice." Aaron M. Powell, the new Quaker editor of the *National*

*Anti-Slavery Standard*, regarded all Southern oaths as ludicrous and the provisions for disfranchisement of Southern traitors as a waste of paper and no guarantee of protection for the freedmen. "To give the negroes land, ballot and education and hold the arm of the Federal government over the whole Southern Territory until these seeds have begun to bear fruit beyond any possibility of blighting is the only safe and practical reconstruction," insisted Powell.[11]

Radicalism reached new heights during the winter of 1866-67 as a result of the midterm election of 1866. Radical Christians rushed into the field to keep the minds of the people focused on the meeting of Congress. In their addresses at the National Loyalist Convention in Philadelphia during the fall of 1866, Anna Dickinson, Frederick Douglass, Tilton, and others laid the groundwork for the ideas to be incorporated in the Reconstruction Act and the Fifteenth Amendment.[12] The radical speakers concentrated primarily on the West. Tilton traveled more than ten thousand miles and spoke more than a hundred times in the West. Dickinson was equally energetic, ranging as far west as Wisconsin and speaking with great effect. She had delivered at least a hundred lectures before the season was over.[13]

Wendell Phillips was also active in promoting the radical cause with his lectures. Phillips had been converted in the great revival of the 1820s after hearing Lyman Beecher, but he had come out of the church and now held devotions in his parlor. He spent most of the lecture season in the West and was welcomed everywhere with enthusiasm when he spoke of the crisis before the nation. To meet the crisis he proposed giving the blacks "Land, ballot and education, and to hold the arm of the Federal government over the whole Southern Territory until these seeds have begun to bear fruit beyond any possibility of blighting." He returned to Boston after giving sixty lectures and traveling more than 12,000 miles.[14]

Christian radicals took more direct action by circulating petitions among their supporters urging Congress to establish universal suffrage as the basis of Radical Reconstruction and asking the states to refuse to ratify the Fourteenth Amendment. The Church Anti-Slavery Society led the way. George Cheever circulated petitions in New York while his brother Henry mounted a petition drive in Massachusetts, urging the state legislature not to ratify the amendment. The Equal Rights Association joined in the petition drive, and the black National Equal Rights League under the leadership of black clergymen held a convention in Washington and petitioned Congress to grant impartial suffrage. As a result of the petition drive and the lectures in the field, by the time Congress had organized, the national legislature was flooded with petitions.[15]

After the election of 1866, Schuyler Colfax returned to Washington for the meeting of the Thirty-ninth Congress. He set the tone for the new Congress by a speech in which he reminded his fellow lawmakers that in the early stage of the war the people were willing to consent to perpetual slavery. "But God willed otherwise [and] the nation rose to a higher plane of duty, and resolved . . . that slavery must die. . . . Does it not seem," he said, "as if again the Creator was leading us in his way rather than our own? . . . He . . . has put all human beings under an equality before the divine law and He demands that we should put all under equality before the human law." On December 3, 1866, when Congress convened, the radicals felt their views had been vindicated by the people. In the House of Representatives the radical Congregational chaplain C.B. Boynton, opened the session with a prayer that set the stage for radical legislation. "We thank Thee for that magnificent uprising of a free people, instructed as they were in reference to every great question presented." He prayed to God, "That there may be no spot in this land that is not wholly consecrated to freedom—Christian freedom. . . . We ask not for harmony that is the result of any compromise, of any yielding of the right."[16]

The president's message did not mention the Fourteenth Amendment or give any indication that his views on the amendment had changed, but it was clear that his basic policy was the same. "I know of no measure more imperatively demanded by every consideration of national interest, sound policy and equal justice than the admission of the loyal members from the now unrepresented States," he informed Congress. The *New York Tribune* thought it was unfortunate that the president did not show the slightest tendency to make peace with Congress. "He clings to his dogmas with as much tenacity as when he hoped to carry the country in the late election," the editor charged.[17]

The Republicans were encouraged to establish federal intervention in the South by stories of atrocities reported by clergymen, teachers, soldiers, and journalists. Reverend J.C. Emerson, a missionary in Florida, wrote to a radical friend who sent the communication on to Sumner. "If Congress will only *destroy these bogus governments*, they may leave us to take care of ourselves for years while they reconstruct. . . . Now we are bound hand and foot in the mercies of the rebels." Emerson wrote to another radical friend in Washington who conveyed the communication to Senator Fessenden. He revealed that the Southern judges scolded and ridiculed loyalists when they asked for protection under the civil rights bill. Another transplanted Northerner wrote, "Let Congress make a clean sweep of it—disfranchise the guilty and *enfranchise* the deserving and leave the results with that Providence who has manifest, during those last five years, such a decided favor for human progress and civil liberty."[18]

While a comprehensive reconstruction bill was being debated and prepared in the committee, the radicals brought forth a black suffrage bill for the District of Columbia. It passed on December 14, 1866, and was promptly vetoed by the president. In his veto message, Johnson chided Republicans, whom he accused of being inconsistent with the principles of right and justice by forcing on the people of the District of Columbia "an experiment which their own constituents have thus far shown an unwillingness to test for themselves." The Senate overrode the veto on the same day that it received the veto message, and the House followed a day later. Charles Slack, the editor of the *Commonwealth* responded in an editorial, "Thank God for this advance." The *Independent* claimed that Congress had exclusive constitutional power over the District of Columbia and that no other president had interfered with that right. Tilton sounded a warning to the president. "The day has dawned. High noon approaches. . . . The country is reluctant to establish the precedent of punishing even a guilty chief magistrate by impeachment. But if acts of wantonness, like this veto-message, are to be continually repeated, it may beget a conviction."[19] The bill was important because it set a precedent for suffrage in the North as well as in the South. The Republicans were applauded by many of their constituents for overriding the president's veto. Some radical Christians expressed sentiments similar to those of the Quaker constituent who urged Congressman Donnelly on to more throughgoing Reconstruction.[20]

In the meantime bills to admit Colorado and Nebraska as states, which had failed to pass the last session of Congress, were introduced again. The admission of Nebraska was more critical because immigrants were flocking in on the new Pacific Railroad and were more likely to furnish two radical senators. The Nebraska bill provided for white suffrage only. Although many radicals supported the Nebraska bill from political expediency, Sumner immediately objected to it. Sumner insisted that it was one of the most disastrous measures that had been introduced into Congress because it would "impair the moral efficiency of Congress, injure its influence, and be something like a bar against adoption of just measures for the rebel States." He reminded his colleagues that they were seeking to obliterate the word 'white' from all institutions. The bill was amended to remove the provision restricting suffrage to whites only. When Johnson vetoed the Nebraska and the Colorado bills, Congress overrode him.[21] The District of Columbia, the Colorado, and the Nebraska bills served to mark the line dividing the Radical Republicans and their opponents.

The radicals feared the South would accept the Fourteenth Amendment and the moderates would declare that the final requirements had been met for readmittance of the Southern states. The *New York Times* advised the moderates that the radicals dreaded nothing as much as the acceptance of the Fourteenth Amendment by the South. "The rejection of the Amendment by the Southern states will not only exclude them from Congress now," warned the editor, "but it will be made a reason for still further exclusions hereafter." The *Times* was very correct in its interpretation of the radicals' fear. After Congress met, the radicals became uneasy and again tried to force the eastern states to reject the amendment. Phillips appeared before the Massachusetts legislative committee and urged the state not to ratify the Fourteenth Amendment. He pleaded with the committee not to make Massachusetts "a party to such a monstrous piece of injustice." The *Commonwealth* joined the protest against ratification with a very telling editorial. Charles Slack had a low opinion of the amendment. "We have outgrown its necessity," he wrote; "It is virtually a dead letter." Tilton protested that the Fourteenth Amendment "commends the political fate of the Negro to the hands of the rebel." He asserted that he knew personally every prominent member of Congress and all leading radicals outside of Congress and they had no intention of making the Amendment the final measure of admission."[22]

The radical Christian physician George B. Loring suggested to Sumner that Massachusetts should ratify the amendment with a proviso that "she considered the proposed amendment not as a finality, but simply an advanced step in the work of reconstruction." This was Sumner's thinking. As early as October he had spoken in the Boston Music Hall and had taken the position that the amendment was not enough and should be followed by impartial suffrage. In January he had written Francis Bird that the Amendment was "only an installment and not a finality." Loring and Bird were members of the Massachusetts committee on federal relations. The Massachusetts legislature ratified the amendment with a protest against the denial of impartial suffrage.[23]

The refusal of the South to ratify the Fourteenth Amendment strengthened radicalism in Congress because the moderate position was undermined by the rejection of the amendment in the Southern states. The radicals were relieved that the South had rejected the amendment. Granville Moody rejoiced that only Tennessee had ratified it. He expressed optimism about the accomplishments of Congress; he believed that God had raised up the Republican party for the millennial age. It was *"radically right* in its record, principles, and progress," he assured his Ohio friends.[24]

With the opening of Congress in December, the radicals prepared to take up the reconstruction bill that had been laid aside in 1866. Stevens informed his colleagues, "I was a Conservative in the last session of this Congress, but I mean to be a Radical henceforth." Many radicals wanted to restrict Johnson's executive power so as to remove options that he could exercise in his administrative capacity. "I hope we shall have as strong a law as Congress can pass regulating appointments and removals from office and restraining abuse of power in that respect," Warner Bateman, of Ohio, wrote to his senator. In the debate on the Tenure-of-Office Act, Sumner asserted that he was willing to act as "a night watchman; and if I could I would save him from Executive tyranny." Sumner promised a radical friend, "All that is possible will be done to limit the Executive power. It is possible that the President may be impeached." The Tenure-of-Office Act passed over the president's veto.[25]

Both Stevens and Sumner introduced ultraradical measures, but they were set aside for more conservative ones. Stevens insisted that black suffrage was necessary to maintain the ascendancy of the party on which the safety of the nation depended. "I am for negro suffrage in every rebel state, . . . every earthly being who has an immortal soul, has an equal right to justice, honesty and fair play. . . . Such is the law of God and such ought to be the law of man."[26] Conservatives and some moderates complained that radical proposals before Congress would demoralize and degrade the people of the South. The Congregational Congressman Josiah Grinnell dismissed the concern with a sharp reply. "I do not fear that; I only fear the wrong of delay to make a compromise with injustice, and I do not want to see the woe we have just borne again brought upon the country by neglect or a compromise which would invite the vengeance of a just God."[27]

A confusing number of amendments and counteramendments to the reconstruction bill were presented for consideration. To many anxious citizens Congress seemed to be stalling or marking time. Many radical Christians expressed impatience with the slow progress of Congress. Edward Pierce reminded Sumner that Congress would be unfaithful to its trust if it neglected, during the current session, "to extinguish the pretended rebel governments" and order new elections for new constitutional conventions. Early in February, a Congregational layman of Illinois complained to David Davis because Congress was doing nothing toward Reconstruction. "The people feel indignant with them," he added angrily. A radical Christian exhorted Senator Richard Yates, "Do Oh Do fearlessly of consequence continue to do right in the fear of God." A constituent advised Congressman Donnelly that everybody was looking for radical measures on Reconstruction and that Congress was far behind the people. " 'We the people' believe it a golden moment" for someone to offer to amend the pending amendment by simply adding "no state shall deny franchise on account of color."[28]

Stevens and Julian introduced a bill that provided for simple territorialization and indefinite military administration of the South. The House passed the bill on February 13. A radical constituent informed Donnelly that the loyal masses would sustain Congress. "This rebellion must be crushed,—killed," he asserted. "No half-way work will do. Nothing short of right in its severity will do." William Dickson informed his congressman that he was sure the House bill would meet the approval of all loyal people. "The South must take military government or must allow their loyal fellow citizens the same right which they claim for themselves," he wrote to Rutherford B. Hayes.[29]

The House bill, however, was too ultraradical to suit the majority in the Senate. John Sherman introduced a substitute for the Stevens-Julian proposal that would readmit the Southern states when they ratified the Fourteenth Amendment and adopted a new constitution guaranteeing black suffrage. With minor changes the bill was passed on February 20, and Johnson's veto was overridden on March 2, the day it returned to Congress.[30]

The sectarian press was uneasy about the progress of Congress in passing the Reconstruction Act. The American Presbyterian lamented that the executive and judiciary departments were paralyzed and argued that Congress should promptly remove any part of the government that was shielding instead of punishing crime. After the Reconstruction Act had passed Congress, the editor of the Watchman and Reflector expressed satisfaction with God's punishment of the South. Austin Blair was of the same opinion. In one of his "Walsingham" articles on Johnson and Reconstruction, he concluded, "The role of Moses has served its purpose . . . and is now played out."[31] Some Christian radicals were dissatisfied with the Reconstruction Act because the Sherman version had been substituted for the Julian-Stevens bill. Senator Timothy O. Howe wrote to his daughter that "the whole will of God was not clearly revealed" to Congress. In an editorial in the *Independent*, Tilton complained that he would not be satisfied until black suffrage had been written into the Constitution.[32]

Radical Christian constituents were of one mind with Howe and Tilton. A radical Methodist citizen in Illinois expressed similar views to his senator. "When the South is reconstructed on the broad ground of equal justice to *all men* then may we expect that peace will reign," he predicted. Another radical Christian from Michigan wanted peace to be restored but only after the Rebels had had their necks broken and equal rights for all mankind had been secured. "I want to see the South granted no right but the right to submit to the Powers that be and hope to see them reconstructed radically," he wrote to Congressman Austin Blair.[33]

The sectarian press were satisfied with the work of the Thirty-ninth Congress. George Day, the editor of the *Morning Star*, wrote that the last Congress had become a ready and faithful servant, and Providence had given it higher and grander tasks. The work that Congress had done testified to "the firmness and patriotism" of that body. Other religious journals were more concerned about the enforcement of the Reconstruction Act. The *Western Christian Advocate* was sure that the legislation, if "fairly interpreted and fully enforced," would extinguish the spirit of rebellion. The *Independent* and the *Northwestern Christian Advocate* assured their readers that the president's refusal to execute, evade, or nullify the act would certainly lead to his impeachment. Even the conservative *New York Observer* grudgingly admitted that "almost any government was better than anarchy."[34] When the religious associations and conferences met early in 1867, those that considered the work of the Thirty-ninth Congress were unanimous in approving Radical Reconstruction.[35] Some of the conferences and associations, however, were silent on the political questions of the day.[36]

The lawmakers of the new Fortieth Congress met immediately upon the adjournment of the Thirty-ninth Congress and promptly undertook the task of amending the Reconstruction Act. On March 23, 1867, a supplementary bill was passed which gave federal military commanders in the South authority to initiate Reconstruction by registering eligible voters and calling state conventions, but Johnson, as the radicals feared, used his presidential powers to obstruct congressional Reconstruction. Basing his action on the investigations of the Military Board and the report of the congressional committee, General Sheridan had removed the governor of Louisiana and local officers responsible for the New Orleans massacre. Johnson ordered Sheridan to defer the removals, but Sheridan answered him with a protest against recalling the order. The president sought the opinion of Attorney General Henry Stanbery, who declared that the military commanders were not authorized to promulgate codes in defiance of civil governments of the states but were to cooperate with the existing governments which were set up under Johnson's plan of Reconstruction. Stanbery's interpretation virtually emasculated the Reconstruction Act. Stanbery also denounced General Daniel Sickles's acts in North Carolina as illegal. The general angrily asked to be relieved of his duties so that he could defend his conduct before a court of inquiry.[37]

The editor of the Baptist *Watchman and Reflector* asserted, "If the President acts on this opinion . . . to obstruct justice, he will . . . inaugurate a new war in Congress." The generally conservative Ohio Baptist *Journal and Messanger* concluded, "The President's conduct from the first has not been such as to inspire confidence in his ability or integrity. Congress has therefore only the more solemn responsibility resting upon it to be calm, vigilant, and unfaltering in its adherence to duty." The editor of the *Zion's Herald* was more direct. "Without doubt, the easiest remedy would be the prompt impeachment and removal of President Johnson." But the editor hardly expected it.[38]

George Fish, a Michigan radical, assured Austin Blair of his faith that Congress would stand up "square to the mark" and not "deliver up the government to unrepented perjured rebels." Most radicals agreed with Fish. When Congress convened, its action was swift and to the point. It met with the approval of most radicals. A Senate caucus agreed to limit the business of the session to amendments to the Reconstruction Act. Congress promptly passed another supplementary reconstruction bill over the president's veto on July 19, 1867, which declared the state governments to be illegal. If they continued at all, they were to be subject to the military commanders. The editor of the Baptist *Christian Times and Witness* explained the reason for the bill. "The necessity for such legislation has arisen in the mistaken and unfortunate action of those in authority who sympathize with the South, and who would restore traitors to their former position without the slightest penalty attached to their crime."[39]

As soon as Congress adjourned, Johnson renewed his tactics of obstruction by asking Secretary of War Edwin Stanton to resign. When he refused, Johnson suspended him on August 12. "It is now universally recognized that there will be no peace, no restoration, no business stability, till something is done to prevent Johnson from enthroning perpetual turmoil," protested the editor of the *Commonwealth*. Henry Dexter, editor of the *Congregationalist and Boston Recorder*, called Johnson "an ignorant and conceited, as well as an obstinate and violent man." He urged the people in states which held elections in the fall of 1867 to make it manifest they were as determined to carry out congressional Reconstruction as they had been in the fall of 1866. In an editorial entitled "Johnsoniana," Tilton announced that the American people were determined to reestablish the Union on an unshakable basis. The removal of a bad president, if necessary, would occasion "no more disturbance than the dismissal of an awkward footman."[40]

When the religious associations met in the fall of 1867, many of the meetings were preoccupied with the subject of Reconstruction. The Cincinnati Conference of the Methodist Episcopal Church met August 31 and deprecated the president for his determination "to misinterpret and refuse to execute according to their true meaning and intent, the laws of Congress respecting reconstruction," and his removal of certain executive officers. The conference called on Congress "to stand firm."[41] The Upper Iowa Conference of the Methodist Episcopal Church also protested against the action of the president in removing men from the government who stood firmly by the principles of freedom. The Cayuga Baptist Association in New York was equally severe in its criticism of the executive department. It charged the Johnson administration with being made up of "wicked rulers" who continued the national strife.[42]

The radicals' discussion of the impeachment of the president started shortly after Johnson's veto of the Freedmen's Bureau bill and his address of February 22, 1866. On February 26, a week after Johnson vetoed the Freedmen's Bureau bill, Garrison delivered a lecture in the Academy of Music in Brooklyn in which he attacked Johnson for opposing Congress. He repeated substantially the same speech in other cities. This attack on Johnson was very bitter, but Garrison did not go so far as to suggest impeachment. He had suggested impeachment earlier in private correspondence, however. Then, in March and April, Garrison wrote articles for the *Independent* in which he called for impeachment.[43] At the same time, through private correspondence, he endeavored to bring public opinion up to the level of impeachment as a means of dealing with Johnson. Early in April he suggested to a friend, "Allow me . . . to offer you the following cold water sentiment: *The speedy impeachment and removal of Andrew Johnson from the office he dishonors and betrays!*"[44]

Many radicals privately agreed with Joseph Medill when he wrote to an Illinois congressman that Johnson was like an aching tooth, and everyone was "impatient to have the old villain out."[45] The election results suggest that such feeling was widespread. After the election, with the meeting of Congress approaching, Wendell Phillips wrote to the editor of the *National Anti-Slavery Standard* that the election results showed the people's desire to see the South reformed. "I say, therefore, impeach the President; and while he is in trial sequester him. What is the advantage? Then we can run the machine." One week later the *Commonwealth* came out for impeaching the president.[46]

A Christian layman wrote Congressman E.B. Washburne that "justice to the sufferers and mercy to mankind" demanded Johnson's impeachment. But some radicals thought Johnson had been made powerless, and they feared making a martyr of him by impeaching him. Henry S. Lane wrote to an Indiana constituent who wanted Johnson removed from office that there was not much sentiment in the capital for impeaching the president. "With the loyal people and a two thirds majority in Congress, we can get along even with Moses," he assured the Indiana citizen. The radical Reverend Samuel Spears held the same opinion. "With more than two-thirds majority against him in both Houses, Congress can better afford to let the President live out his Constitutional days," he concluded in a published sermon. Gerrit Smith was not sure Congress should impeach the president during the next session of Congress. He informed a Presbyterian professor that Congress had some reforming of its own to do before it could reasonably charge the president with crimes.[47]

On January 10, Garrison published an article in the *Independent* in which he regretted that no one in Congress had demanded the impeachment of the president. If the president was not liable to impeachment, he reasoned, "then the phrase 'high crime and misdemeanors' becomes a mockery, and he may act the part of factionist and usurper to any extent with impunity." If Johnson remained in office, "neither union men nor negroes will possess any rights on Southern soil that rebels will be bound to respect." But Garrison believed that the president would not be impeached, "owing to the timidity of the Republicans."[48]

Before Garrison's article was published in the *Independent*, Congress moved against the president. On January 7, Congressman James H. Ashley introduced a resolution to impeach Johnson, and the House Judiciary Committee was charged to investigate allegations against the president. The Washington correspondent reported to the editor of the *Commonwealth* in an animated spirit, "The Rubicon has indeed been passed. 'Let the earth rejoice and all the people give praise unto the Lord.' "[49] The radical Christian population backed the effort to remove Johnson. A radical constituent suggested to Congressman Donnelly that the congressional prayer meeting should "devote one evening a week to earnest and faithful prayer to Almighty God to remove" the great obstacles that the president and the Supreme Court posed to national progress. Reverend S.H. Morse wrote to the editor of the *Boston Radical*, a nondenominational religious journal, that Congress should not be backward about removing Johnson. "What the moral sense of the country privately confesses, may be openly and safely acted upon . . . to save the country from what must otherwise be for years to come an irreparable disaster."[50]

From the time of the presidential veto of the Freedmen's Bureau bill, sectarian journals had suggested that impeachment was a possibility, but not until Johnson undertook to apply his attorney general's interpretation to the Reconstruction Act did any religious newspaper give the idea serious consideration. Some of the religious press still suggested serious reservations. In January 1867, the *Watchman and Reflector* agreed that the president had committed many wrong acts and had been false to the principles underlying his election, but these factors justified his condemnation rather than his impeachment. The "Veteran Observer" informed his readers that he was opposed to the efforts to remove the president from office. "The impeachment must morally fail . . . because the intent is the offence of every crime."[51]

The Baptist *Christian Times and Witness* condemned Johnson's course but still did not think Congress should impeach him, because the president's term was drawing to a close and opinion on the matter remained very divided. "Providence has graciously provided for the protection of the country during the remainder of his term . . . by giving to loyal people such a decided preponderancy in Congress to keep wrong doing in check," explained the editor. But J.W. Barker, editor of the *Christian Freeman*, viewed the crisis differently. "When he who bears the sword bears it so vainly as to be no terror to 'evil doers,' but to cause the good and loyal to quake, he has lost his divine commission as a magistrate," the editor charged. A correspondent for the *Christian Freeman* wrote from Washington that there was a growing sentiment to impeach the president because of the interpretation the attorney general had put on the Reconstruction Act. If Johnson were impeached, a progressive Reconstruction could be set on a firm foundation of universal peace and justice.[52]

As soon as Congress adjourned, Johnson suspended Secretary of

War Edwin Stanton on August 12. "Does he mean to have another rebellion on the question of Executive powers and duties?" James Speed queried Sumner. The dismissal of Stanton made Horace White, the radical Episcopalian editor of the *Chicago Tribune*, into an advocate of impeachment. George Cheever wrote to his brother, Henry, that Johnson had betrayed the moderates, who would now be forced to impeach him—as they should already have done but had not, lacking the pluck. He urged Henry to have his Freedom Club agitate anew. Senator Jacob Howard was also anxious for action in the House. He wrote to the *New York Tribune* that the people's patience could not be infinite. "Perhaps it is the will of Providence that Johnson's madness shall hasten it," he speculated.[53]

The sectarian journals began to campaign for the impeachment of the president after he suspended Stanton. The editor of the *Zion's Herald* catalogued all of Johnson's wrongdoings in an editorial entitled "The Traitorous President." The editors of the *Liberal Christian* and *Christian Register* were convinced that immediate impeachment was unavoidable. Henry Dexter, the editor of the *Congregationalist*, agreed that Johnson's course would lead to his impeachment and that a "multitude of loyal men" would say "amen." The *American Wesleyan* explained that Congress had not only the right to impeach the president but the "imperative duty to do so."[54]

By October 1867, several ecclesiastical bodies were going on record in support of the current objectives of Congress. The New London (Connecticut) Baptist Association, for example, resolved that "the open hostility of the President to the laws of Congress and the consequent hindrance to the peaceful progress of reconstruction fill us with the most painful solicitude." The Grinnell Association of the Congregational Churches characterized Johnson as "an aider and abettor of principles inimical to the best interests of the country."[55]

Attention focused on the elections of 1867 in several states that were shaping up as referenda on black suffrage and Reconstruction. The Democrats denounced the political sermons that were multiplying as the canvas progressed. Reverend H.C. Tilton, in an editorial in the *Northwestern Christian Advocate*, answered that the ballot box was "as sacred as the sacramental table. The cry . . . 'pulpit and politics' . . . cannot deter us from a frank avowal of these Scriptural truths."[56] But in spite of the commitment of the clergy, the Democrats made impressive gains in states where state constitutional referenda and impeachment were the principal issues. The election strengthened the moderates and thereby lessened the will to carry out impeachment.

Although the Judiciary Committee recommended impeachment, on December 7, 1867, the House voted it down.[57]

Horace Greeley expressed the sentiments of many in an editorial written after he had weighed the results of the election. "We cannot resist the conviction that to adopt impeachment now would be to bring . . . greater evils than those we seek to avoid. . . . We shall have burdens enough to carry in the next campaign without making Johnson a martyr and carry him also." George Julian wrote to his wife that Congress had backed down on impeachment. "You . . . can guess the effect of it on the whole South," he lamented. In an editorial on the failure to impeach Johnson, Tilton complained that, "If the great culprit had . . . fired a barn or forged a check, he would have been indicted, prosecuted, condemned, sentenced and punished. But . . . he only oppressed the Negro; . . . conspired with the rebel, . . . betrayed the Union party." The Washington correspondent for the *Commonwealth* explained to the editor, "Johnson defeats Congress at every point. . . . While Congress acts as if he were an obstinate and stupid blockhead he works quietly and steadily . . . to the accomplishment of his wicked ends. . . . While Congress is passing acts to reconstruct the South, the President is drawing a carriage and six through them."[58]

After Johnson made his State of the Union speech in December 1867, the editor of the *Zion's Herald* called attention to "his crimes as a politician and a magistrate against the peace and welfare of the country." His message was described as delivered "in a tone of arrogance and wickedness," but the editor believed that the president would no longer be a threat because his power would diminish as his term of office neared an end. Tilton did not agree with *Zion's Herald*. "Mr. Stanton is said to be Secretary of War. This is not true. He is sitting in his old seat, but not wielding his old power," Tilton informed his readers; "Mr. Johnson must be impeached unless the President consents to act through Mr. Stanton instead of acting *over* him."[59] The dilemma in the ranks of the radicals was soon to be resolved, for Johnson would shortly give Congress a new challenge.

Still, many Christians were impatient for Congress to take action. Horace White, the radical Episcopalian editor of the *Chicago Tribune*, advised his Congressman to fight fire with fire. "Johnson carries all his points by sheer audacity and doggedness," he explained; "it is necessary for Congress to meet him on the same ground, and to be as obstinate as he is." In writing to the editor of the *Boston Advertiser*, the Congregational layman Elizur Wright expressed his impatience for congressional action. "If the executive will not execute there is no possible *seasonable* remedy but to have the lawmakers replace him with something that will execute. . . . All unfit executives or non-executives are removable from office." With Radical Reconstruction all but complete and impeachment certain, the radical Methodist clergyman Granville Moody assured Ben Wade that Congress's work would "out last the pyramids."[60]

On February 21, Johnson ended Stanton's suspension by removing him from office. Three days later the House impeached the president by a party-line vote.[61] The radical Christians were elated. George Fish assured Austin Blair, "Not a loyal tongue will wag against impeachment. . . . Our people ask nothing for vengeance but everything for an abiding well settled peace, resting on the great principle of truth and right." George Cheever was anxious about the progress of the impeachment because some senators might be expected to betray "the cause of truth and righteousness." But he wrote his sister, "Our hope is in God's continued interposition for the salvation of the country in its preparation for the reign of the redeemer." In a letter to William P. Fessenden, the Quaker-reared Congregationalist, Neal Dow of Maine wrote, "Speedy deliverance from his [Johnson's] misrule will bring joy to every loyal heart. . . . Hang Johnson up by the heels like a dead crow in a cornfield to frighten all his tribe." W.C. Howells, an antislavery Ohio editor of Quaker antecedents who had become a Swedenborgian, complained to Garfield that the impeachment charge should have been "a bold and powerful blow for justice and right."[62]

The sectarian press stood behind Congress on impeachment. The *Liberal Christian* explained that Congress had no other course but to bring a charge against Johnson because he threw himself into direct antagonism with the Tenure-of-Office Act. "Congress has not taken a step which it cannot retrace." The *Christian Ambassador* of Auburn, New York, a Universalist journal, also concluded that the president should be tried, for there was "nothing too wicked, too treacherous for this betrayer. . . . Let the High Court decide whether he has sought evil by direct and overt deed." The *Independent* carried an editorial entitled "The Criminal in the White House," in which the editor asserted that the impeachment had "exerted a marked and healthful influence on the public mind," but he added, "If Mr. Johnson is acquitted, reconstruction and the Republican party are destroyed together." A Disciple of Christ and friend of Garfield expressed the same sentiments. If the impeachment movement failed, he was sure the Republican party would be "almost hopelessly demoralized" and divided, and a political revolution would bring the Democrats to power. The *Congregation-*

*alist* charged that Johnson's habitual falseness to his high trust "had nearly ruined the country." The *Christian Register* was equally hostile to Johnson. The editor strongly supported impeachment because the president "had come to proclaim it to be his duty to thwart the execution of the very laws which he had sworn to execute."[63] The Northern Methodist conferences were especially supportive of the effort to remove the president. The New England Methodist Episcopal Conference deeply regretted "the constant and violent hostility of the President . . . to the action of Congress and the will of the people." The conference "heartily and solemnly" approved the action of the House in impeaching the chief executive.[64] The Wesleyan Methodist Church was united in the support of the efforts to remove Johnson.[65]

The trial dragged on through April and May. On May 14, two days before the first vote in the Senate on the removal of the president, a motion was placed before the General Conference of the Methodist Episcopal Church rebuking the chief executive's "tyrannical usurpation," which caused the conference to set aside an hour for prayer "to invoke the mercy of God upon our nation and to beseech Him to save our Senators from error, and so influence them that their decision shall be in truth and righteousness." The African Methodist Episcopal Church, meeting in Washington, addressed a prayer to the Senate asking for the conviction and removal of the president. The general conference probably influenced some votes in the upper house, but its influence was not decisive. On May 16, at 8:00 A.M., George Pendleton of Cincinnati received a telegram from Washington which read: "We have beaten the Methodist Episcopal Church North, hell, Ben Butler, John Logan, Geo[rge] Wilkes, and Impeachment. President Johnson will be acquitted if a vote is had today." On May 16, the Senate voted against impeachment. Johnson remained in office by one vote.[66]

Many church bodies that prayed for the guidance of God during the impeachment crisis, and some that had beseeched God to guide Congress in the removal of the reason for discord in the country, became reconciled to the decision of the Senate, but almost all conferences and associations that met after the trial praised Congress for its efforts to uphold the principles of equal rights and to consummate the union of all the states. The Walworth (Wisconsin) Baptist Association, however, went further. It resolved that honor was due the "noble men in Congress," who showed themselves "of incorruptible principles, whom gold could not buy, while shame and everlasting infamy is due those who have been reduced to the support of a corrupt and corrupting Executive."[67]

In an editorial entitled "The Acquittal," George H. Emerson, editor of the *Christian Ambassador*, declared, the retention of "a wicked ruler and the betrayer of liberty is an offence to the Christian world. It is the duty of Christians to make their convictions felt in a contingency such as just a fraction over one-third of the American Senate has brought upon the nation. . . . We can only regret that the words we write can not more strongly express the disappointment, the mortification, which as citizens of a professedly Christian republic, we feel."[68]

# CHAPTER TEN

# Black Suffrage as a Moral Duty

Black suffrage was one of the most persistent issues during Reconstruction. The debate over suffrage began in 1864 and continued until 1870. To radical Christians, it was a moral and religious issue. The clergy and Christian laymen were in the forefront of the movement to secure the ballot for the freedmen and for all blacks. In April 1863, Gerrit Smith denounced the denial of the suffrage to black soldiers as "unreasonable and unrighteous—a high crime against both the soldiers and the country." The controversy came prominently to public attention when Tilton delivered an address at the Cooper Institute in May. He demanded that the state of New York grant blacks the ballot and the right to hold office. At a Union jubilee in New York in November 1864, Tilton indignantly demanded to know the reason why black soldiers who had shared the perils and hardships of war should not have as much right to vote as the "white scoundrels who stuffed ballot boxes in New York City." On Tilton's extended lecture series during December and January, he was a fearless advocate of universal suffrage and human rights. When he returned from the tour in late January 1865, Tilton explained to Lydia Child that the key to every man's rights was the ballot.[1]

Chase was an early advocate of suffrage for blacks. In a letter to Gerrit Smith in March 1864, he suggested that black soldiers and the intelligent black men should immediately be given the ballot. Early in June he wrote to the organizers of a war meeting in New York that future historians would be amazed at the statesmen's willingness to risk a successful rebellion rather than trust blacks with the ballot. Chases's proposal did not secure the approval of some radicals in Ohio, but he continued his effort to promote black suffrage during the early months of 1865 by giving moral support and encouragement to his old antislavery friends Garrison and Phillips in their quest for black enfranchisement. Chase tried to persuade Lincoln to adopt black suffrage in a reconstruction state as a new experiment in democracy.[2]

The Ohio radical Christians were passionately committed to black suffrage. Francis Parish, a director of the AMA and a deacon in a Congregational church in northern Ohio, informed Senator Sherman that if Congress adopted black suffrage, the public mind would rapidly follow the lawmakers' lead. "Now is the favorable time for public men to plant themselves firmly upon the vital principles of our Republican institutions," he urged. Oberlin radical Christians were in the vanguard of the movement to secure black suffrage. A member of the Oberlin Congregational Church wrote to his antislavery representative in the state legislature, "O how low, unchristian it does seem to be" to deny the blacks their just right, he lamented. Ralph Plumb, another antislavery Christian from Oberlin, told James Garfield that God would give the Union victory in the war as soon as the blacks had suffrage. In May 1864, Charles P. McIlvaine, the liberal Ohio bishop of the Episcopal Church, as chairman of the American Tract Society, in his keynote address at the anniversary of the society, called for the complete enfranchisement of "our colored brethren" because "God is leading us to it."[3]

George Stearns came out boldly with the assertion that "negro suffrage was the only practicable solution of the problem" created by the end of slavery. During the summer of 1864, the Presbyterian Reverend George Duffield of Detroit, in a public letter to his son, wrote that he held "a conviction as deliberate" as it was "irresistible that the cause of freedom and religion, even when it comes to voting and fighting," was a thousandfold safer with the blacks than with the Northern Democratic traitors. Senator Zachariah Chandler was of the same opinion. In a speech in June 1864, he came out in favor of black suffrage in the North as well as in the South.[4]

The Unitarian abolitionist Reverend Samuel J. May urged the New York legislator Andrew White to secure all rights for blacks in the state of New York. "It is folly to attempt to defer what is inevitable, and what is necessary to the perfect peace of our Republic and the entire success of the grand political experiment the Father of all men, has given us. . . . to show the world that *all* men, not white men alone . . . are capable of governing themselves and each other." Wendell Phillips took the lead in trying to enlist the American Anti-Slavery Society in the movement for black suffrage. During the anniversary meeting of the society in May 1863, Phillips called on the society to support the franchise for blacks: "Give the Negro a vote in his hand, and there is not a politician from Abraham Lincoln down to the laziest loafer in the lowest ward of this city, who would not do him honor." By February 1864, Phillips had completed a lecture on a plea for black suffrage which he had prepared for his lecture circuit. In May he pushed the Frémont party convention to join him by advocating suffrage as broad "as possible to whites and blacks" on equal terms.[5]

Some radical Christians were anxious to bring black suffrage forward as a political issue in 1864, but the conservative Republicans were determined to beat the proposal down. James Doolittle met the issue by opposing suffrage for blacks in a speech. Henry Raymond, editor of the *New York Times*, accommodated him by giving his address favorable coverage. Raymond was amazed to see the radicals mounting a contest on black suffrage which would "distract the public mind and divide loyal men." Joseph Medill of the *Chicago Tribune* advised R.H. Oglesby, who was contemplating the race for governor of Illinois, not to "let down an hairs breadth on the 'nigger question,' " but to keep quiet on the question of black suffrage. In Kansas the governor recommended striking out the word "white" in the constitution so that blacks could vote, and many radical missionaries were disappointed when a black suffrage amendment bill lost in the lower house of the legislature. In Montana, a Negro suffrage provision passed in the Senate when it was incorporated in the bill establishing a territorial government but was struck out in the lower house.[6] When the state and national platforms were drawn up, not a single platform proposed black suffrage, and no state submitted a referendum on black suffrage to the people. The radical Baptist minister Samuel Aaron expressed the sentiments of many of his kind when he wrote to a friend that his mind was not clear as to what he would do in the coming election because "both platforms ignored the franchise of the negro," but he firmly believed the nation could never have permanent peace or prosperity until it rendered "equal and impartial justice to all honest men."[7]

In June 1864 the Progressive Friends called upon all the states that disfranchised blacks to amend their constitutions to remove such proscriptions. The Western Yearly Meeting of Friends asked the Indiana General Assembly to repeal all laws which deprived blacks of their "natural rights." Quakers generally classed suffrage as a natural right. Early in 1865 the western yearly meeting was more specific; it called on Indiana to remove the prohibition against Negro suffrage from its laws and constitutions. When the religious bodies convened in the fall of 1864, the Baptist associations took the lead in calling for equal rights for blacks. The Wachusetts Baptist Association of Massachusetts believed that blacks should have "a right to a full investiture of the privileges of the free citizen."[8]

While the abolitionist were debating whether the Anti-Slavery Society would take a stand on making blacks voters, some radical clergy were leading the way with sermons advocating that blacks be granted impartial suffrage. Williard Spaulding, a Universalist clergyman of Salem, Massachusetts, preached a sermon entitled "How Shall We Escape?" in May 1864, in which he advocated complete equality before the law and granting blacks the right to vote. Thanksgiving Day brought a great number of radical sermons, most of which focused on the abolition of slavery. Phillips Brooks, pastor of the Episcopal Holy Trinity Church in Philadelphia, delivered a sermon advocating the enfranchisement of blacks. He told his congregation that freedom must be universal: the blacks should be treated as men and should share the ballot on equal terms with whites. Brooks, who expressed his sentiments without hesitation, said that he was placing his audience "face to face with its Christian duty." He wrote his father concerning his sermon, "It is what some people call politics" but "what I call National Morals." When his father warned him, "Don't go too far," he agreed that his sermon was radical but noted that it was also Christian. A correspondent to the *Independent* who had heard the sermon reported that Brooks "pleaded satirically, pathetically, solemnly for negro suffrage" and "rebuked the church for her shortcomings in refusing to uphold an unpopular cause." The correspondent called the discourse "as logical as it was bold, and profoundly religious."[9]

In a New York sermon in Boston, Gilbert Haven, a Methodist radical minister, also took the position that black suffrage was essential to the true believer in democracy as well as Christianity. In January 1865, Henry Ward Beecher gave a lecture in Music Hall in Boston in which he insisted that the doctrine of human rights was universal and that therefore the right of blacks to suffrage was a God-given natural right, but citizens should not expect legislation to have a moral influence. The North should work to conciliate the South, Beecher counseled, and the section would see the benefit of granting black rights. He brought the same message to his Plymouth Church congregation a few days later. Beecher favored universal amnesty along with impartial suffrage. Reverend Granville Moody spoke before a soldiers' reunion in Ohio early in 1865 and insisted that the blacks should "be elevated to their God-given rights," which included enfranchisement.[10] Reverend Henry Garnett lost no opportunity to advance the cause of black suffrage. In February, William Channing, the chaplain of the House of Representatives, invited Garnett, a black Presbyterian minister, to speak in the hall. Garnett called on Congress to amend the Constitution so that every form of slavery would be eradicated and every American would be enfranchised.[11]

The radical Christians in New England focused on an amendment to the federal constitution granting universal or impartial suffrage primarily because all the New England states except Connecticut granted black suffrage. Sumner would not listen to proposals to amend state constitutions. He wanted a federal measure. A massive universal suffrage meeting was held in Faneuil Hall in June. The list of those who signed the call of the meeting resembled a roster of interdenominational Christians. The convention was read a letter from Governor Andrew in which he asserted that as a radical he believed in suffrage for all men but that he was glad the blacks were not voters in the South. He was certain the experiment undertaken by the executive would fail, and he was thankful that the blacks were not involved in the catastrophe. Henry Ward Beecher spoke in defense of universal suffrage as a natural right. He insisted that suffrage without distinction as to color was "the only rule of safety." He ridiculed the proposal that blacks be required to read and write before they could vote. The meeting drew up an address urging the people to make suffrage impartial.[12]

Despite the fact that blacks could vote in New England, the clergy brought sermons to their congregations in support of black suffrage. Dr. Seth Sweetser of the Central Congregational Church told his church members, "We shall need all the squadrons of freedom to perpetuate our liberties."[13] George Stearns was the chief promoter of efforts in New England to secure black suffrage. In the summer of 1865 he organized a project to distribute literature on Negro suffrage. Stearns organized the Universal and Equal Rights Association to promote the rights of blacks. He took the lead in organizing the Faneuil Hall meeting of June 21, 1865. Stearns also founded the *Nation*, of which Edwin Godkin was editor, and subsidized antislavery newspapers outside New England.[14]

Radical Christians who considered suffrage a natural right demanded universal suffrage for blacks, but many Christians were willing to settle for a system of voting that did not discriminate. Most Northern Baptists were more prone to argue for universal suffrage, but nearly all Northern Methodists came down on the side of impartial suffrage.[15] Congregationalists and Presbyterians were fairly evenly divided on the issue. Rev. I.N. Tarbox, a Boston Congregationalist, considered suffrage for blacks "a matter of right before God and the law." He warned in a sermon printed in the *New Englander* that to deny blacks the right to vote on grounds of color would be to "invite the Lord again to chastise us." Cheever demanded universal suffrage for blacks. He informed his Church of the Puritans congregation that if the people denied blacks suffrage, "We are a slave republic still."[16]

During the summer of 1865 the topic of black suffrage was one of the chief interests of the sectarian press. The editor of the *Congregationalist* concluded that justice would never be done to the Negro, "nor safety be quite gained for the Republic," until suffrage was made strictly universal without regard to color. The *New York Observer* denied that it opposed withholding suffrage from blacks because of color, but to those who argued against black suffrage on the grounds of ignorance, the *Western Christian Advocate* answered that the blacks had "an unerring instinct for liberty and righteousness."[17] The *Pittsburgh Christian Advocate* warned that "the whole nation would seethe and foam with controversies and dissension no less passionate and dangerous than those springing in former days from slavery itself" if blacks were refused the ballot. With a broad segment of Republicans declaring that the freedmen should be granted a right to vote, the *Northwestern Christian Advocate* proposed to *"let the work begin in the loyal states.* Let Ohio, Indiana, Michigan and Kansas ordain it at once."[18]

Most of the evangelist church bodies that met during the summer of 1865 went on record in favor of black suffrage. Some few limited their interest to the freedmen, but the majority encompassed blacks throughout the nation. The New England Methodist Episcopal Church called for the enfranchisement "of the entire colored race within our borders." The General Conference of Congregational Churches of Massachusetts took a similar action.[19] The American Baptist Home Mission Society unanimously adopted resolutions demanding that blacks be invested with the elective franchise to maintain the peace and prosperity of the nation.[20] Almost all other Baptist associations throughout the North went on record in favor of black suffrage.[21] The New School Presbyterian General Assembly unanimously advocated that blacks should "enjoy the right of suffrage in common with all other men" because justice dictates it.[22] The National Congregational Council held a rare meeting in June 1865 and endorsed the granting of suffrage to all blacks.[23] Many state Congregational associations that met in the summer of 1865 followed the lead of their national council.[24] The

United Presbyterian Church, the United Brethren, and the Reformed Presbyterian Church warned that to oppose black suffrage was to go against the will of God.[25] Although the Church Anti-Slavery Society saw slavery as virtually ended, the society asserted that its mission would not end until the word "white" had been "erased from all state constitutions and statutes of legislation."[26] Late in May, the *New York Tribune* carried an editorial entitled "The American Churches on Negro Suffrage," in which the editor described the transformation that churches had undergone on political and public issues and their unanimity on the question of suffrage for blacks.[27]

A Vermont Congregational minister wrote Gerrit Smith, "I go for the religious element, not only in Negro suffrage but in all human institutions." Most radical Christians who wanted federal measures to secure suffrage for blacks looked to Sumner to lead the way in Congress. Chase encouraged Sumner to take the lead in advocating universal suffrage. A liberal vestryman in a Syracuse Episcopal church wrote to Sumner in defense of the equality of blacks. He asserted that the blacks were "entitled to all the Rights that white men are bound to respect." Frank Ballard, a radical Baptist, told Sumner that the war had been fought almost in vain if black suffrage was not secured. Henry Cheever expressed his opinion to Sumner that unless the nation gave the black man "all the power of the Republic," the nation "shall deserve to sink" into the depths of hell.[28]

While Congress was adjourned during the summer of 1865, Sumner tried to rally support among the radicals of Congress. He wrote to Wade and to Stevens, inquiring what could be done to stop Johnson's course. To Senator Edwin Morgan, he charged that Johnson's discrimination against the blacks was flagrantly unconstitutional and a crime "against common sense, common humanity, and openly against God."[29] In June, Sumner spoke before the municipal authorities of Boston and warned that "the battle for equality" was still pending. "The colored suffrage is not a necessity. . . . The cause may be delayed; but it will not be overborne; for it is the cause of humanity." In September he spoke before the Massachusetts Republican convention and urged the party to work for a change in the U.S. Constitution so that the whole nation would be free of discrimination against color in the exercise of suffrage; the document would then be "a covenant with life and a league with Heaven." Sumner was deluged with letters from Massachusetts citizens in praise of his speech.[30]

During the summer of 1865, Chase went East to spend a good part of the summer. From Rhode Island he wrote to his friend Jacob Schuckers that the coming battle would be about universal suffrage. He urged Schuckers to promote the idea that suffrage was the right of every man. In late July the chief justice arranged a meeting with George Stearns and others to suggest measures that would "influence public opinion on Negro Suffrage." Early in August he met for the same purpose with Edward W. Hooper of the New England Freedmen's Union and others. While in New England he spoke at the Dartmouth commencement and limited his comments to advocating suffrage for the freedmen.[31]

The sermons in favor of black suffrage increased during the latter part of 1865, but most of them were limited to suffrage for the freedmen. Samuel Johnson, the radical Unitarian clergyman of Lynn, Massachusetts, advised his congregation, "From every tongue let it be uttered . . . , and from every pulpit . . . let it be spoken, [that] it is not the will of this Republic to end the glorious struggle of Liberty with a new outrage on the poor." The Congregational clergyman Jacob Manning was just as outspoken. Manning spoke on July 4 in Boston and charged that it was inconsistent to demand suffrage for the freedmen simply because the people of the South had been in rebellion while denying it to blacks in the so-called free states. On August 1 in East Abington, Massachusetts, at a West Indies emancipation celebration, Sereno Howe, a Baptist clergyman, concluded his address by saying: "There is just this about it; either the negro is a voter, or the country is a used up concern."[32]

Since Congress did not meet until December 1865, attention was focused on the Northern states where state legislators were meeting and state elections were being held in 1865. The radicals planned to make black suffrage a leading issue in Northern states that did not permit Negroes to vote. In Ohio two radicals were the leading contenders for the Republican nomination for governor. Samuel Galloway, a Presbyterian elder, had advocated Negro equality when he campaigned for Lincoln in 1864.[33] Jacob Cox, the other Republican candidate for governor, was a graduate of Oberlin and the son-in-law of Reverend Charles Finney. While a divinity student, he abandoned a ministerial career to study law. Cox regularly attended the Episcopal church services but never became a member.[34] Galloway withdrew from the contest in June and left Cox as the only serious contender. In the county conventions the question of black suffrage occupied a prominent place in the northern part of the state. The Western Reserve conventions strongly endorsed black suffrage as an objective for the Republican party of Ohio, and the more conservative southern counties were silent on the issue.[35]

In May, Cox's radical friends in Oberlin wrote to him in favor of changing the Ohio constitution to permit black suffrage and asked him where he stood on the issue. Cox answered that he was opposed to any effort to change the Ohio constitution and opposed black suffrage in the South as well. Cox informed Garfield that he favored leaving the question open until Congress met. "If our extreme radicals are determined to make a fight with me on this question, they will find it the most complete specimen of 'cutting off the nose to spite the face,' " he wrote.[36] The Democrats were aware that the Republicans were divided on the issue, and they held a secret meeting in Cincinnati to plan their strategy to profit by the division. In June before the Republican state convention met, the *Cincinnati Enquirer* announced, "The split in the Republican Party promises to be complete. The question of negro suffrage is the wedge."[37]

The conservative and moderate Republicans, and some radicals, saw the danger of a radical platform and planned a strategy of silence on the suffrage question. Advocates of the silence tactic controlled the platform committee and applied their silent treatment to the suffrage question. William Dickinson, chairman of the committee and an advocate of black suffrage, later declared that the majority expected to see Negro suffrage adopted in the future and refrained from any expression of opinion in the interest of harmony.[38] On June 21, William Coggeshall wrote in his diary: "Negro suffrage yielded. I worked to keep it out of the platform," but on June 29, he revealed that on principle he was on the other side. "On principle I fully agree with 'Rads,' color as a basis of suffrage is absurd but a party in Ohio that would commit itself to Negro suffrage would inevitably be defeated." In June, after the Republican convention, Dickinson tried to persuade Cox to make black suffrage an issue.[39]

Late in July a convention met in Oberlin and adopted resolutions to support only men who would use their power to erase from the Ohio constitution the word "white." A committee was appointed to query Cox on the subject of black suffrage. The committee, composed of two of the leading Congregational laymen, addressed a letter to the candidate asking whether he favored black suffrage, but Cox maintained that he backed Johnson's policy because only by this policy could peace and harmony be maintained.[40] Garfield joined those who favored blacks when he spoke at Ravenna, Ohio, on July 4. "In the great crisis of the war, God brought us face to face with the mighty truth. . . . The omniscient witness will appear in judgment against us if we do not fulfill that covenant," he warned. Ten days later Garfield wrote to Cox that he saw no way of settling the vexing problem without giving at least the intelligent blacks the ballot. He sent Cox a paper detailing his position and expressing the opinion that the party could carry the state on black suffrage.[41] On August 15, at Warren, Ohio, at a Republican campaign meeting, Garfield clashed with the Republican candidate and spoke in favor of Negro suffrage.[42] Two days later Cox spoke in Oberlin, and an old black man asked him whether, if he was elected, he would favor an amendment to the constitution of Ohio permitting blacks to vote. He answered that if the matter had to be determined by each state for itself and the South for itself, he would favor the full application of the rights of man in Ohio.[43] The editor of the *Cincinnati Herald and Presbyterian Recorder* criticized Cox for characterizing impartial suffrage as a permanent fusion and amalgamation of the races and insisted that it involved only the political equality of American citizens as set forth in our organic laws. The *Independent* protested Cox's "harsh, pagan" philosophy and added that it was a shame to Christianity that he "should call himself a Christian."[44]

Samuel Plumb and the Western Reserve leaders of the movement to change the Ohio constitution decided the most effective course was to elect radicals to the legislature who would affirm their principles in the local conventions. The local conventions in the Western Reserve held firmly to their principles. The Jefferson County Union Convention repudiated Cox's sentiments and supported an amendment to the state constitution erasing the distinction as to color. The Mahoning Union Convention instructed its legislators to amend the constitution by striking the word "white" from the document. The Western Reserve Synod of the Presbyterian Church called upon the government to confer on blacks every right "which we ourselves possess."[45]

The Republican-controlled legislatures of Minnesota and Wisconsin placed black suffrage on the ballot for the fall elections. The Republican state convention in Minnesota endorsed the proposal. In Minnesota the question was largely an abstract principle, because few blacks lived in the state. The Presbyterian Synod of Minnesota resolved that its members would "fearlessly contend" for the right of black suffrage and denounced any government that deprived a man of suffrage because of color as "rendered unfit for perpetuity and unworthy of the blessing of Almighty God." The proposal lost in Minnesota, but the *St. Paul Press*, the leading journal in the state, acknowledged the clergy's efforts in impressing upon the congregations "their accountability for the use of the ballot."[46]

From Beloit, Wisconsin, a Congregational professor informed the secretary of the AMA that "a great moral warfare" remains to enfranchise the blacks, and conservatism was far from being eliminated even from the church. On July 4, Charles G. Williams, a Methodist layman and later a U.S. congressman, delivered an address on black suffrage in which he warned the people against the danger of a government's "toying with a powder magazine in one hand and the forked lightings of God's wrath" in the other. In Racine, Wisconsin, the Baptist minister of Senator Doolittle's church preached in favor of black suffrage and lamented that a cause of God should set members of the same church against each other and the pastor. Deacon Samuel D. Hastings, an antislavery Congregationalist and the Wisconsin state treasurer, published a strong letter in favor of Negro suffrage. In a July 4 address, Hastings informed a patriotic gathering that if his listeners failed to give the blacks their rights, as sure as there was "a God in Heaven and the truth in His word, He will hold us accountable for our conduct and punish us for our iniquity."[47]

Early in September, the Wisconsin Republican Convention met. A referendum on black suffrage was the chief topic on the agenda. The subject was considered by a committee, and Senator Doolittle, reporting for the majority, advised the convention to oppose black suffrage. A radical Congregational layman, James Paine, reporting for the minority, asked the convention to back black suffrage. Although the majority of the assembly probably favored suffrage for blacks, the convention, which was largely controlled by Doolittle, refused to endorse the minority position. Supporters of black suffrage called another convention to endorse it. When the convention met, it resembled a lay meeting of an interfaith religious gathering. H.E., J.H., and Byron Paine, Sherman Booth, Amasa Cobbs, C.C. Sholes, T.O. Howe, and Samuel Hastings were there. No one spoke against black suffrage. Congressman H.E. Paine asked the convention to endorse what "the great Creator originally" had given the blacks. Congressman Howe urged the convention to do justice to the blacks at the convention and the representatives in Congress would feel stronger. The radical convention called on the people of Wisconsin to give the blacks the ballot.[48]

Several church associations held their convention in September and October of 1865 in Wisconsin. The obligations of the Christian citizen were a prominent topic of discussion. The Wisconsin Methodist Conference, the Monroe Baptist Association, and the Presbyterian and Congregational Convention instructed their communicants that it was a religious duty to grant Wisconsin blacks the right of suffrage. Late in October the *Ripon Commonwealth* ran an editorial on impartial suffrage. In the imminent election, the editor asserted, the people of Wisconsin would determine, by their votes, whether Wisconsin was truly a Christian state.[49] The people of Wisconsin rejected black suffrage in the referendum, but the state supreme court ordered black suffrage in a decision handed down in 1866 based on a referendum in 1849.[50]

The Equal Rights League petitioned the Pennsylvania legislature to grant black suffrage in March 1865, but the petition received no serious consideration. The Abington and the Centre Baptist associations of Pennsylvania warned citizens, lawmakers, and magistrates that they would invoke the displeasure of God by denying suffrage to blacks. Some radical Christians felt that black suffrage should be secured through federal action rather than state referendums, and they placed their grievance before Johnson. A Lutheran layman of Pennsylvania wrote to Johnson that blacks should enjoy suffrage because it was their natural right. Another radical Christian warned the president that the failure to grant blacks political rights was an ingratitude God would "never let go unpunished." When the Republican convention met in Pennsylvania in 1865, Thaddeus Stevens could not control the action of the convention, which bypassed black suffrage as "heavy and premature" in the face of the current state of prejudice. Stevens complained to Sumner that he had failed to rally the convention on the question. "I fear we are ruined," he lamented.[51]

The territory of Colorado voted down a referendum to enfranchise blacks, and in conservative New Jersey a black suffrage resolution was decisively defeated in the Republican party convention of 1865. In Indiana Governor Oliver Morton opposed black suffrage by federal or state action in several speeches. George Julian was the only significant political figure to challenge him. In November, Julian spoke before the state legislature, assembled in special session, and took issue with Morton. Joseph F. Duckwall, editor of the *Delaware Free Press* of Muncie, Indiana, kept the subject of black suffrage before his readers and called the opposition to black suffrage a crime against the colored man crying out "to Heaven in condemnation of the American people." Duckwell was a member of the Methodist Episcopal Church and was regarded as "a conscientious Christian gentleman."[52]

The Iowa Republican State Committee adopted a resolution in favor of black suffrage. The *Independent* applauded Iowa as "a noble state" that was willing "to make a struggle to blot the word *white* from her constitution." Tilton advised other states to do likewise, because the "great argument in the mouths of the opposers of Negro suffrage at the South is, 'You don't permit Negro suffrage at the North.' " In a letter to an opponent of black suffrage, Chester C. Cole, a judge of the Supreme Court of Iowa and a Presbyterian, explained "that in giving the right of suffrage to the negro we obey God's Right— His Eternal Justice." An Iowa citizen informed Johnson that Iowa would be "recognizing and affirming the equality of all men before the law" by taking the word "white" from the Iowa constitution. The Iowa Quakers supported the proposed change in state constitution and earnestly solicited Johnson's support of "equal enfranchisement for all." In September the Upper Iowa and the Des Moines conferences of the Methodist Episcopal Church came out in favor of universal suffrage without regard to color.[53]

In Michigan black suffrage did not become a topic of popular discussion in 1865, although Austin Blair brought it before a July 4 audience in Hudson, Michigan. He told his audience that the nation now stood on holy grounds, but suffrage should be given to blacks because the rights of all men were sacred. When the Michigan Conference of the Methodist Episcopal Church met in September, it recommended that all residents seek an amendment to the Michigan constitution removing the word "white."[54]

The New York constitution discriminated against blacks by imposing an extra residential restriction and a two-hundred-dollar freehold restriction. The Republican party in New York voted down a plank in favor of equal suffrage and avoided the issue when it met in convention. Tilton informed his readers that "New York still blushes at the injustice of her constitution toward the black man."[55] The Baptists took the forefront in New York. The associations of Hudson River, New York, Black River, Buffalo, Franklin, and Broome and Tioga Baptist, as well as the Eastern Association of the Seventh Day Baptists, adopted resolutions favoring equal suffrage.[56]

John Jay, an Episcopal abolitionist, spoke before the inaugural meeting of the American Freeman's Aid Union and asserted that the same Providential hand that had guided the nation through the war would give equal rights to blacks even though malignant politicians stood in the way. Benson Lossing, a radical lawyer and Episcopal vestryman in Christ Church, Poughkeepsie, New York, was also sure Providence would intervene in the matter. He wrote to Henry Wilson that black suffrage was a state affair. Although he felt it was a privilege designed by Providence, he advised patience, but Reverend William Goodell criticized those who counseled patience. "God's time to do justice is the present time," he insisted. He promoted his commitment to black suffrage with a sermon on "The Right of Suffrage and the Duty of Voting." In a sermon in the Church of the Puritans, George Cheever told his listeners that they must give justice to the blacks. If they did not, "God will destroy us," he warned.[57]

Governor William Buckingham of Connecticut, a Congregational church deacon and president of the AMA, asked his legislature to grant the boon of suffrage that had so long been withheld from Connecticut blacks. The Connecticut Republicans were optimistic that suffrage would be granted to blacks. Professor Cyrus Northrop of Yale wrote the editor of the *New Haven Palladium* that prejudice had been softened in the state. He predicted that Negro suffrage would carry by two-thirds of the votes cast in the election. When the proposal was introduced in the legislature, one of the legislators said he believed the bill would end a disease of the body politic that had proved so destructive to the moral and religious character of the nation.[58]

After the black suffrage measure passed the Connecticut legislature, the Republican central committee issued an address to the electorate, urging it to approve the amendment. The mayor of Norwich urged Governor Andrew of Massachusetts to speak in the state of Connecticut in support of black suffrage because a victory there would carry a great weight in influencing the question in all other states. The *Hartford Press*, one of the leading Republican journals in the state, supported the amendment of the state constitution, but most Republican journals as well as the Republican party showed a lack of enthusiasm. Joseph H. Hawley, the publisher of the *Hartford Press*, and his early law partner, William Faxon, a Congregational layman, had been in the antislavery movement since the Free Soil days. Hawley's father, Francis, an antislavery Congregationalist minister, took an active part in promoting black suffrage during 1865.[59] Joseph Hawley's wife was a Congregationalist and Hawley worshiped in that church, although he did not become a member until later. Hawley was deeply religious and regularly preached to his troops while he was an officer in the Union army. Hawley was a political associate and met regularly with a small group of radical Christians that included Francis Gillette, an antislavery Unitarian; John Hooker, an antislavery Congregationalist; Thomas D. Fisher; and Charles D. Warner, Hawley's assistant editor and a leading Congregational layman. Many of them resided at Nook Farm in Hartford, where the discussion of slavery and religion occupied a large part of their time. The group represented the most dedicated faction of the Republican party that was committed to black suffrage.[60]

Reverend G.B. Willcox addressed a public letter to the voters of Connecticut in the *Independent*: "Men and brothers! This is no mere political issue, but a question of moral right. The unseen Christ will stand by the ballot-box watching every vote you deposit." The General Association of Congregational Churches of Connecticut declared that the black race should "be released from all political disabilities" and be granted "the responsibility and privileges of electors" by the several states because of the loyalty of the race during the war. All other religious bodies in the state appeared to be silent on the referendum in Connecticut. Leonard Bacon and other powerful religious leaders in the state remained silent. The publisher of the *Independent*, Henry Bowen, asked Reverend Leonard Bacon to write an article for the *Independent* on the black suffrage referendum. Bacon failed to write the article. Two radical Christians from Pennsylvania wrote Bacon, condemning him for not lending his support to the black suffrage cause.[61]

The editor of the *New York Times* predicted that if black suffrage was defeated in Connecticut, "the moral effect" would be dreadful. The editor of the *Independent* asserted that the election would decide whether religion meant anything. "We appeal to the Christianity of the state . . . to vote on the side of religion and good morals against Paganism and the spirit of slavery," Tilton implored the voters of Connecticut. The question of universal suffrage throughout the country would be largely affected by the decision of Connecticut, Tilton wrote. A correspondent to the *Christian Advocate and Journal* called on Connecticut to lead the nation on the path of righteousness. "Let her not falter. . . . Her refusal to follow the clearest call to duty will put back the cause everywhere. If she obeys this call New York will soon wheel into line; the whole land will follow her lead," he prophesied.[62]

The Connecticut voters rejected the constitutional amendment. The editor of the *Liberator* called the results of the referendum the greatest catastrophe since the assassination of Lincoln. The editor of the *Commonwealth* described the election as "an unworthy, unmanly and discreditable act. . . . We feel humiliated and ashamed." He accused the Republican committee of doing nothing after issuing an address, not even sending one speaker into the field. He charged that Connecticut had stormed Boston begging for election funds to carry every contemptible office in the past, but in this election, where the destiny of the continent was in question, not a cent had been requested. The editor of the *Independent* reminded the Republican party that almost every great representative religious body that had met last Spring had

"voted overwhelmingly in favor of the enfranchisement of the Negro. . . . The Republican party will seek in vain to blot out this Christian record."[63]

The *Boston Transcript* believed that Connecticut had "not only
disgraced herself, but deeply injured the cause of the country." The
editor of the *New Haven Palladium* explained to the disappointed
religious radicals that God "brings all base purposes to naught." A
citizen of New York wrote to Governor Andrew, "The vote on the
colored suffrage question in that 'land of steady habits,' [Connecticut]
is a damper to our people." Reverend Francis Hawley wrote to his son,
"The rebels in Conn. are to be killed . . . not with bullets but with the
weapons of a moral warfare and you know how to do that as well as
you know how to command a regt." Hawley's *Hartford Press* explained
to its readers: "Having got through the war by the grace of God, Connecticut has turned again to the worship of the golden calf." Mark
Howard, a radical Republican friend of Hawley, was more optimistic.
He wrote a correspondent in Charleston, South Carolina, that the contest of 1865 in Connecticut had "done much to purify our politics and
to strengthen us for the future. Let your colored citizens take heart—
for they have an invincible host behind them which is determined that
no man shall be denied an equality before the law."[64]

A correspondent for the *Christian Advocate and Journal* wrote to
the editor that "Connecticut ought to have been a flame of fire . . . ,
the best speakers in the land ought to have lifted the people by their
fervor and their breadth of soul, . . . the ministers should have made
their pulpits ring. . . . Silence in this case was far from golden." During
the week after the election, the Old Colony Baptist Association of
Massachusetts lamented, "We have heard with sorrow and a blush of
shame of the results of the late ballot in Connecticut." Most observers
blamed the loss of the election on a lack of enthusiasm on the part of
the Republicans and the incitement of prejudice by the Democrats,
but the conservative Presbyterian *New York Observer* explained, "The
sober second thought of the American people is that we have already
carried the doctrine of popular suffrage too far."[65]

The usually optimistic Horace White of the *Chicago Tribune* wrote
to William Fessenden after the Connecticut election, "It is useless for
us to hope for Negro suffrage now." White expressed the sentiment of
many Republicans and not a few radicals. The defeat of the Connecticut
amendment was a victory for the position that Johnson was taking,
and the election jeopardized the program the radicals were promoting.
Mansfield French, the radical Methodist minister from the Cincinnati

Conference, wrote to Oliver Howard, "Our freedmen in their upward march to the high table lands of universal freedom have already been told by Connecticut and Wisconsin, you cannot pass by the way of our ballot boxes!! . . . Thus will their journey be prolonged."[66]

In 1867 the editor of the *Commonwealth* explained why the elections in 1865 and 1867 had been lost. The Republicans of Connecticut had not furnished leadership for the effort to secure black suffrage in their state. The address by the Republican state committee was issued "for appearance's sake; but . . . nothing more was done. They did not desire their advice should be followed." The *Commonwealth* complained that Republicans elsewhere had been surprised by the apathy in Connecticut and had offered to organize a campaign, secure speakers, and pay for the expense, but the offer had been declined. Not a meeting was held, nor a speech was made, nor a dollar expended "to secure suffrage for blacks," lamented the editor. After the second defeat of black suffrage and the defeat of Governor Hawley in 1867, a correspondent to the *Commonwealth* blamed the defeat of black suffrage in 1865 and 1867 on the churches. Although there were exceptions among the clergy and some churches that spoke for justice, most of the churches of all denominations were "bond-slaves of the copperhead party." The correspondent explained that the churches in Connecticut were held in vasselage by Copperheads who were not church members but who aided in supporting the church, held the balance of power, forced the church to yield to their political views by threatening to secede from the church, and thus managed to control the pulpit. A clergyman responded the next week that he had spoken for black suffrage and consequently found it necessary to leave the state.[67]

Benedict was correct in believing that the death blow to an early national campaign for Negro suffrage came from the loss of black suffrage in the Connecticut election.[68] The moderates and many Radical Republicans reasoned·that if black suffrage could not carry in a New England state, the people in the nation at large would not support it. When black suffrage referendums lost in all states in which they were considered, all political enthusiasm evaporated, and energetic efforts came to an end to secure black suffrage by an amendment to the federal Constitution. The Christian radicals, however, did not give up. The Congregational *Boston Recorder*, the *Universalist Quarterly*, and the *Christian Register* carried strong editorials in favor of impartial suffrage for the whole nation during the fall of 1865. The Pennsylvania Equal Rights League was busy collecting petitions for universal suffrage, which were sent to Stevens in December 1865.[69]

# CHAPTER ELEVEN

# The Black Suffrage Referenda of 1867

The enthusiasm that was shown by Christians for suffrage early in 1865 was checked after Negro suffrage had been voted down in five referenda in that year. Church members made up less than one-fourth of the population of the country in the 1860s, and the radical Christians could not persuade all the members to follow their lead in 1865. But radical Christians outside political circles still demanded the elimination of color restrictions. In January 1866, the newly organized National Equal Suffrage Association met and called for impartial suffrage. The association was addressed by Albert G. Riddle, a Radical Republican from the Western Reserve. He expressed the opinion that self-government was a natural right and that the elective franchise should be conferred upon all men without regard to color.[1] The spirits of the radicals were lifted by the adoption of black suffrage in the District of Columbia by Congress in January 1866.[2]

During the summer of 1866 the Iowa Republican party adopted a resolution that "the first and highest duty" of the government was to give all people without regard to color or race an equal voice in making the laws.[3] But the legislature had already adjourned for the year. In Michigan, the legislature submitted the question of revising the state constitution to the voters in 1866, as required by the constitution of 1850, and the voters endorsed the proposal for a new constitution. The delegates were elected in April 1867 and were assembled in May. A new constitution was drawn up that provided for black suffrage by omitting the word "white" from the document. The new constitution would not be submitted to the people until April 1868. But the radical Christians took up the work of preparing for the triumph of the suffrage question. Nathan M. Thomas, a Quaker, was one of the most active. Thomas and Dr. S.B. Thayer were seriously organizing their campaign for black suffrage by December 1867.[4] The religious associations continued to be committed to black suffrage as a religious duty. For example, the Walworth Baptist Association, to which Doolittle belonged, declared that "justice and sound policy" demanded that "the right of suffrage be speedily granted" blacks throughout the country.[5] Sermons continued to be preached on the duty of giving blacks the right of suffrage.[6]

But the members of the joint committee in Congress had decided to forgo the effort to secure impartial suffrage in 1866. Jacob Howard presented the committee's report in May 1866 and announced that it was the committee's opinion that "three-fourths of the states of this Union could not be induced to vote to grant the right of suffrage, even in any degree or under any restriction, to the colored race."[7] Gilbert Haven, editor of *Zion's Herald*, was sad because the Republican party had evaded the direct issue of impartial suffrage and because it was trying to reconstruct the Union on a foundation that lacked "the cornerstone of equal justice to all." He predicted that if the blacks were not granted equal justice, another plague would be visited on the nation worse than the war it had just passed through. Impartial suffrage "is as much a moral and religious, as a political question," Haven reminded the faithful.[8]

The success of the Republicans in the election of 1866 gave the radicals a new optimism despite the fact that the victories had nothing to do with black suffrage. Tilton felt that public opinion was favorable to black suffrage in 1867, especially west of the Mississippi River. He was sure that a legislature such as the one which had disgraced Ohio in 1866 could not have been elected in Iowa or Minnesota.[9] There was reason for Tilton's optimism, because Republican platforms endorsed equal suffrage in all but two Northern states in 1867. Others had caught the wave of optimism. The National Equal Rights League, which consisted primarily of black citizens, met in Washington in January 1867 and petitioned Congress to provide for impartial suffrage.[10]

In Connecticut, Governor Joseph Hawley took high ground in his race for reelection. When he came out in favor of black suffrage, he received pamphlet material from Massachusetts to aid him in shaping electoral opinion. Tilton spoke in Connecticut in March for Hawley and black suffrage. He informed his audience that the Republicans deserved to lose the election because they had voted against suffrage in 1865. Back at his editorial desk the next week, he asserted that a loss of the election of 1867 in Connecticut would have serious consequences. "If Connecticut shall vote the wrong way . . . , she will reincite Andrew Johnson to further usurpation, and reanimate the Rebellion to further defiance," he warned. Some Connecticut radical Christians saw the significance of the Connecticut election of 1867

and feared that they would suffer defeat. Charles Johnson, a radical and
a charter member of the Park Congregational Church, Norwich, Connecticut, informed George Cheever that the Copperheads in Connecticut were very confident. He was afraid they would be victorious in the
election.[11]

Tilton's greatest fears came to pass when in April a Democrat was
elected governor of Connecticut. In an editorial entitled "O Backsliding
Connecticut!" Tilton charged that the election was poetic justice; the
Connecticut Republicans were suffering the dishonor that they had
brought upon themselves two years ago. Tilton also quoted Hawley:
"the curse of the Republican Party" in Connecticut was that it had
permitted men to act as its leaders who cared only for offices and "not
for its principles." The Baptist *Watchman and Reflector* explained the
loss of the Connecticut election by saying that the Republicans had
been beaten because they took their stand in favor of the doctrine of
equal suffrage. The two thousand Negroes who would have been enfranchised in 1865 would have turned the scale in the recent election
if the Republicans had exerted themselves two years ago. Although the
Republican leadership in Connecticut had not backed black suffrage
in 1865, it did so in 1867. Gilbert Haven condemned the rejection of
black suffrage as a wicked act, but he commended the political leaders
who had supported it. "Better a thousand fold be defeated with impartial suffrage in the platform than be victorious without it," he insisted.[12]

Aaron Powell, the Quaker editor of the *National Anti-Slavery Standard*, asserted that "the stupid narrow-minded 'Conservatives' of the
Republican fold" had given the Negro one more kick and had bitten
off their own noses. Connecticut Republicans did not have the boldness
to avow and defend great principles and had "not informed or trained
the public conscience," Reverend John Gulliver, a Congregational
clergyman, wrote to Tilton. The Washington correspondent to the *Independent* also told the editor, "Everybody will excuse the President
for excessive delight, for it is the first crumb of comfort he has had
since he turned traitor." Most conservatives were willing to forget
politics for a moment and rejoice, but Gideon Welles, the secretary of
the navy, was concerned about the determination of the radical Christians. On May 2, he wrote in his diary: "The Radicals of Connecticut
are narrow-minded party men of Puritanic Calvinistic notions in politics and religion, intolerant and prejudiced in their opinions. . . . These
fanatics want God to punish, not love, those who do not agree with
them."[13]

Tilton returned to the discussion of black suffrage the week after his Connecticut editorial. "Fellow countrymen, it ought to bring a blush to every white cheek in the loyal North to reflect that the political equality . . . is likely to be sooner achieved in Mississippi than in Illinois. . . . The states that now need reconstruction are the Northern." Sumner wrote to Tilton that since he wanted the North reconstructed he should cease advocating an amendment to secure his objective and hasten to support enfranchisement of the blacks by legislative act because enfranchisement was a corollary to the Thirteenth Amendment. The editor of the *Liberal Christian* echoed Tilton's sentiments. "The States which most need reconstructing now lie North of Mason Dixon's line. Every state that refused to erase the word 'white' must look for the fate of Connecticut," he wrote.[14]

Reverend Francis Hawley encouraged his son Joseph to persist in his efforts to secure black suffrage in the state. He wrote to Governor Hawley, "God . . . had raised you up" for a moral purpose. "I dedicated you to the Gospel ministry but God has answered my prayer by giving you an Editorial chair and . . . as a legislator and a civil ruler . . . for the cause of Christianity and Christian civilization." A Christian radical assured Joseph Hawley that as matters now stood, the Republicans in Connecticut would exert themselves to secure the ballot for blacks. Another radical Christian informed Hawley that he fully believed God would overrule the decision of the people in the Nutmeg State for the good of man. Horace Greeley looked on the results of the Connecticut election as very gloomy. He wrote Joseph Hawley a letter assessing the effects of the election in Connecticut. Greeley concluded that the cowardice of the state in not granting impartial suffrage had postponed Reconstruction a full year.[15]

As a result of the Connecticut election, a correspondent to the *Congregationalist* argued for an amendment to the federal Constitution. The conservative Congregationalist Leonard Bacon answered the correspondent in the *New York Times*. "For my part," wrote Bacon, "much as I desire to see our black citizens sharing equally with whites in all political as well as civil rights, I am not willing to give up that palladium of liberty of the State for the sake of gaining even so desirable an object." Thus one of the most powerful and prestigious Congregational clergyman in Connecticut was opposed to suffrage for blacks in Connecticut by an amendment to the federal Constitution, but he had made no effort to secure a change in the Connecticut constitution to grant black suffrage.[16]

In Iowa, after much hesitation, the legislature passed a constitutional amendment that could not be ratified by the voters until 1868. When the Iowa and the Upper Iowa Methodist Episcopal conferences met in 1867, they went on record in favor of impartial suffrage as a natural right that should be granted to all citizens.[17] The radicals of Minnesota were also working for black suffrage in 1867. They scheduled a lecture on equal rights by Tilton in St. Paul in January 1867. The Minnesota conservatives tried to persuade Tilton to change his topic to literature. When he refused to lecture unless he could speak on the radical program, he had his way. The Minnesota legislature put impartial suffrage on the ballot, but the Democrats met in convention and opposed it. Black suffrage lost in the referendum in this largely Republican state. The *Central Republican* of Minnesota charged that the "weak kneed Republicans" were responsible for the loss.[18]

Early in 1867, the New Jersey legislature received petitions asking that the word "white" be removed from the basic charter, but in April 1867, the lower house of the legislature voted down a provision striking the word "white" from the constitution. The drive for impartial suffrage in New Jersey, however, refused to die. James M. Scovel, the president of the New Jersey senate, took the lead in keeping the issue before the people. Scovel was a Baptist layman who often occupied the pulpit and later became a Baptist evangelist. He spoke at a meeting in Camden, New Jersey, on impartial suffrage and told his listeners that they should forge ahead. "Compromise is the American Devil," he warned the meeting. Scovel issued a circular calling for an impartial suffrage convention to meet early in June.[19]

The refusal to extend suffrage to blacks did not rest easy on the conscience of some Republicans, and a caucus was held at the close of the legislative session. It was decided to call a convention and put the matter before the people, because the popular conviction seemed to be that now was the time to act. When the convention met, Scovel was elected chairman. In his keynote speech he acknowledged that the party regulars were against the Republicans present, "but it is best to be with God and a minority than with the Devil in majority." Reverend Charles H. Thompson, the black moderator of the Presbyterian Presbytery of Newark, was appointed to head a committee of five to address the people on the subject of impartial suffrage. The committee recruited a battery of outstanding speakers, including Governor Marcus Ward, Senator F.T. Frelinghuysen, Joseph Hawley, and Senator Henry Wilson, a Congregational layman. The Republican state central committee finally endorsed the convention.[20]

Governor Marcus Ward, an Episcopal layman, addressed a letter to the Republican central committee and insisted that suffrage should be regarded as the inherent right of all people. When the New Jersey Republican convention met late in July, Senator Frelinghuysen, a Dutch Reformed layman, delivered the most significant speech. "Christianity fostered man's equality. Revelation asserts it. . . . The doctrine of the unity of the race is essential to the maintenance of the true relations to God," he insisted in defense of impartial suffrage. The Republican convention of New Jersey resolved to work for equal suffrage. When the Democratic party convention met, it adopted measures against black suffrage and issued an address to the people in opposition to it.[21] Local free suffrage conventions were held in several towns. One met at Patterson, New Jersey, in August, and the Reverend John Paylor was the featured speaker, but when the New Jersey election was held in November, the Democrats were victorious.[22]

The Pennsylvania legislature discussed equal suffrage in 1867 and set the topic aside as an issue whose time had not come. The *Independent* lamented that the Republican majority had neglected its duty. The editor declared that the Republicans in Pennsylvania had "acted in a base and cowardly manner bringing disgrace upon themselves and their party. Shame on them." The Republicans in the West rebuked the men of the East with their action, wrote Tilton.[23] In spite of the conservative stance of the Pennsylvania Republicans, the Democrats carried the election. Conservative Republican Edgar Cowan, of Pennsylvania, explained the results of the election in 1867 by saying, "After giving ten states to the negroes, to keep the Democrats from getting them, they will lose the rest. . . . Any party with an abolition head and a nigger tail will soon find itself with nothing left but head and tail."[24] Reverend Phillip Brooks saw the election in a different light. "You cannot run principle without men, and there are no prominent men for our principles just now," he wrote to his father.[25]

In New York the voters had approved a new constitutional convention that was to meet in 1867. The *Examiner and Chronicle* urged the Northern states to meet the standard they were imposing on the South. George Cheever wrote to his sister in March 1867 that the radical Christians were beginning to agitate for the righteous claims of blacks in the coming constitutional convention, but many religious men, as usual, were "dead asleep." Cheever was particularly bitter about the opposition at Albany to allowing all blacks to vote in the election to select delegates to the convention. "This is a high-handed outrage," he charged.[26] He spoke on suffrage and the convention at his Church of the Puritans in April. Reverend Samuel J. May urged the people at a meeting in Syracuse to see to it that the new constitution guaranteed equal political rights to blacks and females.[27]

A citizen of Buffalo insisted that some Republicans voted in the convention election for Democratic delegates because they believed the rumors, spread by the Democrats, that a vote for a radical candidate was a vote to elevate Negroes and to disfranchise some whites. Radical citizens sent almost seventy petitions to the convention in favor of equal suffrage.[28] The Republicans controlled the convention. They had enough votes in the convention to put equal suffrage in the constitution, but they chose to adjourn the convention in September and reconvene on November 12, after the election, in order to avoid giving the Democrats an opportunity to make black suffrage a campaign issue. The New York convention removed the property qualification from black suffrage so that equal suffrage was granted to Negroes, but the decision was made to submit the provision to the voters as a separate question rather than to risk seeing the whole constitution voted down because of opposition to the equal suffrage provision. The constitution was completed in February 1868 but was not submitted to the voters until the next election in November 1869. The delay prevented equal suffrage from coming before the electorate during the presidential election of 1868.[29] When the referendum was held in November 1869, the New York voters rejected equal suffrage. The Republicans in the legislature and the Republican delegates in the convention were firmly behind equal suffrage on moral principles. In New York black voters were not sufficient inducement to cause Republicans to support an unpopular cause to secure black votes. Moral concern was a factor in accounting for the Republican commitment in New York and other Northern states.[30]

Since the days of the Kansas-Nebraska controversy, Kansas had been liberally supplied with missionaries. After slavery was abolished, the religious radicals turned their efforts to securing suffrage for blacks in Kansas. The Republican state convention adopted a resolution in favor of removing the word "white" from the Kansas constitution in September 1866. Theodore Tilton lectured in Kansas for black suffrage in November 1866. In his message to the Kansas legislature in January 1867, Governor S.J. Crawford called on the legislature to remove the word "white" from the constitution of the state because the denial of suffrage to blacks was contrary to "the spirit of the laws of God."[31]

The Kansas legislature voted unanimously to remove the restriction on black suffrage from the organic laws of the state and also adopted a resolution to remove the word "male" from the constitution.

The day after the vote was taken on black suffrage, Reverend S.E. MacBurney, a Methodist minister who favored granting the vote to blacks, spoke in the representatives' hall of the legislature and rallied support for the referendum.[32] On April 2, an impartial suffrage convention was held in Topeka, Kansas. Former Governor Charles Robinson, a radical Unitarian, was made president of the convention, and Reverend Lewis Bedwell, a Congregationalist, was elected secretary. Resolutions were passed in support of impartial suffrage, and a mass convention was planned for April 21. The mass convention set up a permanent Impartial Suffrage League with Governor Crawford as president and Samuel Wood, a Quaker legislator, as secretary. The league planned a strategy for supporting both black and female suffrage. Robinson, as one of the executive committee, planned to spend two months in an active canvass for the referenda. The Kansas Congregational Association quickly went on record in support of universal impartial suffrage.[33]

The Republican state committee issued an address supporting black suffrage in Kansas and throughout the Northern states because duty required it and honesty compelled it, since it had been imposed on the South. The committee, however, refused to support woman suffrage.[34] The Impartial Suffrage League brought Reverend Olympia Brown, a Universalist minister, to Kansas from Massachusetts, to canvass the state from July to September in support of both black and female suffrage.[35] In August, Susan B. Anthony and Elizabeth C. Stanton were persuaded to come to Kansas and render support for impartial suffrage. Reverend Parker Pillsbury, Reverend John S. Brown, and Reverend William Starret, as well as Frederick Douglass, C.S. Remond, and S.C. Pomeroy, added their voices to the cause.[36]

Kansas was saturated with speakers for impartial suffrage. Forty-five meetings were held in forty counties at which the featured speakers were Lucy Stone and her husband, Henry Blackwell. The forces for black and female suffrage were strengthened by the addition of the Methodist clergymen of Baker University, Baldwin City, Kansas. President John Horner and Professor Norton lectured for the cause. The radical Calvinist senator Samuel Pomeroy threw himself "boldly and fearlessly into the movement," committing his time and his money. Ministers were among the most active speakers in the movement. Presbyterians, Congregationalists, Baptists, and Methodists were almost unanimous for black suffrage. Religious denominations in Kansas generally supported both black and female enfranchisement from the beginning. At Olathe, Kansas, where the Old School Presbytery was in session when Lucy Stone appeared in town to speak, the presbytery adjourned and allowed her to occupy the church for her lecture.[37]

At the beginning of the campaign to secure impartial suffrage, the Kansas Republican leaders generally favored votes for women, but eventually they began to fear that the issue of female suffrage would prevent the black referendum from passing, and they sought to keep the two questions separate. Some clergymen who worked for suffrage for blacks opposed suffrage for women on the grounds that women should not participate in public life. A grand black suffrage convention held in Atchison, Kansas, at the end of July was dominated by the clergy. The six clergymen who took an active part in the meeting included W.M. Twine, a Presbyterian, and W.K. Marshall, a Methodist.[38] Reverend I.S. Kallach, editor of the Baptist *Home Journal*, who had been sent to Kansas by the Baptist Home Mission Society, and the Methodist Reverend S.E. McBurney were the most active campaigners for black suffrage who opposed female enfranchisement. Reverend D.W. Parker, a Methodist, and Reverend Richard Cordley, a Congregationalist, were very active for black suffrage and voiced some opposition to giving women the vote.[39]

The Republican central committee called a mass meeting on September 5 to defend the proposal that the word "male" be stricken from the constitution of Kansas. A resolution committee was appointed, including Reverend S.E. McBurney and three others. The committee reported a resolution denying that the party opposed female suffrage, but refusing to recognize it as a party measure. The central committee in an address urged the people of Kansas to support black suffrage and announced a new list of speakers who would canvass the state for the cause. P.B. Plumb, a state legislator and a Methodist layman, and Reverend Peter McVicar, an Episcopal clergyman, were the most prominent names added to the list of speakers.[40] The Impartial Suffrage League answered with an appeal to the voters of the country to support suffrage regardless of sex or color. The outstanding clergymen who signed the appeal included Robert Collyer, T.W. Higginson, H.W. Beecher, Calvin Stowe, and Theodore Tilton as well as many radical politicians.[41]

During the last part of the campaign, several clergymen addressed letters to the public through the press. Reverend Cyrus R. Rice, a Methodist Episcopal minister who had lectured in favor of impartial suffrage, addressed a letter to the *Burlington Patriot* urging female suffrage because women as a class had always favored religion and good morals.[42] Reverend D.P. Mitchell, a Methodist, addressed a letter to the *Topeka Record* making a plea for the elimination of both sex and color discrimination in enfranchisement.[43] Reverend Pardee Butler, a Christian Church clergyman, spoke on suffrage in the Atchison church. When rumors were circulated that he opposed extending the right to vote to women, he addressed a letter to the public denying the rumor and stated that he had never said one unkind word against women or blacks. He offered to debate the opponents of woman suffrage.[44] Reverend J.D. Liggett, a Congregationalist of Leavenworth, left no doubt as to where he stood. Just before the election, he preached a sermon against votes for women, which he declared to be wrong in principle.[45]

When the votes were counted, both propositions to extend suffrage lost because the masses were less committed to the principle of equal suffrage than the radical Christians. The fight over votes for women divided the Republicans and dissipated their energy. Although Tilton signed the appeal, the *Independent* said nothing about the efforts to secure woman suffrage in Kansas. The omission was all the more deplored by the friends of woman suffrage because the *Independent* was one of the most widely read journals in Kansas. George F. Train, of Boston, who had worked for equal suffrage in New York, came to Kansas to support the cause early in October. He tried to sell woman suffrage to the Democrats by promising that the woman's movement would vote against black suffrage if the Democrats supported woman's enfranchisement. But the deal fell through and left much suspicion and mistrust.[46]

The radical Christians of Ohio were determined to put the question before the people in 1867. In December 1866, the Western Reserve radicals were busy organizing the Impartial Suffrage Society. Professor G.W. Shurtliff, a Congregational layman, and Reverend Henry Carter were the key figures in the organization of the movement. They sent out circulars explaining the purpose of the organization and recruited men for a board of managers. Douglas Putman, a Congregational deacon from Marietta and vice president of the AHMS, and R.C. Parsons, a Presbyterian layman from northern Ohio, were part of the inner circle. Garfield and Robert Schenck also lent their names to the cause.[47]

In January, at Columbus, a Republican caucus discussed the black suffrage issue. The radicals pressed for a commitment to bring the question before the people in the general election of that year. They also wanted a candidate for governor who would firmly support the measure.[48] When the suffrage measure came before the lower house of the Ohio legislature, the measure failed to win the majority required for a constitutional amendment because some Republicans voted against it. The *Independent* cried out that the lower house had disgraced Ohio. The *Commonwealth* called the Republicans in the lower house who had opposed black suffrage "hypocrites and cowards."[49] William M. Dickson wrote a letter to a member of the legislature from Western Reserve which was published. "We cannot go before the people of Ohio with such a record as yesterday's proceedings. . . . Are we willing that it shall appear to the world that we have imposed negro suffrage upon the South as a punishment? I scorn the idea. . . . Hold at once a caucus of the true men." He suggested that the caucus demand Republican support for the amendment if the caucus was to aid the party in the election. "God forbid" that it should fail, Dickson wrote. There was such an uproar from the radicals that the Senate promptly passed the measure, and the lower house fell in line, but some Republican legislators would not support black suffrage until it had been paired with a proposal to disfranchise army deserters.[50]

Some of the members of the Republican state executive committee were not enthusiastic about supporting black suffrage. A correspondent to the *Commonwealth* from Cincinnati wrote to the editor late in the canvass that the Republican leaders had tended "to dampen rather than inflame the disposition of the people" to do justice. Even after the legislature had committed itself, a portion of the Republican state executive committee was convinced that success could be ensured only by refusal to endorse black suffrage. When the question went before the committee, "shall the word 'white' be stricken out? the answer 'yes' had stuck in their throats so long that the people were unmoved by it." The radical Christians, however, rallied in support of the amendment. The editor of the *Ohio Repository* insisted that equal suffrage was required by an "enlightened Christianity." Thomas N. Davey, a member of the legislature from Lawrence County in southern Ohio and a charter member of a local Methodist church, in a speech in support of the amendment informed his audience, "Providence have forced us across the rubicon, and . . . it now becomes necessary to burn the bridges behind us, and go forward to the conflict. . . . Here, before the great God of Heaven, to whom I must account for this, and every act of my life, I . . . pledge myself now and *forever* to the enfranchisement of all men."[51] Some of the Republican newspapers became discouraged, believing that the black suffrage issue would result in a Democratic victory, allowing the opposition to control the legislature, but in June the Republican state convention met and planted itself on the "broad platform of impartial manhood suffrage" by urging the people to support the amendment. During the summer, when black suffrage appeared unlikely to carry in the election, some candidates abandoned the amendment. Other Republican candidates simply remained silent on the issue or refused to discuss it. Some local Republican campaign committees issued circulars which stated that Republican candidates and voters were not obliged to support the constitutional amendment in the election.[52]

The religious associations fully supported the constitutional change. The Ohio State Christian Association met in July and elected Reverend H.K. McConnell president of the organization. In his message to the association he asserted, "It becomes us to be unflinching in our advocacy and support" of impartial suffrage. The North Ohio Methodist Episcopal Conference pledged to do all it could "by precept and example and vote" to remove discrimination of color from the constitution. The Ohio Methodist Conference passed measures urging the people to end the controversy with God by striking the color restriction from the constitution of Ohio. "We speak to Christian men, not in the interest of party, but for the sake of God and human rights."[53]

In October several religious associations met just before the referendum. The General Conference of the Wesleyan Methodist Church convened in Cleveland and expressed the hope that the question of suffrage would be settled by an amendment to the federal Constitution if the Ohio amendment failed. The Ohio Conference of the Methodist Protestant Church considered the Ohio amendment to be a measure "required by the principles of the Bible, as well as of equity and sound policy." Just before the election the Baptist state convention met and passed a resolution on the suffrage question. It asserted, "We realize more than ever now the need not only of calm and temperate address and wise statesmanship . . . , but also of the direct interposition of Almighty God in our national affairs."[54]

The blacks were not silent on the issue before the voters of Ohio. The Colored Conference of the Methodist Church that was composed of Ohio and three bordering states met in Lexington, Kentucky, and called for the removal of "all obnoxious and unjust laws" against blacks.[55] John Langston, a black Ohio officer in the army, asked Gerrit Smith for funds to sustain a campaign for equal suffrage. The blacks held a state convention in Columbus and appealed for equal political rights so that the people could have the blessing of God. The convention made plans to raise money and send out speakers. Regional and county conventions followed.[56]

George Hoadly, a Unitarian associate of Chase, was in the field speaking for black suffrage. At Mt. Pleasant, Ohio, he asked the people to support the amendment. Hoadly asserted that retribution of the war had been brought on the country for the errors and injustice to the black race. "God's work will never cease," Hoadly informed the audience.[57] Richard Smith, a Presbyterian layman and sometime editorial writer for the *Cincinnati Gazette*, asked a Hamilton County audience to give the Negro the ballot. It was the cause of God, he told them. "We were led by an overruling Providence," he said, in abolishing slavery, and the blacks must have the ballot to protect themselves.[58] Deacon Joseph Root, a former Whig congressman from Ohio and a Congregational layman, spoke in the northern part of the state on black suffrage as a moral question. Thomas Corwin, a former congressman and a Baptist layman, asked a Warren County audience to "remember that God Almighty" would hold voters responsible for the manner in which they discharged their duty as voters.[59] Columbus Delano, a fellow Whig colleague in Congress with Root and Corwin in the 1840s and an active liberal Episcopalian layman, spoke widely for black suffrage in 1867. At Lancaster he said to an audience, "Loyal men, look up! look up! and behold that God is carrying you on the culminating point of this great work of freedom that shall give to every man, who must obey the law or suffer its penalty, a voice in making the law."[60]

Luther D. Griswold, a state senator and Episcopal vestryman, and J.H. Dickson, also an Episcopalian layman, teamed up to speak on the moral and political aspects of the black suffrage question in northern Ohio with good effect.[61] General William H. Gibson, who was licensed to preach in the Methodist church, spoke at the Northern Ohio Methodist Conference in favor of black suffrage and delivered political lectures in the canvass on the subject. At Bellefontaine, Ohio, he urged the people to reconstruct their state "upon the principle of God's eternal justice."[62] Dr. T.B. Fisher of Marion County, a powerful Presbyterian layman who had served in the legislature early in the war, actively supported black suffrage. In October, he wrote a public letter to the *Marion Independent* earnestly entreating the Union men to discharge their whole duty to their country, "God and humanity" by supporting the amendment.[63]

Rutherford Hayes, the Republican candidate for governor, and Deacon C.M. Gray, the Republican candidate for lieutenant governor and a Baptist layman, spoke on the moral aspects of the suffrage question in all their speeches. Hayes, who attended an Episcopal church with his wife, was a committed reformer who had championed impartial suffrage in 1865. In January 1866, he wrote in his diary, "Universal suffrage is sound in principle. The Radical element is right." Congressman Samuel Shellabarger, a Presbyterian layman, Godlove S. Orth, of Indiana, a Methodist layman, Colfax, Chandler, Wade, and Sherman all spoke on the moral aspects of the suffrage question. The *New York Herald* reported that the radicals had imported their heaviest timber because they were badly scared of losing the election.[64]

Even Governor Cox, who had so bitterly opposed black suffrage in 1865, defended his Oberlin letter of the 1865 canvass as not saying a word against black suffrage in Ohio. Cox was now disillusioned with the Johnson Reconstruction and was cursing himself for having backed the president. After the election of 1867, Cox wrote to Garfield that he had "worked earnestly for the adoption of the suffrage amendment" in the recent election.[65]

The abolitionist Reverend Henry C. Wright arrived in Ohio at the beginning of August and lectured on the moral significance of black suffrage until the election was held. As election day drew near the tendency was to emphasize the moral aspects of black suffrage even more. A correspondent to the *National Anti-Slavery Standard* reported that the ablest men were bringing their energies to bear in favor of black suffrage, and "all argued it on moral grounds." He quoted a local minister as having said that a purer gospel was being given at political gatherings than could be found in the churches. Reverend A.G. Byer, a Methodist minister and Reverend E.E. White were featured speakers at several central Ohio Republican rallies in which black suffrage was the chief topic of discussion. The clergy of Greene County were probably the most active in the campaign for black suffrage. Baptists and Methodist clergymen were the most active throughout the state. The radical Reverend W.S. Studley, of the Cincinnati Methodist Conference, wrote a long letter to the *Zion's Herald* about the extensive moral efforts being exerted to secure adoption of the amendment. He was not sure equal suffrage would be victorious, but he did not doubt God would have a controversy with the nation until the people were "ready to obey His will."[66]

Early in September, many who had worked for passage of the amendment began to doubt that it would carry. The *Ohio State Journal* was uncertain whether the appeal to conscience would have any effect. Colfax and others who had rendered aid in the movement for black suffrage began to have apprehensions.[67] Reverend Charles D. McGuffey, a member of the Old School Presbytery of Cincinnati, reported to a friend that "desperate efforts" were being made to defeat black suffrage. A Presbyterian missionary in Ohio wrote to the secretary of the AHMS that there was great alarm among the ignorant and profane part of the community "lest the friends of freedom should place the 'nigger' above the poor white man" and cut wages so that the poor whites could not earn a living. The Democratic press published a bogus card announcing that, according to a secret circular issued by the Republicans, the constitutional amendment was hopelessly lost and the party should concentrate on the state and legislative ticket.[68]

The results of the election showed in no uncertain way that the people of Ohio opposed black suffrage. The Democrats won control of the legislature, and Wade lost his seat in the Senate as a result. Hayes was elected by a majority of 2,083, and the vote for the amendment was 12,000 less than that for the governor.[69] Tilton lamented that the disaster in Ohio was directly attributable to the Republican party. "The Negro, freed in the South, is still a bond-slave to the Republican party of Ohio," he charged. William H. Smith, once the secretary of former governor John Brough of Ohio, confirmed that Tilton was largely correct. Smith, a Quaker and regular lecturer on religious subjects, wrote a friend that he worked diligently to change the minds of six Republicans in his election district, but when the election was held, forty-three other Republicans in the district crossed the "yes" off their ballot and voted against black suffrage.[70]

Black suffrage was coupled with a disfranchisement clause for deserters from the Union army. The Republican convention urged the people to vote for black suffrage but was silent on the disfranchisement of deserters. The *Liberal Christian* and the "Veteran Observer" considered the disfranchise provision one of the reasons for defeat. Mansfield indicated that he and many Ohioans believed that many deserters were entirely innocent because they had left the army after the war was over. The *Commonwealth* praised the Republican leaders for invoking the "indefeasible truth." The editor comforted the radicals everywhere by telling them that "truth and justice cannot be forever crushed."[71]

"It is appalling to see the state of feeling in Ohio as to *Negro suffrage*. . . . It was *purely simple* hatred of the Negro that gave this state to the Democrats," Henry Wright wrote Garrison from Ohio. Garrison was sorry to receive the news of "bitter malignant colorphobia" that still existed in Ohio. Reverend Granville Moody informed Rutherford Hayes that the Negro had vindicated his manhood on the battlefields, and "he will—he must—he shall have the ballot." Stevens was astonished to find so many Republicans in Ohio were not willing to give the blacks suffrage. "Hell is full of such Radicals as we have now," he complained. George Cheever prophesied that New York would "be stirred to its lowest depths of dirt and iniquity by the triumph of the old pro-slavery party" in Pennsylvania and Ohio.[72]

Gilbert Haven wrote an editorial in his *Zion's Herald* expressing his sentiment on the Ohio election. "Terrified by bugbears which their own imagination, inflamed by false and passionate speeches and writings, has conjured up," Ohioans have "cried halt! in the grand career upon which they were marching," complained Haven. But he commended them for being far in advance of Connecticut. "For they not only passed the amendment in the legislature, but defended it before the people. While in the latter there was a silence of the grave on the stump and in the pulpit, in Ohio every pulpit preached and every rostrum" called for justice to the blacks. He concluded with a warning to the churches and Republicans, "Apostacies of the Church have not been uncommon. . . . The Republican party will as surely die, if it yields to the temptation of its baser appetites."[73]

On Thanksgiving Day many ministers in Ohio delivered sermons that were devoted to the subject of black suffrage. A Presbyterian minister of Cincinnati told his congregation that the record of history would show that the Northern people look one way with their swords and the other way with the ballots. "With a glaring and humiliating inconsistency, we demanded the South should do what we were unwilling to do ourselves," he said. A Baptist minister in Columbus insisted that Christians must respond to the demands of Christianity, forget their prejudice, and support black suffrage. A Unitarian minister in the same city informed his people that in the name of a power above all governments, Christians must make a commitment to principle, duty, and right.[74]

The editor of the *Western Christian Advocate* examined the results of the election in Ohio and informed his readers that "The Lord God of Hosts hath a controversy in the north country; a day of vengeance he hath set, and he will avenge the poor of his adversaries." The *Christian Ambassador* concluded that the loss of black suffrage everywhere demanded that Christians rally their papers, preachers, and conventions once more to the defense of the oppressed. Tilton reasoned, "If the Republican party is not to stand for the negro's rights, then it has no better mission than the Democratic," but with words of encouragement Tilton urged the radicals to fight on. The "Party of Justice having God on its side is sure of the final victory," he assured them.[75]

The issue of black political equality had played a significant part in the Republican losses in Pennsylvania and New York, and the rejection of black suffrage amendments in Ohio, Kansas, and Minnesota had slowed the suffrage movement and checked other reform efforts.[76] In an editorial in *Zion's Herald*, Gilbert Haven observed, "In all the land . . . this is a general backsliding. The political revival is seemingly at an end. The people are getting tired of being virtuous. They are forgetting their vows made under the lash of God's wrath." Haven was sure that the battle would go on for the cause of God, and that the middle Atlantic and northwestern states would soon fall in line, but that Kentucky and Maryland would deny suffrage for a quarter of a century or more. Haven also feared that the South would disfranchise blacks when Southern whites gained control of the government. Only a strong remedy, he believed, could prevent this from happening. Haven thought, as did many radical Christians, that the time was right for a federal constitutional amendment guaranteeing the right of suffrage in all the states.[77]

# CHAPTER TWELVE

# The Fifteenth Amendment:
# A Mission Partially Completed

The presidential election of 1868 was of critical importance for the cause of black suffrage.[1] The defeat of the Republican party in 1867 on the issue of Negro suffrage had strengthened the position of the moderate Republicans and had rallied the party behind them in support of the presidential nomination of General Ulysses S. Grant and a moderate platform. The Christian radicals did not follow the majority of the party. In an editorial in the *Independent*, Tilton asked the Christian radicals if they would abandon the Negro for the sake of winning the election. "Better let the [Republican] party be ship-wrecked and go to pieces than haul down its colors from the mast. . . . The only party in this country that can afford a temporary defeat is the Party of Justice; for having God on its side, it is sure of the final victory," he assured them.[2]

Many radicals shared Tilton's optimism. Reverend Octavius Frothingham, a radical Unitarian clergyman, wrote to Moncure Conway late in 1867 that politics were in a "dreadful muddle," but Congress was still strong enough to pass its measures, and the people would be on the right side. The North must agree to black suffrage in the Northern states after forcing it on the South, Parker Pillsbury wrote to Gerrit Smith, or "our whole demeanor toward the southern states" would be "like that of the Pharisee toward the Publican."[3]

Salmon Chase was preferred as a presidential candidate by the antislavery Christians, but the loss of the election of 1867 had led the party to look for someone with popular appeal and Grant was the most available candidate. Chase lost support also because many thought that he had been partial to Johnson in the impeachment trial.[4] But many radical Christians continued to support Chase and criticized Grant during the winter of 1867-68. Wendell Phillips cautioned the people against backing Grant. Phillips acknowledged that he treaded "on hot ashes" when he criticized the great soldier, but he reminded the citizenry that the nation was now a land of graves, widows, and orphans. "You have no right, standing on such a harvest to risk" the fruits which this "great lavish martyrdom gained by your hopeless confidence in any man however beloved." In a guest editorial in the *National Anti-Slavery Standard* in January 1868, Phillips charged Grant with being partially responsible for the riots in the South in 1866. "Grant is the front sinner. . . . The blood at Memphis and New Orleans will blight in history half of his Virginia laurels." During February and March, Phillips lectured in the West, and the chief subject of his lectures was the presidential election of 1868. Phillips demanded Negro suffrage and urged the people to protest against the nomination of Grant because the standard-bearer should be a man who was outspoken on this issue and not a sphinx. Anna Dickinson took to the lecture trail and spoke against the nomination of Grant.[5]

In a published letter to Frederick Douglass, Gerrit Smith threw all of his support to Chase. "In my view, so strikingly supplied is he with all the elements of character for a chief magistrate, that I feel myself to be quite incapable of an unbiased comparison between him and other candidates for the Presidency." The idea of the nomination of Grant was "exceedingly distasteful" to George Julian. Although Sumner made no public statement of his position on Grant as a presidential candidate, he earnestly protested against the support of Grant at a private meeting of Republican leaders held in November 1867.[6]

After the election of 1867, radical journals concentrated on securing black suffrage by federal measures, the impeachment of the president, and the forthcoming presidential election. The *Independent* admitted that the enthusiasm for equal rights was at its low-water mark but encouraged the radicals to hope for better developments. "If the Republican party is to abandon the negro, let it be abandoned of God. But the Republican party has too much brains . . . to commit self-slaughter," he prophesied.[7] The *Commonwealth* charged Grant with furnishing aid to Johnson's policy of obstruction, which made him, in loyal estimation, "an abettor of wrong-doing."[8]

By April 1868 support for Grant had reached a well-advanced stage, and the radicals had to face political reality. Tilton demanded that in case Grant was nominated, the platform on which he stood should "be unequivocally for Impartial Suffrage, North and South." In discussing the responsibility of the Republican convention for adopting a platform that guaranteed the complete enfranchisement of all blacks, Aaron Powell, the Quaker editor of the *National Anti-Slavery Standard*, demanded: "Does Grant stand in the way? Put him aside!" In May, just before the Republican convention, Powell again declared, "We want the negroes enfranchised. If at Chicago it [the party] shall undertake to ignore the question altogether, or to deal with it doubtfully to accommodate any candidate who will demand such a sacrifice, its own doom will be sealed. To such a sacrifice Radicals will not submit." At the anniversary meeting of the American Anti-Slavery Society, the radical Unitarian clergyman Thomas Higginson criticized Northern men who were willing that the black should be regarded as a man in the South despite Southern whites "but not willing that he should be a man at the North, when it offends their prejudices."[9] The editor of the *Independent* considered it of prime importance that the Republican convention should treat the Negro "with unimpeachable fairness. It is a mockery of justice to ordain Negro suffrage in one half of the states and forbid it in the other." Tilton warned the Republicans that "to dodge the issue, or cover it out of sight under some meaningless generality, would be moral depravity and political folly."[10]

The Republican convention met in Chicago late in May. If the delegates were not already determined to take a cautious stance on black suffrage, the newspaper reports of the defeat of the Michigan constitutional amendment on black suffrage in April convinced the majority that a conservative stance was expedient. A bitter struggle took place in the resolution committee, but the conservative faction controlled the resolutions committee, and the dispute was not taken to the floor.[11] The platform explained that suffrage was being granted to Southern blacks from considerations "of public safety, of gratitude, and of justice," but "the question of suffrage in all the loyal States properly belongs to the people of those States."[12]

Tilton denounced the provision on suffrage as a "mean-spirited, . . . foolish and contemptible" plank. As guest editor for the *National Anti-Slavery Standard*, Wendell Phillips denounced the platform in no uncertain terms for failing to advocate black suffrage. He wrote that until the millennial period, "the responsibility rests on us, the loyal masses, to give all the meaning we can to the empty words. We have never gained anything from the justice of the party. So much the more need that we take every advantage of its fear." Tilton predicted that the Republican plank on suffrage would "fall to pieces by its own rottenness." If the national government was to be "just and humane," Tilton reasoned, it was necessary to establish uniform suffrage and make blacks everywhere voters, since the federal government had taken the responsibility of making blacks everywhere citizens.[13] Charles Slack, the editor of the *Commonwealth*, asserted that the

Republican convention knew the expectations entertained by the radicals for black suffrage and "almost insultingly . . . flung their expectations back into their faces." Slack warned the conservatives that the issue would not go away.[14]

The failure of the Chicago convention to guarantee political equality throughout all the states was a repetition of "insulting cowardice, ingratitude, and injustice," Aaron Powell protested to the readers of the *National Anti-Slavery Standard*. He served notice on the conservatives that there could be no peace in the absence of political equality. At the annual meeting of the American Anti-Slavery Society, Powell asserted that Henry Wilson had informed him that the Republican convention had been silent on impartial suffrage because silence was necessary to carry doubtful states. Wilson promised that Congress "would take hold of the matter of negro suffrage" before the next election. Phillips took the lead in condemning the failure of the Republican party to take a forthright stand for impartial suffrage. The Republican party "has yielded, and continues willing to yield," to pressure. "It has never been loyal to a single principle," he charged. Phillips said the party had "proved its utter incompetency to govern" and criticized Grant for not taking a stand on the issue of suffrage. "Of the half dozen catch-words that the Nation has extorted from his lips, not one has any relation to Liberty," Phillips complained. He claimed that public opinion demanded the ballot for the blacks. "The black man without the ballot," is the lamb given over to the wolf, Phillips explained.[15]

Phillips made sure his criticism of the Republicans was not interpreted as support of the Democrats. At the American Anti-Slavery Society convention he advised the radicals that they should not take a chance with Chase if he were the Democratic nominee. "Grant is vastly better as a candidate than Chase," Phillips insisted after Grant received the nomination. He informed the radicals that Grant had "not travelled far, but his face is zionward. . . . Grant's election means progress." Phillips assured the readers of the *Anti-Slavery Standard* that "a vote for Grant means the negro's suffrage is recognized."[16]

The Quaker Friends of Human Progress met shortly after the Republican convention adjourned and denounced the action of the convention in regard to suffrage "as a practical surrender of the whole question as a National issue; as flagrant injustice to disfranchise colored men." So that radical Christians would not forget their commitment to black equality, Aaron Powell wrote an editorial in the *Standard* on the religious duty to see that backs had equal opportunities in the school, in the meetinghouse, in their dwellings, and at work as well as at the polling place. When the AMA held its anniversary meeting, it urged the churches to call for the "instant interposition" of Congress for black equality. Several clergymen spoke on the action the federal government was expected to take on black suffrage during the election campaign, and radical Christians made it clear that they expected congressional action. The South-Eastern Indiana Conference of the Methodist Episcopal Church earnestly prayed for equal rights and justice to all men in the nation. The Wisconsin Conference, as usual "always radical on all the great questions of the day, took advanced ground." The East Maine Conference opposed all methods of Reconstruction which were "not in harmony with the morality of the Gospel, and the rights of every human creature." The General Conference of the Methodist Episcopal Church solemnly protested any Reconstruction which denied equal rights and eligibility of citizens regardless of class or color. The Baptist Associations still showed concern for equal suffrage. The New London Baptist Association in Connecticut, for example, insisted that all people should enjoy the highest privileges of freedom.[17]

Although the Republican convention tried to sidestep the issue, Negro suffrage was the campaign issue in 1868, as it had been since 1866. Some clergy were more radical in their demands for the blacks than the radicals in Congress.[18] Reverend Alexander Clark, a Pittsburgh Methodist minister, insisted that "if we relied upon the bullets of colored troops" during the war, surely "we should be magnanimous enough to give ballots to colored freemen."[19] Reverend Joseph Thompson, a Congregational clergyman and a member of the executive committee of the AHMS, delivered a sermon before the society at its annual meeting in 1868 in which he declared, "Whatever its basis, suffrage must be impartial; whatever its condition, [it] must be the same for all, and open to all alike." Reverend Samuel T. Spear, a Presbyterian minister, challenged the suffrage plank of the Republican platform. He saw no reason why the state should have absolute power to determine the suffrage question, since it was a common question in the nation which should be determined by the whole people through federal action. As soon as the election was over, he urged the Republicans to go forward without pausing and to pass a constitutional amendment granting black suffrage.[20]

The editor of the *Congregationalist* insisted that it remained to be seen whether a nation that had poured out its blood and treasure to defeat the rebels in the field had "the courage to fight with them at the polls." Dallas Lore, editor of the *Northern Advocate*, called on every loyal man to "be as direct with his ballot as he was with his bullet, to check and crush treason." Lore announced that the Methodist ministers were "becoming the most desirable and efficient political speakers of the day." In the end, almost all radical Christians supported Grant, but the Methodist clergy and journals were the most active in the canvass.[21] James Harlan was convinced that "ninety-five hundredths of the members of the M.E. Church, perhaps ninety-nine hundredths of the traveling ministers" were earnest Republicans. The *Free Methodist* urged ministers to help the cause of justice and freedom by voice and vote by enlisting under the banner of Grant and Colfax. Hiram Dunn, a Methodist clergyman from upstate New York, toured the Northwest, whipping up enthusiasm for the Republican ticket and urging the western conferences of the Methodist Church to pass resolutions in favor of the Republicans and equality and justice.[22]

When the Republicans won the election of 1868, the religious journals rejoiced. The *Christian Advocate and Journal* concluded that the election had established that black suffrage would be secured and that peace and goodwill had arrived. The *Congregationalist* agreed that the reign of order had come, and the time was close at hand "when constitutional liberty and personal freedom are to be enjoyed throughout the whole land, by all the people."[23] The editors of the *Anti-Slavery Standard* and the *Commonwealth* did not think that the election of the Republican standard-bearer guaranteed peace and harmony in the nation. They were convinced that peace and security would come only after universal suffrage had been secured for blacks. Powell avowed, "We pledge ourselves never to rest until all legal disabilities" are removed. In a guest editorial Phillips concluded that "every sensible man knows there will be no Peace till this *race* quarrel is taken out of the political arena." Despite the Republican convention's assertion that the question of suffrage properly belonged to the states, the Christian radicals were extremely optimistic after the election of Grant. When the election was over, Alexander Clark turned the early criticism of Grant for his failure to take a stand on equal rights into an advantage by stating that providence would determine the proper time and the action to be taken. Clark saw the new president "as an exponent of right as God reveals it anew and abroad from day to day. We may well thank God for a President who shall have no policy of his own. Surely we have had enough of 'My Policy.' "[24]

The Republican convention was hardly over before Senator Yates spoke in favor of a uniform suffrage provision throughout the nation.

Tilton called the speech one of the most statesmanlike proposals of the Fortieth Congress. As soon as the election was over, Tilton informed the readers of the *Independent* that the first duty of the triumphant Republican party was "to repair the mischief of the Republican platform by adding to its vague and glittering generalities on the state-rights and suffrage, a positive, direct, and manly policy, based on the political equality of all men." Two weeks later Tilton again called for an amendment to guarantee equal suffrage. He accused the leaders of the party of being more committed to success than they were to principles. "God prosper it [the amendment] to a speedy adoption," he prayed. Gilbert Haven, the editor of *Zion's Herald*, wrote, "We have no moral right to impose an obligation on one part of the land which the rest will not accept. We can have no peace till this right is made national." The editor of the *American Presbyterian* counseled Christian men and ministers to cherish no unworthy fear of the radicalism of moral reform. "Be cautious in many respects, but in none more so than to compromise such a precious a thing as principle. And take care always to be more radical than the noisy set who think the removal of a few outward evils will bring on the millennium," he told his readers. The *Presbyterian Evangelist* asserted the work had not ended with victory in the election. Duty extended beyond the mere seeking of peace. The goal of Christian people was to transform the nation into a righteous land.[25]

The Thanksgiving season brought numerous sermons on the meaning of the election. A Baptist minister in Chicago expressed thanks for the suffrage victories in Iowa and Minnesota, but most of all he hailed the day when an amendment would give suffrage to all without distinction as to race or color. A Congregational clergyman informed his congregation that the nation had been unfaithful by "denying suffrage to those whom we admitted to be men, having consciences and souls." Reverend John B. DeMotte instructed his Indiana congregation that Christianity "compels the recognition of the legal and political rights, and equality of all men, upon the sole ground of *Universal manhood.*"[26]

In December 1869 Congress convened for the short session that preceded Grant's inauguration. The advocates of Negro suffrage were encouraged by the adoption of black suffrage in Iowa and Minnesota by referenda in 1868. The activities and growth of the Ku Klux Klan during 1868 had convinced many moderates that an amendment to the Constitution was needed to give the freedman security for the future. The situation in the South appeared immediately menacing for Republican control of Southern states.[27] Radicals in the North were convinced that a federal measure was the only way to secure black suffrage. The Rock River, North Ohio, Cincinnati, and Central Ohio conferences of the Methodist Episcopal Church deplored the lawlessness and violence of the Ku Klux Klan against loyal men in the South and petitioned the government to adopt measures that would bring security to loyal men in the South. The AMA expressed regret that violence was being suffered by the loyal people in the South. It asserted that Christian people should remember them in their "prayers and at the ballot box" and urge the support of measures to bring them security. Edgar Ketchum, an executive officer of the society, wrote to Oliver Howard, the Freedmen's Bureau commissioner, that the AMA had called on Congress for the interposition of measures that would bring security. The *Liberal Christian* was appalled by the violence and asserted that it would end only when all men had been guaranteed their liberties and rights. In October, Henry W. Beecher delivered an address in the Brooklyn Academy of Music and insisted that the terror and violence in the South demonstrated the necessity of a suffrage amendment as a means of self-defense. Senator Henry Wilson, a Congregational layman, informed a political associate that "nothing animated the people more in the canvass than the idea that the rebel outrages should be stopped." Many moderates were converted to advocating a constitutional amendment and laws providing enforcement measures.[28]

Israel Washburn, a former governor of Maine and a Unitarian layman, prepared an article entitled "The Power and Duty of Congress in Respect to Suffrage" that appeared in the *Universalist Quarterly* of January 1869. Washburn wrote that an amendment was the most important, necessary, and just measure Congress could adopt. "Colored men are now *Citizens*, and if they are to enjoy the rights which were understood to be secured to citizens by the Constitution, they must be allowed to vote on precisely the same terms as other citizens," he insisted.[29] On January 9, Governor William Claffin of Massachusetts delivered his inaugural address and took the occasion to influence congressional action. He said that citizens of the Union should have the same privileges, whether they made their homes in Maryland or in Massachusetts. "Deny one man in Maryland his rights to suffrage . . . , and the citizen of Massachusetts suffers as well as the disfranchised. . . . Let it, then, be made a part of the Constitution." Claffin was a powerful radical Methodist layman and a vice president of the AMA.[30]

During January and February 1869, Congress debated the question of a national suffrage amendment. The Massachusetts Anti-Slavery Society exhorted the clergy and members of the churches of all denominations to " 'cry aloud and spare not' against the threatening sins, . . . involving human rights, of uncompromising politicians."[31] Tilton wrote, "The forefinger of the age points unerringly and inexorably to the ultimatum of democracy—Universal Suffrage. . . . Congress has no just excuse for a half-way settlement of the Negro question." The editor of the *Liberal Christian* opposed an educational qualification. "Universal suffrage is the forerunner of universal education," he informed his readers. The editor of the Unitarian *Christian Register* looked on a national amendment establishing uniform national suffrage as a peace measure. "The sooner the question of suffrage to the black man is settled and the negro is taken out of politics . . . , the sooner will the old wounds be healed," he insisted.[32]

Congress passed the Fifteenth Amendment on February 26, 1869. The final form of the amendment was a weak version that left suffrage in the hands of the states but forbade the states to deny the right to vote only on grounds of race, color, or previous condition of servitude. The version of the amendment accepted was the form that moderates preferred. Many radical Christians agreed to it because they had been forced to choose between a weak amendment and no amendment at all. Henry Wilson admitted that the weaker House version was a half-way measure. "We have passed through ten years of struggle; we have had to gather every triumph of human rights step by step, a little at a time; but by the blessing of God the final fruition will come some time, and we will work on for that end." In an editorial in the *National Anti-Slavery Standard*, Wendell Phillips was willing to support the weaker version if the strategy would secure an amendment. "We exhort every man who professes himself a friend of liberty to drop all undue attachment to any form of words and to co-operate, heartily, earnestly . . . , in carrying through . . . any form which includes . . . protection to the voters and the right to office of the colored race. . . . Our urgency comes from . . . the conviction that we are living now in the easiest hour for the accomplishment of a Constitutional Amendment." Phillips beseeched radical congressmen "to be a little more *politicians*—and a little less *reformers*." Congressman George Boutwell was convinced that Phillips had saved the amendment from defeat. He wrote to Phillips in March 1870 that his article had "saved the amendment. . . . Its influence was immediate and potential."[33]

Tilton had originally supported the stronger version of the amendment with officeholding guarantees and measures barring property and educational qualifications. But he yielded to necessity and accepted the weaker version. Early in March 1869 the *Independent* characterized the amendment as "a flood-wave that will float the Constitution still further toward the final high-water mark of Liberty, Equality, and Fraternity."[34] Charles Slack preferred the stronger Senate version, but as a practical matter he was convinced that the weaker House version stood the better chance of being ratified. The *Commonwealth* was willing to accept the weaker version; Congress could take action with appropriate legislation if unjust discrimination came from the Southern states, and the Supreme Court would remedy any flagrant wrong. When fear was expressed that even the weaker version might not be ratified by the required number of states, Slack suggested that the Southern states still out of the Union be admitted only after they had ratified the amendment. "Let the applicants for peace from the hesitating and doubtful States understand that . . . favor will be bestowed upon condition that that amendment is ratified."[35]

Aaron Powell also feared that states would institute property and educational tests to disfranchise blacks. When the amendment was passed by Congress, the *Anti-Slavery Standard* announced that the "paramount duty of the hour for all earnest radicals" was "to concentrate their strength upon the Legislature of the doubtful States." The AMA looked on the Fifteenth Amendment as completing "the grand original aim. . . . It is not only a flag planted on the line of the march of progress, but a fort built to secure the advance." The editor of the *American Missionary* did not deem it out of place to call attention to "the essential and eminent assistance" which the American Missionary Association had rendered in the matter.[36] Grant strongly endorsed the Fifteenth Amendment in his inaugural address on March 4, 1869. The *Anti-Slavery Standard* thanked him for his "frank, prompt and hearty endorsement of the Constitutional Amendment." The editor of the *Congregationalist* praised Grant's endorsement. "Peace, Honesty, Justice . . . , Forbearance, Trust in God! Really, these few simple things seem to be almost as good a 'policy,'" he asserted.[37]

The radical Christians responded to Congress's approval of the Fifteenth Amendment with enthusiasm. A Congregational layman from Illinois could "hardly constrain" himself because of elation resulting from "the last expiring *breath* of the great *apostate* Andy" and the joy over the passage of the suffrage amendment. A radical from western Illinois considered the amendment to be the "primary rock" underlying the Republican system. He commended Congress for requiring the unreconstructed rebel states to ratify the suffrage amendment prior to being received into the Union. A radical from southern Illinois wrote to Richard Yates that the "enfranchisement of all men to equal rights . . . caused every citizen to stand up . . . erect and face towards Heaven inspired by the dignity . . . of his manhood." A Baptist minister in Milwaukee saw the Fifteenth Amendment as also bringing dignity to black citizens. He told his congregation that blacks had "morally as well as politically" acquired "value in the eyes of man by wearing the badge of manhood."[38]

The Republican party supported black suffrage because the party was committed to a moral principle and was not motivated primarily by political expediency to secure the Negro vote in the Northern states. The Republicans saw the Fifteenth Amendment principally as a security measure for the Southern blacks. Concern for black rights and political security coupled with the realization that the permanent federal presence in the South was not practical in a democratic society led to the passage of the Fifteenth Amendment. The amendment and the enforcement laws had been passed in response to the sense of outrage that Ku Klux Klan violence had aroused in Congress and throughout the North. But by supporting black suffrage the Republican party was risking political disaster and defeat. In New York the few black voters historically tended to support the Whig and Republican parties, so that the New York Republicans had very little to gain politically by supporting equal suffrage. After the New York Republican legislature submitted an equal suffrage amendment to the people and ratified the Fifteenth Amendment, it was swept from control in Albany by the Democrats. Although the motives of the Republican voters and lawmakers were mixed, a significant factor was the strong moral idealism which grew to maturity during these critical years.[39] The Democratic party institutionalized race prejudice and exploited the fear of economic competition that swung many doubtful voters into their ranks on the black suffrage referenda. In both New York and Ohio opposition to black suffrage came from the working class, which feared that competition with Negro labor would undermine white labor's economic welfare as the Negro achieved greater prosperity.[40]

The final form of the Fifteenth Amendment prohibited states from denying the right to vote only on grounds of race, color, or previous condition and left loopholes that enabled Southern states, a generation later, to disfranchise the majority of their black voters. Because the courts in the early decisions interpreted the amendment as leaving suffrage to the states, which might prohibit the vote to Negroes on grounds other than race without violating its terms, Negro voting as practiced during the years of radical rule was authorized by state and federal legislation rather than by the amendment. The Southern states denied black suffrage by subterfuges that were clearly contrary to the purpose of the Fifteenth Amendment, however, and could not have done so if the will to enforce the amendment that existed during congressional Reconstruction had persisted at the turn of the twentieth century.[41]

Despite all of the optimism that the radical Christian held for the Fifteenth Amendment as a cure-all for the problems of black rights, it proved to be less significant than the Fourteenth Amendment for all people whose rights would be threatened in the future. This statement was true although the moderate Republicans viewed the Fourteenth Amendment as a makeshift party platform in 1866, but the Radicals and the majority of Republican voters looked on the black man and not their party as the main beneficiary of the Fourteenth Amendment.

With the adoption of the Fifteenth Amendment, many radical Republicans considered their work to be completed and the Northern Republican party began to abandon its preoccupation with the Southern reconstruction issue soon after the election of 1866. With the adoption of the Fifteenth Amendment there was widespread acceptance of the belief that radicalism was superfluous; the Negro could now take care of himself, and there was no further need for vigilance.[42] In August 1869 the *Commonwealth* took issue with the talk about the mission of the Republican party being ended. The editor argued that the spirit of rebellion was reviving and that much work remained to be done. The feeble attempt to restore life to the radical movement was emasculated by the Supreme Court when it rendered the decisions in the *Cruikshank* and *Reese* cases in 1876 and the *Civil Rights* and *Harris* cases in 1883, leaving little for the federal government to enforce in the Fourteenth Amendment and Fifteenth Amendment for half a century.[43] The reconstruction measures, however, proved to be the starting point for modern civil rights law and policy, and the Fourteenth and Fifteenth amendments provided the legal foundations for significant changes in the status of blacks in the twentieth century.[44] In *An American Crisis*, W.R. Brock criticizes the Fifteenth Amendment as a racial proposition rather than a universal one, meaning that the majority of the nation had no particular interest in its enforcement because it failed to link the self-interest of white Americans with their ideological commitment to equal rights as the Fourteenth Amendment did.[45] Although the Fifteenth Amendment was narrow in its scope and a negatively worded measure that was largely nullified in the 1870s and 1880s, the radicals should be credited for their "vision of the equality of all citizens" and for the foundations they erected for the "achievement of their goals" in the twentieth century.[46]

# Epilogue

The Northern churches contributed significantly to the radical movement in the Republican party because the antislavery factions gained control of most evangelical and liberal denominations and threw their weight on the side of the radical program. The churches made antislavery sentiment more respectable in Northern circles. Although anti-Southern sentiment added fuel to the Radical Republican cause, the moral influence of the radical Christians kept the Republican party from following the path of expediency. But the reform movement lost its momentum after the failure to remove Johnson and his retirement from office. Tilton was aware that the cause had reached its pinnacle when he wrote in the *Independent* after the inauguration of Grant that "both President and Congress ought to unite in advertising a joint proposal: 'Wanted—A Moral Purpose.' "[1]

Some radical Christians wanted a paternalistic society with guarantees of black rights. Others wanted to create an integrated society and prevent the formation of a segregated church, but ironically their radicalism hastened the process of the formation of a segregated church. By cultivating self-determinism among the blacks, they encouraged the desire in blacks for an independent church. Radical Reconstruction and its consequences in both the North and the South drove blacks and whites further apart, and no agency played a larger part in ultimately institutionalizing separation than the Protestant churches.[2]

By emphasizing social and human concern instead of concentrating on dogma during the war years, the evangelical churches paved the way for social gospel, which thrived in urban society with the growth of social problems in the late nineteenth century. As a result fundamentalism was somewhat checked in the Northern church. The shattering effects of the war and the loss of the vision of the new Israel led to a revival of premillennialism in the postbellum period with the demise of the dream of a perfect society. The revival of premillennialism encouraged a certain passivity about the social order which had its greatest effect on the concern about race relations and black rights. The clergymen who resisted the fatalism of premillennialism turned to social gospel and were absorbed in dealing with urban social problems.[3]

In the period following the Civil War and Reconstruction, the influence of the churches on politics continued to be more powerful than it had been before the war. The war also broadened the church's concept of charity, opened up new fields of philanthropy, and permanently altered the attitude of churches toward social affairs. The Congregational church experienced the greatest change of view concerning charity and service of any denomination. Unlike some churches, it was not divided on the question of slavery. The South opened up as a field of service and missions, and the Congregational church became a national institution. Although the Congregational church was not able to make many permanent converts among the blacks, it refused to relinquish control of its benevolent institutions and schools to blacks and was more tenacious in this regard than any other denomination. Presbyterians were not particularly successful in converting blacks because their services did not generally allow the emotional expression which blacks desired and which might be enjoyed in the Baptist and Methodist churches. The freedmen were always eager to organize their own churches, and all-black segregated churches were established more quickly in the Baptist church because of the large number of black Baptists and because the Baptist church was congregational.[4]

The vast tide of people flowing into the cities and the subsequent growth of social problems soon occupied the attention of churches as the westward movement had in the antebellum period. Urban social concerns tended to draw much of the attention of reformers. The stubborn Southern resistance to Reconstruction and the encouragement of the spirit of reconciliation by economic interests hastened the end of Reconstruction. The depression of 1873 focused interest on the question of tariffs and monetary problems. Scandals and graft in municipal and state governments as well as in President Ulysses Grant's administration caused many reformers, particularly in the East, to focus on civil service reform. At the same time many western reformers joined the agrarian movement.

The changed circumstances of society caused a rethinking of the radicals' objectives and goals and the ultimate abandonment of Reconstruction. Northerners as well as Southerners were relieved that slavery had been eradicated, but white people became largely indifferent to the fate of black Americans until interest in human rights revived after World War II.[5]

# Abbreviations

| | |
|---|---|
| AASL | American Antiquarian Society Library, Worcester, Mass. |
| *ACAB* | *Appleton's Cyclopedia of American Biography.* New York, D. Appleton and Co., 1887-89. |
| AEDP | Anna E. Dickinson Papers, Library of Congress. |
| AHMSC | American Home Missionary Society Correspondence, Amistad Research Center, Tulane University, New Orleans, La. |
| AJP | Andrew Johnson Papers, Library of Congress. |
| AKFP | Abby Kelley Foster Papers, American Antiquarian Society, Worcester, Mass. |
| ALP | Abraham Lincoln Papers, Library of Congress. |
| AMAC | American Missionary Association Correspondence. Amistad Research Center, Tulane University. |
| BCL | Berea College Library, Berea, Kentucky |
| BFWP | Benjamin F. Wade Papers, Library of Congress. |
| BPL | Boston Public Library, Boston, Mass. |
| B-SC | Beecher-Stowe Collection, Radcliffe College, Cambridge, Mass. |
| CHS | Cincinnati Historical Society, Cincinnati, Ohio |
| CorU | Cornell University, Ithaca, New York |
| CSP | Charles Sumner Papers, Houghton Library, Harvard University, Cambridge, Mass. |
| CU | Columbia University, New York, N.Y. |
| C-WC | Lydia Maria Child-John Greenleaf Whittier Correspondence, Library of Congress. |
| *DAB* | *Dictionary of American Biography* |
| DKEP | David Kirkpatrick Este Papers, Cincinnati Historical Society Library, Cincinnati, Ohio. |
| EBWP | Elihu B. Washburne Papers, Library of Congress. |
| ECSP | Elizabeth C. Stanton Papers, Library of Congress. |
| EMSP | Edwin M. Stanton Papers, Library of Congress. |
| EU | Emory University, Atlanta, Georgia. |
| GBCP | George B. Cheever Papers, American Antiquarian Society, Worcester, Mass. |
| GDD | George Duffield Diary, Detroit Public Library, Detroit, Michigan. |
| G-JP | Joshua Giddings-George Julian Papers, Library of Congress. |
| GMT | George M. Tuthill Journal and Diary, University of Michigan, Ann Arbor, Mich. |
| GSP | Gerrit Smith Papers, Syracuse University Library, Syracuse, N.Y. |
| HGP | Horace Greeley Papers, Library of Congress. |
| HLHU | Houghton Library, Harvard University, Cambridge, Mass. |
| HSP | Historical Society of Pennsylvania, Philadelphia, Pa. |

| | |
|---|---|
| HWBC | Henry W. Bellows Correspondence, Massachusetts Historical Library, Boston, Mass. |
| HWBP | Henry Ward Beecher Papers, Yale University Library, New Haven, Conn. |
| IDP | Ignatius Donnelly Papers, Minnesota Historical Society Library, St. Paul, Minn. |
| InSL | Indiana State Library, Indianapolis, Indiana. |
| Iowa HSL | Iowa Historical Society Library, Iowa City, Iowa. |
| ISHL | Illinois State Historical Library, Springfield, Illinois. |
| JAAP | John Andrew Papers, Massachusetts Historical Library, Boston, Mass. |
| JAGP | James A. Garfield Papers, Library of Congress. |
| JARD | John A. Rogers Diary, Berea College Library, Berea, Kentucky. |
| JGP | Joshua Giddings Papers, Ohio State Historical Library, Columbus, Ohio. |
| JJJP | John J. Janney Papers, Ohio State Historical Library, Columbus, Ohio |
| JMMP | James Miller McKim Papers, Cornell University, Ithaca, N.Y. |
| JMoP | James Monroe Papers, Oberlin College, Oberlin, Ohio. |
| JMP | John McClintock Papers, Emory University Library, Atlanta, Georgia. |
| *JNH* | *Journal of Negro History* |
| *JPH* | *Journal of Presbyterian History* |
| JRHP | Joseph R. Hawley Papers, Library of Congress |
| JSP | John Sherman Papers, Library of Congress. |
| JWWP | J. Watson Webb Papers, Yale University Library, New Haven, Conn. |
| LC | Library of Congress, Washington, D.C. |
| LTP | Lyman Trumbull Papers, Library of Congress. |
| MaHS | Massachusetts Historical Society Library, Boston, Mass. |
| MDCP | Moncure D. Conway Papers, Columbia University Library, New York, N.Y. |
| MHS | Minnesota Historical Society, St. Paul, Minn. |
| MSCP | Missionary Society of Connecticut Papers, Library of Congress. |
| MSP | Matthew Simpson Papers, Library of Congress. |
| *MVHR* | *Mississippi Valley Historical Review* |
| *NASS* | *National Anti-Slavery Standard* |
| *NCAB* | *National Cyclopedia of American Biography*. New York, James T. White and Company, 1891. |
| NYHSL | New York Historical Society Library, New York, N.Y. |
| OCL | Oberlin College Library, Oberlin, Ohio. |
| *OH* | *Ohio History* |
| *OR* | *The War of the Rebellion: A Compilation of the Official Records of the Union and Confederate Armies*. Government Printing Office, 1880-1901. |
| OSHL | Ohio State Historical Library, Columbus, Ohio. |
| PHSL | Presbyterian Historical Society Library, Philadelphia, Pa. |
| RBHL | Rutherford B. Hayes Library, Fremont, Ohio. |
| RC | Radcliffe College, Cambridge, Mass. |
| RDP | Ranson Dunn Papers, University of Michigan, Ann Arbor, Mich. |
| RYP | Richard Yates Papers, Illinois Historical Society, Springfield, Ill. |
| SBAP | Susan B. Anthony Papers, Library of Congress. |
| SHGP | Sydney Howard Gay Papers, Columbia University Library, New York, N.Y. |
| SHLW | State Historical Library of Wisconsin, Madison, Wisconsin. |
| SPCC | Salmon P. Chase Correspondence, Pennsylvania Historical Society, Philadelphia, Pa. |

SPCP  Salmon P. Chase Papers, Library of Congress.
SUL   Syracuse University Library, Syracuse, New York.
TOHP  Timothy O. Howe Papers, Wisconsin State Historical Society, Madison, Wis.
TSP   Thaddeus Stevens Papers, Library of Congress.
TTP   Theodore Tilton Papers, New-York Historical Society Library, New York, N.Y.
UK    University of Kentucky, Lexington, Kentucky
UM    University of Michigan, Ann Arbor, Michigan.
URL   University of Rochester Library, Rochester, New York.
WGP   William Goodell Papers, Oberlin College, Oberlin, Ohio.
W-GP  Theodore Weld-Grimké Papers, University of Michigan, Ann Arbor, Mich.
WHSP  William H. Seward Papers, University of Rochester Library, Rochester, New York
WLGP  William Lloyd Garrison Papers, Boston Public Library, Boston, Mass.
WMPD  William Moody Pratt Diary, University of Kentucky Library, Lexington, Ky.
WVU   West Virginia University, Morgantown, West Virginia.
YU    Yale University, New Haven, Conn.
ZCP   Zachariah Chandler Papers, Library of Congress.

# Notes

## Introduction

1. Avery Craven and Walter Johnson, *The United States: Experiment in Democracy* (Boston: Ginn, 1962), 300.

2. Kenneth M. Stampp, *The Era of Reconstruction, 1865-1877* (New York: Knopf, 1966), 101. George M. Marsden, *The Evangelical Mind and the New School Presbyterian Experience* (New Haven: Yale Univ. Press, 1970), 201.

3. Victor B. Howard, "The Anti-Slavery Movement in the Presbyterian Church, 1835-1861" (Ph.D. diss., Ohio State Univ., 1961), 46-52, 218-20.

4. E. Clifford Nelson, *The Lutherans in North America* (Philadelphia: Fortress Press, 1975), 242. Charles W. Heathcote, *The Lutheran Church and the Civil War* (New York: Fleming H. Revell, 1919), 65-66, 71-76.

5. Mark Mohler, "The Episcopal Church and National Reconciliation, 1865," *Political Science Quarterly* 41 (Dec. 1926), 573-75. Lewis G. Vander Velde, *The Presbyterian Churches and the Federal Union, 1861-1869* (Cambridge, Mass.: Harvard Univ. Press, 1932), 111-12, 126-29.

6. Winifred E. Garrison, *Religious Follows the Frontier: A History of the Disciples of Christ* (New York: Harper, 1931), 220-22. John R. McKivigan, *The War against Proslavery Religion* (Ithaca: Cornell Univ. Press, 1984), 185, 187.

7. McKivigan, *The War against Proslavery Religion*, 199. James Hennesey, *American Catholics: A History* (New York: Oxford Univ. Press, 1981), 156-57. Thomas McAvoy, *A History of the Catholic Church in the United States* (Notre Dame: Notre Dame Univ. Press, 1969), 185.

8. James Moorhead, *American Apocalypse: Yankee Protestants and the Civil War, 1860-1869* (New Haven: Yale Univ. Press, 1978), 11.

9. Lawrence Friedman, *Gregarious Saints* (New York: Cambridge Univ. Press, 1982), 226.

10. Glenn Linden, *Politics or Principles: Congressional Voting on the Civil War Amendments and Pro-Negro Measures, 1838-69* (Seattle: Univ. of Washington Press, 1976), 44-45. Ira V. Brown, "William D. Kelley and Radical Reconstruction," *Pennsylvania Magazine of History and Biography* 85 (July 1961), 324-25.

11. Motivation is very complex. Modern psychologists are convinced that men, rather than being driven or controlled by simple stimuli, are affected by the interaction of many forces over which they may exercise some degree of control. Mature individuals, according to these psychologists, can commit themselves to a certain set of values. Gordon W. Allport, "The Trend in Motivational Theory," in *Measuring Human Motivation*, edited by Robert Birney and Richard Teevan (Princeton: D. Van Nostrand, 1962), 167, 179-80. Erich Fromm, "The Revolutionary Character," in *The Dogma of Christ* (New York: Holt, Rinehart and Winston, 1963), 154, 158, 165. R.S. Peters, *The Concept of Motivation* (London: Routledge, 1958); Gardner Lindsey, ed., *Assessment of Human Motives* (New York: Rinehart, 1958). Martin Duberman, "The Northern Response to Slavery," in *The Antislavery Van-*

*guard: New Essays on the Abolitionists* (Princeton: Princeton Univ. Press, 1965), 410-13. For a profile of the typical Radical Republican, see Allen G. Bogue, *The Earnest Men: Republicans of the Civil War Senate* (Ithaca: Cornell Univ. Press, 1981), 137-43, 331-35. Linden, *Politics or Principles*, 40-46.

12. Ralph H. Gabriel, *The Course of American Democratic Thought* (New York: Ronald Press, 1956), 119. Sydney A. Ahlstrom, *A Religious History of the American People* (New Haven: Yale Univ. Press, 1972), 649.

13. Robert Handy, *A History of the Churches in the United States and Canada* (New York: Oxford Univ. Press, 1977), 268. Clifton E. Olmstead, *History of Religion in the United States* (Englewood Cliffs, N.J.: Prentice-Hall, 1980), 401.

14. George M. Blackburn, "Radical Republican Motivation: A Case History," *JNH* 54 (April 1969), 112-13. Olmstead, *History of Religion*, 401.

15. William A. Russ, Jr., "The Influence of the Methodist Press upon Radical Reconstruction, 1865-68," *Susquehanna University Studies* 1 (Jan. 1937), 51, 62.

16. Marsden, *The Evangelical Mind*, 2, 241.

17. James F. Rhodes, *History of the United States from the Compromise of 1850 to the Final Restoration of Home Rule in the South in 1877*, 7 vols. (New York: Macmillan, 1910), 1:479-80.


## 1. Moral Inevitability and Military Necessity

1. Roy F. Nichols, *The Disruption of American Democracy* (New York: Free Press, 1948), 139-43. Stephen B. Oates, *Our Fiery Trial: Abraham Lincoln, John Brown, and the War Era* (Amherst: Univ. of Massachusetts Press, 1979), 11-12. Carl L. Spricer, "The Great Awakening of 1857 and 1858" (Ph.D. diss., Ohio State Univ., 1935), 223-24, 231. Timothy L. Smith, *Revivalism and Social Reform* (New York: Harper, 1957), 63-69, 202-3. Russell E. Francis, " 'Pentecost,' 1858" (Ph.D. diss., Univ. of Pennsylvania, 1948).

2. Arthur Schlesinger, Jr., "The Cause of the Civil War: A Note on Historical Sentimentalism," *Partisan Review* 16 (1949), 977. Charles C. Cole, Jr., *The Social Ideas of the Northern Evangelist, 1826-1860* (New York: Columbia Univ. Press, 1954), 232-33; Smith, *Revivalism and Social Reform*, 225-37; John R. Bodo, *The Protestant Clergy and Social Issues* (Princeton: Princeton Univ. Press, 1954), 251-52; Marsden, *The Evangelical Mind*, 185-86. Moorhead, *American Apocalyse*, 53-55. C.C. Sholes to J.R. Doolittle, May 21, 1860, James R. Doolittle Papers, SHLW. *Kenosha News* (Wis.), Oct. 12, 1967.

3. John A. Andrew, an anti-Garrison antislavery advocate, was an active member of the Unitarian Church of the Disciples, of which James F. Clarke, an advanced antislavery clergyman, was pastor. Andrew was a regular delegate to the National Unitarian Convention. He helped edit a Unitarian journal early in his career. *DAB*, 1:281; 2:186. For Blair, see obituary, *Jackson Daily Citizen*, Aug. 6, 1894. *Jackson Patriot*, Sept. 17, 1937. Jean Fennimore, "Austin Blair: Civil War Governor, 1861-1862," *Michigan History* 49 (Sept. 1965), 205. *DAB*, 1:330. *Racine Daily Journal*, June 23, 1860. *Chicago Democrat*, June 11, 1860. Linda Evans, "Abolitionism in the Illinois Churches, 1830-1865" (Ph.D. diss., Northwestern Univ., 1981), 204.

4. Chester Dunham, *The Attitude of the Northern Clergy toward the South, 1860-1865* (Philadelphia: Porcupine Press, 1974), 12. *New York Independent*, July 26, Sept. 6, 1860. Donald D. Housley, "The *Independent*: A Study in Religious and Social Opinion, 1848-1870" (Ph.D. diss., Pennsylvania State Univ., 1971), 154-55, 161. Theodore Tilton was a member of Beecher's Congregational Plymouth Church

and a member of the New York Anti-Slavery Society. See James M. McPherson, *The Struggle for Equality* (Princeton: Princeton Univ. Press, 1964), 4.

5. Victor B. Howard, "Presbyterians, the Kansas-Nebraska Act, and the Election of 1856," *JPH* 49 (Summer 1971):141-45, 148-51; "The 1856 Election in Ohio: Moral Issues in Politics," *OH* 80 (Winter 1971):35-44. Dunham, *The Attitude of Northern Clergy*, 110-16. Dale Baum, *The Civil War Party System: The Case of Massachusetts, 1848-1876* (Chapel Hill: Univ. of North Carolina Press, 1984), 97.

6. James B. Stewart, *Joshua R. Giddings and the Tactics of Radical Politics* (Cleveland: Case Western Reserve Univ. Press, 1969), 252-3, 258. *Liberator* (New York), Nov. 17, 1860. Elizabeth C. Stanton to Henry Stanton, Jan. 12, 1861, ECSP, LC. Henry H. Crapo to Son, Nov. 25, 1860, Henry H. Crapo Papers, UM. Henry H. Crapo, *Henry Howland Crapo, 1804-1869* (Boston: Todd, 1933), 71-72. Martin D. Lewis, *Lumber-Man from Flint: The Michigan Career of Henry H. Crapo, 1855-1869* (Detroit: Wayne State Univ. Press, 1958), 14.

7. Howard C. Perkins, ed., *Northern Editors on Secession*, 2 vols. (New York: Appleton-Century, 1942), 2:1,092. *Columbia City News* (Ind.), July 23, 1861, citing the *Chicago Times*. *Crisis* (Columbus, Ohio), Aug. 15, 1861. Moore, *Rebellion Record: A Diary of American Events* (New York: G.P. Putnam, 1861-63; D. Van Nostrand, 1864-68) 1:17. *New York Times*, Dec. 4, 5, 1860. *New York Tribune*, Dec. 4, 1860. *NASS* (N.Y.), Dec. 22, 1860. *Liberator*, Dec. 31, 1860. *Principia* (N.Y.), Dec. 22, 1860.

8. John G. Nicolay and John Hay, *Abraham Lincoln: A History*, 10 vols. (New York: Century, 1886), 6:314-15. Durham, *The Attitude of Northern Clergy*, 73-74. *Liberator*, Dec. 31, 1860; Jan. 11, 1861. Robert Merideth, *The Politics of the Universe: Edward Beecher, Abolition, and Orthodoxy* (Nashville: Vanderbilt Univ. Press, 1963), 223. Charles Beecher to Theodore Tilton, Jan. 11, 1868, TTP, NYHSL. *DAB*, 1:127. Lester Williams, Jr., *Freedom of Speech and the Union: A Discourse Delivered December 30, 1860, at Holden, Massachusetts* (Worcester, Mass.: C. Hamilton, 1861), 11. David F. Estes, *History of Holden, Massachusetts, 1684-1894* (Worcester, Mass.: C.F. Lawrence, 1894), 331-32. A.P. Marvin, ed., *History of Worcester County, Massachusetts* (Boston: C.F. Jewett, 1879), 2:577. See *NASS*, Jan. 12, 19, 1861.

9. J.W. Yeomans to R.J. Breckinridge, Dec. 8, 1860, Breckinridge Family Papers, LC. Vender Velde, *The Presbyterian Churches*, 32. Howard, "The Anti-Slavery Movement in the Presbyterian Church," 323-24. *Presbyterian* (Philadelphia), Jan. 19, 1861. *Philadelphia Inquirer*, Jan. 2, 1861. For conservative sermons, see *New York Tribune*, Jan. 5, 1861; *New York Times*, Jan. 5, 1861; *Philadelphia Press*, Jan. 5, 1861; *New York Herald*, Jan. 5, 6, 1861; *Chicago Tribune*, Jan. 5, 1861; *Cincinnati Gazetta*, Jan. 5, 7, 1861; *Public Ledger* (Philadelphia), Jan. 5, 1861; *Boston Evening Transcript*, Jan. 5, 1861. Henry W. Bellows, *The Advantage of Testing Our Principles, Compensatory of the Evils of Serious Times, a Discourse on February 11, 1861* (Philadelphia: C. Sherman and Son, 1861), 15-17.

10. Charles D. Cleveland to Lincoln, Jan. 5, 1861, ALP. *American Missionary* (N.Y.) 5 (Oct. 1861). Samuel Colt (Presbyterian Clergyman) to Lincoln, Jan. 7, 1861; E.H. Irish to Lincoln, Jan. 9, 1861; John Senff to Lincoln, Feb. 4, 1861; P.B. Ring to Lincoln, Feb. 4, 1861; Joel Manning to Lincoln, Feb. 4, 1861, ALP. *History of Will County, Illinois* (Chicago: William LeBaron, 1878), 306-7.

11. Lincoln's March 4 Inaugural Address, in Basler, *Works of Lincoln*, 4:263. Alden Whitman, ed., *American Reformers* (New York: H.W. Wilson, 1985), 104-6. Emma Brace, ed., *The Life of Charles Loring Brace* (New York: Arno Press, 1976), 232-33, 237, 239. *Minutes of the New England Conference of the Methodist Episcopal Church, April 1861*, 26. (I omit the publication information for church con-

ferences because it serves no useful purpose; see my bibliography.) Robert D. Thomas to Lincoln, April 16, 1861, ALP. Edward E. Hall, *James Freeman Clarke: Autobiography and Correspondence* (Boston: Houghton Mifflin, 1891), 242. *Christian Inquirer*, April 27, 1861.

12. Henry W. Beecher to Emily Drury, May 11, 1861, B-SC, RC. Alexander J. Sessions to Lincoln, April 16, 1861, ALP. Irving K. Annable, *Historical Notes of the Combee Street Congregational Church* (Salem), Essex Institute Historical Collections 76 (July 1941), 203-17. See *Congregational Journal*, May 2, 1861. S.S. Jocelyn to Lincoln, May 14, 1861; Henry T. Cheever to Lincoln, June 6, 1861; General Association of Congregational Churches of Connecticut to Lincoln, June 30, 1861; M.K. Whittlesey to Lincoln, May 6, 1861; Emery S. Hopkins to Lincoln, Aug. 1, 1861, ALP.

13. James D. Richardson, *A Compilation of the Messages of the Presidents, 1789-1908*, 10 vols. (Washington, D.C.: Bureau of National Literature, 1909), 6:31. *New York Tribune*, Sept. 27, 1861. *Independent* (N.Y.), Aug. 21, 1861. George B. Cheever, *Immediate Emancipation: A Discourse* (New York: John A. Gray, 1861), 6, 14. Robert M. York, *George B. Cheever, Religious and Social Reformer, 1807-1890* (Orono: Maine Univ. Press, 1955), 187-88. David K. Este Diaries, XII, Sept. 9, (1861), 20, DKEP, CHS. *Minutes of the General Assembly of the Presbyterian Church, 1860* (N.S.), 385. See also Henry W. Beecher to Emily Drury, Aug. 15, 1861, B-SC. Moncure D. Conway, *Autobiography: Memories and Experiences of Moncure Daniel Conway*, 2 vols. (Boston: Houghton Mifflin, 1904), 1:330. Mary E. Burtis, *Moncure Conway, 1832-1907* (New Brunswick: Rutgers Univ. Press, 1952), 79-80. George M. Fredrickson, *The Inner Civil War: Northern Intellectuals and the Crisis of the Union* (New York: Harper and Row, 1965), 116-17. Horace Greeley to Conway, Aug. 17, 1861, MDCP, CU.

14. *Minutes of the Erie Annual Conference of the Methodist Episcopal Church, 1861*, 23. *Minutes of the Western Iowa Conference of the Methodist Episcopal Church, 1861*, 6, 13. North Ohio Conference of the Methodist Episcopal Church in the *Fremont Journql*, Sept. 20, 1861. *Minutes of the East Genesee Conference of the Methodist Episcopal Church, 1861*, 20. *Western Christian Advocate* (Cincinnati), Aug. 28, 1861. Estel Neace, "A Study of Methodism in Indiana during the Civil War" (masters thesis, Butler Univ., 1961), 49.

15. Gerrit Smith to Lincoln, Aug. 13, 1861, in *Liberator*, Sept. 13, 1861. *NASS*, Sept. 28, 1861. *Principia*, Sept. 28, 1861. Henry Montague to Lincoln, Kalamazoo, Mich., Sept. 17, 1861, ALP. *Compendium of the History and Biography of Kalamazoo Co., Michigan* (Chicago: A.W. Bowen, 1906), 198. John Root to Lincoln, Coldwater, Mich., Sept. 17, 1861, ALP. *Portrait and Biographical Album of Branch Co., Michigan* (Chicago: Chapman Brothers, 1888), 292-95, 485. *Historical Collections, Michigan Pioneer and Historical Society* (Lansing: Wynkoop Crawford, 1905), 34:756-57. Crisfield Johnson, *History of Branch County, Michigan* (Philadelphia: Everts and Abbott, 1879), 135. *Republican* (Coldwater, Mich.), April 29, 1887. Thomas H. Little to Lincoln, Janesville, Wis., Sept. 17, 1861, ALP. *Portrait and Biographical Album of Rock County, Wisconsin* (Chicago: Acme Publishing, 1889), 573-75.

16. Victor B. Howard, *Black Liberation in Kentucky: Emancipation and Freedom, 1862-1884* (Lexington: Univ. Press of Kentucky, 1983), 6-8. A. Harris to Lincoln, Chillicothe, Ohio, Sept. 17, 1861; John L. Williams to Lincoln, Chillicothe, Ohio, Sept. 19, 1861; H.C. Garst to Lincoln, Greenville, Ohio, Sept. 18, 1861; from Cincinnati, a Methodist clergyman penned a concise message: "The proclamation of General Fremont struck the right cord" (Rev. Samuel West to Lincoln, Cincinnati, Oct. 9, 1861, ALP). *History of Ross and Highland Counties, Ohio* (Cleveland: W.W. Williams, 1880), 370. See also Abner Williams to Lincoln, Oct. 11, 1861, ALP.

17. J.G. Roberts to Lincoln, Hillsboro, Ill., Sept. 17, 1861, ALP. William Perrin, *The History of Bond and Montgomery Counties, Illinois* (Chicago: O.L. Baskin, 1881), 344. J.C. Patterson to Lincoln, Wayne Co., Ill., Sept. 21, 1861, ALP. L.H. Parker to Rev. H. Hooker, Oct. 4, 1861, MSCP, LC.

18. *Cincinnati Gazette*, Sept. 2, 1861, cited by *Fond Du Lac Commonwealth* (Wis.), Sept. 11, 1861. *Christian Inquirer*, cited by *NASS*, Oct. 12, 1861. Moncure Conway to Charles Sumner, Sept. 17, 1861, CSP, HLHU. Michael D. Warren, "Moncure Conway: Abolitionist, Reformer" (masters thesis, Morehead State Univ., 1972), 80. *Cincinnati Gazette*, cited by *NASS*, Dec. 7, 1861. George Hoadly to S.P. Chase, Sept. 18, 1861, in "Miscellaneous Letters to Chase, 1842-1870," *Annual Report of the American Historical Association, 1902* 2 (1903), 504; William M. Dickson to Friedrich Hassuarek, Sept. 27, 1861, Friedrich Hassuarek Papers, OSHL.

19. Erastus Wright to Lincoln, Springfield, Ill., Sept. 20, 1861, ALP. *Transactions of the Illinois State Historical Society for 1907* (Springfield: Illinois State Historical Society, 1908), 304. John L. Scripps to Lincoln, Sept. 23, 1861, ALP. *Chicago Tribune*, Sept. 24, 1866. *NCAB*, 7:558. *Rock River Democrat* (Rockford, Ill.), Sept. 24, 1861. John Russell to Lyman Trumbull, Dec. 17, 1862, LTP, LC.

20. *Minutes of the Cincinnati Conference of the Methodist Episcopal Church, 1861*, 16. *Minutes of the Illinois Conference of the Methodist Episcopal Church, 1861*, 15. Rev. James Leaton, Sec., Illinois Methodist Conference, to Lincoln, Sept. 13, 1861, ALP. *Minutes of the Central Ohio Conference of the Methodist Episcopal Church, 1861*, 37. For the Rock River conference, see *Waukegan Gazette*, Oct. 19, 1861. *Minutes of the Michigan Conference of the Methodist Episcopal Church, 1861*, 36. *Minutes of the Detroit Conference of the Methodist Episcopal Church, 1861*, 36. Orville H. Browning to Lincoln, Sept. 30, 1861, Abraham Lincoln Manuscripts, ISHL.

21. *Minutes of the Wisconsin State Baptist Convention, Sept. 1861*, 9. *Minutes of the Grand River (Ohio) Baptist Association, Sept. 1861*, 4. *Minutes of the Oneida (New York) Baptist Association, Sept. 1861*, 10. *Minutes of the Chemung River (New York) Baptist Association, Sept. 1861*, 7-8. Late in September the Free Will Baptist Association of Branch County, Mich., petitioned Lincoln to sustain Fremont in his "bold and righteous proclamation." Ransom Dunn to Sons, Sept. 25, 1861, RDP, UM; H.C. Seefield to Lincoln, Sept. 28, 1861; E.N. Barttells to Lincoln, Oct. 3, 1861; John Fee to Lincoln, Oct. 3, 1861, ALP.

22. James Allen to Lincoln, Bangor, Maine, Sept. 21, 1861, ALP. *History of Penobscot County, Maine* (Cleveland: Williams, Chase, 1882), 723. See also Rev. S. Hines to Lincoln, Middletown, Conn., Sept. 20, 1861, H.W. Chafee to Lincoln, Newton, Mass., Oct. 11, 1861, ALP. Allan Nevins, *Fremont*, 2 vols. (New York: Harpers, 1928), 2:574.

23. *Christian Advocate and Journal* (New York), Sept. 19, 1861. *Maine Evangelist*, cited by *Liberator*, Oct. 4, 1861. Charles Sumner to Francis Lieber, Sept. 17, 1861, in Edward L. Pierce, *Memoir and Letters of Charles Sumner*, 4 vols. (1877; reprt., New York: Arno Press, 1969), 42. In 1833 Sumner told a friend that he was "without religious feeling." David Donald, *Charles Sumner and the Coming of the Civil War* (New York: Knopf, 1960), 18.

24. T. Harry Williams, *Lincoln and the Radicals* (Madison: Univ. of Wisconsin Press, 1960) 41. George Prentice, *The Life of Gilbert Haven* (New York: Phillips and Hunt, 1883), 242. Charles L. Brace to *Independent*, Sept. 12, 1861; Horace Greeley to C.L. Brace, Oct. 7, 1861, in Brace, *The Life of Charles L. Brace*, 244, 247. For Greeley's church membership, see *Western Christian Advocate*, Jan. 23, 1867. John G. Whittier to George Stearns, Sept. 13, 1861, in Frank P. Stearns, *The Life and Public Services of George Luther Stearns* (1907; reprt., New York: Arno Press, 1969), 257. The lawmakers were quick to respond when the Christian radicals

reacted to Lincoln's order. Schuyler Colfax wrote to the president on September 7 that loyal men of all parties were unanimous in favor of Frémont's emancipation decree and that he should at least give the order a qualified approval. When Congress met, Colfax told his fellow lawmakers that Frémont's proclamation should be upheld. "It is, under God, the only means by which we can put down this gigantic, satanic conspiracy and rebellion." When Sumner congratulated him on his speech, he replied, "What I said came from the heart and was prompted by a conviction that justice demanded it. I should have been afraid to sleep . . . if I had not . . . stood forth in Fremont's vindication." Schuyler Colfax to Abraham Lincoln, Sept. 7, 1861, War Dept. Files, 1861, cited by A. Howard Meneely, *The War Department, 1861: A Study in Mobilization and Administration* (New York: Columbia Univ. Press, 1928), 339. *Cong. Globe*, 37th Cong., 2d sess., pt. 2 (March 7, 1862), 1,124. Colfax to Charles Sumner, March 26, 1862, CSP, HLHU.

25. GMT, Diary, Sept. 26, 1861, VI, 1,373, UM. Joel Hawes, *Four Questions Considered: A Sermon Preached in Hartford on the Day of the National Fast, Sept. 26, 1861* (Hartford: Case, Lockwood, 1861), 14-15. *NASS*, Oct. 5, 1861. William N. Patton to Lincoln, Oct. 12, 1861, ALP. *Daily Democratic Union* (Peoria, Ill.), Oct. 12, 1861.

26. Conway, *Autobiography*, 342-43. Burtis, *Conway*, 80-81. Fredrickson, *The Inner Civil War*, 116. Lydia Child to John G. Whittier, Jan. 21, 1862, *Letters of Lydia Maria Child* (Boston: Houghton Mifflin, 1884), 160. Moncure D. Conway, *The Rejected Stone; or, Insurrection vs. Resurrection in America* (Boston: Walter, Wise, 1862), 116-20, 128.

27. For example, see *Minutes of the Oswego Baptist Association, August 28, 29, 1861*, 10. Thomas Waller to Daniel Noyes, Iowa, Sept. 1, 1861, AHMSC, Amistad Archives, Tulane Univ.

28. B.F. Wade to James Monroe, Dec. 11, 1861, JMoP, OCL.

29. *Congregational Journal*, Sept. 12, 1861. *Daily Pittsburgh Gazette*, Oct. 5, 7, 1861. John T. Pressly to Lincoln, Oct. 28, 1861, ALP.

30. George B. Cheever, *Immediate Emancipation*, 9. *New York Times*, Nov. 29, 1861. Charles Sumner to Randolph Schleiden, Nov. 3, 1861; Sumner to John Jay, Nov. 10, 1861, in Pierce, *Memoir and Letters of Charles Sumner*, 49.

31. LeRoy Fischer, *Lincoln's Gadfly, Adam Gurowski* (Normal: Univ. of Oklahoma Press, 1964), 236. Basler, *Works of Lincoln*, 5:48.

32. Theodore Pease and James Randall, ed., *The Diary of Orville Browning*, 2 vols. (Springfield: Illinois Historical Library, 1925), 1:499. John A. Gurley to Lincoln, Oct. 27, 1861, ALP. Benjamin P. Thomas, *Abraham Lincoln* (New York: Modern Library, 1968), 277. George Templeton Strong, *Diary of the Civil War, 1860-1865*, edited by Allan Nevins (New York: Macmillan, 1962), Nov. 6, 1861, p. 191.

33. *Frankfort Commonwealth* (Ky.), Nov. 22, 1861. John Haynes Holmes, *The Life and Letters of Robert Collyer, 1823-1912*, 2 vols. (New York: Dodd, Mead, 1917), 260.

34. *New York Times*, Nov. 28, 1861.

35. DKEP, Diaries, XII, Nov. 28, 1861, p. 51. *New York Times*, Nov. 29, 1861.

36. *Chicago Journal*, Nov. 8, 15, 29, 1861. Edgar C. McMechen, *Life of Governor Evans: Second Territorial Governor of Colorado* (Denver: E.C. McMechen, 1924), 81-83. *NCAB*, 6:445-47. *DAB*, 3:204-5.

37. Lydia Maria Child to John G. Whittier, Jan. 21, 1862. C-WC, LC. *Christian Times and Illinois Baptist* (Chicago), Dec. 11, 1861. George W. Julian, *Political Recollections, 1840-1872* (1883; reprt., Miami: Mnemosyne, 1969), 200, 370. Timothy Howe to Grace Howe, Dec. 13, 1861, TOHP, SHLW. Timothy Howe was a sincere and devout Unitarian. In his letters to his daughter Grace, which were filled

with religious sentiment, Howe expressed his belief in the justice of God and discussed Unitarian sermons by various ministers. He opposed the annexation of Texas, endorsed the principles of the Wilmot Proviso, and was an early advocate of universal emancipation and black suffrage. See Timothy O. Howe to Grace, April 26, 1866, TOHP. *Wisconsin State Journal*, March 26, 28, 1883; *Kenosha Telegraph*, March 30, 1883. William H. Russell, "Timothy O. Howe, Stalwart Republican," *Wisconsin Magazine of History* 35 (Winter 1951), 91, 94-95, 99. Albert Erlebacher, "Senator Timothy Otis Howe and His Influence on Reconstruction, 1861-1877" (masters thesis, Marquette Univ., 1956), 7. Strong, *Diary*, December 14, 1861, p. 194.

38. Kirk H. Porter and Donald B. Johnson, *National Party Platforms, 1840-1968* (Urbana: Univ. of Illinois Press, 1972), 32. Julian, *Political Recollections*, 200, 370. Richardson, *Messages*, 6:55.

39. Marsden, *The Evangelical Mind*, 207. Rowland Berthoff, "Peasants and Artisans, Puritans and Republicans: Personal Liberty and Communal Equality in American History," *Journal of American History* 49 (Dec. 1982), 586. George Marsden, "Kingdom and Nation: New School Presbyterian Millennialism in the Civil War Era," *JPH* 46 (Dec. 1968), 254.

40. George Bancroft to Lincoln, Nov. 15, 1861, ALP.

## 2. Radical Christians and the Emancipation Proclamation

1. Basler, *Works of Lincoln*, 5:48-49.

2. James C. Conkling to Lyman Trumbull, Dec. 16, 1861, LTP. Joseph Wallace, *Past and Present of the City of Springfield and Sangamon County, Illinois* (Chicago: S.J. Clarke Publishing, 1904), 54. Shubal York to Trumbull, Dec. 5, 1861; P.A. Allaire to Trumbull, Dec. 10, 1861, LTP. Richard Edward, *Aurora Census Report and Directory of the City* (Aurora, Ill.: Fox River Printing, 1872), 80. J.M. Sturtevant to Lyman Trumbull, Dec. 18, 1861; Wait Talcott to Trumbull, Feb. 4, 1862, LTP.

3. James M. McPherson, *Ordeal by Fire: The Civil War and Reconstruction* (New York: Knopf, 1982), 79, 82, 89, 270. W. Hunger in *Christian Advocate and Journal*, Jan. 2, 1862. *Independent*, Jan. 16, 1862. George I. Rockwood, "George Barrel Cheever: Protagonist of Abolition," *American Antiquarian Society Proceedings*, n.s., 46 (April 1936), 82-113. *Presbyterian Witness* (Cincinnati), Jan. 14, 1862. Rev. E.J. Goodspeed to Editor, *Milwaukee News*, Dec. 31, 1861, in *Janesville Daily Gazette*, Jan. 8, 1862. S. Willard Segur, *The Nation's Hope: A Sermon Preached in the Congregational Church, Tallmadge, Ohio* (Akron: Beebe and Elkins, 1863), 12-13. W.G. Cochrane, "Freedom without Equality: A Study of Northern Opinion and the Negro Issue, 1861-1870" (Ph.D. diss., Univ. of Minnesota, 1957), 43. *Boston Courier*, cited in *LaCrosse Tri-Weekly Democrat*, Feb. 5, 1862.

4. W.A. Crofut to George Cheever, Nov. 25, 1861; Roscoe Conkling, Owen Lovejoy, et al. to George Cheever, Jan. 9, 1862; Congressmen and Senators to George Cheever, Jan. 14, 1862, GBCP, AASL. *New York Tribune*, Jan. 15, 1862. *Independent*, Jan. 16, 1862. *Jackson Standard* (Ohio), Jan. 23, 1862. Elizabeth Washburn to George Cheever, Feb. 17, 1862; W.A. Crofut to George Cheever, March 5, 1862, GBCP. *NASS*, Feb. 17, 1862. Susan B. Anthony to George Cheever, March 6, 1862; George Cheever to Elizabeth, April 10, 1862, GBCP. Julian, *Political Recollections*, 191. York, *George Cheever*, 191-92. William H. Cheever to George Cheever, April 26, 1862, GBCP. "Our Special Correspondent," Washington, D.C., Jan. 15, 1862, *New York Tribune*, Jan. 17, 1862. Moncure Conway to Ellen Conway, Jan. 22, 1862, MDCP, CU.

5. G.S. Berry to George Cheever, Jan. 13, 1862; John B. Dales to Cheever,

Jan. 29, 1862, GBCP. York, *George B. Cheever*, 192. Moncure Conway to wife, Jan. 15, 16, 21, 22, 24, 27, 1862, MDCP. *New York Times*, Jan. 31, 1862. *New York Tribune*, Feb. 1, 1862. *Cincinnati Gazette*, April 3, 1862. R.W. Lyman to George Cheever, March 23, 1862; James Allen to George Cheever, March 27, 1862; J.B. Johnson to Cheever, April 1, 1862; A.M. Powell to George Cheever, March 6, 1862, GBCP. *Fond Du Lac Commonwealth* (Wis.), Feb. 19, 1862. Moncure Conway to Wife, March 13, 17, 24, 25, 27, 28, 1862, MDCP. Fanny Garrison to Theodore Tilton, April 6, 1862, TTP. Richard Smith to Joseph H. Barrett, Feb. 9, 1862; March 21, 1862, in Muriel B. Drell, "Letters by Richard Smith of the *Cincinnati Gazette*," *MVHR* 26 (March 1950), 543, 545; also p. 537.

6. *Congregational Journal*, Jan. 30, 1862; *Zion's Herald and Wesleyan Journal* (Boston), Jan. 29, 1862; *Presbyterian Quarterly Review* (Philadelphia) 10 (Jan. 1862), 491; *Religious Telescope* (Dayton, Ohio), Jan. 29, 1862. *Lutheran and Missionary* (Philadelphia), May 15, 1862. *Journal of the Annual Session of the Franckean Evangelic Lutheran Synod, 1862*, 22. Cochrane, "Freedom with Equality," 351. *Minutes of the Berkshire Baptist Association, June 1862*, 7. *Minutes of the Ashford Baptist Association, June 1862*, 6. *Minutes of the Central Union Association of Independent Baptist Churches, June 1862*, 10. *Minutes of the Pittsburgh Regular Baptist Association, June 1862*, 5. *Minutes of the St. Joseph River Baptist Association, June 1862*, 4. *Minutes of the Broome and Tioga Baptist Association, June 1862*, 14.

7. Basler, *Works of Lincoln*, 5:144-45. David Donald, *Charles Sumner and the Rights of Man* (New York: Knopf, 1970), 51.

8. *New York Tribune*, March 7, 1862; *New York Times*, March 7, 1862. New York Citizens at Cooper Institute, March 6, 1862, ALP.

9. *Independent*, March 13, 1862. Edwin W. Terry, "Theodore Tilton as Social Reformer, Radical Republican, Newspaper Editor, 1863-1872" (Ph.D. diss., St. John's Univ., 1971), 21. Horace Greeley to S.H. Gay, March 7, 1862, SHGP, CU. *Christian Advocate and Journal*, March 20, 1862. *Minutes of the New England Conference of the Methodist Church, April 1862*, 24. John McClintock to Emory, March 24, 1862; McClintock to Rev. W. Arthur, March 22, 1862, JMP, EU.

10. Moncure Conway to wife, March 8, 12, 1862, *Fall River News* clipping attached to March 12 letter, MDCP. A.C. Hand to S.S. Jocelyn, March 13, 1862, AMAC. Rev. W. Hunter to W.T. Willey, March 27, 1862, W.T. Willey Papers, UWV. Abraham Folson to Lincoln, March 20, 1862, ALP. P. Weton to George Cheever, March 29, 1862, GBCP.

11. *Lutheran and Missionary* (Philadelphia), May 15, 1862. *Journal of the Annual Session of the Franckean Evangelic Lutheran Synod, 1862*, 22. Cochrane, "Freedom without Equality," 351. *Minutes of the New England Conference of the Methodist Episcopal Church, April 1862*, 24. Rev. John F. Hill to Lincoln, May 20, 1862, ALP. *Pittsburgh Gazette*, May 24, 1862. *Banner of the Covenant*, June 28, 1862. *Minutes of the New York Conference of the Methodist Episcopal Church, April 1862*, 25-26. *Minutes of the North Indiana Conference of the Methodist Episcopal Church, 1862*, 32.

12. *Minutes of Berkshire Baptist Association, June 1862*, 7. *Minutes of the Ashford Baptist Association, June 1862*, 6. *Minutes of the Central Union Association of Independent Baptist Churches, June 1862*, 10. *Minutes of the Pittsburgh Regular Baptist Association, June 1862*, 5. *Minutes of the St. Joseph River Baptist Association, June 1862*, 4. *Minutes of the Broome and Tioga Baptist Association, June 1862*, 14. Congress passed the joint resolution the president asked for and Lincoln approved the resolution on April 10. *Cong. Globe*, 37th Cong., 2d sess. (May 2, 1862), p. 1,919. Nathan M. Thomas to S.B. Thayer, Jan. 22, 1862, N.M. Thomas Correspondence, UM. Edward Brown to Executive Committee, March 28,

1862, AHMSC. J.R. Giddings to Milton Sutliff, June 3, 1848; Jan. 22, Feb. 5, 1862, Milton Sutliff Letters, Western Reserve Historical Society Library. Joshua R. Giddings, *History of the Rebellion: Its Authors and Causes* (New York: Follet, Foster, 1864), 478.

13. *Independent,* Jan. 9, March 20, April 7, 1862. John McClintock to Emory, Feb. 17, 1862, JMP. *Minutes of the New England Conference of the Methodist Episcopal Church, April 1862,* 24. *Watchman and Reflector,* cited by *Independent,* April 24, 1862. *Western Christian Advocate,* May 7, 1862. *Morning Star* (Dover, N.H.), April 2, 16, 1862. Congregational Churches of Cuyahoga and Lorain Counties to Lincoln, April 18, 1862, ALP. *Christian Advocate and Journal,* April 24, 1862. George Cheever to Elizabeth Cheever, April 4, 1862, GBCP. *Minutes of the Vermont Conference of the Methodist Episcopal Church, May 1862,* 27. *Minutes of the Erie (Ohio) Conference of the Methodist Episcopal Church, July 1862,* 15. *Mahoning Register* (Youngstown, Ohio), July 24, 1862. *Minutes of the North Indiana Methodist Conference, 1862,* 32. Congregational Association of Grand Rapids, Mich., *Charlotte Republican,* May 30, 1862. *NASS,* May 10, 1862, *New York Herald,* May 7, 1862. *Minutes of the East New Jersey Baptist Association, June 1862,* 9. C.C. Knowles to Elizabeth B. Chace, April 20, 1862, in Lillie Buffum Chace Wyman and Arthur C. Wyman, *Elizabeth Buffum Chace, 1806-1899,* 2 vols. (Boston: W.B. Clark, 1914), 234.

14. Basler, *Works of Lincoln,* 5:222-23. David Hunter to E.M. Stanton, May 9, 1862, *OR,* Ser. 1, 14:341. David Hunter to E.M. Stanton, Jan. 29, 1862, EMSP, LC. *DAB,* 5:399-400. *New York Evening Post,* May 20, 1862. S.P. Chase to Lincoln, May 16, 1862, ALP. David Donald, *Inside Lincoln's Cabinet: The Civil War Diaries of Salmon P. Chase* (New York: Longmans, Green, 1954), 20. John A. Andrew to E.M. Stanton, May 19, 1862, in *New York Tribune,* May 24, 1862. John Andrew to E.M. Stanton, May 19, 1862; A.W. Albee to Andrew, May 24, 1862, JAAP, MaHS. Edward F. Haywood, *History of the Second Parish Church, Marlborough, Massachusetts* (Marlboro, Mass.: Parish, 1906), 38. Peleg W. Chandler, *Memoir of Governor Andrew, with Personal Reminiscences* (Boston: Roberts Brothers, 1880), 55. Charles Blake to John Andrew, May 27, 1862; U.T. Clark to Andrew, May 28, 1862; Charles Sumner to Andrew, May 28, 1862; N.H. Whiting to Andrew, June 15, 1862; David Scounehill to Andrew, June 19, 1862; David Wellman, Jr., to Andrew, June 26, 1862; William E. Whitcomb to Andrew, June 14, 1862, JAAP. Katherine W. Ross, *History of the Centre Congregational Church, 1720-1970,* 21. *New Bedford Mercury,* cited by *Boston Evening Transcript,* Aug. 12, 1862. *Proceedings of the Pennsylvania Yearly Meeting of Progressive Friends, June 1862,* 23. *New York Tribune,* May 20, 1862.

15. Lorenzo Wood to Elihu Washburne, June 3, 1862, EBWP, LC. *History of Lee County, Illinois* (Chicago: H.N. Hill, 1881), 193. M. French to S.P. Chase, June 13, 1862, SPCP; *NCAB,* 2:549. *American Missionary* (New York) 6 (Sept. 1862), 200-1. J.H. Jordan to S.P. Chase, July 6, 1862, SPCP. Edward D. Mansfield to S.P. Chase, July 8, 1862, SPCP. *Cincinnati Gazette,* Oct. 28, 30, 1880. Mansfield and his father were Episcopalians, but Edward Mansfield joined the Presbyterian church as a young man. Edward D. Mansfield, *Personal Memories, 1803-1843* (1879; reprint., Freeport, N.Y.: Books for Libraries Press, 1970), 60, 154. Henry H. Crapo to Son, July 18, 1862, GDD, Henry H. Crapo Papers, UM. George Duffield's Diary, July 21, 1862, GDD, Detroit Public Library.

16. *Proceedings of the Pennsylvania Yearly Meeting of Progressive Friends, 1862,* 13-14. Minutes of the Genesee Convention of the Free Methodist Church, Sept. 18-22, 1862, p. 7, Manuscript Record, Free Methodist Church Archives, Winona Lake, Ind. Journal of Samuel G. Wright, June 3, 1862, Knox College. *Minutes*

*of the Walworth Baptist Association (Wis.) June 1862*, 6. *Minutes* of the following Baptist Associations: Central Union (Pa.), 10. Dane (Wis.), 3; Fox River (Ill.), 10; Northumberland (Pa.), 11. Clearfield (Pa.), 9; Hudson, South, 20.

17. *Northern Independent Methodist* (Auburn, N.Y.), May 22, 1862. *Independent*, May 22, 1862. Alexander K. McClure, *Abraham Lincoln and Men of War Times* (Philadelphia: Times Publishing, 1892), 104. A.W. Thayer to William S. Thayer, May 30, 1862, William S. Thayer Papers, Univ. of Virginia Library (microfilm copy).

18. *Northwestern Christian Advocate* (Chicago), March 12, 1862. *Independent*, June 12, 1862. William B. Dodge to Elihu B. Washburne, June 12, 1862, EBWP, LC. Newton Bateman and Paul Selby, *Historical Encyclopedia of Illinois and the History of Lake County* (Chicago: Munsell Publishing, 1902), 676. John Montelius to Elihu Washburne, July 4, 1862, EBWP. George Candee to J.J. Jocelyn, July 8, 1862, AMAC, Amistad Archives.

19. C.G. Ryman to B.F. Wade, June 27, 1862, BFWP, LC. John Blair Linn, *History of Centre and Clinton Counties, Pennsylvania* (Philadelphia: J.B. Lippincott, 1883), 369. *New York Herald*, May 8, 1862. David Root to B.F. Wade, May 5, 1862, BFWP. *Exercises Commemorative of the First Congregational Church in Cheshire, Connecticut, 1724-1924* (Hartford: George C. Williams, 1925), 33. *New York Herald*, May 8, 1862. Lyman Trumbull to Wife, July 13, 1862, LTP, LC.

20. *New York Tribune*, July 16, 17, 1862. *New York Times*, July 16, 1862.

21. C.R. Robert to S.P. Chase, July 23, 1862, SPCP, *NCAB*, 10:492. *Thirty-Sixth Report, 1862*, AHMS (New York: John A. Grey, 1862), 8. Samuel Plumb to Ransom Dunn, July 25, 1862, RDP. J.T. Connell to Richard Yates, Aug. 4, 1862, RYP, ISHL.

22. Minutes of the Zanesville Conference of the Wesleyan Connection, 1849-63, Manuscript Record, Marion College. J.W. Caffin to Lincoln, Felicity Church, Miami Conference, Wesleyan Church, Sept. 6, 1862, ALP. A. Worth, Indiana Conference, Wesleyan Church to Lincoln, Sept. 6, 1862, ALP. E.R. Ames, Bishop, Cincinnati Methodist Episcopal Conference, to Lincoln, Sept. 8, 1862, ALP. West Wisconsin Methodist Episcopal Church to Lincoln, Sept. 18, 1862, ALP.

23. *Minutes of the Keokuk Baptist Association, 1962* (Iowa), 5. *Minutes of the Davenport Baptist Association, Sept. 1862*, 7. *East Liverpool Mercury* (Ohio), July 24, 1862.

24. Zachariah Chandler to Lyman Trumbull, Sept. 17, 1862, LTP. Mary George and Wilmer Harris agreed that Chandler was an exponent of practical politics and a power broker, but he was also a devoted Christian. Chandler liberally supported the Underground Railroad and gave large sums of money to defend those who were prosecuted because they helped fugitive slaves. He contributed freely to erect and sustain the Fort Street Presbyterian Church and engaged in volunteer work only when he could serve that institution or promote causes he identified with it. Chandler knew the Bible well and quoted from the Scripture to reinforce the objectives of the radicals. Wilmer C. Harris, *Public Life of Zachariah Chandler, 1851-1875* (Lansing: Michigan Historical Commission, 1917), 3, 125; Mary K. George, *Zachariah Chandler: A Political Biography* (East Lansing: Michigan State Univ. Press, 1969), 4, 271, 359. *Zachariah Chandler: An Outline Sketch of His Life and Public Service* (Detroit: Post and Tribune, 1880), 45, 75. Walter Buell, "Zachariah Chandler," *Magazine of Western History* 4 (1886), 276-77. Donald H. Smith, "Senator Zachariah Chandler, Yankee Unionist, 1813-1879" (masters thesis, Georgetown Univ., 1942).

25. S.P. Chase to R.C. Parsons, July 20, 1862, SPCC, HSP. Joseph H. Geiger to S.P. Chase, July 26, 1862, SPCP. Sidney H: Gay to Lincoln, July 30, 1862, ALP.

"Enquirer" [Anonymous] to Editor, *New York Tribune*, July 28, 1862, ALP. Reuben Hitchcock to Wife, Aug. 31, Sept. 7, 1862, Peter Hitchcock Family Papers, Western Reserve Historical Society Library. A.H. Thrasher to A.G. Riddle, July 13, 1862, Albert Riddle Papers, Western Reserve Historical Society Library. Parker Pillsbury to Theodore Tilton, Sept. 16, 1862, TTP. Proclamation of the Act to Suppress Insurrection, July 25, 1862, Basler, *Works of Lincoln*, 5:341.

26. W.A. Croffut to Ignatius Donnelly, Aug. 10, 1862, IDP, MHS. *NASS*, Aug. 9, 1862. *Liberator*, Aug. 8, 1862.

27. Basler, *Works of Lincoln*, 5:370-75. *Congregationalist*, Aug. 29, 1862. Williams, *Lincoln and the Radicals*, 171. Donald, *Inside Lincoln's Cabinet*, Aug. 15, 1862, p. 112. Louis S. Gerteis, "Salmon P. Chase, Radicalism, and the Politics of Emancipation, 1861-1864," *Journal of American History* 60 (June 1973), 51. John McClintock to Lemuel, Sept. 10, 1862, JMP.

28. *New York Tribune*, Aug. 20, 1862. Herbert Mitgang, ed., *Lincoln as They Saw Him* (New York: Rinehart, 1957), 300-1. *National Intelligencer* (Washington, D.C.), Aug. 23, 1862. Basler, *Works of Lincoln*, 5:388-89. James R. Gilmore [Edmund Kirke, pseud.], *Personal Recollections of Abraham Lincoln and the Civil War* (Boston: L.C. Page, 1898), 98. Ralph R. Fahrney, *Horace Greeley and the Tribune in the Civil War* (1936; reprt., New York: Da Capo Press, 1970), 127-28. John Hope Franklin, *The Emancipation Proclamation* (Garden City, N.Y.: Doubleday, 1963), 136.

29. *Evangelist* (N.Y.), Aug. 28, 1862.

30. S.I. Prime to Lincoln, Aug. 21, 1862, ALP. *New York Observer*, Aug. 21, 1862. Records of the Synod of Buffalo, 1843-1870 (O.S.), Aug. 21, 1862, Manuscript Record, Presbyterian Historical Society, 217. C.J. Phelps, President of Middlebury College Alumni, to Lincoln, Aug. 13, 1862, ALP. *NCAB*, 1:180, 438. *New York Times*, April 5, 1887. *General Catalogue of Middlebury College* (1950). *Lake Geneva Herald* (Wis.), Oct. 20, 1899. *Burlington Gazette*, March 2, 1891. *Annual* (1862), Christ Episcopal Church, Burlington, Iowa, 13, 15.

31. *Minutes of the Oneida Baptist Association, Sept. 1862*, 10. *Minutes of the Oskaloosa Baptist Association, Sept. 1862*, 10. *Minutes of the Bridgewater Baptist Association, 1862*, 6. *Minutes of the Chemung River Baptist Association, Sept. 1862*, 10. *Minutes of the Wisconsin Baptist State Convention, Sept. 1862*, 10. *Minutes of the Lake George Baptist Association, Sept. 1862*, 6. *Minutes of the Dutchess Baptist Association, Sept. 1862*, 8. See also *Minutes of the Centre Baptist Association, Sept. 1962*, 9. *Minutes of the Lafayette Baptist Association, Sept. 1862)*, 6.

32. Benjamin A. West to Lincoln, Aug. 27, 1862; J.G. Davis to Lincoln, Sept. 5, 1862, ALP. Citizens of Washington County, Pa., to Lincoln, Aug. 28, 1862, ALP. General Association of Congregational and Presbyterian Ministers of New Hampshire, Aug. 28, 1862, ALP. Timothy Stillman to Lincoln, Sept. 18, 1862, ALP. Records of the Wisconsin Synod, 1857-69, 1:95. Manuscript Record, PHSL. *NASS*, Sept. 6, 1862, citing *Independent*.

33. *Chicago Tribune*, Sept. 8, 23, 1862. Christian Citizens of Chicago to Lincoln, Sept. 8, 1862, ALP. *Aurora Beacon* (Ill.), Sept. 18, 1862. Christian Residents of Bureau Co., Ill., Sept. 14, 1862, ALP. W.C. McCarthy to Lincoln, Sept. 16, 1862, ALP. Methodist Protestant Conference of Illinois to Lincoln, Sept. 14, 1862, ALP. William B. Dodge to Lincoln, Sept. 14, 1862, ALP. *Banner of the Covenant*, Oct. 4, 1862. W.W. Bucknell to John Andrew, Sept. 15, 1862, JAAP.

34. *Christian Instructor and United Presbyterian*, Sept. 13, 20, 1862. *Northwestern Christian Advocate*, Sept. 17, 1862. *Minutes of the Methodist Episcopal Conference of Iowa, Sept. 1862*, 17. J.K.W. Levane to Lincoln, Sept. 21, 1862, ALP.

35. Howard Beale, *Diary of Gideon Welles*, 3 Vols. (New York: Norton, 1960), Sept. 22, 1862, 1:145. Chase, *Civil War Diary*, July 22, 1862, 97.

36. James Speed to William Herndon, Feb. 9, 1866, Herndon-Weik Correspondence, LC. Gary L. Williams, "James and Joshua Speed: Lincoln's Kentucky Friends" (Ph.D. diss., Duke Univ., 1971), 128. Charles Sumner to John M. Forbes, Dec. 25, 28, 1862, in Sarah Forbes Hughes, ed., *Letters and Recollections of John Murray Forbes*, 2 vols. (Boston: Houghton Mifflin, 1899), 1:348-49, 352-53. "Preliminary Draft of Final Emancipation Proclamation" (Dec. 30, 1862), in Basler, *Works of Lincoln*, 6:24-25; "Emancipation Proclamation." S.P. Chase to Lincoln, Dec. 31, 1862, ALP. Dec. 31, 1863, Basler, *Works of Lincoln*, 6:30.

37. *Minutes of the Illinois Baptist Association, October 1862*, 22. *Minutes of the Woodstock, Vermont, Baptist Association, September 1862*, 6. *Independent*, Oct. 9, 1862. See also Records of the Synod of Ohio, 1849-69 (N.S.), II, Manuscript Record, PHSL.

38. *Presbyterian Witness* (Cincinnati), Sept. 24, 1862. *Pittsburgh Christian Advocate*, Sept. 30, 1862. *Christian Times and Illinois Baptist*, Oct. 1, 1862. *Presbyterian*, Sept. 27, 1862. *New York Observer*, Oct. 2, 1862. *Presbyterian Banner* (Philadelphia), Sept. 27, Oct. 4, 11, 1862. *Christian Herald and Presbyterian Recorder* (Cincinnati), Sept. 25, Oct. 2, 1862. *Christian Intelligencer* (New York), Oct. 2, 1862. See also the *Religious Herald* (Hartford, Conn.), Oct. 2, 1862. *American Presbyterian* (Philadelphia), Oct. 9, 1862. *Presbyter* (Cincinnati), Oct. 2, 1862. *Evangelist* (N.Y.), Sept. 25, 1862. *United Presbyterian* (Pittsburgh), Oct. 1, 1862. *Presbyterian Witness* (Pittsburgh), Oct. 8, 1862. *Christian Advocate and Journal*, Oct. 2, 1862. *Western Christian Advocate*, Oct. 1, 1862. *Northwestern Christian Advocate*, Oct. 1, 1862. *Northern Independent* (Auburn, N.Y.), Oct. 2, 1862. (Baptist) *Examiner* (N.Y.), Oct. 23, 1862. *Morning Star*, Oct. 1, 1862. *Lutheran and Missionary* (Philadelphia), Oct. 16, 1862. *Christian Ambassador* (Auburn, N.Y.), Oct. 4, 1862. *Universalist* (Boston) 19 (Oct. 1862), 362. *Christian Inquirer* (N.Y.), Oct. 4, 1862. *Boston Recorder*, Oct. 2, 1862. *Congregational Journal* (Concord, N.H.), Oct. 9, 1862. *Congregationalist* (Boston), Oct. 2, 1862.

39. George Cheever to Elizabeth, Sept. 29, 1862, GBCP. George Cheever to Lincoln, Nov. 22, 1862, ALP. Conway, *Autobiography*, 1:370-71. William H. Channing to G.B. Cheever, Nov. 25, 1862, GBCP. Burtis, *Conway*, 90-91. William Goodell to Daughter, Sept. 24, 1862, WGP, BCL.

40. Edward E. Hale, *James Freeman Clarke* (Boston: Houghton Mifflin, 1891), 243. Goodell claimed that he had met with Lincoln shortly before the Emancipation Proclamation was issued and that he later found some of his own phrases in the document. See William Goodell to Wife, March 17, 1863, and unpublished biography by Lavinia Goodell, WGP. Gerald Sorin, *The New York Abolitionists: A Case Study of Political Radicalism* (Westport, Conn.: Greenwood, 1971), 61. Alice H. Henderson, "History of New York State Anti-Slavery Society" (Ph.D. diss., Univ. of Michigan, 1963), 388.

41. Joseph Medill to Ozias Hatch, Oct. 13, 1862, Ozias Hatch Papers, ISHL. *Chicago Tribune*, March 2, 1899. John Wilson to Richard Yates, Oct. 8, 1862, RYP. *Biographical Sketches of the Leading Men of Chicago* (Chicago: Wilson and St. Clair, 1868), 425. *Commonwealth*, Oct. 25, 1862.

42. *Christian Advocate and Journal*, Nov. 20, 1862. C.C. Goen, *Broken Churches, Broken Nation* (Macon, Ga.: Mercer Univ. Press, 1985), 6, 13.

43. William W. Sweet, *The Story of Religions in America* (New York: Harper and Brothers, 1930), 10. Alhstrom, *Religious History of the American People*, 677. *Minutes, General Assembly of the Presbyterian Church* (O.S.) 17 (1863), 77. Moorhead, *American Apocalypse*, 70-75.

44. Ira V. Brown, *Lyman Abbott: Christian Evolutionist* (Cambridge, Mass.:

Harvard Univ. Press, 1953), 31. Arthur C. Cole, *The Irrepressible Conflict, 1850-1865* (1934; reprt., Freeport, N.Y.: Books for Libraries Press, 1971), 306.

## 3. The Election of 1862

1. Thomas Savan to B.F. Wade, July 26, 1862, BFWP.
2. Joseph Medill to Lyman Trumbull, June 5, 1862, LTP.
3. Jacque Voegeli, *Free but Not Equal* (Chicago: Univ. of Chicago Press, 1967), 53.
4. *Lutheran Observer* (Baltimore), Oct. 3, 1862.
5. *Christian Instructor and United Presbyterian* (Philadelphia), Aug. 9, 1862. *Presbyterian Standard* (Philadelphia), Sept. 4, 1862. *Christian Intelligencer*, Sept. 4, 1862. *Independent*, Sept. 18, 1862.
6. See: *Atlas and Argus* (Albany, N.Y.), Sept. 18, 1862, for example. *Harper's Weekly*, Dec. 20, 1862, 802.
7. *Daily Wisconsin* (Milwaukee), Oct. 8, 1862.
8. C.L. Scholes to James Doolittle, Sept. 8, 1862, James R. Doolittle Papers. H. Barber to Lyman Trumbull, Oct. 30, 1862, LTP.
9. *Minutes of the Dodge, Wisconsin, Baptist Association, Sept. 3-4, 1862*, 6. *Minutes of the Columbus Baptist Association, 1862*, 6.
10. *Worcester Palladium*, Sept. 17, 1862. *Christian Review* (Boston) 27 (Oct. 1862), 585.
11. John Nevin, Moderator, and John Douglas, Clerk, to Lincoln, Oct. 1, 1862, ALP.
12. Minutes of the Synod of Illinois (N.S.), Oct. 1862, 2:176, Manuscript Record, McCormick Theological Seminary Library.
13. *Minutes of the Illinois Conference of the Methodist Episcopal Church, Oct. 1862*, 21.
14. *Western Christian Advocate*, Oct. 1, 1862. *Wolverine Citizen* (Flint, Mich.), Oct. 25, 1862. *United Presbyterian*, (Pittsburgh), Oct. 29, 1862.
15. *Western Christian Advocate*, Oct. 22, Nov. 5, 1862.
16. Minutes of the Synod of Pennsylvania, (N.S.), Oct. 1862, pp. 8-9, Manuscript Record, PHSL. John C. Smith, Moderator (N.S.), to Lincoln, Oct. 28, 1862, ALP.
17. *New York Tribune*, Oct. 16, 1862. Voegeli, *Free but Not Equal*, 60. *Western Christian Advocate*, Jan. 7, 1863. *Christian Instructor and United Presbyterian*, Nov. 1, 1862. *Presbyterian Standard*, Nov. 12, 1862.
18. *Western Christian Advocate*, Oct. 1, 1862. *Ladies' Repository*, (Cincinnati), March 1863, p. 192.
19. *Wabash Express* (Terre Haute, Ind.), Sept. 16, 1862.
20. *Boston Evening Transcript*, Oct. 10, 1862. *Western Episcopalian* (Gambier, Ohio), Oct. 23, 1862.
21. *Ladies' Repository* (Cincinnati) 22 (Oct. 1862), 494.
22. *Christian Instructor and United Presbyterian*, Oct. 4, 1862.
23. *Independent*, Oct. 30, 1862. *Cincinnati Gazette*, Nov. 8, 1862. J.R. Wood to Richard Yates, Nov. 3, 1862, RYP.
24. John McClintock to Lamuel, Oct. 2, 1862, JMP. Henry W. Bellows to Son, Oct. 19, 1862, HWBC, MaHS. Oliver Johnson to William L. Garrison, Sept. 25, 1862, WLGP, BPL.
25. Baum, *The Civil War Party System*, 63-65. Moorfield Storey, *Charles Sumner* (Boston: Houghton Mifflin, 1900), 233. Archibald H. Grinke, *The Life of Charles Sumner* (New York: Funk and Wagnalls, 1892), 24-25. Walter G. Shotwell, *Life of*

*Charles Sumner* (New York: Crowell, 1910), 723. S. Holmes to Charles Sumner, Oct. 6, 1862, CSP.

26. *Boston Evening Transcript*, Oct. 1, 1862. *Janesville Daily Gazette*, Oct. 1, 1862. *Marietta Times* (Ohio), Oct. 2, 1867. *The Massachusetts Manual for the Use of General Court, 1862-63*, 219.

27. John B. DeMotte, Journal or Brief Private Diary, Oct. 18, 1862, DePauw Univ.; William Graham, Personal Memoirs (1862), 104, DePauw Univ. Edward McPherson, *The Political History of the United States of America during the Great Rebellion* (Washington, D.C.: Phillip and Solomons, 1865), 499. C.D. Hubbard to Son, Nov. 11, 1862, C.D. Hubbard Correspondence, WVU.

28. Theodore Tilton to William L. Garrison, Sept. 25, 1862. Theodore D. Weld to William L. Garrison, Oct. 8, 30, 1862, WLGP. *Liberator*, Oct. 31, Nov. 7, 14, 21, 28, Dec. 12, 19, 1862. Benjamin P. Thomas, *Theodore Weld: Crusader for Freedom* (New Brunswick, N.J.: Rutgers Univ. Press, 1950), 244. *Boston Evening Transcript*, Dec. 8, 1862. *NASS*, Dec. 6, 20, 22, 29, 1862. *Worcester Daily Spy* (Mass.), Dec. 4, 1862.

29. *Liberator*, Nov. 14, Dec. 12, 22, 26, 1862. James H. Young, "Anna Elizabeth Dickinson and the Civil War" (Ph.D. diss., Univ. of Illinois, 1941), 261, 265. Fanny Garrison to Anna E. Dickinson, Oct. 12, 1862, AEDP, LC. Anna E. Dickinson to Abby K. Foster, Oct. 21, 1862, AKFP, AASL.

30. Voegeli, *Free but Not Equal*, 61-63, Baum, *The Civil War Party System*, 67-68. McPherson, *Ordeal by Fire*, 297. Allan Nevins, *The War for the Union*, 2 vols. (New York: Scribner's, 1960), 2:322. George H. Porter, *Ohio Politics during the Civil War Period* (1911; reprt., New York, AMS Press, 1968), 106.

31. H.W. Bellows to Son, Oct. 19, 1862; Henry W. Foote to Henry W. Bellows, Nov. 7, 1862, HWBC. Lyman Trumbull to Zachariah Chandler, Nov. 9, 1862, ZCP, LC. George Bancroft to Francis Lieber, Oct. 29, 1862, Francis Lieber Papers, Huntington Library. McPherson, *The Political History of the United States of America during the Great Rebellion*, 476.

32. Annie Fields, ed., *Life and Letters of Harriet Beecher Stowe* (Boston: Houghton Mifflin, 1898), 262.

33. Ralph Plumb to J.R. Giddings, December 1, 1862, JGP, OSHL. *Biographical and Genealogical Record of La Salle Co., Illinois* (Chicago: Lewis Publishing, 1900), 1:13, Garrison to Fanny Garrison, Sept. 25, 1862; Oliver Johnson to Garrison, Nov. 10, 1862, WLGP. Sallie Holly to Abby Kelley Foster, Sept. 30, 1862, AKFP, Worcester Historical Society.

34. "D.B." to William Goodell, Oct. 11, 1862, in the *Principia*, Nov. 6, 1862. George W. Nichols to John Andrew, Oct. 27, 1862, JAAP. *DAB*, 7:494. *Cincinnati Enquirer*, Sept. 18, 1885.

35. *Cong. Globe*, 37th Cong., 3d sess. (1862), 15, 92.

36. J.M. Ashley to George Cheever, Dec. 23, 1862, GBCP.

37. Basler, *Works of Lincoln*, 5:529-31.

38. *Boston Commonwealth*, Dec. 6, 1862. Parker Pillsbury to Theodore Tilton, Dec. 12, 1862, TTP.

39. J.M. Ashley to George Cheever, Dec. 23, 1862, GBCP. Robert F. Horowitz, *The Great Impeacher: A Political Biography of James M. Ashley* (New York: Brooklyn College Press, 1979), 84. Franklin, *The Emancipation Proclamation*, 137.

40. *Presbyter*, Dec. 11, 1862.

41. *New York Observer*, Dec. 11, 1862.

42. D. Heaton to I. Donnelly, Dec. 9, 1862, IDP. *NASS*, Dec. 13, 1862. For Putnam's and Hatfield's sermons, see *New York Tribune*, Nov. 28; Dec. 19, 1862.

43. Israel Washburn to Hamlin, Dec. 20, 1862, Israel Washburn Papers, LC.

Gaillard Hunt, *Israel, Elihu, and Cadwallader Washburn: A Chapter in American Biography* (New York: Macmillan, 1925), 13. Hannibal Hamlin to J. Watson Webb, Nov. 29, 1862, JWWP, YU. Charles E. Hamlin, *The Life and Times of Hannibal Hamlin* (Cambridge, Mass.: Riverside Press, 1899), 81.

44. Ben Birdsall to Zachariah Chandler, Dec. 22, 1862, ZCP. Franklin Ellis, *History of Genesee County, Michigan* (Philadelphia: Everts and Abbott, 1879), 230.

45. T.W. Cheney to B.F. Wade, Dec. 25, 1862, BFWP. *The History of Union County, Ohio* (Chicago: W.H. Beers, 1883), 495-96.

46. Thomas Maple to Lyman Trumbull, Dec. 28, 1862, LTP. Charles Sedgwick to J.M. Forbes, Dec. 22, 1862; Charles Sumner to J.M. Forbes, Dec. 28, 1862, in Hughes, *Letters and Recollections of John Murray Forbes*, 1:344-45, 352. Samuel Hooper to John Andrew, Dec. 27, 1862, JAAP. George Stearns to Lysander Spooner, Oct. 1, 1861, Lysander Spooner Correspondence, NYHSL. Samuel Hooper to John Andrew, Dec. 27, 1862, JAAP.

47. New Bedford, Mass. Citizens to Lincoln, Dec. 12, 1862, ALP. Forty-one citizens signed the memorial. Four can be identified as clergy, eight occupied a lay office in church bodies, and others were members of churches. See Leonard B. Ellis, *History of New Bedford and Its Vicinity* (Syracuse: Mason, 1892), 40, 58, 93, 544, 548, 561-63, 573, 601, 630. Samuel Fessenden to Lincoln, Dec. 15, 1862, ALP. Charles A. Jellison, *Fessenden of Maine: Civil War Senator* (Syracuse: Syracuse Univ. Press, 1962), 131. Francis Fessenden, *Life and Public Service of William Pitt Fessenden*, 2 vols. (Boston: Houghton Mifflin, 1907), 1:6. Society of Friends of Prairie Grove, Iowa, to Lincoln, Dec. 27, 1862, ALP. Johnson Brigham, *James Harlan* (Iowa City: State Historical Society of Iowa, 1913), 23-24. *DAB*, 4:268.

48. "EDM," Morrow, Ohio, Dec. 1862, "The Proclamation," *Cincinnati Daily Gazette*, Dec. 30, 1862.

49. *Principia*, Dec. 25, 1862. *New York Tribune*, Dec. 22, 1862. *New York Times*, Dec. 23, 1862. *Liberator*, Dec. 26, 1862. *NASS*, Jan. 10, 1863.

50. *New York World*, cited by the *Principia*, Dec. 25, 1862.

51. Hughes, *Letters and Recollections of John Murray Forbes*, 1:352.

52. Franklin, *The Emancipation Proclamation*, 103-4. McPherson, *The Struggle for Equality*, 124, 127.

### 4. Rise Up O Man of God

1. John Rankin to William L. Garrison, Nov. 19, 1863, in *Proceedings of the American Anti-Slavery Society at the Third Decade Held in the City of Philadelphia* (New York: American Anti-Slavery Society, 1864), 15. *Independent*, June 25, 1863. A.N. Arnold, *Place the Fruit of Righteousness: A Sermon, Westboro, Massachusetts, 1863* (Boston: John Whittemore, 1863), 13.

2. Basler, *Works of Lincoln*, 6:30. Beale, *Diary of Gideon Welles*, 1:210. Thomas, *Abraham Lincoln*, 359.

3. *Daily Pittsburgh Post*, Jan. 12, 1863. *Liberator*, Jan. 2, 1863. *Independent*, Jan. 1, 1863. Theodore Tilton to W.L. Garrison, Jan. 9, 1863, WLGP, BPL. G.R. Crooks to John McClintock, Jan. 2, 1863, John McClintock Correspondence, Drew Univ. Library. *NASS*, Jan. 3, 1863. *New York World*, Jan. 2, 1863. R.C. Waterston to Charles Sumner, Jan. 2, 1863, CSP. Rudolf Schleiden, Dispatch No. 3, Jan. 2, 1863, Schleiden Papers, microfilm, LC. cited by H.L. Trefousse, *Benjamin Franklin Wade* (New York: Twayne, 1863), 190. See George Tuthill's Diary, GMT, 6:1506, Jan. 1, 1863.

4. Basler, *Works of Lincoln*, 6:30. Gayle Thornbrough, *The Diary of Calvin Fletcher* (Indianapolis: Indiana Historical Society, 1972), 8:6, Jan. 2, 1863. *New York*

*Times*, Feb. 20, 1863. William Parker Cutler's Diary, Feb. 2, 1863, in Allan G. Bogue, "William Parker Cutler's Congressional Diary of 1862-63," *Civil War History* 33 (Dec. 1987), 316, 329. George F. Hoar, *Charles Sumner: His Complete Works*, 20 vols. (1900; reprt., New York: Negro Univ. Press, 1969), 262, 264.

5. *New York Post*, Jan. 7, 1863. *New York Times*, Jan. 6, 1863. See *Daily Morning Chronicle*, Jan. 5, 1863, for Channing's sermon. For similar remarks, see Rev. William W. Patton, Chicago, *Chicago Evening Journal*, Jan. 13, 1863, at proclamation meeting; also see Meeting at Revenna, Ohio, in *Portage County Democrat*, Jan. 14, 1863. *Philadelphia Inquirer*, Jan. 2, 1863. For religious effects of the proclamation in Wisconsin, see Rev. Wesson G. Miller, *Thirty Years in the Itineracy* (Milwaukee: I.L. Hauser, 1875), 244; Rev. P.S. Bennett, *History of Methodism in Wisconsin* (Cincinnati: Cranston and Stowe, 1890), 200-2.

6. Samuel S. Cox, *Puritanism in Politics: Speech of the Hon. S.S. Cox of Ohio, before the Democratic Association, January 13, 1863* (New York: Van Evrie Horton, 1863). *Cong. Globe*, 37th Cong., 3d sess., 1862-63, pp. 94-100, 281, 626, 916. Samuel S. Cox, *Eight Years in Congress from 1857-1865* (New York: D. Appleton, 1865), 259-61, 281-300. *Crisis* (Columbus, Ohio), Jan. 21, 1863. *Ohio State Journal* (Columbus), Jan. 20, 1863. David Lindsey, *"Sunset" Cox: Irrepressible Democrat* (Detroit: Wayne Univ. Press, 1957), 70-71. *New York Times*, Jan. 14, 1863. *New York Tribune*, Jan. 14, 1863. *Zion's Herald*, Sept. 14, 1863.

7. *Pittsburgh Christian Advocate*, Feb. 7, 1863.

8. *Christian Advocate and Journal*, Jan. 8, 1863. *Boston Recorder*, Jan. 8, 1863. *Evangelist*, Jan. 8, 1863. *Independent*, Jan. 8, 1863. *Christian Inquirer*, Jan. 10, 1863. *Presbyter*, Jan. 7, 1863; cited by the *Christian Herald and Presbyterian*, Jan. 8, 1863. *Principia*, Jan. 8, 1863. *Morning Star* (Dover, N.H.), Jan. 14, 1863. See also *Congregationalist*, Jan. 9, 1863. Theodore Tilton to Susan B. Anthony, Jan. 11, 1863, SBAP, LC. Fredrickson, *The Inner Civil War*, 118.

9. *Christian Advocate and Journal*, Feb. 5, 1863. *Boston Recorder*, Feb. 12, 1863. Rev. Edmund B. Fairchild, *Christian Patriotism: A Sermon Delivered in the Representatives' Hall* (Lansing, Mich.: John Kerr, 1863), 37, 46.

10. *New York Times*, March 7, 1863. George Cheever to Henry Cheever, Feb. 26, 1863, GBCP. John McClintock to Jane (daughter), Jan. 20, 1863, JMP. Henry G. Pearson, *The Life of John A. Andrew* (Boston: Houghton Mifflin, 1904), 2:51. Samuel May, Jr., to Richard Webb, Sept. 23, 1862, Samuel May, Jr., Papers, BPL; Samuel May, Jr., Robert Wollcut, and Edmund Quincy to Abraham Lincoln, Jan. 29, 1863, ALP.

11. *The Diary of Orville Browning*, 2:600. William Fessenden to Family, Jan. 10, 1863, in Fessenden, *Life and Public Services of William Pitt Fessenden*, 1:265-66. A.H. Dunlevy to John Sherman, Jan. 13, 1863, JSP. Henry Ford, *History of Hamilton Co., Ohio* (Cleveland: H.Z. Williams, 1881), 350. A.H. Dunlevy, *History of the Miami Baptist Association*. William P. Cutler, Diary, Jan. 26, 1863, in Julia P. Cutler, *Life and Times of Ephraim Cutler, from His Journal and Correspondence* (Cincinnati: R. Clarke, 1890), 298-300. Donald V. Smith, *Chase and Civil War Politics* (1931; reprt., Freeport, N.Y.: Books for Libraries Press, 1972), 69.

12. E.S. James to John McClintock, Jan. 12, 1863, JMP. James Pike to William P. Fessenden, Jan. 13, 1863, James S. Pike Papers, Calasis Free Library. Alexander K. McClure, *Abraham Lincoln and Men of War-Times: Some Personal Recollections of War and Politics during the Lincoln Administration* (Philadelphia: Times Publishing, 1892), 109.

13. *Cong. Globe*, 37th Cong., 3d sess. (Jan. 29, 1863), 593.

14. Mark Krug, *Lyman Trumbull: Conservative Radical* (New York: A.S. Barnes, 1965), 216.

15. J.M. Forbes to Sumner, Feb. 17, 1863, CSP. Edward Archibald to B.F. Wade,

Feb. 15, 1863, BFWP. Storey, *Charles Sumner*, 238. Donald, *Charles Sumner*, 120-21. Sumner, *Works*, 9:268-69. *Northern Independent*, July 16, 1863.

16. Samuel C. Pomeroy to Anna Dickinson, May 27, 1863, AEDP, LC. Sheffield Ingalls, *History of Atchison County, Kansas* (Lawrence: Standard Publishing, 1916), 245. Clinton Rice to S.P. Chase, Oct. 29, 1863, SPCP.

17. Conway, *Autobiography*, 1:377-78. *Liberator*, Jan. 30, March 20, 1863. *NASS*, Feb. 28, 1863.

18. Giraud Chester, *Embattled Maiden: The Life of Anna Dickinson* (New York: G.P. Putnam's Sons, 1951), 45-48. *NASS*, Jan. 3, March 14, 28, 1862. *Hartford Daily Post*, March 24, 1862.

19. *NASS*, March 28, April 4, 11, 25, 1862. *Liberator*, April 18, May 8, July 31, Oct. 2, Dec. 26, 1862. *Hartford Daily Courant*, March 25, 26, 1862. J. Robert Lane, *A Political History of Connecticut during the Civil War* (Washington, D.C.: Catholic Univ. of American Press, 1941), 233. *Independent*, April 23, 1863. *New York Times*, May 1, 3, 24, 1863. *Daily Morning Chronicles*, May 5, 1863. *New York Tribune*, May 25, 1863.

20. Theodore D. Weld to J.M. McKim, Feb. 14, 1862, JMMP, CorU. Robert H. Abzug, "Theodore Weld: A Biography" (Ph.D. diss., University of California at Berkeley, 1977), 334-47. Benjamin Thomas, *Theodore Weld* (New Brunswick, N.J.: Rutgers Univ. Press, 1950), 244, 249-50. *NASS*, Jan. 3, 10, 31; Feb. 7, 21, 28; March 7, 28; May 2; June 13, 20; Aug. 15; Nov. 14, 1863. *Liberator*, Jan. 9, 16; Feb. 27; March 13; May 22; Aug. 21; Oct. 9; Nov. 13, 1863. Oliver Johnson to William L. Garrison, April 9, 1863, WLGP, BPL. William L. Garrison to Samuel J. May, April 6, 1863; Garrison to Theodore Weld, Sept. 29, 1863, in Walter M. Merrill, ed., *The Letters of William Lloyd Garrison* (Cambridge: Belknap Press, 1979), 5:142-43, 144. Samuel May, Jr., to Mrs. Chace, Jan. 6, 1863, in Lillie B. Chace Wyman and Arthur C. Wyman, *Elizabeth Buffum Chace, 1806-1899* (Boston: W.B. Clarke, 1914), 2:245. Merton L. Dillon, *The Abolitionist: The Growth of a Dissenting Minority* (DeKalb: Northern Illinois Univ. Press, 1974), 266.

21. Chester, *Embattled Maiden*, 49. McPherson, *The Struggle for Equality*, 130. *NASS*, Jan. 3, 31; May 9, 23, 1863. Susan B. Anthony to Theodore Tilton, Jan. 30, 1863; Frederick Douglass to Tilton, June 20, 1863, TTP. *Proceedings of the American Anti-Slavery Society, 1863* (New York: American Anti-Slavery Society, 1863), 100. George Cheever to wife, June 17, 1863, GBCP. York, *Cheever*, 195.

22. *Christian Times*, Jan. 4, 1863.

23. *New York Recorder and Examiner*, Feb. 19, 1863. *Pittsburgh Christian Advocate*, Feb. 7, 1863.

24. *Northwestern Christian Advocate*, April 29, 1863. *American Baptist*, cited by the *Liberator*, July 31, 1863. *Boston Recorder*, July 3, 1863.

25. *Press* (Philadelphia), May 1, 1863. Eugene H. Roseboom, *The Civil War Era, 1850-1873* (Columbus: Ohio State Archeological Society, 1944), 421. Porter, *Ohio Politics during the Civil War Period*, 189. *Dayton Empire* (Ohio), March 16, 1863.

26. James S. Gibbons, "Journal," in Sarah Hopper Emerson, *Life of Abby Hopper Gibbons*, 2 vols. (New York: G.P. Putnam's Sons, 1897), 29-30.

27. *Daily Morning Chronicle*, May 2, 1863. *Minutes of the General Assembly of the Presbyterian Church* (N.S.) 13 (1863), 242-43.

28. Susan H. Ward, *George H. Hepworth, Preacher, Journalist, Friend of the People* (New York: E.P. Dutton, 1913), 65.

29. John Cross to S.S. Jocelyn, March, 1863, AMAC.

30. *New York Observer*, cited by the *Christian Watchman and Reflector*, Sept. 24, 1863.

31. *Minutes of the Pittsburgh Conference of the Methodist Episcopal Church,*

*March 1863*, 22; William W. Sweet, *The Methodist Episcopal Church and the Civil War* (Cincinnati: Methodist Book Concern, 1963), 73. *Christian Advocate and Journal*, April 23, 1863. *New York Tribune*, April 20, 1863.

32. Sweet, *The Methodist Episcopal Church*, 71. George Peck, *The Life and Times of Rev. George Peck, D.D.* (New York: Nelson and Phillips, 1874), 374.

33. *Northern Ohio Methodist Episcopal Conference, Sept. 1863*, 30-32. Northern Ohio Methodist Episcopal Conference to Lincoln, Sept. 7, 1863, ALP.

34. E.E. Reed and Reuben Tompson to Lincoln, June 20, 1863, ALP. *Minutes of the New London Baptist Association, Sept. 1863*, 5.

35. Minutes of the Congregational and Presbyterian Convention, 1862-73, Manuscript Record, SHLW. *Minutes of the General Association of Congregational Churches of Michigan, May 1863*, 13. *Minutes of the Congregational Conference of Ohio, 1863*, 16-17. *Minutes of the Presbytery of Columbus (Ohio), 1856-1865*, (N.S.) 1 (June 1863), 156, Manuscript Record, PHSL. See also Charles A. Hanna, *Historical Collection of Harrison County in the State of Ohio, 1900*, 152.

36. McPherson, *The Political History of the United States of America during the Great Rebellion*, 502. William Miller to Lincoln, Sept. 25, 1863, ALP.

37. Lyman Trumbull to Zachariah Chandler, Aug. 4, 1863, ZCP. Chandler to Trumbull, Aug. 6, 1863, LTP. Joshua Giddings to George Julian, March 22, 1863, G-JP, Giddings to S.P. Chase, July 21, 1863, SPCP; Chase to Giddings, July 17, 1863, JGP. Stewart, *Giddings and the Tactics of Radical Politics*, 276. Benjamin F. Butler Correspondence, 3:112-13. John A. Andrew, Sept. 14, 1863, JAAP. *Cincinnati Gazette*, Sept. 26, 1863. John Morgan to Theodore Weld, July 29, 1863, W-GP, UM. York, *Cheever*, 195. *Liberator*, July 3, 1863.

38. Frank L. Klement, "Clement L. Vallandigham," in *For the Union: Ohio Leaders in the Civil War*, edited by Kenneth W. Wheeler (Columbus: Ohio State Univ. Press, 1968), 49. Frank L. Klement, *The Limits of Dissent* (Lexington: Univ. Press of Kentucky, 1970), 235-36.

39. *Daily Chronicle*, July 7, 1863. J.G. Balwin and J. Carter to Lincoln, Oct. 10, 1863, ALP. Klement, *The Limits of Dissent*, 236.

40. Klement, *The Limits of Dissent*, 2, 35-36.

41. *Daily Capital Fact* (Columbus, Ohio), Sept. 21, 1863. James A. Woodburn, "The Scotch-Irish in Monroe County, Indiana," *Indiana Historical Publications* (Indianapolis: Bobbs-Merrill, 1906), 4:517-19.

42. Klement, *The Limits of Dissent*, 236. Bruce C. Flack, "The Attitude of the Methodist Episcopal Church in Ohio toward the Civil War, 1861-1865" (masters thesis, Ohio State Univ., 1962).

43. *Western Standard* (Ohio), Aug. 13, 1863, citing *Piqua Enquirer* (Ohio), Aug. 6, 1863. *Western Christian Advocate*, April 29, 1863. *Daily Capital Fact*, July 14, 1863. *Zanesville Courier* (Ohio), Oct. 1, 1863. *Ohio State Journal* (Columbus), Oct. 9, 16, 1863. *Cincinnati Gazette*, Aug. 7, 1863. *Chicago Tribune*, Nov. 11, 1863.

44. Minutes of the Zanesville Conference of the Wesleyan Connection, 1849-1863, Aug. 26, 1863, Manuscript Record, Archives, Marion College. Klement, *Limits of Dissent*, 236.

45. *Zanesville Daily Courier*, Oct. 29, 1863.

46. Thornbrough, *Diary of Calvin Fletcher*, 228-30.

47. *NASS*, Nov. 14, 1863. *Daily Sandusky Register* (Ohio), Oct. 15, 1863.

48. *Pittsburgh Gazette*, Sept. 21, 1863.

49. Forrest G. Wood, *Black Scare* (Berkeley: Univ. of California Press, 1968), 36. *Daily Pittsburgh Gazette*, Oct. 10, 13, 1863. *DAB*, 5:212-13; 8:125. *Liberator*, Oct. 7, 1863. McPherson, *The Political History of the United States of America during the Great Rebellion*, 493-94. Alexander V. Allen, *Life and Letters of Phillips Brooks* (New York: E.P. Dutton, 1901), 1:461-62. *Independent*, Jan. 16, 1868. *Phila-*

*delphia Age*, June 29, Aug. 13, Sept. 29, 1863. William Dusinberre, *Civil War Issues in Philadelphia, 1856-1865* (Philadelphia: Univ. of Pennsylvania Press, 1865), 172. John H. Hopkins, Jr., *The Life of the Late Right Reverend John Henry Hopkins* (New York: F.J. Huntington, 1873), 331-36.

50. *Pittsburgh Daily Dispatch*, Jan. 26, 1864.

51. *Minutes of the Philadelphia Baptist Association, Oct. 1863*, 21. *Minutes of the North Philadelphia Baptist Association, Sept. 1863*, 11.

52. *Pittsburgh Gazette*, Oct. 1, 2, 3, 8, 9, 10, 1863. Allen, *Life and Letters of Phillips Brooks*, 1:462.

53. Daniel D. Addison, *The Clergy in American Life and Letters* (London: Macmillan, 1900), 348. Lincoln to Nathaniel P. Banks, Aug. 5, 1863, in Basler, *Works of Lincoln*, 6:365.

54. Lincoln to James C. Conkling, Aug. 26, 1863, ALP.

55. Stephen B. Oates, *With Malice toward None: The Life of Abraham Lincoln* (New York: Harper and Row, 1977), 360. *Evangelist*, Sept. 10, 1863. *Principia*, Sept. 10, 1863.

56. Horace Greeley, *A History of the Great Rebellion in the United States of America, 1860-1865*, 2 vols. (Hartford: O.D. Case, 1865-66), 2:254-55. Strong, *Diary*, 408. Lincoln's Annual Message to Congress, Dec. 8, 1863, Basler, *Works of Lincoln*, 7:49-50. *Western Christian Advocate*, Oct. 21, 1863.

57. Basler, *Works of Lincoln*, 7:51. Rev. William H. Pearne quoted in Union League Meeting, *Proceedings of the State Council of the Union League of America for the State of New York on the 25th Day of November, 1863* (New York: Davies and Kent, 1863), 10-11. Theodore Tilton to Henry W. Beecher, Aug. 7, 1863, HWBP, YU.

58. Basler, *Works of Lincoln*, 7:51. Henry Wright to Lincoln, Dec. 16, 1863, ALP. Whitman, *American Reformers*, 910, 912. Henry C. Hubbart, *The Older Middle West, 1840-1880* (1936; reprt., New York: Russell and Russell, 1963), 216.

59. McPherson, *The Struggle for Equality*, 124.

60. *Crisis*, Oct. 7, 1863; Sept. 4, 1867. Flack, "The Attitude of the Methodist Episcopal Church in Ohio toward the Civil War," 42.

61. *Crisis*, Sept. 4, 1867. Flack, "The Attitude of the Methodist Episcopal Church in Ohio toward the Civil War," 48.

## 5. The Election of 1864

1. S.P. Chase to Abraham Lincoln, Nov. 23, 1863, ALP. "Proclamation of Amnesty and Reconstruction," Dec. 8, 1863, in Basler, *Works of Lincoln*, 7:53-56. Simon Nash to John Sherman, Feb. 4, 1864, JSP. John G. Fee to Wendell Phillips in the *Liberator*, March 18, 1864; Whitelaw Reid to Anna E. Dickinson, April 3, 1864, AEDP.

2. Abraham Lincoln to Albert G. Hodges, April 4, 1864, in Basler, *Works of Lincoln*, 7:281-82.

3. *Cong. Globe*, 38th Cong., 1st sess. (Feb. 15, 1864), 19-21, 1,313-14. Ashley's father was a Campbellite clergyman, but James rebelled against the proslavery teaching of the Disciples of Christ and his father's strict discipline. Under the guidance of his mother, the young man read the Bible and interpreted the Scripture as antislavery. He focused on the moral aspect of the antislavery movement and believed slavery a great sin. His moral opposition to slavery was strengthened by Quaker abolitionists and refined by his radicalism when he became a member of the Unitarian Church. Horowitz, *The Great Impeacher*, 5-7, 174. "Life and Activities of James F. Wilson," Document W-50, Iowa HSL. Mark M. Krug, *Lyman Trumbull*, 219.

4. *Cong. Globe*, 38th Cong., 1st sess. (March 19, 1864), 1,203. James F. Wilson's parents and their family were active members of the Methodist Episcopal Church, but later Senator Wilson and his family attended the Congregational church, of which Mrs. Wilson and the children were members. Wilson was a man of broad philanthropy and devotion to humanitarian causes. He often spoke on religious subjects and was remembered for his commencement address on Genesis, in which he firmly held that a personal God alone created all things. When Wilson died, he was held in such high regard by the Christian community that commemoration services were conducted by the Congregational, Presbyterian, and Methodist churches, and Rev. George F. Magoun, a Congregational minister and former president of Grinnell College, wrote a tribute to him that was widely circulated. See *Portrait and Biographical Album of Jefferson and Van Buren Counties, Iowa* (Chicago: Lake City Publishing, 1890), 169-70. *Fairfield Ledger* (Iowa), April 24, May 15, 1895. *Iowa State Register* (Des Moines), April 26, 1895. John P. Hale rejoiced that the nation was now listening to the voice of God and was preparing to put itself in alliance with Providence and come up to "the high standard of Christian duty" (*Cong. Globe*, 38th Cong., 1st sess. [April 6, 1864], 1,443-44). Early in life he became a compulsive churchgoer and was a warden in the Unitarian church in Dover, New Hampshire. Religion was an intensely personal affair for Hale. When he became an antislavery Christian, Hale hated slavery passionately. Richard E. Sewell, *John P. Hale and the Politics of Abolition* (Cambridge, Mass.: Harvard Univ. Press, 1965), 33.

5. Harold M. Dudley, "The Election of 1864," *MVHR* 18 (March 1932), 501. Jacob W. Schuckers, *The Life and Public Services of Salmon Portland Chase* (New York: Appleton, 1874), 450, 494. Greeley, Tilton, and Sydney Gay favored Chase. See James G. Randall and David Donald, *The Civil War and Reconstruction* (Boston: Heath, 1961), 465. James G. Randall, *Lincoln, the President: The Last Full Measure* (New York: Dodd, Mead, 1955), 96-97. Don Piatt, *Memories of the Men Who Saved the Union* (New York: Bedford, Clark, 1887), 99.

6. S.P. Chase Diaries, July 12, 14, 15, 26, Aug. 4, 29, Dec. 25, 1840, pp. 104-5, 167-69, 172-77, LC.

7. S.P. Chase to Charles Sumner, Jan. 21, March 15, 1850, CSP. After studying Chase's career, Robert Gruber found that Chase's motives were very complex. Chase consciously committed himself to serving humanity, but he often had difficulty distinguishing between what would advance humanity and what would advance his career. Robert H. Gruber, "Salmon P. Chase and the Politics of Reform" (Ph.D. diss., Univ. of Maryland, 1969), 353. See also John R. Russell, "Free Soil: Politics and Beliefs" (Ph.D. diss., Johns Hopkins Univ. 1973), 140.

8. Donald, *Inside Lincoln's Cabinet: Chase's Diary*, 19.

9. Nevins, *The War for the Union*, 2:336.

10. Schuckers, *Life of Salmon P. Chase*, 476. Beale, *Diary of Gideon Welles*, Feb. 15, 1964, 1:502. Rev. William H. Brisbane (Baptist) to S.P. Chase, Jan. 10, 1864; Rev. Mansfield French (Methodist) to S.P. Chase, Jan. 22, 1864, SPCP. L. Maria Child to Gerrit Smith, n.d., GSP, SUL. See letters of radical Presbyterian layman Col. Henry B. Carrington to S.P. Chase, Dec. 18, 24, 1863, SPCP. *NCAB*, 22:254. Edgar Ketchum, Treasurer of the AMA, to Chase, Dec. 30, 1863, SPCP. *American Missionary* 11 (Oct. 1867), 241. Presbyterian layman George H. Stuart to Chase, Dec. 21, 1863, SPCP. Robert E. Thompson, *The Life of George H. Stuart* (Philadelphia: J.M. Stoddart, 1890), 348. George Morgan, *Fifty Years in Philadelphia Journalism* (Philadelphia: Historical Society of Philadelphia, 1926), 167. Presbyterian clergyman E.D. MacMaster to Chase, Nov. 13, 1863; H.W. Beecher to Chase, Dec. 28, 1863, SPCP.

11. Beale, *Diary of Gideon Welles*, Aug. 22, 1863, 1:413. Henry W. Beecher to S.P. Chase, Dec. 28, 1863; John Jay to Chase, Oct. 6, 1863, SPCP. George Cheever to Theodore Tilton, [n.d.] 1864, TTP. Terry, "Theodore Tilton," 35.

12. *Independent*, Feb. 4, 18, 1864. Terry, "Theodore Tilton," 35.

13. *Boston Commonwealth*, Feb. 26, 1864, citing *Independent*.

14. *Principia*, March 3, 24; April 21, 1864. Leon Perkal, "William Goodell: A Life of Reform" (Ph.D. diss., City College of New York, 1972), 319-20. William L. Garrison to James McKim, Feb. 27, 1864, in *Philadelphia Press*, March 17, 1864. *Liberator*, March 18, 1864.

15. Schuyler Colfax to S.H. Gay, Feb. 6, 1864, SHGP. In 1846 Colfax joined a Presbyterian church during a revival but later withdrew and helped organize a Dutch Reformed church. For twelve years he served as a Sabbath school teacher in the Reformed Church of South Bend, Indiana. Colfax published and edited the *St. Joseph Valley Register* early in his career and kept it on the highest moral plane. He was elected to Congress as a Free Soiler and resolved to stop making concessions to slavery. Colfax was one of the most respected Christian laymen during the Civil War years and was generally called "the Christian statesman." He was in demand as chairman of national benevolent and religious meetings. Colfax was sincere in his religious beliefs, and much of his humanitarism and passion for justice and equality for the blacks reflected commitment to his religious principles. Linus P. Brocket, *Men of Our Day* (Philadelphia: Zeigler McCurdy, 1868), 267. Rev. A.Y. Moore, *The Life of Schuyler Colfax* (Philadelphia: T.B. Peterson, 1868), 41. Harriet B. Stowe, *Men of Our Times* (Hartford: Hartford Publication, 1868), 349-50. Edward W. Martin, *The Life and Public Service of Schuyler Colfax* (New York: U.S. Publishing, 1868), 19. Ovando J. Hollister, *Life of Schuyler Colfax* (New York: Funk and Wagnalls, 1886), 345. Willard H. Smith, *Schuyler Colfax: The Changing Fortunes of a Political Idol* (Indianapolis: Indiana Historical Bureau, 1952), 445.

16. H.H. Houghton to Elihu B. Washburne, March 27, 1864, EBWP. *Galena Weekly Gazette* (Ill.), May 9, 1879. Union League Council, Allentown, N.J., to Abraham Lincoln, Feb. 15, 1864, ALP. Franklin Ellis, *History of Monmouth County, New Jersey* (New York: R.T. Peck, 1885), 341.

17. A. Belcher to Elihu B. Washburne, Feb. 1, 1864, EBWP. David M. Martin to Thaddeus Stevens, Jan. 15, 1864, TSP, LC. David M. Martin to John Sherman, Jan. 15, 1864; Henry Wheeler to Sherman, Feb. 8, 1864; R.W. Clark to Sherman, Feb. 20, 1864; John Howard to Sherman, Feb. 22, 1864; James C. Devin to Sherman, Feb. 26, 1864; E. Ingmand to Sherman, Feb. 14, 1864, JSP. J.P. Plummer to Ignatius Donnelly, March 10, 1864; William S. Timerman to Donnelly, March 16, 1864; S. Miller to Donnelly, Feb. 16, 1864; D.J. Higgins to Donnelly, Feb. 16, 1864, IDP, MHS. Christian Sans to Rev. Horace Hooker, Jan. 6, 1864, MSCP, LC. Owen Lovejoy to W.L. Garrison, Feb. 22, 1864, in W.P. Garrison and F.J. Garrison, *William L. Garrison, 1805-1879: The Story of His Life Told by His Children*, 4 vols. (New York: Century, 1885-89), 4:98. H.G. McPike to Lyman Trumbull, Feb. 1, 1864; Jonathon B. Turner to Trumbull, Feb. 1, 1863, LTP. *Daily State Register* (Des Moines, Iowa), June 18, 1864, citing Washington correspondent for *Boston Watchman and Reflector*.

18. *Atlas and Argus* (Albany, N.Y.), Sept. 17, 1864. *Connecticut Register and Manual* (1984), 144. Samuel Plumb to James Monroe, April 9, 1864, JMoP. Joseph R. Hawley to William Faxon, Jan. 30, 1864, JRHP, LC.

19. William M. Dickson to Friedrich Hassuarek, Feb. 15, 1864, Friedrich Hassuarek Papers, OSHL.

20. Lewis B. Gunckel to John Sherman, Feb. 29, 1864, JSP. Dudley, "The Election of 1864," 503.

21. Shuckers, *Life of Salmon P. Chase*, 476. *American Annual Cyclopaedia and Register of Important Events* (New York: D. Appleton, 1864), 4:784. Dudley, "The Election of 1864," 502-3. Beale, *Diary of Gideon Welles*, Feb. 22, 1864, 1:529. *Pittsburgh Gazette* clipping in JSP, February 24, 1864. J. Cutler Andrews, *Pittsburgh's Post-Gazette: "The First Newspaper West of the Alleghenies"* (1936; reprt., Westport, Conn.: Greenwood Press, 1970), 153, 186. Whitelaw Reid to Anna Dickinson, April 3, 1864, AEDP.

22. R.C. Parsons to S.C. Chase, March 2, 1864, SPCP.

23. J.W. Gasley to S.P. Chase, March 1, 1864, SPCP.

24. James F. Clarke to S.P. Chase, Feb. 26, 1864, SPCP.

25. George L. Stearns to Mary Elizabeth Stearns, Jan. 23, 1864, in Stearns, *The Life and Public Services of George Luther Stearns*, 326. George L. Stearns to William L. Garrison, Sept. 12, 1864, in the *Commonwealth*, Sept. 23, 1864. Tyler Dennett, *Lincoln and the Civil War in the Diaries and Letters of John Hay* (New York: Dodd, Mead, 1939), May 14, 1864, p. 181.

26. Isaac Glass to John Sherman, Feb. 29, 1864; Lewis B. Gunckel to John Sherman, Feb. 29, 1864, JSP. J.R. Giddings to Mrs. G.W. Julian, March 7, 1864, G-JP, LC.

27. S.P. Chase to James C. Hall, March 8, 1864 in *New York Post*, March 10, 1864, cited by *Appleton Motor* (Wis.), March 17, 1864. *American Annual Cyclopaedia* 4 (1864), 783.

28. L. Maria Child to Gerrit Smith, April 22, 1864, GSP. Theodore Tilton to Parker Pillsbury, May 22, 1864, Parker Pillsbury Manuscripts, NYHSL. Extract of letter from Henry Ward Beecher in the *Liberator*, May 27, 1864. *Principia*, May 26, 1864. *Woodstock Sentinel* (Ill.), August 17, 1864. Dennett, *Diaries and Letters of John Hay*, 181, 184. S.P. Chase to William Buckingham, May 9, 1864, William Buckingham Correspondence, Connecticut State Library.

29. Jesse Hawley to John Sherman, March 13, 1864, JSP.

30. D.B. Hill to Elihu B. Washburne, Feb. 29, 1864, EBWP.

31. *Minutes of the New York East Conference, April 1864*, 41-42. Asahel Moore, Secretary, Methodist Episcopal Church, Maine Conference, to Abraham Lincoln, April 14, 1864, ALP. *Minutes of the East Maine Conference of the Methodist Episcopal Church, June 1864*, 20. *Minutes of the New York Conference of the Methodist Episcopal Church, April 1864*, 32. McPherson, *The Political History of the United States of America during the Great Rebellion*, 498. *Ripon Commonwealth* (Wis.), June 10, 1864. Sylvester Weeds, ed., *A Life's Retrospect: Autobiography of Rev. Granville Moody* (Cincinnati: Cranston and Stowe, 1890), 444-45, 473. *Journal of the General Conference of the Methodist Episcopal Church, May 1864*, 383.

32. J.M. Sturtevant, Tri-annual Congregational Convention to Abraham Lincoln, April 28, 1864, ALP. *Chicago Tribune*, April 28, 1864. *Minutes of the General Association of Congregational Churches . . . of Indiana, May 1864*, 5. Constantine Blodgett and James P. Root, Rhode Island Congregational Conference, to Abraham Lincoln, June 20, 1864, ALP. *Christian Herald* (Cincinnati), June 16, 1864. *Minutes of the General Conference of Congregational Churches of Maine, June 1864*, 9.

33. *Proceedings of the Pennsylvania Yearly Meeting of Progressive Friends, Longwood, Chester Co., Pennsylvania, June, 1864*, 15. *Minutes of the Seventh Day Baptist Central Association, June 1864*, 7. *Minutes of the Rock River Baptist Association, 1864*, 7. Samuel Harris and E.F. Duren to Abraham Lincoln, July 1, 1864, ALP. *Principia*, June 16, 1864.

34. Primitive Methodist Conference to Abraham Lincoln, May 24, 1864; R.Z. Williams, Clerk, Reformed Presbyterian Synod of New York, to Abraham Lincoln,

June 3, 1864, ALP. *Pittsburgh Dispatch*, May 26, 1864. *Pittsburgh Gazette*, May 26, 27, 1864. John Clayton, Secretary, Protestant Episcopal Convention, to Abraham Lincoln, June 8, 1864, ALP.

35. *Cong. Globe*, 38th Cong., 1st sess., pts. 3, 4 (April 29, June 15, 1864), 1,979, 2,988-89. Burton A. Konkle, *The Life and Speeches of Thomas Williams* (Philadelphia: Campion, 1905), 512. *Chicago Tribune*, July 2, 1864.

36. F.D. Parish to John Sherman, June 16, 1864, JSP. Virgil A. Bogue to Elihu B. Washburne, June 21, 1864, EBWP.

37. Pittsburgh Conference of the Methodist Episcopal Church to Abraham Lincoln, March 16, 1864, ALP. *Minutes of the Troy Conference of the Methodist Episcopal Church, April 1864*, 47.

38. Conference of Brownmansville United Brethren in Christ to Abraham Lincoln, April 11, 1864, ALP.

39. Theodore Weld to Samuel Johnson, Feb. 4, 1864, Samuel Johnson Papers, Essex Institute Library. *New York Tribune*, Feb. 22, 1864. *NASS*, Jan. 23, Feb. 20, Nov. 14, 1864. *Liberator*, Feb. 19, Nov. 25, 1864. *New York Independent*, Jan. 21, 1864. Emerson, *Life of Abby Hopper Gibbons*, 81. Young, "Anna Dickinson," 174.

40. *Morning Chronicle* (Washington, D.C.), May 10, 1864. *New Era* (Washington, D.C.), May 10, 1864.

41. Whitelaw Reid to Anna Dickinson, April 3, 1864, AEDP. Dennett, *Diaries and Letters of John Hay*, May 14, 1864, p. 181. Theodore Tilton to Anna E. Dickinson, July 13, 1864; B.F. Prescott to Anna E. Dickinson, March 13, 30, 1864, AEDP. Elizabeth B. Chace to Lucy F. Lovell, July 2, 1864, in Wyman, *Elizabeth Buffum Chace*, 1:263.

42. Thomas H. McKee, *The National Conventions and Platforms of All Political Parties, 1789-1905* (1906; reprt., St. Clair Shore, Mich.: Scholarly Press, 1970), 127. *New York Tribune*, June 1, 1864.

43. *Harper's Weekly* 8 (June 1864): 386. *New York Tribune*, June 1, 1864. Six radical clergymen can be identified.

44. Elizabeth C. Stanton to the Central Fremont Club, May 14, 1864, in *New York Tribune*, May 18, 1864. Whitman, *American Reformers*, 752-53. Elizabeth C. Stanton to Caroline Dall, May 7, 1864, in *Liberator*, June 3, 1864. McPherson, *Ordeal by Fire*, 407. Edwin Cowles to Montgomery Blair, May 31, 1864, in ALP. *NCAB*, 23:51. Theodore Tilton to Anna Dickinson, June 3, 1864; B.F. Prescott to Dickinson, June 10, 1864, AEDP. Susan B. Anthony to Elizabeth Stanton, June 14, 1864, ECSP, LC.

45. McKee, *The National Conventions and Platforms*, 124-25. *Autobiography of Andrew Dickson White*, 2 vols. (New York: Century, 1922), 1:117. James G. Blaine, *Twenty Years of Congress, from Lincoln to Garfield*, 2 vols. (Norwich, Conn.: Henry Bill Publishing, 1884-86), 1:518. *New Jersey Journal* (Elizabeth), June 14, 1864. *Ohio Repository* (Canton), June 14, 1864. James C. Klotter, *The Breckinridges of Kentucky, 1760-1981* (Lexington: Univ. Press of Kentucky, 1986), 86.

46. Samuel Aaron to Charles S. Bates, June 4, 1864 in L.C. Aaron, *Rev. Samuel Aaron: His Life, Sermons, and Correspondence* (Norristown, Pa.: Morgan Wills, 1890), 194.

47. Susan B. Anthony to Anna Dickinson, April 14, 1864, AEDP. Abraham Lincoln to A.G. Hodges, April 4, 1864, in Basler, *Works of Lincoln*, 7:281-82. Susan B. Anthony to Elizabeth C. Stanton, June 12, 1864, ECSP. Whitman, *American Reformers*, 27. *NASS*, June 18, 1864. G.B. Stebbins to W.L. Garrison, July 15, 1864, in the *Liberator*, July 22, 1864. Gerrit Smith to E. Cady Stanton, June 6, 1864, in the *Liberator*, June 17, 1864. John Keep to Gerrit Smith, Sept. 19, 1864. L. Maria Child to Gerrit Smith, July 23, 1864, GSP. Gerrit Smith to Elizabeth C. Stanton,

Oct. 3, 1864, ECSP. Lydia Maria Child to Eliza Scudder, n.d., 1864, in John G. Whittier, ed., *Letters of Lydia Maria Child* (Boston: Houghton Mifflin, 1883), 183-84. Charles R. Denton, "American Unitarians, 1830-1865: A Study of the Religious Opinion on War, Slavery, and the Union" (Ph.D. diss., Michigan State Univ., 1969), 147. Mott in the *Liberator*, May 20, 1864.

48. June 30, July 7, 1864, 7:1,716, GMT.

49. Basler, *Works of Lincoln*, 7:433-34.

50. Henry Cheever to Gerrit Smith, July 20, 1864, GSP. Henry Wilson to George B. Cheever, July 27, 1864, Henry W. Davis to George Cheever, July 21, 1864, GBCP. Amasa Walker to Theodore Tilton, July 22, 1864, TTP.

51. *Principia*, July 14, Aug. 25, 1864. George Cheever to William Claflin, Aug. 11, 1864, William Claflin Papers, RBHL. William Goodell to Maria, Oct. 12, 1864, WGP.

52. George W. Julian, *Political Recollections*, 237-38. Grace Julian Clarke, *George Julian* (Indianapolis: Indiana Historical Commission, 1923), 250-51. *Centreville* (Ind.) *Republican*, June 16, 1864. Kenneth Stampp, *Indiana Politics during the Civil War* (Bloomington: Indiana Univ. Press, 1978), 219.

53. *American Baptist*, cited by the *Commonwealth*, Aug. 14, 1864. *NASS*, Sept. 17, 1864.

54. Henry B. Curtis to John Sherman, July 30, 1864, JSP. N.N. Hill, Jr., *History of Knox County* (Mt. Vernon, Ohio: A.A. Graham, 1881), 413. *NASS*, Aug. 6, 1864.

55. For example, see *Minutes of the Walworth Baptist Association, June, 1864*, 6. *Proceedings of the Saratoga Baptist Association, June 1864*, 7-8.

56. Horace Greeley to Abraham Lincoln, July 8, Aug. 8, 1864, ALP; Lincoln to Greeley, July 9, 18, 1864, in Basler, *Works of Lincoln*, 7:435-51. Edward C. Kirkland, *The Peacemakers of 1864* (New York: Macmillan, 1927), 67-68.

57. Kirkland, *The Peacemakers of 1864*, 105. *Christian Advocate and Journal*, Aug. 4, 1864.

58. President's Fast Day Proclamation, July 8, 1864, in Basler, *Works of Lincoln*, 7:433. *New York Times*, Aug. 5, 1864. *Boston Daily Journal*, Aug. 5, 1864. *Cincinnati Gazette*, Aug. 10, 1864. See the *Philadelphia Inquirer*, Aug. 5, 8, 1864; and *Freeport Journal* (Ill.), Sept. 28, 1864. Samuel Landes to James J. Embree, Aug. 16, 1864, Lucius C. Embree Papers, ISHL. *Wabasha County Herald*, Aug. 25, 1864, citing *Watchman and Reflector*.

59. *Ashland Times* (Ohio), Sept. 1, 1864, citing *Christian Advocate and Journal*. *Pittsburgh Christian Advocate*, Oct. 8, 1864. *American Presbyterian*, Sept. 1, 1864.

60. Frank L. Klement, *The Copperheads in the Middle West*, 235-36. McKee, *The National Conventions and Platforms*, 122. East Genesee, Detroit, Iowa, and Ohio conferences. See *Elmira Advertiser*, Sept. 6, 1864. *Minutes of the Detroit Conference, 1864*, 12; *Iowa Conference, 1864*, 14; *Ohio Conference*, (1864) 21. Pittsburgh Conference, *Newark Advertiser*, Sept. 26, 1864; Rock River (Ill.) Conference, *Galena Gazette*, Oct. 20, 1864. *Journal of the General Conference, 1864*, 883.

61. *Minutes of Iowa State Baptist Conventions (1864)*, 6, and *Minutes of the Monongahela Association (1864)*, 11.

62. See Minutes of the Genesee Free Methodist Conference, 1864, p. 21, Manuscript, Free Methodist Church Archives. Minutes of the Michigan Conference of the Wesleyan Connection, 1852-1867, Oct. 1864, unpaginated, Wesleyan Methodist Church Archives. *Minutes of the General Conferences of Seventh-Day Baptists, Sept. 1864*, 6. Russell E. Miller, *The Larger Hope: The First Century of Universalists* (Boston: Unitarian Universalist Association, 1979), 636. *Liberator*, Oct. 21, 1864.

63. *Christian Advocate and Journal*, Sept. 15, Oct. 13, 1864. *Western Christian*

*Advocate,* Oct. 19, 1864. *Zion's Herald,* Sept. 28, 1864. *Ladies' Repository* (Nov. 1864), 702. See *Pittsburgh Christian Advocate,* Nov. 5, 1864; and Unitarian *Christian Examiner,* (Nov. 1864), 76:361.

64. See *Detroit Advertiser and Tribune,* Oct. 19, 1864; *Liberator,* Oct. 21, 1864; *Worcester Spy,* Oct. 21, 1864; *Auburn Advertiser* (N.Y.), Oct. 25, 1864; *New York Tribune,* Sept. 27, 1864. *Pittsburgh Gazette,* Sept. 11, 1864. *Elyria Independent Democrat* (Ohio), Oct. 28, 1864. *New York Herald,* Oct. 22, 1864. Nicolay and Hay, *Abraham Lincoln,* 6:317-18. Minutes of the Michigan Conference of the Wesleyan Connection, Manuscript Record, unpaginated, Wesleyan Methodist Church Archives. See Robert L. Stanton, *The Church and the Rebellion* (1864; reprt., Freeport, N.Y.: Books for Libraries Press, 1911), 408 (p. 413 for the part Elder Stanley Matthews played in the Old School Presbyterian General Assembly report). *Minutes of the General Assembly, Presbyterian Church* (N.S.) 13 (1864), 465-66.

65. Seneca Baptist Association in *Daily Commercial Register,* (Sandusky, Ohio), Oct. 27, 1864. *Minutes of the French Creek Baptist Association, 1864,* 9.

66. *Western Christian Advocate,* Sept. 7, Oct. 12, 1864. *Ladies' Repository* (Nov. 1864), 702. *American Presbyterian,* Sept. 8, 1864. *Ohio Signal* (Zanesville, Ohio), Oct. 20, 1864, citing the *New York Observer.* "The New Rule," *Presbyter,* Nov. 9, 1864. See also March 25, 1863; May 18, July 13, 1864.

67. Gilmore, *Personal Recollections,* 102. Randall and Donald, *The Civil War and Reconstruction,* 473, citing *New York Sun,* June 30, 1889.

68. Parke Goodwin and Theodore Tilton to John Andrew, Sept. 2, 1864; John M. Forbes to Andrew, Sept. 2, 1864; Theodore Tilton to Andrew, Sept. 5, 1864, JAAP. John Andrew to Greeley, Tilton, and Goodwin, Sept. 3, 1864, HGP, NYHSL, and JAAP. William Buckingham to Horace Greeley, Sept. 3, 1864, William Buckingham Correspondence and HGP. Richard Yates to Greeley, Goodwin, and Tilton, Sept. 6, Theodore Tilton Correspondence, New York Public Library, HGP. Guy J. Gibson, "Lincoln's League: The Union League Movement during the Civil War" (Ph.D. diss., Univ. of Illinois, 1957), 494. Joseph A. Gilmore to Theodore Tilton, Sept. 5, 1864, TTP. Strong, *Diary,* 481, Sept. 5, 1864. *NCAB,* 3:523. James C. Conkling to Abraham Lincoln, Sept. 6, 1864, ALP.

69. George Stearns to William L. Garrison in the *Liberator,* Sept. 12, 1864. *Boston Commonwealth,* Sept. 23, 1864. John P. Gulliver to Abraham Lincoln, Sept. 12, 1864, ALP.

70. Arhtur C. Cole, "President Lincoln and the Illinois Radical Republicans," *MVHR* 4 (March 1918), 434-35. George B. Cheever to Elizabeth Washburne, Sept. 12, 1864, GBCP. Gilmore, *Personal Recollections,* 99-100. Rev. L.H. Parker to Rev. Horace Hooper, Oct. 3, 1864, MSCP. E.C. Fisher to John McClintock, Oct. 1, 1864, John McClintock Correspondence. James R. Doolittle, Speech, Springfield, Ill., Oct. 4, 1864, in *Chicago Tribune,* Oct. 7, 1864.

71. Henry W. Davis to Zachariah Chandler, Aug. 24, 1864; Zachariah Chandler to Wife, Aug. 27, 28, Sept. 2, 6, 8, 24, 1864; Benjamin Wade to Chandler, Oct. 2, 1864, ZCP. Winfred A. Harbison, "Zachariah Chandler's Part in the Reelection of Abraham Lincoln," *MVHR* 22 (June 1935), 268-70. Henrietta M. Dilla, *The Politics of Michigan, 1865-1878* (New York: Columbia Univ. Press, 1912), 15.

72. *Minutes of the Mad River (Ohio) Baptist Association, Sept. 1864,* 8. *New York Tribune,* Sept. 29, 1864.

73. "Records of the Peoria Synod, 1860-1869," vol. 2, p. 135, McCormick Theological Seminary Library. *Chicago Tribune,* Oct. 23, 1864.

74. *Detroit Advertiser and Tribune,* Oct. 1, 1864. *Minutes of the Michigan Conference of the Methodist Episcopal Church, Sept. 1864,* 36. *Hartford Courant,* Sept. 10, 1864.

75. Basler, *Works of Lincoln*, 7:533.

76. *Zanesville Courier* (Ohio), Sept. 8, 1864. *New York Tribune*, Sept. 5, 1864.

77. Sermon by W.A. Davidson in *Pittsburgh Christian Advocate*, Sept. 17, 1864. Gilbert Haven, *National Sermons, Speeches, and Letters on Slavery and Its War* {Boston: Lee and Shepard, 1869}, 482. Herrick Johnson, *The Shaking of the Nations: A Sermon* (Pittsburgh: W.S. Haven, 1864), 20.

78. Joseph P. Thompson to Elihu B. Washburne, Sept. 12, 1864, EBWP. For other fast day sermons, see *New York Times*, Sept. 20, 1864; *Daily Commercial Register* (Sandusky, Ohio), Sept. 27, 1864; *Independent*, Sept. 22, 1864. Roswell D. Hitchcock to Gerrit Smith, Oct. 14, 1864, GSP.

79. Lucius Fairchild to Abraham Lincoln, Sept. 13, 1864, ALP. Henry T. Cheever to William H. Seward, Sept. 10, 1864; John D. Baldwin to Frederick Seward, Sept. 10, 1864; Seward to Baldwin, Sept. 24, 1864, WHSP, URL. *NCAB*, 6:275; 13:483. *DAB*, 1:537. John Cox and Lawanda Cox, *Politics, Principles, and Prejudice, 1865-1866* (Glencoe, Ill.: Free Press, 1963), 4. See *Albany Journal*, cited by the *Liberator*, Sept. 16, 1864, for Seward speech, and *Commonwealth*, Sept. 16, 1864, for resolutions of Freedom Club (request that Seward explain statement).

80. Abraham Lincoln to William Dennison, Chairman of the Convention, June 9, 1864; Annual Message to Congress, Dec. 6, 1864, in Basler, *Works of Lincoln*, 7:380; 8:151-52. *New York Tribune*, June 10, 1864. James G. Randall and Richard N. Current, *Lincoln the President: Last Full Measure* (New York: Mead, 1955), 307. William A. Clebsch, "Baptism of Blood: A Study of Christian Contribution to the Interpretation of the Civil War" (Ph.D. diss., Union Theological Seminary, 1957), 254. See George Cheever to *Boston Recorder*, in the *Mankato* (Minn.) *Record*, Sept. 24, 1864, and *Saint Paul* (Minn.) *Pioneer*, Sept. 18, 1864, on rumors that Cheever's church was against his position on the presidential election.

81. Wyman, *Elizabeth B. Chace*, 215. Lillie B. Chace to Anna Dickinson, Aug. 21, 1864. William D. Kelley to Dickinson, July 24, 1864; Theodore Tilton to Dickinson, Aug. 8, Sept. 3, 5, 1864; Kennett H. Square to Dickinson, Sept. 1, 1864; B.F. Prescott to Dickinson, Sept. 4, 1864, AEDP. Anna E. Dickinson to T.V. Reavis, Aug. 29, 1864, T.V. Reavis Papers, Chicago Historical Society Library.

82. *Independent*, Sept. 8, 1864. T.B. Pugh to Anna Dickinson, Sept. 8, 1864; Edwin R. Hawkins to Dickinson, Sept. 9, 1864; Whitelaw Reid to Dickinson, Sept. 11, 1864; Oliver Johnson to Dickinson, Sept. 22, 1864; William Hay to Dickinson, Oct. 16, 1864; B.F. Prescott to Dickinson, Oct. 2, 1864; Lillie B. Chace to Dickinson, Oct. 29, 1864, AEDP. *Hartford Courant*, Sept. 28, Oct. 24, 1864. *NASS*, Oct. 10, 29, Nov. 7, 1864.

83. *Liberator*, Sept. 16, Oct. 7, 28, Nov. 4, 1864; Feb. 3, 17, 1865. Gerrit Smith to Garrison, Oct. 10, 1864, WLGP. Giles B. Stebbins, *Upward Steps of Seventy Years* (New York: John Lovell, 1890), 165. Theodore Tilton to Dickinson, Sept. 14, 1864, AEDP. Tilton to John Nicolay, Nov. 12, 1864, ALP. Young, "Anna E. Dickinson," 269. Oliver Johnson to Anna Dickinson, Sept. 22, 1864; Lillie B. Chace to Anna Dickinson, Oct. 29, 1864, AEDP. *NASS*, June 25, July 25, Sept. 24, 1864. Horace Mack, *History of Columbiana Co., Ohio* (Philadelphia: D.W. Ensign, 1879), 226-27. *Dunn County Lumberman* (Wis.), Oct. 1, 15, 22, 1864. *Eau Claire Free Press* (Wis.), Oct. 13, 20, 1864. *Wabasha County Herald* (Minn.), Oct. 27, 1864. McPherson, *The Struggle for Equality*, 284.

84. *Pittsburgh Gazette*, Oct. 17, 1864. Calvin Fairbank, *During Slavery Times* (1890; reprt., New York: Negro Univ. Press, 1969), 162-68. Katherine L. Herbig, "Friends for Freedom: The Lives and Careers of Sallie Holley and Caroline Putnam" (Ph.D. diss., Claremont Graduate School, 1977), 237. John A. Rogers, Manuscript Diary, 1850-1864, Sept. 6, 1864, 2:2, JARD, BCL.

85. *New York Tribune*, Sept. 9, 1864. *Chicago Tribune*, Sept. 13, 1864. *Auburn Advertiser*, Sept. 15, 1864.

86. See, for example, *Commercial Register*, Oct. 8, 1864. *New York Tribune*, Sept. 6, 1864. S.H. Gay to Elizabeth Gay, Sept. 9, 1864, SHGP. J.R. Sikes to Abraham Lincoln, Sept. 10, 1864. See also Benjamin B. French to Lincoln, Oct. 11, 1864. George W. Egleston to Lincoln, Oct. 25, 1864; Joseph B. Maxfield to Lincoln, Oct. 21, 1864; Benjamin Tatham to Isaac Newton, Oct. 28, 1864, in ALP. See also Rev. Christian Sans to Rev. Horace Hooker, Nov. 24, 1864; Rev. J.H. Payne to Hooker, Nov. 4, 1864, MSCP.

87. *Boston Journal*, Sept. 24, 27, 28, 29; Oct. 7, 10, 11, 13, 18, 19, 20, 31, 1864. *Boston Advertiser*, Sept. 7, 21, Oct. 6, 10, 12, 17, 20, 29, 1864. *Boston Evening Transcript*, Oct. 20, 1864. *Liberator*, Oct. 7, 14, 21, 1864. *Commonwealth*, Sept. 9, 1864. *New York Tribune*, Sept. 7, 1864. Ward, *George H. Hepworth*, 83. Arthur S. Bolster, Jr., *James Freeman Clarke: Disciple to Advancing Truth* (Boston: Beacon Press, 1954), 248.

88. See *Pittsburgh Gazette*, Sept. 11, 15, Oct. 7, 10, 13, 25, 26, 27, 1864. *Pittsburgh Dispatch*, Oct. 26, 29, 31, 1864.

89. *Ohio State Journal* (Columbus), Sept. 2, 1864. *New York Tribune*, Sept. 22, 1864. *Auburn Advertiser and Union* (N.Y.), Sept. 30, 1864. *Ashland Times* (Ohio), Sept. 29, 1864. *Commercial Register*, Oct. 5, 1864. Weeks, *Autobiography of Rev. Granville Moody*, 448. Granville Moody to Abraham Lincoln, Nov. 2, 1864, ALP. *Ohio State Journal*, Nov. 4, 1864. *Cleveland Leader*, Oct. 10, 1864. *Portage County Democrat* (Ohio), Oct. 19, 1864.

90. Henry W. Beecher to Emily Drury, Oct. 25, 1864, B-SC, RC. *New York Tribune*, Oct. 17, 24, 1864. *New York Times*, Oct. 23, 31, 1864. *Hartford Courant*, Oct. 29, 1864. *NASS*, Oct. 15, 22, 29, 31, 1864. Thomas W. Knox, *Life and Works of Henry Ward Beecher* (New York: Wilson and Ellis, 1887), 222.

91. *Elmira Advertiser* (New York), Aug. 9, Sept. 6, 1864. Document no. 17241-1-2, Oct. 1864, "The National Crisis," Address by Bishop Simpson, Mozart Hall, Cincinnati; S.W. Thomas to Matthew Simpson, Oct. 7, 1864; R.A. Brick to Simpson, Oct. 24, 1864, MSP, LC. *Pittsburgh Dispatch*, Oct. 18, 1864. *Pittsburgh Gazette*, Oct. 19, 1864. *New York Tribune*, Nov. 4, 7, 1864. *New York Herald*, Nov. 4, 1864. *Independent*, Nov. 7, 1864. Robert D. Clark, "Bishop Matthew Simpson and the Emancipation Proclamation," *MVHR* 35 (Sept. 1948), 269. Robert D. Clark, *The Life of Matthew Simpson* (New York: Macmillan, 1956), 240, 256.

92. William Moody Pratt Diaries, III, unpaginated, Sept. 12, 1864, UK. *Cincinnati Gazette*, Sept. 29, 1864. Veteran Observer [Edward D. Mansfield], *New York Times*, Oct. 30, 1864.

93. *Chicago Tribune*, Sept. 22, Oct. 31, 1864. *New York Tribune*, Sept. 20, 23, 29, Oct. 4, 18, 28, 1864. *Hartford Courant*, Oct. 12, 26, 1864. *Detroit Tribune*, cited by *Rochester Advertiser and Union*, Sept. 16, 1864. *Auburn Advertiser*, Sept. 20, Oct. 3, 1864. *Eau Claire Free Press* (Wis.), Sept. 3, 29, 1864. *Daily Pantagraph* (Bloomington, Ill.), Oct. 22, 1864. *Galena Gazette* (Ill.), Sept. 23, Oct. 16, 20, 1864. *Howard Tribune* (Ind.), Sept. 22, 1864.

94. Clara M. DeBoer, "The Role of Afro-Americans in the Origin and Work of the American Missionary Association" (Ph.D. diss., Rutgers Univ., 1973), 1:226.

95. For examples, see, *Auburn Advertiser and Union*, Sept. 8, 1864. *Ashland Union*, Oct. 5, 1864.

96. Moorhead, *American Apocalypse*, 151. Adam Gurowski, *Diary: 1863-'64-'65* (Washington: Morrison, 1866) 2:294; 3:345. Henry Ward Beecher to Frances Lieber, Oct. 25, 1864, etc., Francis Lieber Papers, Huntington Library. Alfred C. Abbe, "The Influence of Henry Ward Beecher on Theology" (masters thesis, Drew

Theological Seminary, 1928), 53, citing Stephen W. Griswold, "Sixty Years with Plymouth Church."

97. *Elmira Advertiser*, Oct. 31, 1864. *Auburn Advertiser*, Sept. 20, 1864, citing *New York Express*. Henry W. Beecher to Emily Drury, April 18, 1863, B-SC.

98. Francis M. Sykes to Richard Yates, Oct. 10, 1864, RYP. Baum, *The Civil War Party System*, 85, 99, 212. Vander Velde, *The Presbyterian Churches*, 131.

99. *Cincinnati Enquirer*, Oct. 5, 1864. *Western Advocate*, Nov. 16, 23, 1864. Stephen Starr, "Was There a Northwest Conspiracy?" *Filson Club Historical Quarterly* 38 (Oct. 1964), 323-24.

100. Hubbart, *The Older Middle West*, 234-37. Porter, *Ohio Politics during the Civil War*, 202. Emma L. Thornbrough, *The Negro in Indiana* (Indianapolis: Indiana Historical Bureau, 1957), 204. Voegeli, *Free but Not Equal*, 153-54. For Tilton's speech, see *NASS*, Nov. 5, 1864.

101. Basler, *Works of Lincoln*, 8:149, 150.

## 6. Churches and Presidential Reconstruction.

1. *Universalist Quarterly and General Review* (Boston) 22 (Jan. 1865), 92. William H. Channing to William L. Garrison, Feb. 3, 1865, in the *Liberator*, Feb. 24, 1865.

2. Fred Carlisle to William Henry Smith, Nov. 1864, William Henry Smith Correspondence, OSHL. *Detroit Illustrated: The Commercial Metropolis of Michigan* (Detroit: Hook, 1891), 135. Preston King to James Doolittle, Nov. 29, 1864, James R. Doolittle Correspondence, New York Public Library. *Ogdensburg Journal* (New York), May 17, 1866. John A. Andrew to Lewis Hayden, Dec. 21, 1864, in the *Liberator*, Jan. 20, 1865. James L. Phillips, "The Presidential Election in 1864," *Free Will Baptist Quarterly* 13 (Jan. 1864), 80.

3. *Presbyterian Witness* (Cincinnati), Jan. 4, 1865. *Religious Herald* (Hartford, Conn.), Jan. 26, 1865.

4. *Morning Star* (Dover, N.H.), Jan. 11, 1865. "M" to Editor, *American Presbyterian*, Jan. 18, 1865. *Examiner* (N.Y.), Feb. 23, 1865. Luther Newcomb to Secretary, Jan. 18, 1865, AHMSC.

5. *Zion's Herald*, Feb. 8, 22, 1865. "Bridgewater" to Editor, *Christian Herald and Presbyterian Recorder*, Feb. 2, 1865. Gerrit Smith to J.M. Ashley, Feb. 6, 1865, in the *Liberator*, Feb. 24, 1865.

6. *NASS*, Jan. 14, 1865. *Alton Telegraph* (Ill.), Jan. 2, 1865. *St. Louis Journal*, Jan. 2, 1865. *St. Louis Democrat*, Jan. 2, 1865. *Chicago Tribune*, cited by the *Liberator*, Jan. 20, 1865. *Cleveland Herald*, cited by *Ohio Repository*, Jan. 18, 1865. Theodore Tilton to Horace Greeley, Jan. 6, 1865, TTP; Theodore Tilton to S.H. Gay, Jan. 14, 1865, SHGP.

7. Abraham Lincoln's Annual Message, Dec. 6, 1864; Speech, April 11, 1865, in Basler, *Works of Lincoln*, 8:152, 399-405. George L. Sterns to Richard Yates, Jan. 6, 1865, RYP. J.M. Ashley to Editor, Feb. 27, 1865, *Commonwealth*, March 4, 1865. Michael L. Benedict, *A Compromise of Principle: Congressional Republicans and Reconstruction, 1863-1869* (New York: Norton, 1874), 91-93.

8. Eric L. McKitrick, *Andrew Johnson and Reconstruction* (Chicago: Univ. of Chicago Press, 1960), 47-48. George L. Stearns to Charles Sumner, April 30, 1865, CSP.

9. Charles Sumner to George Cheever, Jan. 6, 1865; George B. Cheever to Elizabeth, Feb. 23, 1865, GBCP. Hans L. Trefousse, *The Radical Republicans: Lincoln's Vanguard for Racial Justice* (New York: Knopf, 1969), 299. Howard, *Black Liberation*, 77. Isaac N. Arnold, *The History of Abraham Lincoln and the Over-Throw of Slavery* (Chicago: Clarke, 1866), 346-48.

10. *Boston Recorder*, Jan. 27, 1865. GMT, 7:1817, Feb. 1, 1865, *Christian*

*Intelligencer* (N.Y.), Feb. 2, 1865. *Christian Register* (Boston), Feb. 4, 1865. Sermon of Rev. John W. Chadwick, Feb. 5, 1865, in *Christian Inquirer* (N.Y.), Feb. 18, 1865. *Christian Watchman and Reflector* (Boston), Feb. 9, 1865.

11. *Zion's Herald*, Feb. 8, 1865. *Morning Star*, Feb. 8, 1864.

12. *Minutes of the New England Conference of the Methodist Episcopal Church, March 1865*, 25. *Minutes of the New Hampshire Conference of the Methodist Episcopal Church, April 1865*, 24. *Newark Advertiser*, March 28, 1865. *Christian Advocate and Journal*, April 6, 1865. *Zion's Herald*, April 19, 1865. *Minutes of the New Jersey Baptist State Convention, 1865*, 7.

13. B. Grinnell to George Whipple, Jan. 28, 1865. M.E. Strieby to Whipple, Feb. 24, 1865, AMAC. *Examiner* (N.Y.), Feb. 9, 1865. Robert Schenck was not primarily motivated by religious sentiments.

14. W.S. Post to M.E. Strieby, Jan. 26, 1865; William Holmes to Secretaries, Feb. 6, 1865, AMAC. R.C. Dunn to Secretaries, Jan. 9, 1865, AHMSC. *Ottawa Republicans* (Ill.), Jan. 28, 1865. Norman D. Harris, *The History of Negro Servitude in Illinois* (1904; reprt., New York: Negro Univ. Press, 1969), 240. *New York Times*, Jan. 26, 1865.

15. David, *Charles Sumner and the Rights of Man*, 220. Trefousse, *Benjamin Franklin Wade*, 248. Zachariah Chandler to Wife, April 23, 1865, ZCP. See also Julian, *Political Recollections*, 255. *New York Tribune*, April 21, 1865.

16. For example, see sermons of Rev. M.P. Gaddis, Rev. J.H. Mac El'Rey, and Rev. C.A. Holmes in the *Wooster Republican* (Ohio), May 4, 1865. *Pittsburgh Christian Advocate*, April 29, 1865.

17. *Elyria Independent Democrat* (Ohio), May 10, 1865. *Illinois Gazette* (Lacon), May 17, 1865. George B. Loring, *The Present Crisis: A Speech Delivered at Lyceum Hall, Salem, Massachusetts, April 26, 1865* (South Danvers, Mass., 1865), 6, 12. *Boston Daily Advertiser*, May 30, 1866. J. Michael Quill, *Prelude to the Radicals: The North and Reconstruction during 1865* (Washington, D.C.: Univ. Press of America, 1980), 140.

18. Silas Johnson to Andrew Johnson, June 21, 1865; A.J. Brown et al. to Johnson, June 20, 1865; William Johnson to Johnson, June 6, 1865, B. Shaw to Andrew Johnson, May 1, 1865, AJP, LC. *Biographical and Genealogical History, Morris County, New Jersey* (New York: Lewis, 1899), 698. George L. Stearns to Johnson, May 17, 1865, AJP. Horace Greeley to Gerrit Smith, June 21, 1865, GSP.

19. T. Gilbert to Charles Sumner, June 3, 1865; J.J. Twiss to Sumner, June 6, 1865; J.W. Alden to Sumner, June 14, 1865; Edgar Ketchum to Sumner, June 17, 1865, CSP. Charles Sumner to Carl Schurz, June 22, 1865, Carl Schurz Papers, LC.

20. J.W. Hall to Charles Sumner, June 25, 1865, in SPCP. *Liberator*, June 16, 1865. James Harlan to Charles Sumner, June 15, 1865, CSP. Brigham, *James Harlan*, 171. J.M. Howard to C. Sumner, June 22, 1865, CSP. Charles Sumner to S.P. Chase, June 25, 1865, SPCP. Felice A. Bondaio, *North of Reconstruction: Ohio Politics, 1865-1870* (New York: New York Univ. Press, 1970), 53.

21. *Northwestern Christian Advocate*, May 24, 1865. *Western Christian Advocate*, May 10, 1865. See also *Northern Advocate and Journal*, June 8, 1865. *Zion's Herald*, May 31, June 28, 1865. *Independent*, June 22, 1865. *Rochester Union and Advertiser*, June 9, 1865. Ralph E. Morrow, *Northern Methodism and Reconstruction* (East Lansing: Michigan State Univ. Press, 1865), 205.

22. *Minutes of the General Assembly* (N.S.) 14 (1865), 352-56. Vander Velde, *The Presbyterian Churches*, 375. Rev. E.F. Hatfield to Andrew Johnson, May 27, 1865, AJP. *Detroit Tribune*, June 30, 1865. *Cincinnati Gazette*, June 27, 1865.

23. *Minutes of the Sussex Baptist Association, June, 1865*, 6-7. *Minutes of the North-Western Seventh Day Baptists, June, 1865*, 7.

24. *Minutes of the Genesee Baptist Association, June 1865*, 8-9. *Newark Daily*

*Advertiser*, June 8, 1865. *Minutes of the Niagara Baptist Association, June 1865*, 9. *Central Union Baptist Association, June 1865*, 8. Bogue, *The Earnest Men*, 194, 203. *Cong. Globe*, 38th Cong., 1st sess., pt. 2 (March 17, 1864), p. 1,161. *Commonwealth*, July 1, 1865.

25. John A. Andrew to Dear Sir, June 19, 1865, JAAP.

26. George S. Stearns to Andrew Jackson, Aug. 16, 1865, AJP. Charles F. Adams, *Richard H. Dana: A Biography*, 2 vols. (Boston: Houghton Mifflin, 1890), 1:21. *Commonwealth*, June 24, 1865. Stearns, *The Life and Public Service of George Luther Stearns*, 346-50. *Cincinnati Gazette*, July 13, 1865. *New York Times*, June 22, 25, 1865. McPherson, *The Struggle for Equality*, 326. Benedict, *A Compromise of Principle*, 110-11.

27. S.P. Chase to James W. Webb, July 9, 1865, JWWP, YU.

28. *Christian Advocate and Journal*, July 6, 1865. *Congregationalist* and *New York Christian Advocate* cited by the *Presbyter*, July 26, 1865. *Independent*, cited by *Commercial Register* (Sandusky, Ohio), July 25, 1865.

29. Charles Brooks to Andrew Johnson, July 7, 1865, AJP. *NCAB*, 16:287. D.M. Woolley to Johnson, July 31, 1865, AJP. *Keokuk Constitution* (Iowa), May 17, 1880. Granville Moody to Johnson, July 31, 1865; Luther Wiswell to Johnson, Aug. 22, 1865, AJP. Samuel T. Dole, *Windham in the Past* (1916; reprt., Windham, Maine: Windham Historical Society, 1974), 124-24. Joseph Medill to Andrew Johnson, Sept. 15, 1865, AJP.

30. John Covode to B.F. Wade, July 11, 1865, BFWP. *Biographical Directory of the American Congress, 1774-1961* (Washington: GPO, 1961), 851. *DAB*, 2:470. Charles E. Norton to Charles Sumner, July 7, 1865, CSP. *Boston Evening Transcript*, July 6, 1865. "Veteran Observer," *New York Times*, July 15, 1865. Bland Ballard to Charles Sumner, Sept. 14, 1865, CSP.

31. B.F. Wade to Charles Sumner, July 29, 1865; M.W. Howard to Sumner, July 26, 1865, CSP. Sumner to Edwin D. Morgan, July 12, 1865, Edwin D. Morgan Papers, New York State Library. Sumner to B.F. Wade, July 29, 1865, BFWP.

32. *Minutes of the Erie Conference of the Methodist Episcopal Church, July 1865*, 19-21. *Minutes of the Iowa Conference of the Methodist Episcopal Church, Sept. 1865*, 20. Minutes of the Illinois Conference of the Free Methodist Church, Sept. 1865, p. 6, Free Methodist Church Archives.

33. *Annual Report of the Chemung River Baptist Association, Sept. 1865*, 10. *Annual Report of the New Jersey Baptist State Convention, Oct. 1865*, 7.

34. *Daily Morning Chronicle*, Nov. 23, Dec. 8, 1865. *New York Times*, Dec. 11, 1865. *Auburn Daily Advertiser* (N.Y.), Oct. 25, 1865.

35. O.B. Frothingham to Charles Sumner, Aug. 3, 1865, CSP. J.R. Gilmore to James Garfield, Oct. 27, Dec. 16, 1865, JAGP, LC. *DAB*, 4:310.

36. *Alton Telegraph* (Ill.), June 23, 1865.

37. "SGA" to Editor, Sept. 4, 25, 1865, in *Toledo Blade*, Sept. 6, 28, 1865. S.G. Arnold to Columbus Delano, Oct. 2, 1865, Columbus Delano Papers, LC. S.G. Arnold, "The Suffrage Qualification," *Methodist Quarterly Review* 47 (Oct. 1865), 586, 590, 593. S.G. Arnold to Andrew Johnson, Oct. 24, 1865, AJP.

38. *Indiana True Republican* (Centreville, Ind.), Dec. 7, 1865. Julian was a Quaker in his youth, but in early manhood he searched for religious truths with which he would be more comfortable. Julian's Unitarianism was of great importance in leading him into the ranks of the antislavery movement and political reform. Clark, *Julian*, 70-72, 420. Patrick Riddleberger, *George Washington Julian, Radical Republican* (Indianapolis: Indiana Historical Bureau, 1966), 8-11, 34-36, 41-42.

39. Harold M. Hyman, *A More Perfect Union: The Impact of the Civil War and Reconstruction on the Constitution* (New York: Knopf, 1873), 296-300. Herman

Belz, *Emancipation and Equal Rights: Politics and Constitutionalism in the Civil War Era* (New York: Norton, 1979), 100. Theodore B. Wilson, *The Black Codes of the South* (University: Univ. of Alabama Press, 1865), 72-74, 76, 78-79.

    40. *Liberator*, Dec. 15, 1865. *Chicago Tribune*, Nov. 17, 1865. *Cleveland Leader*, Nov. 9, 1865. William L. Garrison to Helen Garrison, Nov. 24, 27, 29, Dec. 1, 1865, and Garrison to Charles Sumner, Dec. 14, 1865, in Merrill, *The Letters of William L. Garrison*, 5:341-43, 346-48, 350-52, 361.

    41. William L. Garrison to Helen Garrison, Oct. 31, Nov. 5, 9, 10, 13, 16, 17, 24, 27, Dec. 1, 1865; Garrison to James M. McKim, Nov. 17, 1865, in Merrill, *The Letters of William L. Garrison*, 5:311-13, 317-44, 346-49, 350-52. Richard I. Bonner, ed., *Memoirs of Lenawee County* (Madison, Wis.: Western Historical Association, 1909), 1:502.

    42. McPherson, *The Struggle for Equality*, 339. *Cincinnati Commercial*, cited by *Liberator*, Nov. 10, 1865.

    43. James A. Garfield to S.P. Chase, Oct. 4, 1865, SPCP. W.M. Grosvenor to Charles Sumner, Nov. 5, 1865, CSP.

    44. *American Missionary* 9 (Dec. 1865), 268. David O. Mears, *Life of Edward Norris Kirk, D.D.* (Boston: Lockwood, Brooks, 1877), 315.

    45. Smith, *Schuyler Colfax*, 222-23. That Colfax spoke the sentiment of the radical Christians is shown by the reception given his speech by the Christian public. Charles D. Cleveland, a Presbyterian and vice president of the AMA, thanked Colfax and informed the congressman that he hoped Congress would delay Reconstruction until the Southerners showed themselves to be penitent. C.D. Cleveland to Schuyler Colfax, Nov. 22, 1865, Schuyler Colfax Papers, LC. T.J. McLain to John Sherman, Nov. 28, 1865, JSP. H.P. Bennet to Thaddeus Stevens, Nov. 26, 1865, TSP. L.C.

    46. McPherson, *Ordeal by Fire*, 505.

    47. *Presbyterian* (Philadelphia), July 22, 1865.

    48. McKitrick, *Andrew Johnson and Reconstruction*, 21.

    49. Sidney Andrews, *The South since the War* (Boston: Ticknor and Fields, 1866), 384. J. Michael Quill, *Prelude to the Radicals*, 140, 142.

## 7. The Christian Opposition to Johnson

    1. Pierce, *Memoir and Letters of Charles Sumner*, 4:273.

    2. W.E. Walker to Charles Sumner, Dec. 11, 1865; J.D. Fulton to Sumner, Dec. 27, 1865, CSP.

    3. John A. Andrew to Dear Sir, Dec. 26, 1865, JAAP. John Binney to Thaddeus Stevens, Jan. 5, 1866, TSP.

    4. *New York Times*, Jan. 1, 1866. *Nass*, Jan. 13, 1866. E. Burt to Charles Sumner, Jan. 1, 1866, CSP.

    5. *Cleveland Leader*, Jan. 16, 1865. John J. Janney to Samuel Shellabarger, Jan. 16, 1866, JJJP, OSHL.

    6. John Binney to Thaddeus Stevens, Jan. 5, 1866, TSP. *Cong. Globe*, 39th Cong., 1st sess. (Jan. 10, 1866), 180. *New York Times*, Jan. 22, 1866. Kelley was fully devoted to the moral and humanitarian cause of uplifting the blacks. He was an active and radical member of the Second Presbyterian Church of Philadelphia. Kelley eventually decided not to commune with any church that was not fully devoted to these fundamental truths, that would not urge its members to help the poor, and that would not work to change institutions which breed evil. He left the Calvinism of his ancestry and became a member of F.A. Eustice's Unitarian church but joined William H. Furness's First Unitarian Church when Furness became an abolitionist. Michael R. Greco, "William Darrah Kelley: The Antebellum

Years" (Ph.D. diss., Johns Hopkins Univ., 1974), 38, 69-72, 119, 170. *Philadelphia Inquirer*, Jan. 10, 1890.

7. *Cong. Globe*, 39th Cong., 1st sess. (Jan. 16, 1866), p. 259. *NASS*, Jan. 20, 1866. William L. Garrison to George Julian, Feb. 11, 1866, in Merrill, *Letters of William L. Garrison*, 5:382.

8. See, for example, *Cong. Globe*, 39th Cong., 1st sess. (Dec. 20, 1865), p. 88; (Jan. 11, 1866), p. 184; (Jan. 19, 1866), p. 312. "DWB," Washington, D.C., Jan. 22, 1866; *Independent*, Jan. 25, 1866.

9. *Congregationalist*, Jan. 26, 1866.

10. *Zion's Herald*, Jan. 24, 1866.

11. *NASS*, June 23, 1866.

12. *Cong. Globe*, 39th Cong., 1st sess. (Dec. 19, 1865), p. 79. Hoar, ed., *Charles Sumner: His Complete Works*, 13:48, 52-54.

13. Pierce, *Memoir and Letters of Charles Sumner*, 4:275.

14. *Cong. Globe*, 39th Cong., 1st sess. (Feb. 6, 1866), p. 673. Hoar, *Charles Sumner*, 13:119-20. Donald, *Charles Sumner and the Rights of Man*, 227, 245-47. Thesta Dana to Charles Sumner, Jan. 9, 1866; see also letter of another female "J.S." to Sumner, Jan. 24, 1866, CSP.

15. Rev. Jonathan K. Wellman to Charles Sumner, Jan. 13, 1866, CSP. *Brown's Adrian, Michigan, City Directory, 1870*.

16. Unidentified correspondent to Charles Sumner, Jan. 19, 1866; Rev. George N. Richardson to Sumner, Jan. 19, 1866; Richard L. Storrs to Sumner, Jan. 22, 1866, CSP. Bernard S. Halperin, "Andrew Johnson, the Radicals, and the Negro, 1865-1866" (Ph.D. diss., Univ. of California, Berkeley, 1966), 118.

17. Thaddeus Stevens to Charles Sumner, Aug. 26, 1865, CSP. Amos Tuck to Thaddeus Stevens, Jan. 26, 1866, TSP. *Manual of the First Church in Exeter, New Hampshire, 1638-1888* (Exeter, N.H.: Gazette Job Print, 1888), 33.

18. *Daily Morning Chronicle*, Feb. 21, 1866. M.M. Coppueh to Ignatius Donnelly, Feb. 21, 1866, IDP.

19. *Congregationalist*, Jan. 19, 1866. *Presbyterian Witness*, Jan. 31, 1866. *Christian Examiner* (Boston) 1 (Jan. 1866), 104-5, 116.

20. *Independent*, Jan. 25, Feb. 1, 1866. *Christian Advocate*, Feb. 1, 1866. *New York Observer*, Feb. 1, 1866. *Christian Intelligencer* (N.Y.), Feb. 8, 1866. After the Radical Republicans had demonstrated their power, the address that Colfax delivered on February 11 as chairman of the U.S. Christian Commission met with uniform approval when he announced that "our Constitution has become the New Testament of our freedom" (Moore, *The Life of Schuyler Colfax*, 309).

21. *New York Independent*, Feb. 8, 1866. Theodore Tilton to Charles Sumner, Feb. 3, 1866, CSP. *New York Times*, Feb. 4, 1866. Sharon A. Carroll, "Elitism and Reform" (Ph.D. diss., Cornell Univ., 1970), p. 123. McPherson, *The Struggle for Equality*, 351.

22. *Boston Recorder*, Feb. 9, 1866. *Christian Times and Witness* (Chicago), Feb. 15, 1866.

23. William C. Child to E.B. Washburne, Feb. 1, 1866, EBWP. Charles Wittlesay to John Sherman, Feb. 1, 1866, JSP. William G. Rose, *Cleveland: The Making of a City* (New York: Word Publishing, 1950), 136. *ACAB*, 6:496.

24. William Rose to Richard Yates, Feb. 2, 1866, RYP. *History of Pike County, Illinois* (Chicago: Charles C. Chapman, 1880), 200, 782. Thomas S. Malcom to Richard Yates, Feb. 20, 1866, RYP. Samuel B. Tobey to T.A. Jenckes, Feb. 21, 1866, Thomas Jenckes Papers, LC. *Providence Journal* (R.I.), June 24, 1867. Charles Durkee to Thaddeus Stevens, Feb. 20, 1866, TSP. *Kenosha Telegraph* (Wis.), Jan. 20, 1870.

25. Dr. Henry A. Hartt to Charles Sumner, Feb. 16, 1866, CSP. Gerrit Smith to Sumner, Feb. 5, 1866, in AMAC.

26. George Duffield to Charles Sumner, Feb. 17, 1866. See also W.A. Lloyd, Feb. 17, 1866; Lyman W. Johnson, Feb. 18, 1866; W.H. Beaman, Feb. 20, 1866, CSP.

27. McPherson, *The Political History of the United States of America during the Great Rebellion*, 69-72.

28. James M. McKim to Joseph Simpson, Feb. 16, 1866; J.R. Shipherd to McKim, Feb. 19, 1866, JMMP.

29. James M. McKim to Joseph Simpson, Feb. 23, 28, 1866, JMMP.

30. GMT, 8:33, Feb. 22, 1866. Gayle Thornbrough, *The Diary of Calvin Fletcher*, 9 vols. (Indianapolis: Indiana Historical Soc., 1972-81) 9:225.

31. Samuel May, Jr., to James M. McKim, Feb. 20, 1866, JMMP. Theodore Tilton, to Horace Greeley, Feb. 21, 1866, HGP, New York Public Library. William L. Garrison to Theodore Tilton, March 8, 1866, in Walter Merrill, *The Letters of William Lloyd Garrsion*, 5 vols. (Cambridge: Belknap, 1971) 5:397. Thomas Richmond's letter was printed in the *Independent*, March 8, 1866. Thomas Richmond to John Sherman, Feb. 27, 1866, JSP.

32. A. Huster to Lyman Trumbull, Feb. 22, 1866, LTP. U.P. Miller to John Sherman, Feb. 22, 1866, JSP. R.E. Lowry, *History of Preble County, Ohio* (Indianapolis: B.F. Bowen, 1915), 283-85. William D. Kelley to Wendell Phillips, in *NASS*, May 12, 1866.

33. *Detroit Advertiser and Tribune*, March 2, 1866. *Adridn Times and Expositor* (Mich.), Sept. 30, 1882. *Hillsdale Standard* (Mich.), March 20, 1866. Clark Waggoner to John Sherman, Feb. 28, 1866, JSP. *Toledo Blade*, July 2, 1903.

34. R.S. Rust to John Ogden, Feb. 27, 1866, AMAC. William Faxon to Mark Howard, Feb. 22, 1866, Mark Howard Papers, Connecticut Historical Society Library. Hannibal Hamlin to J.W. Babson, Feb. 26, 1866, Hannibal Hamlin Papers, University of Maine. Editorial in *Zion's Herald*, Feb. 28, 1866, and *Western Christian Advocate*, Feb. 28, 1866.

35. W. Jones to H.W. Beecher, Dec. 25, 1865, in *Commonwealth*, Jan. 20, 1866. For speech at Troy, N.Y., see *Macomb Eagle* (Ill.), Jan. 20, 1866, citing *Rochester Union*. Harriet Beecher Stowe to Duchess of Argyle, Feb. 19, 1866, in Annie Fields, ed., *Life and Letters of Harriet Beecher Stowe* (Boston: Houghton Mifflin, 1898), 275.

36. *Evening Post* (N.Y.), Feb. 21, 1866. *New York Times*, Feb. 21, 1866. C.H. Bullard to Leonard Bacon, Feb. 27, March 14, 1866, S. Guiteau to Bacon, March 2, 1866, Leonard Bacon Papers, YU. *New York Times*, March 2, 1866. *Hartford Evening Press*, March 1, 1866.

37. F.G. Russell to John W. Longyear, Feb. 24, 1866, John W. Longyear Correspondence, UM. W. McCaulley to Thaddeus Stevens, Feb. 24, 1866, TSP. I.A.W. Buck to Yates, Feb. 25, 1866, RYP. Joseph Warren to William H. Seward, Feb. 24, 1866, WHSP, URL. M.S. Wilkinson to H.S. Lane, March 14, 1866, H.S. Lane Papers, Indiana Historical Society Library. *Western Christian Advocate*, Feb. 28, March 4, 1866. *New York Independent*, Feb. 29, 1866. *Christian Inquirer*, March 1, 1866. *American Wesleyan* (Syracuse, N.Y.), March 7, 1866, printed editorials from almost all of the religious press.

38. For example, see J.M. Snyder to John D. Strong, Feb. 27, 1866, John D. Strong Papers, ISHL. E.H. Gilbert to B.F. Butler, Feb. 27, 1866, B.F. Butler Papers, LC. *Chicago Journal*, Feb. 27, 1866, *Cleveland Leader*, March 5, 13, 1866.

39. *Congregationalist*, March 2, 1866. *Evangelist*, March 8, 1866. *New York Independent*, Feb. 29, 1866.

40. Terry, "Theodore Tilton," 74. Tilton to Hugh McCulloch, March 6, 1866,

TTP. Henry Bowen to Zachariah Chandler, May 2, 1866, ZCP. H.C. Bowen to Theodore Tilton, June 27, 1866; Theodore Tilton to Edwin D. Morgan, March 6, 1866, TTP. H.W. Beecher to William Claflin, July 14, 1866, AMAC. William P. Fessenden to Hugh McCulloch, Aug. 9, 1866, Hugh McCulloch Papers, LC. Housley, "The Independent," 183. Jellison, Fessenden of Maine, 212-13. Lewis D. Campbell to Andrew Johnson, April 25, 1866, AJP. L.E. Pease to Gideon Welles, July 23, 1866, Gideon Welles Papers, LC.

41. Benedict, A Compromise of Principle, 157-58.

42. Western Christian Advocate, Feb. 28, 1866.

43. Congregationalist, March 16, 1866. Christian Register, March 17, 1866.

44. J.J. Meade to John Longyear, March 1, 1866, John W. Longyear Papers. Edwin C. Larned to Lyman Trumbull, March 3, 1866, LTP. A.T. Andreas, History of Chicago, 3 vols. (Chicago: Andreas, 1866), 3:608-9. Commonwealth, March 3, 1866. Freeport Weekly Bulletin (Ill.), March 8, 1866.

45. Detroit Advertiser and Tribune, March 1, 1866.

46. Ralph Plumb to James Garfield, March 5, 1866, JAGP. Adoniran J. Joslyn to Richard Yates, March 12, 1866; J.B. Turner to Yates, March 17, 1866, RYP. E.C. Alft, Elgin: An American History, 1835-1984 (Elgin, Il.: Courier-News, 1984), 33, 37, 47. Harvey Milligan, Historic Morgan and Classic Jacksonville (Jacksonville, Ill.: Charles Eames, 1885), 313-14. Turner was ordained as a Presbyterian minister and for several years was pastor of two small Congregational churches. While serving as a professor at Illinois College, he taught a Bible class on Sundays. Mary Turner Carriel, The Life of Jonathan Baldwin Turner (Jacksonville, Ill.: Mary T. Carriel, 1911), 61, 62.

47. Moses Thacher to Charles Sumner, March 12, 1866; S. Kelley to Sumner, March 12, 1866, CSP.

48. H. Whitney to Charles Sumner, March 14, 1866; Amos Dresser to Sumner, March 27, 1866, CSP. Louis Fuller, The Crusade against Slavery, 1830-1860 (New York: Harper and Row, 1960), 75.

49. Morning Chronicle, March 16, 1866.

50. R.M. Pearson to E.B. Washburne, March 19, 1866, EBWP. History of Ogle County, Illinois (Chicago: H.F. Kett, 1878), 570. Halperin, "Andrew Johnson," 100. Rev. R. Norton to Andrew Johnson, March 19, 1866, AJP.

51. Commercial Register (Sandusky, Ohio), March 23, 1866. Tilton to Independent, March 19, 1866, in Independent, March 22, 1866.

52. H.W. Beecher to Andrew Johnson, March 17, 1866, AJP. Examiner and Chronicle, March 22, 1866. McPherson, Political History, 74-78.

53. Diaries of William T. Coggeshall, IV, April 5, 1866, William T. Coggeshall Papers, OSHL. Freda P. Koch, Colonel Coggeshall: The Man Who Saved Lincoln (Columbus, Ohio: Poko Press, 1985), 16-20, 22, 73. R.S. Storrs to Charles Sumner, March 30, 1866, CSP. Warner Bateman to John Sherman, March 30, 1866, JSP. Charles Sumner to the Duchess of Argyle, April 3, 1866, in Pierce, Memoir and Letters of Charles Sumner, 4:275.

54. Cong. Globe, 39th Cong., 1st sess., pt. 2 (April 5, 1866), p. 1,786. Trefousse, Benjamin Franklin Wade, 269.

55. Nass, April 14, 1866. Boston Daily Journal, April 2, 1866. Boston Daily Transcript, April 6, 1866. Christian Register, April 14, 1866. George Hepworth to Charles Sumner, April 9, 1866, CSP. Halperin, "Andrew Johnson," 150.

56. Dilla, The Politics of Michigan, 53. Henry H. Crapo to William W. Crapo, April 8, 1866, Henry H. Crapo Papers, UM. Detroit Post, April 6, 1866. Wolverine Citizen (Flint, Mich.), April 14, 1866. Pamela Charles, "Governor Henry H. Crapo: The Republican" (masters thesis, Univ. of Michigan, 1980), 8. "Walsingham," in the Detroit Advertiser and Tribune, April 12, 1866.

57. Simon E. Baldwin to Mother, March 28, 1866, Simon E. Baldwin Papers, YU. *Independent*, March 29, 1866. Thornbrough, *The Diary of Calvin Fletcher*, 9:246, April 3, 1866.

58. E.D. Morgan to Ransom Balcom, April 3, 1866; Morgan to T. Weed, April 8, 1866, Edwin D. Morgan Papers, New York State Library.

59. Rev. Francis Vinton to Edward D. Morgan, April 7, 1866; Samuel Osgood to Morgan, April 18, 1866, Edwin D. Morgan Papers. James A. Rawley, *Edwin D. Morgan, 1811-1883* (1955; reprt., New York: AMS Press, 1968), 219-21, 265-66. Beale, *Diary of Gideon Welles*, 2:475-76, 477-87. James A. Rawley, "Senator Morgan and Reconstruction," *New York History* 34 (Jan. 1953), 27-53. John Cox and Lawanda Cox, *Politics, Principles, Prejudice*, 205.

60. Edgar Ketchum to Charles Sumner, April 7, 1866, CSP. *New York Times*, March 4, 1882. See Hugh White to George D. Hill, April 9, 1866, George D. White Correspondence, UM.

61. B.F. Sheets to E.B. Washburne, April 24, 1866, EBWP. *Hisory of Ogle County, Illinois*, 347, 495. D.J. Pinckney to Richard Yates, May 7, 1866, RYP. Henry Snapp to Lyman Trumbull, May 3, 1866, LTP. *Genealogical and Biographical Record of Will County, Illinois* (Chicago: Biographical Publishing, 1900), 518. Paul C. Brownlow, "The Northern Protestant Pulpit on Reconstruction, 1865-1877" (Ph.D. diss., Purdue Univ., 1970), 149.

62. *Christian Advocate*, March 29, 1866. For an equally bitter editorial, see *Western Christian Advocate*, April 4, 1866. *Congregationalist*, March 30, April 6, 1866.

63. *Zion's Herald*, April 18, 1866. *Christian Advocate*, April 19, 1866. *Evangelist*, April 12, 1866. *Presbyterian Witness*, April 11, 18, 1866.

64. For example, see *Examiner and Chronicle*, April 12, 1866. *Western Christian Advocate*, April 11, 1866. *Congregationalist*, April 13, 1866.

65. *Christian Herald and Presbyterian Recorder*, April 19, 1866. *Congregationalist*, April 13, 1866. Samuel B. Burnham to Charles Sumner, April 13, 1866, CSP.

66. *New Englander* (New Haven) 25 (April 1866), 362.

67. *Minutes of the New England Conference of the Methodist Episcopal Church, March 28, 1866*, 38. *Minutes of the New York Conference of the Methodist Episcopal Church, April 1866*, 20. *Minutes of the New York East Conference of the Methodist Episcopal Church, April 1866*, 23. *Minutes of the Troy Conference of the Methodist Episcopal Church, April 1866*, 52. *Minutes of the Maine Conference of the Methodist Episcopal Church, May 1866*, 7.

68. *Minutes of the Burlington, Iowa, Baptist Association, June 1866*, 4. *Minutes of the Northumberland Baptist Association, June 1866*, 19.

69. Miller, *The Larger Hope*, 9. Cochrane, "Freedom without Equality," 276. *American Annual Cyclopedia* 6 (1866), 760.

70. Otis D. Swan to Edwin D. Morgan, May 3, 1866, Edwin D. Morgan Papers. *New York Times*, Dec. 29, 1876, p. 8.

71. *New York Tribune*, May 22, 1866. *Independent*, May 17, 1866. *Christian Watchman and Reflector*, May 17, 1866. William W. Thayer to Charles Sumner, May 14, 1866, CSP. Thomas M. Edwards to J.S. Morrill, May 18, 1866, J.S. Morrill Papers, LC.

72. *Independent*, June 14, 1866.

73. Charles Slack to Charles Sumner, Feb. 28, 1866, CSP. *Pittsburgh Christian Advocate*, March 17, 1866. *Minutes of the East Maine Methodist Episcopal Church, May 1866* (Boston: James Magee, 1866), 24.

74. David Plumb to Charles Sumner, April 12, 1866, CSP. *NASS*, April 7, 1866.

75. S.P. Chase to Wendell Phillips, May 1, 1866, in the *Commercial Register* (Sandusky, Ohio), May 11, 1866. *Cincinnati Daily Gazette*, April 12, 1866.

76. "DWB," Washington, D.C., April 28, 1866, in the *Independent*, May 3, 1866.

77. George Stearns to Charles Sumner, May 1, 1866; William Claflin to Charles Sumner, May 1, 1866, CSP. *NCAB*, 1:119. W.C. Stacy to Richard Yates, May 7, 1866, RYP. Thomas Richmond to Lyman Trumbull, May 12, 1866, LTP.

78. *New York Times*, May 7, 1866. *New York Tribune*, May 7, 1866. *NASS*, Feb. 3, 1866.

79. Theodore Tilton to Charles Sumner, Feb. 2, 1866, CSP. *Independent*, May 3, June 7, 14, 21, 1866. Tilton's June 15 speech in *Auburn Advertiser and Union*, June 20, 1866.

80. *Cong. Globe*, 39th Cong. 1st. sess., pt. 4 (June 16, 1866), pp. 3,208-9.

81. *Boston Daily Journal*, May 31, 1866. *Boston Advertiser*, June 1, 1866. *Right Way* (Boston), March 17, 1866. Halperin, "Andrew Johnson," 93. McPherson, *The Struggle for Equality*, 356.

82. Alexander C. Twining to Lyman Trumbull, June 1, 1866, LTP. *NCAB*, 19:18. S.E. Sewall to Charles Sumner, June 1, 1866, CSP. *Morning Star*, June 20, 1866.

83. *American Presbyterian* (Philadelphia), June 21, 1866.

84. *Cong. Globe*, 39th Cong., 1st sess. (June 22, 1866), p. 3,349. W.R. Brock, *An American Crisis: Congress and Reconstruction, 1865-1867* (London: Macmillan, 1963), 148. Lyman Trumbull to Wife, June 28, 1866, LTP.

85. *Wolverine Citizen*, July 14, 1866. George M. Blackburn, "Michigan: Quickening Government in a Developing State," in *Radical Republicans in the North: State Politics During Reconstruction*, edited by James C. Mohr (Baltimore: Johns Hopkins Univ. Press, 1976), 120. For D.F. Reid's attack on the Democrats, see *St. Clairsville Gazette*, cited by *Cleveland Plain Dealer*, July 10, 1866. J.A. Caldwell, *History of Belmont and Jefferson Counties, Ohio* (Wheeling, W.Va.: Historical Publishing, 1880), 383.

86. Granville Moody to Andrew Johnson, July 12, 1866, AJP. Moody to Johnson, July 12, 1866, in the *Ironton Register* (Ohio), Aug. 30, 1866. *Congregationalist*, July 20, 1866. *Christian Register*, July 21, 1866.

87. Rev. E.P. Tenney to J.S. Morrill, July 17, 1866, J.S. Morrill Papers.

88. Henry Snapp to Lyman Trumbull, July 17, 1866, LTP. W. Jones to B.F. Butler, May 18, 1866, B.F. Butler Papers, LC.

89. Joseph Medill to Lyman Trumbull, May 2, 1866, LTP. Joseph Medill to E.B. Washburne, July 17, 1866, EBWP. Andreas, *History of Chicago*, 2:51.

90. W.M. Dickson to Benjamin F. Wade, July 16, 1866, BFWP. Charles T. Greve, *Centennial History of Cincinnati and Representative Citizens*, 2 vols. (Chicago: Biographical Publishing, 1904), 2:769. *Cincinnati Enquirer*, Oct. 17, 1889. D.L. Phillips to Lyman Trumbull, July 14, 1866, LTP. Alexander G. Cattell to Charles Sumner, July 18, 1866, CSP.

91. *Northwestern Christian Advocate*, July 25, 1866.

92. *Minutes of the General Association of Congregational Ministers and Churches of Iowa*, 9. *Minutes of the Congregational Conference of Ohio*, 8. *Minutes of the Central Union Association of Baptist, 1866*, 8. Michigan Free Will Baptists in the *Detroit Tribune*, June 9, 1866. *Minutes of the Eastern Association of Seventh Day Baptists, June 1866*, 6.

93. Julian, *Political Recollections*, 265-66.

94. McKitrick, *Andrew Johnson and Reconstruction*, 355. McPherson, *The Struggle for Equality*, 357. Joseph James, *The Framing of the Fourteenth Amendment* (Urbana: Univ. of Illinois Press, 1956), 201.

## 8. The Fourteenth Amendment and the Election of 1866

1. Stephen Field to S.P. Chase, June 30, 1866, SPCP. Warner Bateman to John Sherman, July 9, 1866, JSP. James Speed to Francis Lieber, May 26, 1866, Francis Lieber Papers, Huntington Library. James Speed was a man of principle who tried throughout his life to do what was morally right and worried when he thought he had not done so. Speed was often a delegate to the Unitarian National Convention in the 1860s. After the Civil War, Speed's radicalism matured, and he wanted blacks to have political and civil rights. Williams, "James and Joshua Speed," 40, 232. Howard, *Black Liberation*, 88, 138, 148, 165, 171.

2. *New York Times*, May 2, 1866. *New York Herald*, May 2, 1866. McKitrick, *Andrew Johnson and Reconstruction*, 351, 357.

3. M.C. Canfield to James Garfield, June 4, June 22, 1866; Peter Hitchcock to Garfield, June 26, 1866, JAGP. For Phillips's address, see *NASS*, July 21, 1866.

4. *New York Tribune*, June 29, 1866. McKitrick, *Andrew Johnson and Reconstruction*, 406. Howard K. Beale, *The Critical Year: A Study of Andrew Johnson and Reconstruction* (New York: Ungar Publishing, 1930), 360-61, 370. Henry Raymond to Ransom Balcom, July 17, 1866, in *New York Times*, Oct. 15, 1866. *Christian Watchman and Reflector*, Aug. 23, 1866. See also, for example, *Congregationalist*, Aug. 24, 1866. *Christian Advocate*, 30, 1866.

5. McPherson, *Political History of the United States of America during the Great Rebellion*, 118-19. Beale, *The Critical Year*, 131-38. McKitrick, *Andrew Johnson and Reconstruction*, 417. Benedict, *A Compromise of Principle*, 196.

6. *New York Tribune*, Sept. 5, 6, 1866. *New York Times*, Sept. 4, 1866. *New York Herald*, Sept. 6, 1866. *Independent*, Sept. 13, 1866. *Commonwealth*, Sept. 15, 1866. Beale, *The Critical Year*, 185-86, 330-31. Beale, *Diary of Gideon Welles*, 2:540. McPherson, *The Struggle for Equality*, 360-63.

7. McKitrick, *Andrew Johnson and Reconstruction*, 426-27. Charles Sumner to John Bright, Sept. 3, 1866, in Pierce, *Memoir and Letters of Charles Sumner*, 4:298.

8. Gerrit Smith in *NASS*, Sept. 1, 1866. Rev. M. French to George Whipple, Aug. 8, 1866, AMAC. Letter from Elizur Wright in *New York Independent*, Aug. 16, 1866. Gerrit Smith to William L. Garrison, Aug. 5, 1866, WLGP. For Henry Lane's speech, see *New York Tribune*, Aug. 14, 1866. For Collier's sermon, see *Chicago Tribune*, Sept. 24, 1866. For L.N. Breakman's lecture, see *Kalamazoo Telegraph*, Sept. 24, 1866. For the New Orleans mass meeting, see *New York Tribune*, Aug. 14, 1866.

9. *Christian Instructor and Western United Presbyterian* (Philadelphia), Aug. 4, 1866.

10. *Examiner and Chronicle*, Aug. 9, Sept. 6, 20, 1866. *Morning Star*, Aug. 8, 15, 1866. *Pittsburgh Christian Advocate*, Sept. 1, 1866. *New York Independent*, Aug. 9, 1866. *Congregationalist*, Aug. 10, 24, 1866.

11. *Examiner and Chronicle*, Aug. 9, Sept. 6, 20, 1866. *Pittsburgh Christian Advocate*, Oct. 22, 1866.

12. Lucinda Moses to Mary, Aug. 10, 1866, Kingsley S. Bingham Correspondence, UM. *North-Western Christian Advocate*, Aug. 5, 1866. *Christian Advocate*, Aug. 30, 1866. See *Joliet Signal* (Ill.), Aug. 14, 1866, for Phillips's call to the clergy.

13. Minutes of the Central Ohio Wesleyan Methodist Conference, Aug. 1866, p. 381, Manuscript Record, Wesleyan Methodist Church Records, 1864-95, Wesleyan Methodist Church Historical Society. *Minutes of the Cincinnati Conference of the Methodist Episcopal Church, August 1866*, 36. For the Rock River Methodist Conference, see *Chicago Tribune*, Sept. 23, 1866. *Minutes of the Huron, Ohio, Baptist Association, September 1866*, 9. *Minutes of the New London, Connecticut,*

*Baptist Association, September 1866*, 6. *Minutes of the General Conference of Congregational Churches of Maine, June 1866*, 15.

14. *Minutes of the Oswego, New York, Baptist Association, 1866*, 8. *Minutes of the Bridgewater, Pennsylvania, Baptist Association, September 1866*, 5.

15. *Wisconsin State Journal* (Madison), Sept. 12, 1866. "Minutes of the White River Conference of the United Brethren in Christ, 1866," p. 16, United Methodist Church Commission on Archives and Historical Library.

16. "Walsingham," in the *Detroit Advertiser and Tribune*, Sept. 8, 1866. John B. Scott to Samuel Hunt, Sept. 10, 1866, AMAC. James B. Porter to Austin Blair, Sept. 13, 1866, Austin Blair Papers, UM. *Olivet College Catalogue, 1866*.

17. *Independent*, Sept. 6, 1866.

18. *Christian Register*, Nov. 10, 1866. *American Presbyterian*, Aug. 30, 1866. *Christian Times and Witness*, Sept. 27, 1866. *Morning Star*, Oct. 3, 1866. *Western Christian Advocate*, cited by *Mahoning Courier* (Youngstown, Ohio), Oct. 17, 1866. *Central Advocate*, Oct. 10, 24, 1866. *Christian Herald and Presbyterian Recorder*, Sept. 6, Oct. 4, 1866.

19. *Minutes of the Michigan Conference of the Methodist Episcopal Church, September 1866*, 13. For the Wisconsin Methodist Episcopal Conference, see *Ripon Commonwealth*, Sept. 14, 1866. *Minutes of the Cincinnati Conference of the Methodist Episcopal Church, August 1866*, 36. For the Illinois Methodist Episcopal Conference, see *Carlinville Free Democrat* (Ill.), Oct. 4, 1866. Minutes of the Genesee Conference of the Free Methodist Church, Oct. 1866, p. 18, Archives of the Free Methodist Church.

20. For the Central Iowa Baptist Association, see the *Chicago Journal*, Oct. 31, 1866. For the Ohio State Baptist Convention, see the *Zanesville Courier* (Ohio), Nov. 1, 1866.

21. Benedict, *A Compromise of Principle*, 202. James, *The Framing of the Fourteenth Amendment*, 158, 161, 164-65, 167.

22. *Independent*, Aug. 2, 23, 30, 1866.

23. *Christian Advocate*, Sept. 6, 1866.

24. Albert Smith to Andrew Johnson, July 17, 1866, AJP. *Cincinnati Commercial*, ed., *Speeches of the Campaign of 1866 in the States of Ohio, Indiana, and Kentucky* (Cincinnati: Cincinnati Commercial, 1866), 13. *Centennial of the Methodist Episcopal Church, 1825-1925*, (Crawfordsville, Ind.: First United Methodist Church, 1925), unpaginated.

25. *NASS*, Oct. 6, 1866.

26. *Independent*, Sept. 12, 1866.

27. *Chicago Tribune*, Sept. 24, 1866.

28. *Cincinnati Gazette*, Sept. 12, 1866.

29. For Frothingham's sermon, see *New York Tribune*, Sept. 11, 1866. Augustus Woodbury, *The President and Congress* (Providence: Whitney, 1866), 8.

30. Spear, *The Citizen's Duty*, 12. Woodbury, *The President and Congress*, 17.

31. *Chicago Tribune*, July 31, 1866. *Peoria Transcript*, June 30, Aug. 28, 1866. *Cincinnati Gazette*, Sept. 20, 1866.

32. *Clermont Courier*, cited by the *Ohio Repository*, Sept. 12, 1866. *Cincinnati Gazette*, Sept. 24, 28, 1866. *Chicago Times*, cited by the *Fairfield Ledger*, Nov. 1, 1866.

33. H.W. Beecher to Charles G. Halpine, Chairman of the Executive Committee of the Cleveland Convention, Aug. 30, 1866, in *Albany Journal* (N.Y.), Sept. 3, 1866. *Chicago Tribune*, Sept. 2, 1866. For an example of Beecher's support for black suffrage in 1865, see *New York Times*, Sept. 25, 1865. Stephen H. Tyng to

Henry W. Beecher, Sept. 6, 1866; Henry W. Beecher to Leonard Bacon, Sept. 21, 1866, HWBP, YU. Edward Beecher to Henry Ward Beecher, in *Chicago Tribune,* Sept. 26, 1866. *Independent,* Sept. 7, 14, 21, 1866.

34. *Independent,* cited by *Worcester Spy,* Sept. 12, 1866.

35. *Daily Pantagraph* (Bloomington, Ill.), Sept. 28, 1866. "Veteran Observer," Sept. 12, 1866, in *New York Times,* Sept. 21, 1866.

36. *Racine Journal* (Wisconsin), Sept. 19, 1866. *Independent,* March 18, 1869.

37. *Grand Rapids Daily Eagle,* Sept. 17, 1866.

38. *Auburn Advertiser and Union,* Sept. 6, 8, 11, 19, 1866.

39. Allen, *Life and Letters of Phillips Brooks,* 2:60. *Miami Union* (Troy, Ohio), Oct. 6, 1866.

40. *Ohio Statesmen,* cited by *Ohio State Journal* (Columbus), May 29, 1866. *Cincinnati Gazette,* Sept. 20, 1866.

41. *Examiner and Chronicle,* Nov. 1, 1866. *Christian Examiner* 81 (Nov. 1866), 407.

42. *Minutes of the Woodstock, Vermont, Baptist Association, 1866,* 6.

43. *New York Evening Post,* Oct. 18, 1866. *Chicago Tribune,* Sept. 21, 1866. *Boston Advertiser,* Oct. 13, 1866.

44. *Chicago Tribune,* Oct. 13, 1866. *New York Tribune,* Oct. 19, 1866. *Daily Wisconsin,* Oct. 10, 1866.

45. *Chicago Evening Journal,* Oct. 31, 1866.

46. Records of the Peoria Synod, 1860-1869, 2:191, Manuscript Records, McCormick Theological Seminary. *Minutes of the General Assembly, 1866* (N.S.) (New York: John Grey, 1866), 264.

47. *Minutes of the Iowa Synod of the United Presbyterian Church, October 1866,* 24. *Chicago Evening Journal,* Oct. 8, 1866.

48. *New York Tribune,* Sept. 26, 1866. *New York Times,* Sept. 26, 1866. For the Republican National Committee address, see *New York Tribune,* Aug. 17, 1866.

49. *Independent,* Sept. 27, 1866.

50. *Christian Advocate,* Oct. 4, 1866. *Commonwealth,* Oct. 6, 1866.

51. *Pittsburgh Commercial,* cited by the *Chicago Tribune,* Oct. 22, 1866. For Sumner's speech, see *Commonwealth,* Oct. 6, 1866. *New York Herald,* Sept. 29, 1866.

52. *New York Independent,* cited by *NASS,* Sept. 29, 1866.

53. Patrick W. Riddleburger, *1866: The Critical Year Revisited* (Carbondale: Southern Illinois Univ. Press, 1979), 227-28. *Northwestern Christian Advocate,* Oct. 17, 1866. *Christian Advocate,* Oct. 17, 1866. For Chandler's speech, see the *Detroit Advertiser* and *Tribune,* Sept. 5, 1866. John H. Thurber, "The Public Speaking of Zachariah Chandler" (Ph.D. diss., Univ. of Michigan, 1965), 127. *Independent,* Oct. 4, 1866.

54. *Congregationalist,* Nov. 2, 1866.

55. Samuel May, Jr., to J. Miller McKim, Nov. 5, 1866, JMMP.

56. *Independent,* Nov. 15, 1886.

57. *Zion's Herald,* Nov. 14, 28, 1866. *Evangelist,* Nov. 15, 1866. *Independent,* Nov. 9, 1866.

58. Benedict, *A Compromise of Principle,* 208.

59. Beale, *The Critical Year,* 315-16. Brownlow, "The Northern Protestant Pulpit on Reconstruction," 159-60. Stampp, *The Era of Reconstruction,* 188.

60. Terry, "Theodore Tilton," 81. McKitrick, *Andrew Johnson and Reconstruction,* 488.

61. Brock, *An American Crisis,* 154.

62. Julian, *Political Recollections,* 263.

63. McKitrick, *Andrew Johnson and Reconstruction*, 449. Avery Craven, *Reconstruction: The Ending of the Civil War* (New York: Holt, Rinehart and Winston, 1969), 196.

64. Sorin, *Abolitionists*, 163.

## 9. Impeachment and the Churches

1. Rev. E.P. Tenney to Justin Morrill, June 29, 1866, Justin Morrill Papers. *NCAB*, 7:530-31. James Speed to Charles Sumner, Nov. 28, 1866, CSP.

2. *New York Tribune*, Nov. 30, 1866. *New York Times*, Nov. 30, 1866.

3. *Boston Advertiser*, Nov. 28, 1866. LaRoy Sunderland, Sermon, in *Addresses and Ceremonies at the New Year's Festival to the Freemen* (Washington, D.C.: McGill and Witherow, 1867), 18.

4. *New York Tribune*, Nov. 30, 1866. *New York Herald*, Nov. 30, 1866.

5. *Boston Journal*, Nov. 30, 1866. *Cincinnati Commercial*, Nov. 30, 1866.

6. James Cruickshank, *A Humble Thanksgiving* (Boston: Charles Moody, 1866), 8. *Boston Review* 7 (Jan. 1867), 113.

7. *New York Tribune*, Nov. 30, 1866.

8. Beale, *Diary of Gideon Welles*, 2:618. James Doolittle to Thomas Ewing, Nov. 5, 1866, Thomas Ewing Papers, LC. James Doolittle to Orville O. Browning, Nov. 8, 1866, Orville O. Browning Correspondence, ISHL.

9. *Illinois State Register* (Springfield), Nov. 22, 1866. *American Missionary* 10 (Nov. 1866), 266. For the Unitarian convention, see: *NASS*, Nov. 10, 1866.

10. *Examiner and Chronicle*, Nov. 15, 1866. *New York Independent*, Nov. 15, 1866. *Christian Examiner* (Nov. 1866), 2:412.

11. *Boston Commonwealth*, Nov. 10, Dec. 15, 22, 1866. *Independent*, Jan. 27, 1867. *NASS*, Jan. 5, 1867. Aaron M. Powell, *Personal Reminiscences* (New York: Caulton Press, 1899), 209-11. Merrill, *The Letters of William Lloyd Garrison*, 5:28. Stampp, *The Era of Reconstruction*, 128. McPherson, *The Struggle for Equality*, 372-73.

12. Chester, *Embattled Maiden*, 14. McPherson, *The Struggle for Equality*, 367-68.

13. William L. Garrison to Fanny G. Villard, Feb. 19, 1867, in Merrill, *The Letters of William Lloyd Garrison*, 5:458. *St. Louis Democrat*, Dec. 20, 1866, cited by *NASS*, Dec. 29, 1866, March 16, 30, 1867. Chester, *Embattled Maiden*, 89. A.H. Forman to Anna E. Dickinson, Nov. 25, 1866, AEDP.

14. *New York Times*, Nov. 7, 23, 1866. *NASS*, Jan. 5, March 2, April 27, June 8, July 17, 1867. *New York Tribune*, Feb. 22, 1867. *Independent*, Jan. 17, 1867. Wendell Phillips to Charles Sumner, Dec. 27, 1866, CSP. Lorenzo Sears, *Wendell Phillips* (New York: Benjamin Blom, 1909), 13. Irving H. Bartlett, *Wendell Phillips: Brahmin Radical* (Boston: Beacon Press, 1961), 306-7. Carlos Martyn, *Wendell Phillips: The Agitator* (New York: Funk and Wagnalls, 1890), 41, 355-58.

15. Henry Cheever to Gerrit Smith, Dec. 22, 1866, GSP. James L. Child to Henry Cheever, Dec. 26, 1866; Henry Cheever to Elizabeth C. Washburne, Dec. 29, 1866, GBCP. *NASS*, Feb. 2, 1867. Alma Lutz, *Created Equal: A Biography of Elizabeth Cady Stanton* (New York: Farrar, Straus and Giroux, 1974), 138-40. *Cong. Globe*, 39th Cong., 2d sess., pt. 1 (Jan. 9, 10, 11, 14, 15, 16, 17, 21, 1867), 353, 378, 401, 421, 430, 450, 482, 514, 629; (Feb. 11, 15, 1867), 1,134, 1,262.

16. Moore, *The Life of Colfax*, 288. See *Tiffin Tribune* (Ohio), May 7, 1868. *Cong. Globe*, 39th Cong., 2d sess. (Dec. 3, 1866), 3.

17. Richard, *Messages and Papers of the Presidents*, 6:445. *New York Tribune*, Dec. 4, 1866.

18. Rev. J.C. Emerson to Liberty Billings, Dec. 21, 1866, in CSP. Emerson to

D. Richards, Jan. 11, 1867; C.L. Robinson to Richards, Jan. 8, 1867; Norman Brownson to Richards, Jan. 12, 1867; Richards to William P. Fessenden, Jan. 15, 1867, William P. Fessenden Papers, LC.

19. Richardson, *Messages and Papers of the Presidents*, 6:474. *Commonwealth*, Dec. 15, 1866. *Independent*, Jan. 17, 1867.

20. Pierce, *Memoir of Charles Sumner*, 309-12. McPherson, *Political History of the United States of America during the Great Rebellion*, 154-60.

21. *Cong. Globe*, 39th Cong., 2d sess., pt. 1 (Dec. 14, 1866), 124. McPherson, *Political History of the United States of America during the Great Rebellion*, 164-66.

22. *New York Times*, cited by *NASS*, Nov. 10, 1866, Feb. 2, 1867. *Boston Commonwealth*, March 9, 16, 1867. *New York Independent*, Jan. 10, 1867.

23. George Loring to Charles Sumner, Feb. 9, 1867, CSP. Sumner to Frank W. Bird, Jan. 10, 1867, in Pierce, *Memoirs of Charles Sumner*, 311. Wendell Phillips to Sumner, Feb. 1, 1867, CSP. For Sumner's address, see *New York Herald*, Oct. 26, 1866. James, *The Framing of the Fourteenth Amendment*, 173. McPherson, *The Struggle for Equality*, 373.

24. Benedict, *A Compromise of Principles*, 215. McPherson, *The Struggle for Equality*, 374. Granville Moody to D.M. Fleming and others, Jan. 24, 1867, in *Miami Union* (Troy, Ohio), Feb. 16, 1867.

25. Washington Correspondent, *New York World*, Dec. 3, 1866, cited by Ellis P. Oberholtzer, *A History of the United States since the Civil War*, 3 vols. (New York: Macmillan, 1926), 1:422. Warner Bateman to John Sherman, Dec. 7, 1866, JSP. Sumner to W.W. Story, Dec. 16, 1866, in Pierce, *Memoir of Charles Sumner*, 4:307.

26. *Cong. Globe*, 39th Cong., 2d sess., pt. 1 (Jan. 3, 1867), 252. Stevens's mother was a pious Baptist, but he followed no doctrinaire religion and seldom attended any church. Stevens held a pew in the local Presbyterian church and generously aided religious institutions, Catholic as well as Protestant. Yet he was no churchgoer. Ralph Korngold, *Thaddeus Stevens* (New York: Harcourt, Brace, 1955), 11; Fawn Brodie, *Thaddeus Stevens* (New York: Norton, 1959), 30, 55-56. See Donald K. Pickens, "The Republican Synthesis and Thaddeus Stevens," *Civil War History* 31 (March 1985), 59, 72-73. William Gribbin, "Republicanism, Reform, and the Sense of Sin in Ante-Bellum America," *Cithara* 14 (Dec. 1974-May 1975), 25-41.

27. *Cong. Globe*, 39th Cong., 2d sess., pt. 1 (Jan. 17, 1867), 536-37.

28. Edward L. Pierce to Charles Sumner, Jan. 25, 1867, CSP. L.G. Fisher to David Davis, Feb. 2, 1867, David Davis Papers, ISHL. *NCAB*, 14:119. J.H. Rhodes to Richard Yates, Feb. 12, 1867, RYP. M.J. Cronwell to Ignatius Donnelly, Feb. 7, 1867, IDP.

29. Nathan Stanton to Donnelly, Feb. 21, 1867, IDP. W.M. Dickson to R.B. Hayes, Feb. 25, 1867, R.B. Hayes Papers, RBHL.

30. James G. Randall, "John Sherman and Reconstruction," *MVHR* 19 (Dec. 1932), 387-88.

31. *American Presbyterian*, Feb. 7, 1867. *Watchman and Reflector*, Feb. 28, 1867. *Detroit Advertiser*, March 1, 1867.

32. Timothy O. Howe to Grace, March 5, 1867, TOHP. *Independent*, Feb. 21, April 4, 1867.

33. J.A. Burnham to Richard Yates, March 3, 1867, RYP. *The Past and Present of Woodford County, Illinois* (Chicago: William LeBaron, 1878), 596. D.S. Varnum to Austin Blair, March 17, 1867, Austin Blair Papers.

34. *Morning Star*, March 6, 13, 1867. *Western Christian Advocate*, March 13, 1867. *Independent*, March 7, 1867. *Northwestern Christian Advocate*, March 20, 1867. *New York Observer*, March 7, 1867.

35. For example, see *Minutes of the Pittsburgh Conference of the Methodist Episcopal Church, March 1867*, 20.

36. *Minutes of the New England Conference of the Methodist Episcopal Church, March 1867*, 33. *New York Times*, April 7, 1867.

37. Benedict, *A Compromise of Principle*, 252.

38. *Watchman and Reflector*, June 27, 1867. *Journal and Messenger*, June 27, 1867. *Zion's Herald*, June 26, 1867.

39. George W. Fish to Austin Blair, July 15, 1867, Austin Blair Papers. *Christian Times and Witness*, July 25, 1867.

40. *Commonwealth*, Aug. 17, 1867. *Independent*, Aug. 29, 1867. *Congregationalist and Boston Recorder*, Oct. 17, 1867.

41. *Urbana Union* (Ohio), Sept. 18, 1867.

42. *Cincinnati Gazette*, Oct. 3, 1867. *Minutes of the Cayuga Baptist Association, Sept. 1867*, 6.

43. For Garrison's speech, see *NASS*, Feb. 10, 1866, and *New York Times*, Feb. 28, 1866. *Independent*, March 29, April 26, 1866.

44. William L. Garrison to Edwin A. Studwell, April 13, 1866, in Merrill, *The Letters of William Lloyd Garrison*, 5:412.

45. Joseph Medill to John Logan, March 16, 1868, cited by George Milton, *Age of Hate* (New York: Coward, McCann, 1930), 518.

46. *NASS*, Nov. 3, 1866. *Commonwealth*, Nov. 10, 1867.

47. J. Weldon to E.B. Washburne, Nov. 20, 1866, EBWP. Charles C. Church, *Past and Present of the City of Rockford, Illinois* (Chicago: S.J. Clark, 1905), 656. H.S. Lane to Aaron H. Blair, Nov. 30, 1866, H.S. Lane Papers. Samuel Spear, "The President and Congress," *American Presbyterian and Theological Review*, n.s., 5 (Jan. 1867), 44. Gerrit Smith to Taylor Lewis, Nov. 6, 1866, AMAC.

48. *Independent*, Jan. 10, 1867. William L. Garrison to Fanny G. Villard, Nov. 30, 1866, in Merrill, *The Letters of William Lloyd Garrison*, 433.

49. *NASS*, Jan. 10, 1867. *Cong. Globe*, 39th Cong., 2d sess. (Jan. 7, 1867), 320. *Commonwealth*, Jan. 12, 1867.

50. Orville Brown to Ignatius Donnelly, Jan. 17, 1867, IDP. Rev. S.H. Morse to Editor of the *Radical* (Boston), cited by *NASS*, Feb. 16, 1867.

51. *Watchman and Reflector*, Jan. 17, 1867. "Veteran Observer," Jan. 24, 1867, in *New York Times*, Feb. 7, 1867.

52. *Christian Times and Witness*, Aug. 1, 1867. *Christian Freeman* (Boston), June 27, Aug. 1, 1867.

53. James Speed to Charles Sumner, Sept. 12, 1867, CSP. Horace White to Zachariah Chandler, Aug. 20, 1867, ZCP. George Cheever to Henry Cheever, Aug. 28, 1867, GBCP. Jacob Howard to Editor, Sept. 25, 1867, in *New York Tribune*, Sept. 26, 1867.

54. *Zion's Herald*, Aug. 22, 1867. *Liberal Christian*, Sept. 7, 1867. *Christian Register*, Sept. 28, 1867. *Congregationalist*, Sept. 5, 1867. *American Wesleyan*, Oct. 2, 1867.

55. *Minutes of the New London Baptist Association, Sept. 1867*, 11. *Chicago Tribune*, Oct. 6, 1867.

56. *Northwestern Christian Advocate*, Oct. 9, 1867.

57. *Cong. Globe*, 40th Cong., 2d sess., pt. 1. (Dec. 7, 1867), 68.

58. *New York Tribune*, Dec. 9, 1867. George Julian to Grace, Dec. 8, 1867, George Julian Papers, InSL. *New York Independent*, Dec. 12, 1867. "Moses," Dec. 31, 1867, to Editor, *Boston Commonwealth*, Jan. 4, 1868.

59. *Zion's Herald*, Dec. 12, 1867. *Independent*, Jan. 23, 1868.

60. Horace White to E.B. Washburne, Jan. 16, 1868, EBWP. Granville Moody

to Wade, Feb. 21, 1868, BFWP. Elizur Wright to Editor of the *Boston Advertiser*, Jan. 7, 1868, cited by *Commonwealth*, March 14, 1868.

61. Benedict, *A Compromise of Principle*, 297.

62. George W. Fish to Austin Blair, March 3, 1868, Austin Blair Papers. George B. Cheever to Elizabeth, March 21, 1868, GBCP. Neal Dow to W.P. Fessenden, April 6, 1868, in Fessenden, *Life of William Pitt Fessenden*, 2:186. *The Reminiscences of Neal Dow: Recollections of Eighty Years* (Portland, Maine: Evening Express, 1898), 87-102. W.C. Howells to J.A. Garfield, March 10, 1868, JAGP. *DAB*, 5:306.

63. *Liberal Christian*, Feb. 29, March 7, 28, 1868. *Christian Ambassador*, March 7, 1868. *Independent*, March 5, 1868. B.A. Hinsdale to James Garfield, May 16, 1868, JAGP. *Congregationalist*, May 14, 1868. *Christian Register* 47 (May 2, 1868), 2.

64. *Minutes of the New England Conference of the Methodist Episcopal Church, March 1868*, 33.

65. *American Wesleyan*, April 29, 1868.

66. *Journal of the General Conference of the Methodist Episcopal Church, 1868*, 152-53. Charles H. Ambler, *Waitman Thomas Willey: Orator, Churchman, Humanitarian* (Huntington, W.Va.: Standard Printing, 1954), 132-33. *Cong. Globe*, 40th Cong., 2d sess., pt. 3 (May 18, 1868), 521. Charles S. Smith, *A His:ory of the African Methodist Episcopal Church* (Philadelphia: Book Concern of the AME Church, 1922), app., 554. 8:00 A.M., May 16 [1868], Washington, D.C., Charley to Hon. Geo. H. Pendleton, Cincinnati, "Raising of Money to be Used in Impeachment," *House Report* 75 (40th Cong., 2d sess.), p. 48. David M. DeWitt, *The Impeachment and Trial of Andrew Johnson* (New York: Macmillan, 1903), 531.

67. *Minutes of the Walworth, Wisconsin, Baptist Association, 1868*, 6.

68. *Christian Ambassador*, June 6, 1868.

## 10. Black Suffrage as a Moral Duty

1. Gerrit Smith to the Editor, April 20, 1863, *NASS*, May 16, 23, 1863. *Proceedings of the American Anti-Slavery Society* (New York: American Anti-Slavery Society, 1863), 16. Terry, "Theodore Tilton," 16. *New York Tribune*, Nov. 12, 1864. For Tilton's lecture tour, see *NASS*, Jan. 3, 28, 1865, and *Independent*, Jan. 19, 1865. Tilton to L.M. Child, Jan. 22, 1865, in *Liberator*, March 3, 1865. L. Maria Child to Tilton, March 7, 1865, TTP.

2. S.P. Chase to Gerrit Smith, March 2, 1864, in J.W. Schuckers, *The Life of Salmon Portland Chase*, 399. Frederick J. Blue, *Salmon P. Chase: A Life in Politics* (Kent, Ohio: Kent State Univ. Press, 1987), 196. S.P. Chase to James Woodworth and James T. Brady, June 3, 1864, in *New York Times*, June 5, 1864. Chase to William Garrison, Jan. 22, 1865; Chase to Wendell Phillips, Feb. 7, 1865, SPCC, Historical Society of Pennsylvania. Chase to Lincoln, April 11, 1865, in Schuckers, *Chase*, 514-15. Chase to Lincoln, April 12, 1865, in Basler, *Works of Lincoln*, 8:399-401.

3. F.D. Parish to John Sherman, June 6, 1864; Jan. 17, 1865, JSP. John E. Patterson to James Monroe, April 1, 1864, JMoP. R. Plumb to James Garfield, May 14, 1864, JAGP. For Bishop McIlvaine's address, see *Daily Commercial Register*, May 28, 1864.

4. Stearns, *The Life and Public Service of George L. Stearns*, 341. George Duffield to George Duffield, Jr., in *Detroit Tribune*, cited by *Rochester Union and Advertiser*, Sept. 16, 1864. John H. Thurber, "The Public Speaking of Zachariah Chandler," 56. Wilmer C. Harris, *The Public Life of Zachariah Chandler, 1851-1875* (Lansing: Michigan Historical Commission, 1917), 256.

5. Samuel J. May to A.D. White, March 11, 1864, Andrew D. White Papers, CorU. *Liberator*, May 29, 1863. Wendell Phillips to Elizabeth C. Stanton, Feb. 8, 1864, ECSP. Wendell Phillips to Judge Stallo, in the *Liberator*, May 13, 1864.

6. H.J. Raymond to James Doolittle, April 30, 1864, James R. Doolittle Papers, LC. J. Medill to R.H. Oglesby, May 28, 1864, R.H. Oglesby Papers, ISHL. J.W. Fox to S.S. Ridgeway, Jan. 29, 1864; Fox to S.S. Jocelyn, Feb. 8, 1864, AMAC. *Milwaukee Daily Life*, cited by the *Liberator*, June 17, 1864.

7. Samuel Aaron to Charles T. Bates, June 10, 1864, in L.C. Aaron, *Rev. Samuel Aaron*, 195.

8. *NASS*, July 2, 1864. "Minutes of the Western Yearly Meeting of the Society of Friends, Sept. 19, 1864," p. 19, Manuscript, Earlham College. *Indianapolis Journal*, Jan. 17, 26, 1865. Thornbrough, *The Negro in Indiana*, 203. *Worcester Spy* (Mass.), Sept. 21, 1864.

9. *Boston Advertiser*, May 27, 1864. "Oscar" to Editor, Nov. 27, 1864, in *National Anti-Slavery Standard*, Dec. 10, 1864. Phillips Brooks to William Brooks, Nov. 23, 1864; William G. Brooks to Phillips Brooks, Dec. 13, 19, 1864, in Allen, *Life and Letters of Phillips Brooks*, 1:520-23. *Independent*, Dec. 1, 1864.

10. *New York Times*, Jan. 2, 1865. For Beecher's Music Hall lecture, see *Boston Advertiser*, Jan. 17, 1865. For Beecher's Plymouth church sermon, see *New York Times*, Feb. 21, 1865. Knox, *Life and Work of Henry Ward Beecher*, 223. Weeks, ed., *Autobiography of Rev. Granville Moody*, 425.

11. Earl Ofari, *Let Your Motto Be Resistance: The Life of Henry H. Garnet* (Boston: Beacon Press, 1972), 115.

12. *Boston Transcript*, June 21, 1865. *Worcester Spy*, June 22, 1865. *Commonwealth*, June 24, 1865. *Albany Argus* (New York), July 6, 1865.

13. *Liberator*, June 16, 30, Sept. 15, 1865. *NASS*, June 24, 1865.

14. McPherson, *The Struggle for Equality*, 326.

15. Donald Jones, *The Sectional Crisis and Northern Methodists* (London: Scarecrow Press, 1979), 293.

16. I.N. Tarbox, "Universal Suffrage," *New Englander* 24 (1865), 166. *New York Times*, May 8, 1865.

17. *Congregationalist*, May 19, 1865. *New York Observer*, June 8, 1865. *Western Christian Advocate*, May 17, 1865.

18. *Pittsburgh Christian Advocate*, June 17, 1865. *Northwestern Christian Advocate*, July 12, 1865. See also *Central Christian Advocate*, June 28, 1865. *Independent*, June 15, 1865. *Christian Watchman and Reflector*, May 25, 1865.

19. *Minutes of the New England Conference of the Methodist Episcopal Church, March 1865*, 25. *Minutes of the General Conference of Congregational Churches of Massachusetts, Sept. 1865*, 15.

20. *Annual Report of the American Baptist Home Mission Society, May 1865*, 44.

21. For example, see *Proceedings of the Chicago Baptist Association, June 1, 1865*, 9. *Minutes of the Pittsburgh Regular Baptist Association, June 1865*, 9. *Minutes of the Broome and Tioga, New York, Baptist Association*, 14. *Minutes of the Dane, Wisconsin, Baptist Association, June 1865*, 6. *Minutes of the Ottawa, Illinois, Baptist Association, June 1865*, 8.

22. *Minutes of the General Assembly* (N.S.) 14 (1865), 352-55. E.F. Hatfield to Andrew Johnson, May 27, 1865, AJP.

23. *Congregational Quarterly* 7 (Oct. 1865), 362. *Boston Transcript*, June 20, 1865.

24. See, for example, Illinois Congregational Association to Andrew Johnson, May 29, 1865, AJP.

25. Vander Velde, *The Presbyterian Churches*, 386-90. *New York Tribune*, June

7, 1865. General Synod of the Reformed Presbyterian Church to Andrew Johnson, June 2, 1865; Committee of the Washington Conference of the Methodist Episcopal Church to Johnson, Oct. 25, 1865, AJP.

26. *Worcester Palladium* (Mass.), June 14, 1865.

27. *New York Tribune*, May 29, 1865. See also *Presbyter*, July 12, 1865.

28. Samuel March to Gerrit Smith, Oct. 25, 1865, GSP. S.P. Chase to Charles Sumner, April 12, 1865; A.P. Granger to Sumner, April 14, 1865; Frank Ballard to Sumner, June 26, 1865; Henry Cheever to Sumner, Aug. 23, 1865; see also Rev. I.R.W. Sloane to Sumner, Dec. 20, 1865 (Reformed Presbyterian); Benjamin F. Hall to Sumner, Dec. 1865 (Episcopalian); Charles W. Upham to Sumner, Dec. 7, 1865 (Unitarian), CSP. Dwight H. Bruce, *Onondaga's Centennial: Gleamings of a Century*, 2 vols. (Boston: Boston History, 1896), 1:527.

29. Charles Sumner to B.F. Wade, Aug. 3, 1865, BFWP. Sumner to Thaddeus Stevens, Aug. 20, 1865, TSP. Sumner to Edwin Morgan, July 12, 1865, E.D. Morgan Papers.

30. *Chilton Times* (Wis.) June 24, 1865. For Sumner's convention speech, see: *Worcester Palladium* (Mass.), Sept. 27, 1865. Charles Stearns, Sept. 15, 1865; John Sargent, Sept. 15, 1865; Henry Wilson, Sept. 1865; Charles Brooks, Sept. 15, 1865, all to Charles Sumner, CSP.

31. S.P. Chase to Jacob Schuckers, July 7, 18685, SPCP. Chase to Schuckers, Oct. 14, 1865, Jacob Schuckers Papers, LC. George Stearns to John Andrew, July 28, 1865; Edward Hooper to Andrew, Aug. 1, 1865, JAAP. *Enquirer* (Dover, N.H.), cited by *NASS*, Aug. 5, 1865.

32. *NASS*, Aug. 12, 1865. *Boston Advertiser*, July 6, 1865. *Liberator*, Aug. 11, 1865.

33. *Marietta Times* (Ohio), Oct. 20, 1865.

34. *NCAB*, 22:232.

35. Porter, *Ohio Politics during the Civil War*, 206.

36. J.D. Cox to James Garfield, May 30, 1865, JAGP.

37. William Dickinson to J.D. Cox, May 31, 1865, J.D. Cox Papers, OCL. *Cincinnati Enquirer*, June 2, 16, 1865.

38. Roseboom, *The Civil War Era*, 450. Porter, *Ohio Politics during the Civil War*, 211-13. William Dickinson to Editor, Aug. 10, 1865, *Cincinnati Commercial*, cited by *Boston Commonwealth*, Aug. 26, 1865.

39. June 21, 29, 1865, Diary of William Coggeshall, William Coggeshall Papers. William Dickinson to Jacob Cox, June 17, 1865, J.D. Cox Papers.

40. *Elyria Independent Democrat*, July 26, 1865. E.H. Fairchild and Samuel Plumb to J.D. Cox, July 24, 1865; J.D. Cox to E.H. Fairchild and Samuel Plumb, July 25, 1865, in *Canfield Herald*, Aug. 12, 1865.

41. *Medina Gazette*, July 22, 1865. *Portage County Democrat*, July 12, 1865. James Garfield to J.D. Cox, July 14, 1865, J.D. Cox Papers. See also James Garfield to Dear Friend, Oct. 14, 1865, JAGP.

42. Porter, *Ohio Politics during the Civil War*, 216-17.

43. *Indianapolis Journal*, Aug. 24, 1865.

44. *Christian Herald and Presbyterian Recorder*, Aug. 10, 1865. *Independent*, Aug. 17, 1865.

45. Samuel Plumb to James Garfield, Aug. 7, 1865, JAGP. *Ohio State Journal*, Aug. 29, 1865. Records of the Presbyterian Synod of the Western Reserve, 1846-67 (N.S.), 2:469, PHSL.

46. Records of the Presbyterian Synod of Minnesota, 1858-69 (N.S.), Sept. 30, 1865, PHSL. *St. Paul Press*, Aug. 20, 1865, cited by *St. Paul Pioneer*, Aug. 23, 1865.

47. John Silsby to George Whipple, May 23, 1865, AMAC. *Janesville Gazette*, Aug. 14, 1865. *The History of Rock County, Wisconsin* (Chicago: Western History,

1879), 728. *Racine Journal*, July 26, 1865. *Dictionary of Wisconsin Biography* (Madison: State Historical Society of Wisconsin, 1960), 232-33. For Hastings's letters and addresses, see *Detroit Advertiser and Tribune*, Aug. 12, 1865. *Janesville Gazette*, Aug. 10, 1865. *NCAB*, 10:142. *Argus* (Albany, N.Y.), July 3, Sept. 19, 1865.

48. *Daily Wisconsin*, cited by the *Hartford Times*, Sept. 20, 1865. *Wisconsin Lumberman* (Stevens Point, Wis.), Sept. 16, 1865. J. Pease to Gideon Welles, Sept. 8, 1865, Gideon Welles Papers, LC. Byron Paine to Charles Sumner, Oct. 7, 1865, CSP. Edward Palmer to Moses M. Davis, July 28, 1865, Moses M. Davis, Papers; M.M. Davis to John F. Potter, Sept. 3, 1865, John F. Potter Papers, SHSW. *Ripon Commonwealth*, Oct. 6, 1865. *Chicago Tribune*, Sept. 28, 1865. *NASS*, Oct. 7, 1865. Halbert E. Paine was affiliated with the Presbyterian church, and James H. Paine and his son Byron Paine were Congregationalists. See *Washington Post*, April 18, 1905; *DAB*, 7:148-49, and *NCAB*, 10:54, for H.E. Paine. For J.H. and Byron Paine, see Henry Holcomb Papers, Manuscript Collection MSS3368, Western Reserve Historical Society Library; Sherman M. Booth was a Congregationalist who lectured for the New York Temperance Society and the Connecticut Anti-Slavery Society in the 1830s. Later he edited several antislavery newspapers in Wisconsin. He is best known for the Glover rescue, after which he said, "Whatever aid and comfort I may have rendered . . . , it was only such . . . as humanity dictates and as the plainest precepts of Christian religion required of me on peril of my soul." See *Evening Wisconsin* (Milwaukee), Aug. 11, 12, 1904; *Dictionary of Wisconsin Biography* (Madison: State Historical Society of Wisconsin, 1960), 42. T.O. Howe and C.C. Sholes were Unitarians, Samuel Hastings was a Congregationalist, and Amasa Cobbs was an Episcopalian but was probably motivated primarily by nationalism. Howe, a man of high moral character, attended the Unitarian church with regularity wherever he was. See T.O. Howe to Grace Howe, Feb. 21, April 26, 1866; Feb. 5, 16, 1867, TOHP; *NCAB*, 6:191. *Evening News* (Lincoln, Nebr.), July 6, 1905; *Nebraska State Journal* (Lincoln), Oct. 22, 1905. Other antislavery Christians who reportedly attended the Janesville convention included: Rev. Benjamin E. Hale, Congregationalist; Rev. Joseph J. Baker, Universalist; Rev. William C. Whitford, Seventh Day Baptist; Judge David Noggle, Episcopalian; Elisha Keyes, Baptist trustee; John B. Cassoday and James Sutherland, Congregationalists.

49. For the Methodist Conference, see *Wisconsin State Journal*, Sept. 11, 1865. *Minutes of the Monroe Baptist Association, Oct. 1865*, 16. Minutes of the Presbyterian and Congregational Convention, Oct. 1865, Manuscript Record, SHLW. *Ripon Commonwealth*, Oct. 20, 1865.

50. William Gillette, *The Right to Vote: Politics and the Passage of the Fifteenth Amendment* (Baltimore: Johns Hopkins Univ. Press, 1965), 27.

51. Ira V. Brown, "Pennsylvania and the Rights of the Negro, 1865-1887," *Pennsylvania History* 28 (Jan. 1961), 50. *Minutes of the Abington Baptist Association, Aug., 1865*, 6. L.O. Greenell to Andrew Johnson, Aug. 24, 1865, AJP. *Minutes of the Centre Baptist Association of Pennsylvania, Aug. 1865*, 10. Lewis S. Hartman to Andrew Johnson, Aug. 21, 1865; H.B. Sherman to Johnson, July 4, 1865, AJP. Thaddeus Stevens to Charles Sumner, Aug. 26, Oct. 7, 1865, CSP. Leslie H. Fishel, "Northern Prejudice and Negro Suffrage, 1865-1878," *JNH* 39 (Jan. 1954), 13.

52. Marion T. Wright, "Negro Suffrage in New Jersey, 1776-1875," *JNH* 31 (April 1948), 201-4. Gillette, *The Right to Vote*, 25. Fishel, "Northern Prejudice and Negro Suffrage," 13. Julian, *Political Recollections*, 263-65. *Indianapolis Journal*, Nov. 3, 18, 22, 1865. Clarke, *George Julian*, 281-91. Emma L. Thornbrough, *Indiana in the Civil War Era, 1850-1880* (Indianapolis: Indiana Historical Bureau, 1965), 230. *Delaware Free Press* (Muncie, Ind.), June 29, 1865. *A Portrait and Bio-*

*graphical Record of Delaware and Randolph Counties, Indiana* (Chicago: A.W. Bowen, 1894), 251.

53. James Harlan to George B. Edwards, Aug. 26, 1865, in the *Ottawa Republican* (Ill.), Sept. 16, 1865. *Independent*, Aug. 24, 1865. C.C. Cole to J.M. Windor in *Iowa State Register*, cited by the *Dubuque Times*, Aug. 17, 1865. Thomas H. Benton to Andrew Johnson, Sept. 16, 1865; Eli Jessup to Johnson, Sept. 12, 1865, AJP. *Minutes of the Upper Iowa Conference of the Methodist Episcopal Church, Sept. 1865*, 13. For Des Moines conference resolutions, see *Christian Advocate and Journal*, Sept. 21, 1865. William D. Heinzig, "Iowa's Response to Reconstruction, 1865-1868" (masters thesis, Iowa State Univ., Ames, Iowa, 1971), 79, 81-82. J.W. Cattel to S.J. Kirkwood, Des Moines, Aug. 14, 1865; Rev. A. Kenyon to Kirkwood, Iowa City, Feb. 21, 1866, Dr. Jesse Bowen to Kirkwood, Dec. 3, 1865, Samuel J. Kirkwood Papers, Iowa State Historical Library.

54. *Jackson Citizen* (Mich.), Aug. 5, 1865. *Journal of the Michigan Conference of the Methodist Episcopal Church, Sept. 1865*, 18.

55. Phyllis Field, *The Politics of Race in New York* (Ithaca: Cornell Univ. Press, 1982), 162. *Independent*, Aug. 24, 1865.

56. *Minutes of the Hudson River Baptist Association, June 1865*, 16, 19. *Minutes of the Franklin Baptist Association, June 1865*, 6. *Minutes of the New York Baptist Association, 1865*, 15. *Liberator*, June 30, 1865. Edna Farley, "Methodist and Baptist on the Issue of Black Equality in New York, 1865-1866," *JNH* 61 (Oct. 1976), 375-76.

57. *New York Post*, May 11, 1865. John Jay, the grandson of Chief Justice John Jay, was a radical Episcopal layman. He was recognized as a leader of the laity in the state of New York and was active in benevolent work of the Episcopal church all of his life. *DAB*, 5:10; *NCAB*, 7:347. *New York Times*, May 6, 1894. Benson Lossing to Henry Wilson, June 19, 1865, Henry Wilson Papers, LC. *Year Book* 30 (1945), 86, Dutchess County, NYHSL. *NCAB*, 4:324. William Goodell to Maria Frost, June 22, 1865, WGP, BCL. For Goodell's sermon, see William Goodell, Manuscript Sermon, in WGP, OCL. *Principia*, July 6, 1865. For Cheever's sermon, see *NASS*, July 1, 1865.

58. *Norwich Courier* (Conn.), May 4, 1865. *New Haven Palladium*, May 15, 1865. Buckingham was a charter and corporate member of the American Board of Commissioners of Foreign Missions, president of the AMA, and moderator of the first National Council of Congregational Churches in 1865. He taught a Sabbath school class in the Second Congregational Church of Norwich, Connecticut. *DAB*, 2:229. *NCAB*, 10:340. Increase N. Tarbox, "William Alfred Buckingham" *Congregational Quarterly*, April 1876, p. 216.

59. James L. Greene to John Andrew, Sept. 22, 1865, JAAP. Francis Hawley to Joseph Hawley, July 26, 28, Sept. 24, 1865, JRHP. For address to voters, see *New Haven Palladium*, Sept. 6, 1865. *New York Tribune*, Sept. 9, 1865. For Francis Hawley's religious affiliation, see *ACAB*, 3:124. Francis Hawley was originally a Baptist but became a Congregationalist minister later in his career. Elias S. Hawley, *The Hawley Record* (Buffalo: E.H. Hutchinson, 1890), 107. See John A. Nicolson, "New England Idealism in the Civil War: The Military Career of Joseph Roswell Hawley" (Ph.D. diss., Claremont Graduate School, 1970), 4.

60. Nicolson, "New England Idealism during the Civil War," 22, 38, 255. John Hooker, *Some Reminiscences of a Long Life* (Hartford: Belknap and Warfield, 1899), 58-59, 170-71, 282. Kenneth Andrew, *Nook Farm: Mark Twain's Hartford Circle* (Cambridge, Mass.: Kenneth Andrew, 1950), 2-6. For Warner's religion, see *Representative Men of Connecticut, 1861-1894* (Everett: Massachusetts Publishing, 1894), 275.

61. *Independent*, Sept. 28, 1865. *Minutes of the General Association of Congregational Churches of Connecticut, June 1865*, 20. H.C. Bowen to Leonard Bacon, Sept. 22, 1865; Joseph Mann to Bacon, Sept. 18, 1865; Jonathan S. Mauer to Bacon, Sept. 18, 1865, Leonard Bacon Papers.

62. *New York Tribune*, Sept. 12, 1865. *Independent*, Sept. 28, 1865. *Christian Advocate and Journal*, Sept. 28, 1865.

63. *Liberator*, Oct. 13, 1865. *Commonwealth*, Oct. 7, 1865. *Independent*, Oct. 12, 1865.

64. *Boston Transcript*, Oct. 4, 1865. *New Haven Palladium*, Oct. 3, 1865. John W. Harbracke to John Andrew, Oct. 5, 1865, JAAP. F. Hawley to Joseph Hawley, Oct. 22, 1865, JRHP. *Hartford Press*, Oct. 3, 1865. Mark Howard to unknown correspondent, April 5, 1866, Mark Howard Correspondence, Connecticut Historical Society Library.

65. *Christian Advocate and Journal*, Oct. 12, 1865. *Minutes of the Old Colony Baptist Association, Oct. 1865*, 6. *New York Observer*, Oct. 12, 1865.

66. Horace White to W.P. Fessenden, Oct. 9, 1865, Horace White Papers, ISHL. M. French to O.O. Howard, Dec. 2, 1865, AMAC.

67. *Commonwealth*, April 6, June 1, 8, 1867.

68. Benedict, *A Compromise of Principles*, 115.

69. *Congregationalist*, Sept. 1, 1865. *Boston Recorder*, Sept. 22, 1865. *Universalist Quarterly* 22 (Oct. 1865), 460. *Christian Register*, Nov. 11, 1865. Joseph C. Bustill to Thaddeus Stevens, Dec. 22, 1865, TSP.

## 11. The Black Suffrage Referenda of 1867

1. Church membership was estimated at 23 percent in 1860 and 18 percent in 1870. *Yearbook of American Churches, 1865* (New York: National Council of Churches, 1965), 280. *Morning Chronicles*, Jan. 11, 1866. *NASS*, Jan. 2, 1866.

2. Porter, *Ohio Politics*, 219.

3. Robert Rutland, "Iowans and the Fourteenth Amendment," *Iowa Journal of History* 51 (Oct. 1953), 292-93.

4. Willis F. Dunbar, with William G. Shade, "The Black Man Gains the Vote: The Centennial of 'Impartial Suffrage' in Michigan" *Michigan History* 61 (Jan. 1972), 47. Nathan M. Thomas to S.B. Thayer, Dec. 23, 1867, Nathan M. Thomas Correspondence, UM.

5. *Minutes of the Walworth Baptist Association, June 1866*, 9.

6. See, for example, *National Principia*, June 14, 1866.

7. *Independent*, May 31, 1866.

8. *Zion's Herald*, Nov. 28, 1866.

9. *Independent*, March 14, 1867.

10. McPherson, *Ordeal by Fire*, 529. *NASS*, Feb. 2, 1867. Martin E. Mantell, "The Election of 1868: The Response to Congressional Reconstruction" (Ph.D. diss., Columbia Univ., 1970), 82. Only in California and Pennsylvania did the Republican conventions fail to endorse black suffrage in 1867. *American Annual Encyclopaedia* (1867), under states' names.

11. Alpheus Crosby to Joseph R. Hawley, Feb. 19, 1867, JRHP. O.D. Case to Horace Greeley, March 14, 1867, HGP, LC. *Independent*, March 14, 21, 1867. C. Johnson to George Cheever, March 9, 1867, GBCP. *Norwich Bulletin* (Conn.), Dec. 9, 1921.

12. *Independent*, April 11, 1867. *Watchman and Reflector*, April 11, 1867. *Zion's Herald*, April 17, 1867.

13. *NASS*, April 6, 1867. *Independent*, April 11, 1867. Beale, *Diary of Gideon Welles*, 3:88.

14. *Independent*, April 18, 1867. Charles Sumner to Theodore Tilton, April 20, 1867, TTP. *New York Times*, May 3, 1867. *Liberal Christian*, April 27, 1867.

15. Francis Hawley to Joseph Hawley, April 7, 1867; J.B. Cleveland to Joseph Hawley, April 4, 1867; H.L. Wayland to Joseph Hawley, April 8, 1867; Horace Greeley to Joseph Hawley, Nov. 17, 1867, JRHP.

16. *New York Times*, May 12, 1867.

17. Fishel, "Northern Prejudice and Negro Suffrage," 21-22. *Minutes of the Iowa Conference of the Methodist Episcopal Church, Sept. 1867*, 26. For the Upper Iowa Conference, see *Cincinnati Gazette*, Oct. 3, 1867.

18. *NASS*, Jan. 26, March 23, 1867. *Saint Paul Pioneer*, June 20, 1867. *Central Republican* (Faribault, Minn.), Nov. 20, 1867.

19. Charles M. Knapp, *New Jersey Politics during the Period of the Civil War and Reconstruction* (Geneva, N.Y.: W.F. Humphrey, 1924), 168. Hamilton Eckenrode, *Rutherford B. Hayes, Statesman of Reunion* (New York: Dodd, Mead, 1930), 85. *New York Tribune*, May 3, 24, June 5, 1867. For Scovel's obituary, see *New York Times*, Dec. 3, 1904.

20. Wright, "Negro Suffrage in New Jersey," 215-17.

21. Marcus Ward to the Republican state central committee, July 19, 1867, in the *New York Tribune*, July 25, 1867. *New York Times*, July 24, 1867. For Ward's obituary see *Newark Advertiser*, April 26, 1884. For Frelinghuysen's speech, see *Cleveland Leader*, July 30, 1867. Fishel, "Northern Prejudice and Negro Suffrage," 21.

22. *NASS*, Aug. 24, 1867.

23. *Independent*, Feb. 21, March 14, 1867.

24. Erwin S. Bradley, "Post-Bellum Politics in Pennsylvania, 1866-1872" (Ph.D. diss., Pennsylvania State Univ., 1952), 110-11. Brown, "Pennsylvania and the Rights of the Negro," 49.

25. Allen, *Life and Letters of Phillips Brooks*, 2:73.

26. *Examiner and Chronicle*, Jan. 17, April 4, 1867. George Cheever to Elizabeth, March 4, 1867, GBCP. *NASS*, April 6, 1867.

27. *New York Times*, May 8, 1867.

28. "J.W.B." to Editor, Nov. 16, 1867, in *Christian Freeman*, Nov. 28, 1867.

29. *New York Times*, June 27, 1867. *NASS*, Sept. 28, 1867. J.C. Mohr, *The Radical Republicans and Reform in New York during Reconstruction* (Ithaca: Cornell Univ. Press, 1973), chap. 8. Phyllis F. Field, "Republicans and Black Suffrage in New York State: The Grass Roots Response," *Civil War History* 22 (June 1975), 147.

30. Field, *The Politics of Race in New York*, 170-71.

31. *Leavenworth Times*, Sept. 7, Nov. 22, 1866; Jan. 10, 1867.

32. *New York Times*, Jan. 18, Feb. 15, 1867. *State Record* (Topeka), Feb. 15, 1867.

33. *Wyandotte Commercial Gazette*, April 6, 1867. Samuel A. Johnson, *The Battle Cry of Freedom: The New England Emigrant Aid Company in the Kansas Crusade* (Lawrence: Univ. of Kansas Press, 1954), 88. *Minutes of the General Association of Congregational Ministers and Churches in Kansas*, 34. *New York Tribune*, June 5, 1867. *Tiffin Tribune* (Ohio), June 13, 1867. Sister Jeanne McKenna, "With the Help of God and Lucy Stone," *Kansas Historical Quarterly* 36 (Spring 1970), 13-14.

34. *Leavenworth Times*, May 18, 1867. Ida H. Harper, *The Life and Work of Susan B. Anthony*, 3 vols. (Indianapolis: Hollenbeck Press, 1898), 1:284.

35. *Kansas Record*, cited by *Wyandotte Commercial Gazette*, July 20, Aug. 31, 1867. Harper, *Susan B. Anthony*, 1:286.

36. *Wyandotte Commercial Gazette*, Aug. 24, 31, 1867. Alma Lutz, *Susan B.*

*Anthony* (Boston: Beacon Press, 1959), 129. Harper, *Susan B. Anthony*, 1:283, 287. *Kansas Record* (Topeka), Oct. 30, 1867.

37. McKinna, "With the Help of God and Lucy Stone," 15. *New York Tribune,* June 5, 1867. Samuel Pomeroy to Anna Dickinson, Oct. 16, 1867, AEDP. "Reminiscences by Helen Starrett," in Elizabeth C. Stanton, ed., *History of Woman Suffrage,* 5 vols. (New York: Fowler and Wells, 1882), 2:251.

38. *Freedom's Champion,* Aug. 1, 1867. Sheffield Ingalls, *History of Atchison County, Kansas* (Lawrence: Standard Publishing, 1916), 247. Rev. James Shaw, *Early Reminiscences: Pioneer Life in Kansas* (Atchison: Haskel, 1886), 214-15.

39. *Freedom's Champion,* Aug. 15, Sept. 12, 19, 26, 1867. *Leavenworth Times,* Dec. 1, 1867. *White Cloud Kansas Chief,* Sept. 12, Oct. 3, 1867. Rev. H.D. Fisher, *The Gun and the Gospel: Early Kansas and Chaplain Fisher* (Kansas City: Hudson-Kimberly, 1902), 156. R.S. Tenney to Susan B. Anthony, Nov. 23, 1881, SBAP. Stanton, *History of Woman Suffrage,* 2:257. Emory Landquist, "Religion in Kansas during the Era of the Civil War," *Kansas Historical Quarterly* 25 (Autumn, 1959); 319.

40. *Wyandotte Commercial Gazette,* Sept. 21, 1867. *Leavenworth Times,* Sept. 21, 25, 1867. *New York Times,* Oct. 12, 1867. Fisher, *The Gun and the Gospel,* 232.

41. *New York Tribune,* Oct. 1, 1867, cited by *Wyandotte Commercial Gazette,* Oct. 12, 1867.

42. *Wyandotte Commercial Gazette,* Sept. 21, 28, 1867. W.G. Cutler, *History of Kansas* (Chicago: Andreas, 1883), 859.

43. D.P. Mitchell to J.H. Watson, Sept. 21, 1867, in *Kansas Record,* Oct. 23, 1867. Shaw, *Early Reminiscences,* 214-15.

44. *Freedom's Champion,* Oct. 17, 1867. *White Cloud Kansas Chief,* Oct. 3, 1867. Landquist, "Religion in Kansas," 319. Rosetta Hastings, *Personal Recollections of Pardee Butler* (Cincinnati: Standard Publishing, 1889), 38-39.

45. *White Cloud Kansas Chief,* Nov. 7, 1867. Landquist, "Religion in Kansas," 318.

46. Harper, *Susan B. Anthony,* 1:281-82. *DAB,* 9:626.

47. James A. Garfield to G.W. Shurtliff, Dec. 31, 1866; R.C. Parson to G.W. Shurtliff, Dec. 26, 1866; Douglas Putnam to Rev. Henry Carter, Dec. 27, 1866; Robert C. Schenck to Shurtliff, Jan. 14, 1867, in the *Portage County Democrat,* Feb. 13, 1867. *History of Lorain County, Ohio* (Cleveland: Williams Brothers, 1879), 182. *History of Washington County, Ohio* (Marietta: Washington County Historical Society, 1881), 485.

48. Gen. R. Hastings to R.B. Hayes, Jan. 31, 1867, Rutherford Hayes Papers. *Elyria Independent Democrat,* Jan. 9, 23, 1867.

49. *Ohio Repository,* Feb. 27, 1867. *Portage County Democrat,* March 6, 1867. *Ironton Register,* March 21, 1867. *Independent,* March 14, 1867. *Commonwealth,* March 2, 1867.

50. *New York Times,* March 11, April 4, 6, 11, 1867. For Dickson's letter, see *Times,* March 11, 1867. David Gerber, *Black Ohio and the Color Line, 1860-1915* (Urbana: Univ. of Illinois Press, 1976), 38.

51. "Sprague," Sept. 22, 1867, in the *Commonwealth,* Sept. 28, 1867. *Ohio Repository,* April 10, 1867. *Ironton Register,* April 18, 1867. *Ironton Tribune,* Nov. 19, 1903.

52. *Cleveland Herald,* April 22, 1867. *New York Times,* June 20, 1867. Bonadio, *North of Reconstruction,* 99-100.

53. *Cincinnati Gazette,* July 4, 1867. *Minutes of the North Ohio Conference of the Methodist Episcopal Church, August 1867,* 23. For the Ohio conference, see

*Western Christian Advocate*, Sept. 25, 1867. See *Urbana Union*, Sept. 18, 1867, for the support of the amendment by the Cincinnati conference.

54. Records of the Wesleyan Methodist Convention of America, 1842-1887, p. 236, Wesleyan Methodist Church Archives. *American Wesleyan*, Oct. 16, 1867. For the Methodist Protestant Church, see *Marion Independent* (Ohio), Oct. 3, 1867. For the Ohio Baptist convention, see *Cincinnati Gazette*, Oct. 26, 1867.

55. *Elyria Independent Democrat*, May 1, 1867.

56. John M. Langston to Gerrit Smith, March 1, 1867, GSP. *Morning Journal* (Columbus), July 3, Oct. 1, 1867. *Cincinnati Gazette*, July 4, 16, 1867.

57. *Cincinnati Gazette*, Oct. 5, 1867.

58. *Cincinnati Commercial*, Sept. 11, 1867. Greve, *Centennial History of Cincinnati*, 2:604.

59. *Carroll Union Press* (Carrolton), Sept. 18, 1867. *Western Star* (Lebanon), Sept. 19, 1867.

60. *Cincinnati Commercial*, Aug. 29, 1867. *New York Times*, Sept. 7, 1867.

61. *Elyria Independent Democrat*, Sept. 11, 1867. *History of Lorain County, Ohio*, 115. *History of Medina County, Ohio* (Chicago: Baskin and Battery, 1881), 258.

62. *Cincinnati Gazette*, Sept. 5, 1867. *Cincinnati Commercial*, Sept. 7, 1867.

63. *Marion Independent*, Oct. 3, 1867. *History of Marion County, Ohio* (Chicago: Leggett, Conway, 1883), 393.

64. *Morning Journal* (Columbus), July 18, 31, 1867. *Western Star*, Sept. 26, 1867. Gertrude Van Rensselaer Wickham, *The Pioneer Families of Cleveland, 1796-1840* (Cleveland: Evangelical Publishing, 1914), 605. C.R. Williams, *Rutherford Hayes*, 2 vols. (Boston: Houghton Mifflin, 1914), 1:279. For Shellabarger's speeches, see *Salem Republican*, Oct. 2, 1867, and *Cincinnati Commercial*, Aug. 30, 1867. *Biographical Cyclopaedia of Ohio* (Cincinnati: Western Biographical Publishing, 1887). *NCAB*, 2:357. For Orth's speech, see *Cincinnati Gazette*, Oct. 1, 1867. *Indianapolis Journal*, Dec. 18, 1882. For Wade's speeches, see *Cincinnati Gazette*, Sept. 11, 1867. *NASS*, Aug. 31, 1867. *Ashtabula Sentinel*, Oct. 2, 1867. *Cadiz Republican*, Oct. 30, 1867. For Sherman's speech, see *Cincinnati Gazette*, Aug. 21, 1867. For Colfax's speech, see *Urbana Union*, Sept. 25, 1867. *Warren Republican*, Sept. 26, 1867. *Ohio Repository*, Sept. 25, 1867. Z. Chandler to R.B. Hayes, Oct. 5, 1867, R.B. Hayes Papers. *New York Herald*, Oct. 1, 1867.

65. *Portage County Democrat*, June 12, 1867. J.D. Cox to Friedrich Hassuarek, May 13, 1867, Friedrich Hassuarek Papers. J.D. Cox to James Garfield, Nov. 22, 1867, JAGP.

66. Henry C. Wright to Editor, Aug. 18, 1867; "N" to Editor, Aug. 25, 1867, in *NASS*, Sept. 14, Oct. 5, 1867. *Ohio State Journal*, Oct. 5, 1867. Charles Robertson, *History of Morgan County, Ohio* (Chicago: L.H. Watkins, 1886), 389. *Cincinnati Gazette*, Sept. 6, Oct. 3, 1867. W.S. Studley to Editor, Oct. 1, 1867, *Zion's Herald*, Oct. 17, 1867.

67. *Ohio State Journal*, Sept. 11, 1867. Schuyler Colfax to James Garfield, Sept. 11, 1867; Harmon Austin to Garfield, Sept. 22, 1867, JAGP. Gerber, *Black Ohio and the Color Line*, 38.

68. Charles D. McGuffey to John Eaton, Oct. 1, 1867, John Eaton Papers, Univ. of Tennessee. *Minutes of the Old School General Assembly of the Presbyterian Church* (1866), 23. Wood, *Black Scare*, 26. Levi S. Fay to Milton Badger, Oct. 6, 1867, AHMSC. *NASS*, Oct. 5, 1867.

69. Porter, *Ohio Politics*, 242, 248.

70. *Independent*, Oct. 17, 1867. William H. Smith to R.B. Mussey, Oct. 21, 1867, William Henry Smith Letterbooks, OSHL. *NCAB*, 19:442. Edgar L. Gray,

"The Career of William Henry Smith, Politician-Journalist" (Ph.D. diss., Ohio State Univ., 1951), 4, 6, 11.

71. *Liberal Christian*, Nov. 16, 1867. "Veteran Observer," Oct. 10, 1867, *New York Times*, Oct. 15, 1867. *Commonwealth*, Oct. 19, 1867.

72. Henry C. Wright to William L. Garrison, Dec. 5, 1867, WLGP. Jayme A. Sokolow, "Henry Clarke Wright: Antebellum Crusader," *Essex Institute Historical Collection* 3 (April 1975), 136. Lewis Perry, *Childhood, Marriage, and Reform: Henry Clarke Wright, 1797-1870* (Chicago: Univ. of Chicago Press, 1980), 165. William L. Garrison to Henry C. Wright, Dec. 9, 1867, in Merrill, *The Letters of William Lloyd Garrison*, 5:555. Granville Moody to R.B. Hayes, Nov. 27, 1867, R.B. Hayes Papers. See *New York World*, Nov. 9, 1867, for Stevens. George Cheever to Elizabeth, Oct. 7, 1867, GBCP.

73. *Zion's Herald*, Oct. 17, 1867.

74. *Cincinnati Gazette*, Nov. 29, 1867. *Ohio State Journal*, Nov. 2, 1867.

75. *Western Christian Advocate*, Oct. 16, 24, 1867. *Christian Ambassador*, Oct. 26, 1867. *Independent*, Nov. 14, 1867.

76. Gillette, *The Right to Vote*, 32. Baum, *The Civil War Party System*, 125.

77. *Zion's Herald*, Oct. 17, Nov. 28, 1867. William B. Gravely, "Gilbert Haven, Racial Equalitarian: A Study of His Career in Racial Reform, 1850-1880" (Ph.D. diss., Duke Univ., 1869), 193.

## 12. The Fifteenth Amendment

1. McPherson, *The Struggle for Equality*, 385, 417.

2. *Independent*, Nov. 14, 1867.

3. Octavius B. Frothingham to M.D. Conway, Oct. 29, 1867, MDCP. Parker Pillsbury to Gerrit Smith, Nov. 27, 1867, GSP.

4. Frederick J. Blue, *Salmon P. Chase: A Life in Politics*, 280, 284. Charles H. Coleman, *The Election of 1868: The Democratic Effort to Regain Control* (1933; reprt., New York: Octagon Books, 1971), 79-81.

5. *NASS*, Dec. 28, 1867, Jan. 18, Feb. 22, March 28, 1868. Martyn, *Wendell Phillips*, 363.

6. *NASS*, Feb. 29, 1868. Julian, *Political Recollections*, 319. Pierce, *Memoir and Letters of Charles Sumner*, 4:358.

7. *Independent*, Oct. 24, Dec. 5, 1867.

8. *Commonwealth*, Jan. 4, Feb. 15, 1868.

9. *Independent*, April 9, 1868. *NASS*, April 11, 18, May 9, 30, 1868.

10. *Independent*, May 14, 1868.

11. Dunbar, "The Black Man Gains the Vote," 47. Gillette, *The Right to Vote*, 37.

12. Porter, *National Party Platforms, 1840-1968*, 39. *Commonwealth*, May 30, 1868. Martin E. Mantell, "The Election of 1868: The Response to Congressional Reconstruction" (Ph.D. diss., Columbia Univ., 1969), 157.

13. *Independent*, May 28, 1868, June 18, 1868. *NASS*, May 30, 1868.

14. *Commonwealth*, June 6, 1868.

15. *NASS*, Aug. 11, 1866; June 13, Aug. 15, 29, Sept. 26, 1868; May 22, 1869.

16. *NASS*, June 13, Aug. 29, Sept. 26, 1868.

17. *NASS*, June 13, Sept. 26, Nov. 7, 1868. *Proceedings of the Pennsylvania Yearly Meeting of the Progressive Friends, 1868*, 11. *Minutes of the South-Eastern Indiana Conference of the Methodist Episcopal Church 1868*, 151. For the Wisconsin Methodist Conference, see Miller, *Thirty Years in the Itineracy*, 269, 275. *Minutes of the East Maine Methodist Episcopal Conference, 1868*, 16. *Journal of*

the *General Conference of the Methodist Episcopal Church, 1868,* 343. *Minutes of the New London Baptist Association, 1868,* 8.

18. Brownlow, "The Northern Protestant Pulpit," 125, 127.

19. Alexander Clark, "Radical Reconstruction," in *The Radical Republicans and Reconstruction, 1861-1870,* edited by Harold Hyman (Indianapolis: Bobbs-Merrill, 1967), 471.

20. Joseph P. Thompson, *The Theocratic Principle; or, Religion, the Bond of the Republic* (New York: Trow and Smith, 1868), 12. *Independent,* Aug. 27, 1868.

21. *Congregationalist,* July 16, 1868. *Northern Advocate,* Oct. 8, 1868. Morrow, *Northern Methodism and Reconstruction,* 212-14.

22. James Harlan to William E. Chandler, June 24, 1868, William E. Chandler Papers, LC. *Free Methodist* (Rochester, N.Y.), Oct. 15, 1868. Morrow, *Northern Methodism,* 213.

23. *Christian Advocate and Journal,* Nov. 12, 1868. See also the *Northwestern Advocate,* Nov. 11, 1868. *Congregationalist,* Nov. 12, 1868.

24. *Commonwealth,* Dec. 26, 1868; Jan. 23, 1869. *NASS,* Dec. 12, 1868; Jan. 16, 1869. Clark, "Radical Reconstruction," 471-72.

25. *Independent,* June 18, Nov. 5, 1868. *Zion's Herald,* Dec. 10, 1868. *American Presbyterian,* Dec. 17, 1868. *Evangelist,* Nov. 19, 1868.

26. *Chicago Tribune,* Nov. 28, 1868. John B. DeMott's Sermon, Nov. 27, 1868, DeMott's Diary, DePauw Univ.

27. Benedict, *A Compromise of Principle,* 327. Allen W. Trelease, *White Terror: The Ku Klux Klan Conspiracy and Southern Reconstruction* (New York: Harper and Row, 1971), 111-85.

28. *Register of the Rock River Conference of the Methodist Episcopal Church, Sept. 1868,* 22. *Minutes of the North Ohio Conference of the Methodist Episcopal Church, Sept. 1868,* 31. *Minutes of the Cincinnati Conference of the Methodist Episcopal Church, Aug. 1868,* 52. For the Central Ohio conference, see *Miami Union,* Sept. 26, 1868. *American Missionary* 12 (Dec. 1868), 266. Edgar Ketchum to O.O. Howard, Nov. 18, 1868, Freedmen's Bureau Papers, National Archives. *Liberal Christian,* Sept. 5, 1868. For the Beecher lecture, see *Minneapolis Tribune,* Oct. 16, 1868. Henry Wilson to A.A. Terry, May 14, 1869, in *American Missionary* 14 (Jan. 1870), 17.

29. Hunt, *Israel, Elihu, and Cadwallader Washburn,* 125.

30. *New York Times,* Jan. 10, 1869. *American Missionary* 14 (July 1870), 2-3.

31. Cited by the *New York Times,* Jan. 29, 1869.

32. *Independent,* Feb. 11, 1869. *Liberal Christian,* Feb. 13, 1869. *Christian Register,* Feb. 13, 1869.

33. *Cong. Globe,* 40th Cong., 3d sess. (Feb. 26, 1869), 1,627. *NASS,* Feb. 20, 1869. George S. Boutwell to Wendell Phillips, March 13, 1870, in George S. Boutwell, *Reminiscences of Sixty Years,* 2 vols. (1902; reprt., New York: Greenwood Press, 1968), 2:48-50.

34. *Independent,* Feb. 11, March 4, 11, 1869.

35. *Commonwealth,* Feb. 6, 13, 20, April 24, 1869.

36. *NASS,* Feb. 6, March 6, 1869. *American Missionary* 14 (May 1870), 82.

37. Gillette, *The Right to Vote,* 79. *NASS,* March 13, 1869. *Congregationalist,* March 11, 1869.

38. Sylvester Tallcott to Richard Yates, March 5, 1869; Anson Miller to Yates, April 10, 1869; J.W. Strevelle to Yates, July 3, 1869, RYP. *Portrait and Biography Record of Winnebago and Boone County, Illinois* (Chicago: Biographical Publishing, 1892), 605. "Suffrage," Sermon 22, March 7, 1869, William C. Gannet Sermons, Colgate Divinity School Library.

39. John Cox and LaWanda Cox, "Negro Suffrage and Republican Politics: The

Problem of Motivation in Reconstruction Historiography," *Journal of Southern History* 33 (Aug. 1967), 319, 322, 330. Field, *The Politics of Race in New York*, 170-71. Dixon R. Fox, "The Negro Vote in Old New York," *Political Science Quarterly* 32 (June 1917), 275. Linden, *Politics or Principle*, 41. Brock, *An American Crisis*, 14. William Gillette, *Retreat from Reconstruction, 1869-1879* (Baton Rouge: Louisiana State Univ. Press, 1979), 46. Herman Belz, *Emancipation and Equal Rights: Politics and Constitutionalism in the Civil War* (New York: Norton, 1978), 126.

40. Joanna D. Cowden, "Civil War and Reconstruction in Connecticut, 1863-1863" (Ph.D. diss., Univ. of Connecticut, 1975), 254. Robert Dykstra and Harlan Hahn, "Northern Voters and the Negro Suffrage Question: The Case of Iowa, 1868," *Public Opinion Quarterly* 22 (Summer 1963), 212. Sylvia Cohn, "The Reaction of New York and Ohio to the Ratification of the Fifteenth Amendment" (masters thesis, Univ. of Chicago, 1944), 74. Frank Klement, "Western Copperheadism and the Genesis of the Granger Movement," *MVHR* 30 (March 1952), 679.

41. McPherson, *Ordeal by Fire*, 546. Sorin, *Abolitionists*, 163.

42. Trefousse, *The Radical Republicans*, 443-46. Charles Blank, "The Waning of Radicalism: Massachusetts Republicans and Reconstruction Issues in the Early 1870's" (Ph.D. diss., Brandeis Univ., 1972), 20.

43. *Commonwealth*, Aug. 21, 1869. Cochrane, "Freedom without Equality," 392. Hyman, *A More Perfect Union*, 543-44. Gillette, *Retreat from Reconstruction*, 23-24, 295-99. Stanley I. Kutler, *Judicial Power and Reconstruction Politics* (Chicago: Univ. of Chicago Press, 1968), 159, 166.

44. Belz, *Emancipation and Equal Rights*, 113.

45. Brock, *An American Crisis*, 288, 297-98.

46. Trefousse, *The Radical Republicans*, 470.

## Epilogue

1. *Independent*, March 25, 1869.

2. Gravely, "Gilbert Haven," 326. Marty, *Righteous Empire*, 140.

3. Marty, *Righteous Empire*, 140. William G. McLoughlin, Jr., *Modern Revivalism* (New York: Ronald Press, 1959), 106. Premillennialists believed Christ's return would precede and usher in the millennium. Postmillennialists believed Christ's second coming would occur after a period of reform.

4. William W. Sweet, *The Story of Religion in America* (New York: Harper, 1930), 470. Ahlstrom, *A Religious History*, 681. Williston Walker, *A History of the Congregational Churches in the United States* (New York: Christian Literature, 1894), 395. James M. McPherson, *The Abolitionist Legacy: From Reconstruction to the NAACP* (Princeton: Princeton Univ. Press, 1975), 263, 265, 271, 273. Oliver S. Heckman, "The Presbyterian Church in the United States of America in the Southern Reconstruction, 1860-1880," *North Carolina Historical Review* 20 (July 1947), 228-29.

5. Ralph L. Moellering, *Christian Conscience and Negro Emancipation* (Philadelphia: Fortress Press, 1965), 184.

# Bibliography

This bibliography lists only sources used in the present book. As prolific as scholarship and professional collators of reference aids have been in recent decades, there is no want of bibliographies on the Civil War era. John D. Smith's *Black Slavery in the Americas: An Interdisciplinary Bibliography, 1865-1880* is one of the most recently published. Although I made extensive use of monographs and articles in twentieth-century periodicals, I have not included this material in the bibliography. I drew on political newspapers such as the *New York Times, New York Tribune, Chicago Tribune, Boston Transcript*, and *Cincinnati Gazette*, to name a few of the most important, and on smaller publications, including a large number of county newspapers. More than 125 newspapers provided useful material. The notes list secondary sources and nineteenth-century political newspapers in full.

## ARCHIVES

*American Antiquarian Society Library*, Worcester, Mass.: George B. Cheever Papers; Abby Kelley Foster Papers.

*Amistad Research Center, Tulane University*, New Orleans, LA.: American Home Missionary Society Correspondence; American Missionary Association Correspondence.

*Berea College Library*, Ky.: William Goddell Papers; John A. Rogers Journal.

*Boston Public Library*, Mass.: William L. Garrison Papers; Samuel May, Jr., Papers.

*Calasis Free Public Library*, Me.: James Pike Papers.

*Chicago Historical Society Library*, Ill.: T.V. Reavis Correspondence.

*Cincinnati Historical Society Library*, Ohio: David K. Este Diaries.

*Samuel Colgate Baptist Memorial Library*:, William C. Gannet Sermons.

*Columbia University Library*, N.Y.: Moncure D. Conway Papers; Sydney H. Gay Papers.

*Connecticut Historical Society Library*, Hartford, Ct.: William Buckingham Correspondence; Mark Howard Papers.

*Cornell University*, Ithaca, N.Y.: James M. McKim Papers; Andrew D. White Papers.

*DePauw University Library*, Greencastle, Ind.: Journal of Brief Private Diary of John B. DeMotte; Personal Memoirs of William Graham.

*Detroit Public Library*, Mich.: George Duffield Diary.

*Drew University Library*, Madison, N.J.: John McClintock Correspondence.

*Emory University Library*, Atlanta, Ga.: John McClintock Papers.

*Essex Institute Library*, Essex, Mass.: Samuel Johnson Papers.

*Houghton Library, Harvard University*, Cambridge, Mass.: Charles Sumner Papers.

*Huntington Library*, San Marion, Calif.,: Francis Lieber Papers.

*Illinois State Historical Library*, Springfield, Ill.: Orville O. Browning Correspondence; David Davis Papers; Lucius C. Embree Papers; Ozias Hatch Papers; Abraham Lincoln Manuscripts; Richard J. Oglesby Papers; John D. Strong Papers; Horace White Papers; Richard Yates Papers.

*Indiana Historical Society Library*, Indianapolis, Ind.: Henry S. Lane Papers.

*Indiana State Historical Library*, Indianapolis, Ind.: George Julian Papers.

*Iowa State Historical Library*, Des Moines, Iowa: Samuel J. Kirkwood Papers.

*Iowa State Historical Society Library*, Iowa City, Iowa: James F. Wilson, "Life and Activities of James F. Wilson," Document W-50.

*Knox College Library*, Galesburg, Ill.: Journal of Samuel G. Wright.

*Library of Congress*: Susan B. Anthony Papers; Nathaniel Bank Papers; Breckinridge Family Papers; Benjamin F. Butler Papers; Zachariah Chandler Papers; William E. Chandler Papers; Salmon P. Chase Diaries; Salmon P. Chase Papers; Lydia M. Child-John G. Whittier Correspondence; Columbus Delano Papers; Anna E. Dickinson Papers; James R. Doolittle Papers; Thomas Ewing Papers; William P. Fessenden Papers; James A. Garfield Papers; Giddings-Julian Papers; Horace Greeley Papers; James R. Hawley Papers; Herndon-Weik Correspondence; Joseph Holt Papers; Thomas Jenckes Papers; Andrew Johnson Papers; Abraham Lincoln Papers; Hugh McCulloch Papers; Missionary Society of Connecticut Papers; Justin S. Morrill Papers; Rudolf Schleiden Papers (Microfilm); Jacob Schuckers Papers; Carl Schurz Papers; William H. Seward Papers; John Sherman Papers; Matthew Simpson Papers; Edwin M. Stanton Papers; Elizabeth C. Stanton Papers; Thaddeus Stevens Papers; Lyman Trumbull Papers; Benjamin F. Wade Papers; Israel Washburn Papers; Elihu B. Washburne Papers; Gideon Welles Papers; Henry Wilson Papers.

*Massachusetts Historical Library*, Boston, Mass.: John A. Andrew Papers; Henry W. Bellows Papers.

*Minnesota Historical Society Library*, St. Paul, Minn.: Ignatius Donnelly Papers.

*National Archives*: Freedmen's Bureau Papers.

*New York Historical Society Library*, N.Y.: Horace Greeley Papers; Parker Pillsbury Manuscript; Lysander Spooner Correspondence; Theodore Tilton Papers.

*New York Public Library*, N.Y.: James R. Doolittle Correspondence; Horace Greeley Papers.

*New York State Library* Albany, N.Y. Edwin D. Morgan Papers.

*Oberlin College Library*, Oberlin, Ohio: J.D. Cox Papers, William Goodell Papers; James Monroe Papers.

*Ohio State Historical Library*, Columbus, Ohio: William T. Coggeshall Diary; Joshua R. Giddings Papers; Friedrich Hassuarek Papers; John J. Janney Papers; William Henry Smith Correspondence.

*Pennsylvania Historical Society Library*, Philadelphia, Pa: Salmon P. Chase Correspondence.

*Radcliffe College Library*, Cambridge, Mass.: Beecher-Stowe Correspondence.

*Rutherford Hayes Library*, Fremont, Ohio: Rutherford B. Hayes Papers; William Claflin Papers.

*Syracuse University Library*, N.Y.: Gerrit Smith Papers.

*University of Kentucky Library*: William M. Pratt Diaries.

*University of Maine*, Orono, Maine: Hannibal Hamlin Papers.

*University of Michigan*, Ann Arbor, Mich.: Kingsley S. Bingham Correspondence; Austin Blair Papers; Henry H. Crapo Papers; Ransom Dunn Papers; John Longyear Correspondence; Nathan M. Thomas Correspondence; George Tuthill Diaries; Weld-Grimké Papers; George D. White Correspondence.

*University of Rochester Library*, N.Y.: William H. Seward Papers.

*University of Tennessee Library*, Knoxville, Tenn.: John Eaton Papers.

*University of Virginia*, Charlottesville, Va.: William S. Thayer Papers (Microfilm copy).

*West Virginia University Library*, Morgantown, W.V.: C.D. Hubbard Correspondence; Waitman T. Willey Papers.

*Western Reserve Historical Society Library*, Cleveland, Ohio: Peter Hitchcock Family Papers; Henry Holcomb Papers; Albert Riddle Papers; Milton Sutliff Letters.

*Wisconsin State Historical Society Library*, Madison, Wis.: Moses M. David Papers; James R. Doolittle Papers; Timothy O. Howe Papers; John Fox Potter Papers.

*Worcester Historical Society Library*, Mass.: Abby Kelley Foster Papers.

*Yale University Library*, New Haven, Ct.: Leonard Bacon Papers; Simon E. Baldwin Papers; Henry Ward Beecher Papers; J. Watson Webb Papers.

## CHURCH RECORDS

Minutes of the Central Ohio Wesleyan Methodist Conference, 1864-95, Wesleyan Church Archives, Marion College, Marion, Indiana.

Minutes of the Champlain Conference of the Wesleyan Connection, 1868-82, Marion College, Marion, Indiana.

Minutes of the Congregational and Presbyterian Convention, 1862-73, Wisconsin State Historical Society, Madison.

Minutes of the Genesee Convention of the Free Methodist Church, 1861-70, Free Methodist Church Archives, Winona Lake, Indiana.

Minutes of the Illinois Conference of the Free Methodist Church, 1862-70, Marion College, Marion, Indiana.

Minutes of the Indiana Conference of the Wesleyan Connection, 1884-67, Marion College, Marion, Indiana.

Minutes of the Michigan Conference of the Wesleyan Connection, 1852-67, Marion College, Marion, Indiana.

Minutes of the Presbyterian Presbytery of Columbus, Ohio, 1856-65, N.S., Presbyterian Historical Society Library, Philadelphia, Pa.

Records of the Presbyterian Synod of Buffalo, 1843-70, O.S., Presbyterian Historical Society Library.

Minutes of the Presbyterian Synod of Illinois, 1861-70, McCormick Theological Seminary, Chicago, Ill.

Records of the Presbyterian Synod of Minnesota, 1858-69, Presbyterian Historical Society Library.

Records of the Presbyterian Synod of Ohio, 1849-69, Presbyterian Historical Society Library.

Records of the Presbyterian Synod of Peoria, 1860-69, McCormick Theological Seminary Library.

Minutes of the Presbyterian Synod of Pennsylvania, 1861-62, Presbyterian Historical Society Library.

Minutes of the Presbyterian Synod of Wabash, 1860-66, Indiana State Presbyterian Office, Indianapolis, Ind.

Records of the Presbyterian Synod of Western Reserve, 1846-67, Presbyterian Historical Society Library.

Records of the Presbyterian Synod of Wisconsin, 1857-69, Presbyterian Historical Society.

Records of the Wesleyan Methodist Convention of America, 1842-67, Marion College, Marion, Indiana.

Minutes of the Western Yearly Meeting of the Society of Friends, 1864, Earlham College, Richmond, Indiana.

Minutes of the White River Conference of the United Brethren in Christ, 1866, United Methodist Church Archives, Drew University, Madison, New Jersey.

Minutes of the Zanesville Conference of the Wesleyan Church, 1861-70, Marion College, Marion, Indiana.

## RELIGIOUS SERIAL PUBLICATIONS

*American Missionary* (New York)

*American Presbyterian* (Philadelphia)

*American Presbyterian and Theological Review* (New York)

*American Wesleyan* (Syracuse)

*Banner of the Covenant* (Philadelphia)

*Boston Commonwealth*

*Boston Recorder*

*Christian Advocate and Journal* (New York)

*Christian Ambassador* (Auburn, N.Y.)

*Christian Examiner* (Boston)

*Christian Freeman* (Boston)

*Christian Herald and Presbyterian Recorder* (Cincinnati)

*Christian Inquirer* (New York)

*Christian Instructor and United Presbyterian* (Pittsburgh)

*Christian Intelligencer* (New York)

*Christian Register* (Boston)

*Christian Review* (Boston)

*Christian Times and Illinois Baptist* (Chicago)

*Christian Watchman and Reflector* (Boston)

*Congregational Journal* (Concord, N.H.)
*Congregational Quarterly* (Boston)
*Congregationalist* (Boston)
*Episcopal Record* (Philadelphia)
*Examiner* (New York)
*Free Methodist* (Rochester)
*Journal and Messenger* (Columbus, Ohio)
*Ladies' Repository* (Cincinnati)
*Liberal Christian* (New York)
*Liberator* (Boston)
*Lutheran and Missionary* (Philadelphia)
*Lutheran Observer* (Baltimore)
*Methodist* (New York)
*Methodist Quarterly Review* (Louisville, Ky.)
*Morning Star* (Dover, N.H.)
*National Anti-Slavery Standard* (New York)
*New Englander* (New Haven)
*New York Evangelist*
*New York Examiner and Recorder*
*New York Independent*
*New York Observer; Northern Independent Methodist* (Auburn, N.Y.)
*Northwestern Christian Advocate* (Chicago)
*Pittsburgh Christian Advocate*
*Presbyter* (Cincinnati)
*Presbyterian* (Philadelphia)
*Presbyterian Banner* (Philadelphia)
*Presbyterian Quarterly Review* (Philadelphia)
*Presbyterian Standard* (Philadelphia)
*Presbyterian Witness* (Cincinnati)
*Principia* (New York)
*The Religious Herald* (Hartford, Ct.)
*Religious Telescope* (Dayton, Ohio)
*United Presbyterian* (Pittsburgh)
*Universalist* (Boston)
*Universalist Quarterly and General Review* (Boston)
*Western Christian Advocate* (Cincinnati)
*Western Episcopalian* (Gambier, Ohio)
*Zion's Herald* (Boston)

## PUBLISHED RECORDS AND PROCEEDINGS OF CHURCHES AND ANTISLAVERY SOCIETIES

The publishing information has been omitted because it serves no useful purpose. Baptist published records are in the American Baptist Historical Society, the Dargan-Carver Library of the Southern Baptist Historical Commission, and the Boyce Centennial Library of the Southern Baptist Theological Seminary. The Congregational published records are housed in the Congregational Library of the American Congregational Association.

Methodist records will be found in the Library of the General Commission on Archives and History of the United Methodist Church and the United Library of Garrett Theological Seminary. Presbyterian published records are in the Presbyterian Historical Society.

## American Anti-Slavery Society

*Proceedings of the American Anti-Slavery Society*, 1863.
*Proceedings of the American Anti-Slavery Society at the Third Decade Meeting Held in the City of Philadelphia*, 1864.

## Baptist Church

*Annual Report of the American Baptist Home Mission Society*, 1865.
*Minutes of the Allegany, Pa., Baptist Association*, 1865.
*Minutes of the Ashford, Conn., Baptist Association*, 1862.
*Minutes of the Ashtabula, Ohio, Baptist Association*, 1864.
*Minutes of the Berkshire, Mass., Baptist Association*, 1862.
*Minutes of the Bradford, Pa., Baptist Association*, 1865.
*Minutes of the Bridgewater, Pa., Baptist Association*, 1862, 1866.
*Minutes of the Broome and Tioga, New York, Baptist Association*, 1862, 1865.
*Minutes of the Burlington, Iowa, Baptist Association*, 1866.
*Minutes of the Central Union Association of Independent Baptist Churches of Masschusetts*, 1862, 1865, 1866.
*Minutes of the Centre Baptist Association of Pennsylvania*, 1862, 1864, 1865.
*Minutes of the Chemung River, New York, Baptist Association*, 1862, 1865.
*Proceedings of the Chicago Baptist Association*, 1865.
*Minutes of the Clearfield, Pa., Baptist Association*, 1862.
*Minutes of the Columbus, Ohio, Baptist Association*, 1862.
*Minutes of the Dane, Wis., Baptist Association*, 1862, 1865.
*Minutes of the Davenport, Iowa, Baptist Association*, 1862.
*Minutes of the Dodge, Wis., Baptist Association*, 1862.
*Minutes of the Dutchess, N.Y., Baptist Association*, 1862.
*Minutes of the East New Jersey Baptist Association*, 1862.
*Minutes of the Erie, N.Y., Baptist Association*, 1866.
*Minutes of the Fox River, Ill., Baptist Association*, 1862.
*Minutes of the Franklin, N.Y., Baptist Association*, 1865.
*Minutes of the French Creek, Pa., Baptist Association*, 1864.
*Minutes of the Genesee, N.Y., Baptist Association*, 1865.
*Minutes of the Grand River, Ohio, Baptist Association*, 1861.
*Minutes of the Hudson River Baptist Association*, 1862, 1865.
*Minutes of the Huron, Ohio, Baptist Association*, 1866.
*Minutes of the Illinois Baptist Association*, 1862.
*Minutes of the Iowa State Baptist Convention*, 1864.
*Minutes of the Keokuk, Iowa, Baptist Association*, 1862.
*Minutes of the Lafayette, Pa., Baptist Association*, 1862.
*Minutes of the Lake George, N.Y., Baptist Association*, 1862.
*Minutes of the Mad River, Ohio, Baptist Association*, 1864.
*Minutes of the Monongahela Baptist Association*, 1864.
*Minutes of the Monroe Baptist Association*, 1865.
*Minutes of the New Jersey Baptist State Convention*, 1865.

*Minutes of the New London, Conn., Baptist Association,* 1863, 1865, 1866, 1868.
*Minutes of the New York Baptist Association,* 1865.
*Minutes of the Niagara, N.Y., Baptist Association,* 1865.
*Minutes of the North Philadelphia Baptist Association,* 1863, 1864.
*Minutes of the Northumberland, Pa., Baptist Association,* 1862, 1866.
*Minutes of the Old Colony Baptist Association,* 1865.
*Minutes of the Oneida, N.Y., Baptist Association,* 1861, 1862.
*Minutes of the Onondaga, N.Y., Baptist Association,* 1866.
*Minutes of the Oskaloosa, Iowa, Baptist Association,* 1862.
*Minutes of the Oswego Baptist Association,* 1861, 1866.
*Minutes of the Ottawa, Ill., Baptist Association,* 1865.
*Minutes of the Philadelphia Baptist Association,* 1863.
*Minutes of the Pittsburgh Regular Baptist Association,* 1865.
*Minutes of the Rhode Island Baptist Association,* 1864.
*Minutes of the Rock River Baptist Association,* 1864.
*Minutes of the St. Joseph River, Mich., Baptist Association,* 1862.
*Proceedings of the Saratoga Baptist Association,* 1864.
*Minutes of the Shaftsbury, Vt., Baptist Association,* 1864.
*Minutes of the Sussex, New York, Baptist Association,* 1865.
*Minutes of the Vermont State Baptist Convention,* 1861, 1864.
*Minutes of the Walworth, Wisconsin, Baptist Association,* 1862, 1864, 1866, 1868.
*Minutes of the Warren, Rhode Island, Baptist Association,* 1866.
*Minutes of the Wisconsin State Baptist Convention,* 1861, 1862.
*Minutes of the Woodstock, Vt., Baptist Association,* 1862, 1864, 1866.
*Minutes of the Wyoming, Pa., Baptist Association,* 1863.

## Congregational Church

*Minutes of the General Association of Congregational Churches of Connecticut,* 1865.
*Minutes of the General Association of Congregational Churches . . . of Indiana,* 1864, 1866.
*Minutes of the General Association of Congregational Churches of Michigan,* 1863.
*Minutes of the General Association of Congregational Ministers and Churches of Iowa,* 1866.
*Minutes of the General Conference of Congregational Churches of Maine,* 1864, 1866.
*Minutes of the General Conference of Congregational Churches of Massachusetts,* 1864, 1865.
*Minutes of the Congregational Conference of Ohio,* 1863, 1866.
*Minutes of the Wisconsin Congregational and Presbyterian Convention,* 1866.

## Evangelical Lutheran Church

*Journal of the Annual Session of the Franckean Evangelic Lutheran Synod,* 1862.

## Methodist Episcopal Church

*Centennial of the Methodist Episcopal Church of Crawfordsville*, 1825-1925.

*Journal of the General Conference of the Methodist Episcopal Church*, 1864, 1868.

*Minutes of the Central Ohio Conference of the Methodist Episcopal Church*, 1861, 1863.

*Minutes of the Cincinnati Methodist Episcopal Church*, 1861, 1863, 1866, 1868.

*Minutes of the Detroit Conference of Methodist Episcopal Church*, 1861, 1863.

*Minutes of the East Genesee Conference of the Methodist Episcopal Church*, 1861.

*Minutes of the East Maine Conference of the Methodist Episcopal Church*, 1864, 1866, 1868.

*Minutes of the Erie Conference of the Methodist Episcopal Church*, 1861, 1862, 1863, 1865.

*Minutes of the Illinois Conference of the Methodist Episcopal Church*, 1861, 1862.

*Minutes of the Indiana Conference of the Methodist Episcopal Church*, 1863.

*Minutes of the Maine Conference of the Methodist Episcopal Church*, 1866, 1868.

*Minutes of the Methodist Episcopal Conference of Iowa*, 1862, 1863, 1865, 1866, 1867.

*Minutes of the Michigan Conference of the Methodist Episcopal Church*, 1864, 1865, 1866.

*Minutes of the Newark, N.J., Conference of the Methodist Episcopal Church*, 1865.

*Minutes of the New England Conference of the Methodist Episcopal Church*, April 1861, 1862, 1865, 1866, 1867.

*Minutes of the New Hampshire Conference of the Methodist Episcopal Church*, 1865.

*Minutes of the New York Conference of the Methodist Episcopal Church*, 1862, 1864, 1866, 1867.

*Minutes of the New York East Conference of the Methodist Episcopal Church*, 1861, 1868.

*Minutes of the Northern Ohio Methodist Episcopal Conference*, 1863, 1867, 1868.

*Minutes of the North Indiana Conference of the Methodist Episcopal Church*, 1862.

*Minutes of the Ohio Conference of the Methodist Episcopal Church*, 1862, 1863.

*Minutes of the Pittsburgh Conference of the Methodist Episcopal Church*, 1863.

*Register of the Rock River Conference of the Methodist Episcopal Church*, 1868.

*Minutes of the South-Eastern Indiana Conference of the Methodist Episcopal Church*, 1868.

*Minutes of the Troy Conference of the Methodist Episcopal Church*, 1864, 1866

*Minutes of the Upper Iowa Conference of the Methodist Episcopal Church*, 1865.

*Minutes of the Vermont Conference of the Methodist Episcopal Church*, 1862.

*Minutes of the Western Iowa Conference of the Methodist Episcopal Church*, 1861.

## Presbyterian Church

*Minutes of the General Assembly of the Presbyterian Church* (N.S.), 1861-66.

*Minutes of the General Assembly of the Presbyterian Church* (O.S.), 1861-66.

*Minutes of the Iowa Synod of the United Presbyterian Church*, 1866.

## Progressive Friends Society

*Proceedings of the Pennsylvania Yearly Meeting of Progressive Friends*, 1862, 1864, 1865, 1868.

## Seventh Day Baptist Church

*Minutes of the Eastern Association of the Seventh Day Baptists*, 1866.

*Minutes of the General Conference of the Seventh Day Baptists*, 1864.

*Minutes of the Seventh Day Baptists, Central Association*, 1864.

## Union League of America

*Proceedings of the State Council of the Union League of America for the State of New York, Nov. 1863*, 1863.

## AUTOBIOGRAPHIES, BIOGRAPHIES, AND REMINISCENCES

Aaron, L.C. *Rev. Samuel Aaron: His Life, Sermons, Correspondence, etc.* Norristown, Pa.: Wills, 1890.

Adams, Charles F. *Richard H. Dana: A Biography.* 2 vols. Boston: Houghton Mifflin, 1890.

Allen, Alexander V. *Life and Letters of Phillips Brooks.* New York: E.P. Dutton, 1901.

Blaine, James G. *Twenty Years of Congress: From Lincoln to Garfield.* 2 vols. Norwich, Conn.: Henry Bill, 1884-86.

Brace, Emma, ed. *The Life of Charles Loring Brace.* 1894. Reprint. New York: Arno Press, 1976.

Butler, Harriet, ed. *A Retrospect of Forty Years, 1825-1865.* New York: Scribner's, 1911.

Chace, Lillie Buffum, and Arthur C. Wyman. *Elizabeth Buffum Chace, 1806-1899.* 2 vols. Boston: W.B. Clark, 1914.

Chandler, Peleg W. *Memoir of Governor Andrew, with Personal Reminiscences.* Boston: Roberts Brothers, 1880.

Clarke, Grace Julian. *George Julian.* Indianapolis: Indiana Historical Commission, 1923.

Conway, Moncure D. *Autobiography: Memories and Experiences of Moncure Daniel Conway.* 2 vols. Boston: Houghton Mifflin, 1904.

Cox, Samuel S. *Eight Years in Congress from 1857-1865*. New York: D. Appleton, 1865.

Cutler, Julia P. *Life and Times of Ephraim Cutler from His Journal and Correspondence*. Cincinnati: R. Clarke, 1890.

Dow, Neal. *The Reminiscences of Neal Dow: Recollections of Eighty Years*. Portland: Evening Express Publishing, 1898.

Emerson, Sarah Hopper. *Life of Abby Hopper Gibbons*. 2 vols. New York: G.P. Putnam's Sons, 1897.

Fairbank, Calvin. *During Slavery Times*. 1890. Reprint. New York: Negro Univ. Press, 1969.

Fessenden, Francis. *Life and Public Service of William Pitt Fessenden*. Boston: Houghton Mifflin, 1907.

Field, Henry M., ed. *The Life of David D. Field*. New York: Scribner's, 1989.

Fisher, H.D., Rev. *The Gun and the Gospel: Early Kansas and Chaplain Fisher*. Kansas City: Hudson-Kimberly, 1902.

Gilmore, James R. [Edmund Kirke, pseud.] *Personal Recollections of Abraham Lincoln and the Civil War*. Boston: L.C. Page, 1898.

Hale, Edward E. *James Freeman Clarke*. Boston: Houghton Mifflin, 1891.

Hamlin, Charles E. *The Life and Times of Hannibal Hamlin*. Cambridge, Mass.: Riverside Press, 1899.

Hastings, Rosetta. *Personal Recollections of Pardee Butler*. Cincinnati: Standard Publishing, 1889.

Hollowell, Anna Davis. *James and Lucretia Mott*. New York: Houghton Mifflin, 1884.

Holmes, John Haynes. *The Life of Robert Collyer, 1823-1912*. 2 vols. New York: Dodd, Mead, 1917.

Hooker, John. *Some Reminiscences of a Long Life*. Hartford: Belknap and Warfield, 1899.

Hopkins, John H., Jr. *The Life of the Late Right Reverend John Henry Hopkins*. New York: F.J. Huntington, 1873.

Hughes, Sarah F., ed. *Letters and Recollections of John Murray Forbes*. 2 vols. Boston: Houghton Mifflin, 1899.

Julian, George W. *Political Recollections, 1840-1872*. 1883. Reprint. Miami: Mnemosyne, 1969.

Knox, Thomas. *Life and Work of Henry Ward Beecher*. New York: Wilson and Ellis, 1887.

Konkle, Burton A. *The Life and Speeches of Thomas Williams*. Philadelphia: Campion, 1905.

McClure, Alexander K. *Abraham Lincoln and Men of War Times*. Philadelphia: Times Publishing, 1892.

McMechen, Edgar C. *Life of Governor Evans: Second Territorial Governor of Colorado*. Denver: E.C. McMechen, 1924.

Mears, David O. *Life of Edward Norris Kirk, D.D.* Boston: Lockwood, Brooks, 1872.

Merriam, George S. *The Life and Times of Samuel Bowles*. New York: DaCapo Press, 1970.

Miller, Rev. Wesson G. *Thirty Years in the Itineracy*. Milwaukee: I.L. Hauser, 1875.

Peck, George. *The Life and Times of Rev. George Peck, D.D.* New York: Nelson and Phillips, 1874.

Piatt, Don. *Memories of the Men Who Saved the Union.* New York: Clark, 1887.

Pierce, Edward L. *Memoir and Letters of Charles Sumner.* 4 vols. 1877. Reprint. New York: Arno Press, 1969.

Powell, Aaron M. *Personal Reminiscences.* New York: Caulton Press, 1899.

Prentice, George. *The Life of Gilbert Haven.* New York: Phillips and Hunt, 1883.

Schuckers, Jacob W. *The Life of Salmon Portland Chase.* New York: D. Appleton, 1874.

Shaw, Rev. James. *Early Reminiscences: Pioneer Life in Kansas.* Atchison: Haskel, 1886.

Shaw, Rev. James. *Twelve Years in America, being observations on the county, the people, institutions and religion, with notices of slavery and the late war.* London: Hamilton, Adams, 1867.

Stearns, Frank P. *The Life and Public Services of George Luther Stearns.* 1907. Reprint. New York: Arno Press, 1969.

Stebbins, Giles B. *Upward Steps of Seventy Years.* New York: John W. Lovell, 1890.

Thompson, Robert E. *The Life of George H. Stuart.* Philadelphia: J.M. Stoddart, 1890.

Ward, Susan H. *George H. Hepworth, Preacher, Journalist, Friend of the People.* New York: E.P. Dutton, 1913.

Weeks, Sylvester, ed. *Autobiography of Rev. Granville Moody.* Cincinnati: Cranston and Stowe, 1890.

## SERMONS

Arnold, A.N. *Place the Fruit of Righteousness: A Sermon, Westboro, Mass., 1863.* Boston: John Whittemore, 1863.

Bellows, Henry W. *The Advantage of Testing Our Principles, Compensatory of the Evils of Serious Times, A Discourse on February 11, 1861.* Philadelphia: C. Sherman and Son, 1861.

Bouton, Nathaniel. *Days of Adversity: A New Year's Sermon, Preached in Concord, N.H., Jan. 6, 1861.* Concord: P.B. Cogswell, 1861.

Cheever, George B. *Immediate Emancipation: A Discourse.* New York: John A. Gray, 1861.

Cheever, George B. *Protest against the Robbery of the Colored Race by the Proposed Amendment of the Constitution.* New York: Robert Johnson, 1866.

Chesebrough, A.S. *Christian Politics: A Sermon Preached on Fast Day.* Hartford: Case, Lockwood, 1863.

Clark, Frederick G. *Gold in the Fire: A Sermon Preached in the Twenty-Third Presbyterian Church, New York, Nov. 27, 1862.* New York: J.H. Daychinck, 1862.

Conway, Moncure D. *The Rejected Stone; or, Insurrection vs. Resurrection in America.* Boston: Walter, Wise, 1862.

Cruickshank, James. *A Humble Thanksgiving*. Boston: Charles Moody, 1866.

Fairchild, Edmund B. *Christian Patriotism: A Sermon Delivered in the Representative Hall*. Lansing, Mich.: John Kerr, 1863.

Haven, Gilbert. *National Sermons, Speeches, and Letters on Slavery and Its War*. Boston: Lee and Shepard, 1869.

Hawes, Joel. *Four Questions Considered: A Sermon Preached in Hartford on the Day of National Fast, Sept. 26, 1861*. Hartford: Case and Lockwood, 1861.

Johnson, Herrick. *The Shaking of the Nations: A Sermon*. Pittsburgh: W.S. Haven, 1864.

Quint, A.H. "Southern Chivalry, and What the Nation Ought to Do With It." *Three Sermons Preached in the North Congregational Church*. New Bedford: Mercury Press, 1865.

Quint, Alonzo. *A Sermon*. Boston: Wright and Potter, 1866.

Segur, S. Willard. *The Nation's Hope: A Sermon Preached in the Congregational Church, Tallmadge, Ohio*. Akron: Beebe and Elkins, 1863.

Spear, Samuel T. *The Citizen's Duty in the Present Crisis*. New York: Tibbals, 1866.

Sunderland, La Roy. Sermon. In *Addresses and Ceremonies at the New Year's Festival to Freemen*. Washington, D.C.: McGill and Witherow, 1867.

Williams, Jr., Lester. *Freedom of Speech and the Union: A Discourse Delivered December 30, 1860, at Holden, Massachusetts*. Worcester, Mass.: C. Hamilton, 1861.

## OTHER CONTEMPORARY DOCUMENTS

Arnold, Isaac N. *The History of Abraham Lincoln and the Over-Throw of Slavery*. Chicago: Clarke, 1866.

Beale, Howard K., ed. *Diary of Gideon Welles*. New York: Norton, 1960.

Child, Lydia Maria. *Letters of Lydia Maria Child*. Boston: Houghton Mifflin, 1883.

Cox, Samuel S. *Puritanism in Politics: Speech of the Hon. S.S. Cox of Ohio before the Democratic Association, January 13, 1863*. New York: Van Evrie Horton, 1863.

Dennett, Tyler. *Lincoln and the Civil War in the Diaries and Letters of John Hay*. New York: Dodd, Mead, 1939.

Giddings, Joseph R. *History of the Rebellion: Its Authors and Causes*. New York: Follet, Foster, 1864.

Greeley, Horace. *A History of the Great Rebellion in the United States of America, 1860-1865*. 2 vols. Hartford: D.D. Case, 1865-66.

Gurowski, Adam. *Diary: From March 4, 1861 to 1865*. 3 vols. 1866. Reprint. New York: Burt Franklin, 1862-65.

Hoar, George F. *Charles Sumner: His Complete Works*. 20 vols. 1900. Reprint. New York: Negro Univ. Press, 1969.

Loring, George B. *The Present Crisis: A Speech Delivered at Lyceum Hall, Salem, Mass., April 26, 1865*. South Danvers, Mass., 1865.

McPherson, Edward. *Political History of the United States of America during the Great Rebellion*. Washington, D.C.: Phillip and Solomons, 1865.

Marshall, Jessie Ames. *Private and Official Correspondence of Benjamin F. Butler during the Period of the Civil War.* 5 vols. Norwood, Mass.: Plimpton Press, 1917.

Merrill, Walter M., ed. *The Letters of William Lloyd Garrison.* Cambridge, Mass.: Belknap Press, 1979.

Nevins, Allan, ed. *George Templeton Strong: Diary of the Civil War, 1860-1865.* New York: Macmillan, 1962.

Norton, Charles E., ed. *Letters of James Russell Lowell.* 3 vols. New York: AMS Press, 1966.

Pease, Theodore, and James Randall, eds. *The Diary of Orville Browning.* 2 vols. Springfield: Illinois Historical Library, 1925.

Richardson, James. *A Compilation of the Messages and Papers of the Presidents.* 11 vols. Washington: Bureau of National Literature and Art, 1909.

*Speeches of the Campaign of 1866 in the States of Ohio, Indiana and Kentucky.* Cincinnati: Cincinnati Commercial, 1866.

Stanton, Robert L. *The Church and the Rebellion.* New York: Derby and Miller, 1864.

Thornbrough, Gayle. *The Diary of Calvin Fletcher.* Indianapolis: Indiana Historical Society, 1972.

*The War of the Rebellion: A Compilation of the Official Records of the Union and Confederate Armies.* 69 vols. Washington: Government Printing Office, 1880-1901.

# Index